TENTH EDITION

MARKETING MISTAKES AND SUCCESSES

Robert F. Hartley
Cleveland State University

WILEY

JOHN WILEY & SONS, INC.

Associate Publisher	Judith Joseph
Senior Acquitions Editor	Jayme Heffler
Director of Marketing	Frank Lyman
Senior Designer	Kevin Murphy
Senior Production Editor	Patricia McFadden
Senior Editorial Assistant	Ame Esterline
Senior Media Editor	Allison Morris
Production Management	Hermitage Publishing Services

This book was set in 10/12 New Caledonia by Hermitage Publishing Services and printed and bound by Courier/Westford. The cover was printed by Courier/Stoughton.

This book is printed on acid-free paper. ∞

To order books or for customer service please, call 1-800-CALL WILEY (225-5945).

ISBN-13 978- 0-471-74321-7
ISBN-10 0-471-74321-6

Printed in the United States of America

10 9 8 7 6 5 4 3 2 1

PREFACE

Welcome to this tenth edition of *Marketing Mistakes and Successes*. It has now been around for almost 30 years. Who would have thought that interest in mistakes would have been so enduring? I know that many of you are past users and hope you will find this new edition a worthy successor to the earlier editions.

After so many years of investigating mistakes, and more recently some successes as well, it might seem like a monumental challenge to keep these new editions fresh and interesting and still provide good learning experiences. But the task of doing so, and the joy of the challenge, has made this an intriguing labor through the decades. It is always difficult to abandon interesting cases that have stimulated student discussions and provided good learning experiences, but newer case possibilities are ever competing for inclusion. Examples of good and bad handling of problems and opportunities are always emerging, but occasionally we bring back an oldie.

For new users, I hope the book will meet your full expectations and be an effective instructional tool. Although case books abound, you and your students may find this one somewhat unique and very readable. It is a book that can help transform dry and rather remote concepts into practical reality, lead to lively classroom discussions, and even contribute to debates amid the arena of decision making.

NEW TO THIS EDITION

In contrast to the earlier editions, which examined only notable mistakes, and based on your favorable comments about recent editions, I have again included some well-known successes. While mistakes provide valuable learning insights, we can also learn from successes. We can learn by comparing the unsuccessful with the successful.

We have brought back Marketing Wars, where the moves and countermoves of direct competitors are examined. We have also continued the Managing Change and Crises section. We have added a new section, Competitive Uncertainties, where four firms face an uncertain future. By popular demand we have brought back Entrepreneurial Adventures from earlier editions of the book. Three of these cases are so current we had to keep updating the cases until the manuscript left our hands for the production process. Other cases we have tried to keep as current as possible by including Postscripts, Later Developments, and Updates where they are appropriate.

A number of you have asked that I identify which cases would be appropriate for the traditional coverage of topics as organized in most marketing texts. With most cases it is not possible to truly compartmentalize the mistake or success to merely one topic. The patterns of success or failure tend to be more pervasive. Still, I think you will find the following classification of cases by subject matter to be helpful. I thank those of you who made this and other suggestions.

Classification of Cases by Major Marketing Topics

Topics	Most Relevant Cases
Marketing Research and Consumer Analysis	Coca-Cola, Disney, McDonald's, Toys "R" Us
Product	Nike/Reebok, Coke/Pepsi, McDonald's, Maytag, Perrier, Boeing/Airbus, Southwest Air, Vanguard, Firestone/Ford, Gateway, Harley-Davidson, Merck, Toy "R" Us, Boston Beer, Snapple, Newell Rubbermaid, Hewlett-Packard, Kmart/Sears
Distribution	Nike/Reebok, Coke/Pepsi, Toys "R" Us, Wal-Mart, Snapple, Newell Rubbermaid, Vanguard, Gateway, Kmart/Sears, Perrier, OfficeMax, Boston Beer
Promotion	Gateway, Coke/Pepsi, Nike/Reebok, Maytag, Vanguard, Wal-Mart, Merck, Boston Beer, Snapple, Harley-Davidson, McDonald's
Price	Disney, Gateway, Vanguard, Southwest, Wal-Mart, Boeing/Airbus, McDonald's, Perrier, Boston Beer, Newell Rubbermaid, Hewlett-Packard, Toys "R" Us
International	Coke/Pepsi, Nike, Disney, Maytag, Boeing/Airbus, McDonald's, Wal-Mart, Nike, Harley-Davidson, Firestone/Ford, Perrier
Customer Relations	Newell Rubbermaid, Vanguard, Maytag, Harley, Southwest, Wal-Mart, Firestone/Ford, OfficeMax
Change and Crisis Management	Scott/Sunbeam, Perrier, Maytag, Boeing, Disney, Firestone/Ford, Merck, Toys "R" Us, Coke, Gateway
Non-product	Disney, Southwest, Hewlett-Packard
Social and Ethical	Wal-Mart, Merck, Scott/Sunbeam, Firestone/Ford

TARGETED COURSES

As a supplemental text, this book can be used in a variety of undergraduate and graduate courses. These range from introduction to marketing courses to those in marketing management and strategic marketing. It can also be used as a text in international marketing courses. Retailing, entrepreneurship, and ethics courses could use a number of these cases and their learning insights in their syllabus. Training programs for nonprofessionals who are looking for a good read about well-known firms and personalities, would find this book both interesting and useful.

TEACHING AIDS

As in the previous editions, this edition contains a number of teaching aids both within and at the end of each chapter. Some of these are applicable to several cases, illustrating that certain successful and unsuccessful practices tend to cross company lines.

Information Boxes and Issue Boxes are included within each chapter to highlight relevant concepts and issues or related information. Learning insights help students see how certain practices, errors and successes, cross company lines and are prone to be either traps for the unwary or success modes. Discussion Questions and Hand-On Exercises encourage and stimulate student involvement. A pedagogical feature is the Team Debate Exercise in which formal issues and options can be debated. In some cases a *Devil's Advocate* exercise appears in which students can argue against a proposed course of action to test its merits. Invitation to Research suggestions allow students to take the case a step further, to investigate what has happened since the case was written. In the final chapter, the various learning insights are summarized and classified into general conclusions.

An Instructor's Manual written by the author accompanies the text to provide suggestions and considerations for the pedagogical material within and at the ends of chapters. The IM is available online only at: www.wiley.com/college/hartley.

ACKNOWLEDGMENTS

It seems fitting to acknowledge all those who have provided encouragement, information, advice, and constructive criticism throughout the years since the first edition appeared. I hope you all are well and successful. I truly appreciate your contributions. I apologize if I have missed anybody and would be grateful to know about this oversight so I can rectify this in future editions. I also welcome any updates of present affiliations.

Michael Pearson, Loyola University, New Orleans; Beverlee Anderson, University of Cincinnati; Y.H.Furuhashi, Notre Dame; W. Jack Duncan, University of Alabama-Birmingham; Mike Farley, Del Mar College; Joseph W. Leonard, Miami University (OH); Abbas Nadim, University of New Haven; William O'Donnell, University of Phoenix; Howard Smith, University of New Mexico; James Wolter, University of Michigan, Flint; Vernon R. Stauble, California State Polytechnic University; Donna Giertz, Parkland College; Don Hantula, St. Joseph's University; Milton Alexander, Auburn University; James F. Cashman, University of Alabama; Douglas Wozniak, Ferris State University; Greg Bach, Bismark State College; Glenna Dod, Wesleyan College; Anthony McGann, University of Wyoming; Robert D. Nale, Coastal Carolina University; Robert H. Votaw, Amber University; Don Fagan, Daniel Webster University; Andrew J. Deile, Mercer University; Samuel Hazen, Tarleton State University; Michael B. McCormick, Jacksonville State University.

I would also like to acknowledge Barnett Helzberg, Jr. of the Shirley and Barnett Helzberg Foundation, and my colleagues from Cleveland State University: Ram Rao and Benoy Joseph. From Wiley, I acknowledge the hard work of Judith Joseph, Jessica Bartelt, and Ame Esterline.

Robert F. Hartley, Professor Emeritus
College of Business Administration
Cleveland State University
Cleveland, Ohio
RFHartley@aol.com

ABOUT THE AUTHOR

Bob Hartley is Professor Emeritus at Cleveland State University's College of Business Administration. He taught a variety of undergraduate and graduate courses at Cleveland State in management, marketing, and ethics. Prior to that he taught at the University of Minnesota and George Washington University. His received his MBA and Ph.D. from the University of Minnesota, with a BBA from Drake University.

Before moving into academia, Bob spent 13 years employed in retailing with the predecessor of Kmart (S. S. Kresge), as well as with JCPenney, Dayton-Hudson, and its Target subsidiary. He held positions in store management, central buying, and merchandise management.

His first textbook, *Marketing: Management and Social Change*, was published in 1972. It was ahead of its time in introducing social and environmental issues to the study of marketing. Other books, *Marketing Fundamentals, Retailing, Sales Management*, and *Marketing Research* have followed.

In 1976, the first *Marketing Mistakes* edition was published. This book brought a new approach to case studies. They were more student-friendly books, and more relevant to career enhancement than existing books. In 1983, *Management Mistakes* was introduced. These books are now in their tenth and eighth editions, respectively, and have been widely translated. In 1992, Professor Hartley wrote *Business Ethics: Violations of the Public Trust*. *Business Ethics Mistakes and Successes* was published in 2005. He is listed in Who's Who in America and Who's Who in the World.

CONTENTS

CHAPTER ONE

Introduction

$\mathbf{A}$t this writing, *Marketing Mistakes* is nearing its thirtieth anniversary. The first edition, back in 1976, was 147 pages and included such long-forgotten cases as Korvette, W. T. Grant, Edsel, Corfam, Gilbert, and the Midi.

In this tenth edition, seven cases from the ninth edition have been dropped, and seven were added, several of these being modified from earlier editions. Other cases have been updated and, in some instances, reclassified. The popular section on "Marketing Wars," which was introduced in the eighth edition, is again included and follows major competitors in their furious struggles. Two new parts are introduced: Part III Competitive Uncertainties, and Part VI Entrepreneurial Adventures, brought back by popular demand. Some cases are as recent as today's headlines; several still have not come to complete resolution. In response to your feedback, the section on notable successes has also been continued.

We continue to seek what can be learned—insights that are transferable to other firms, other times, other situations. What key factors brought monumental mistakes to some firms and resounding successes for others? Through such evaluations and studies of contrasts, we may learn to improve batting averages in the intriguing, ever-challenging art of decision making.

We will encounter organizational life cycles, with an organization growing and prospering, then failing (just as humans do), but occasionally resurging. Success rarely lasts forever, but even the most serious mistakes can be (but are not always) overcome.

As in previous editions, a variety of firms, industries, mistakes, and successes are presented. You will be familiar with most of the organizations, although probably not with the details of their situations.

We are always on the lookout for cases that can bring out certain points or caveats in the art of marketing decision making, and that give a balanced view of the spectrum of marketing problems. The goal is to present examples that provide somewhat different learning experiences, where at least some aspect of the mistake or success is unique. Still, we see similar mistakes occurring time and again. From the prevalence of such mistakes, it is hard to say how much decision making has really improved over the decades.

Let us then consider what learning insights we can gain, with the benefit of hindsight, from examining these examples of successful and unsuccessful marketing practices.

LEARNING INSIGHTS

Analyzing Mistakes

In looking at sick companies, or even healthy ones that have experienced difficulties with certain parts of their operations, it is tempting to be overly critical. It is easy to criticize with the benefit of hindsight. Mistakes are inevitable, given the present state of decision making, and the dynamic environment facing organizations.

Mistakes can be categorized as errors of omission and of commission. *Mistakes of omission* are those in which no action was taken and the status quo was contentedly embraced amid a changing environment. Such errors, often characteristic of conservative or stodgy management, are not as obvious as the other category of mistakes. They seldom involve tumultuous upheaval; rather, the company's competitive position slowly fades, until management finally realizes that mistakes having monumental impact have been allowed to happen. The firm's fortunes often never regain their former luster.

Mistakes of commission are more spectacular. They involve hasty decisions, poor support and follow-up, misdirected expansion, and the like. Although the costs of eroding competitive position due to errors of omission are difficult to calculate precisely, the costs of errors of commission are often fully evident. For example, with Euro Disney, in 1993 alone the loss was $960 million from a poorly planned venture; it improved in 1994 with only a $366 million loss. With Maytag's overseas Hoover Division, the costs of an incredibly bungled sales promotion were more than $200 million, and still counting. Then there was the reckless purchase of Snapple by Quaker Oats' CEO, William Smithburg, for $1.7 billion; Quaker sold the product less than three years later for $300 million.

Although they may make mistakes, organizations with sharp managements follow certain patterns when confronting difficult situations:

1. Looming problems or present mistakes are quickly recognized.
2. The causes of the problem(s) are carefully determined.
3. Alternative corrective actions are evaluated in view of the company's resources and constraints.
4. Corrective action is prompt. Sometimes this requires a ruthless axing of the product, the division, or whatever is at fault.
5. Mistakes provide learning experiences. The same mistakes are not repeated, and future operations are consequently strengthened.

Slowness to recognize emerging problems leads us to think that management is incompetent or that controls have not been established to provide prompt feedback at strategic control points. For example, a declining competitive position in one or a few geographical areas should be a red flag that something is amiss. To wait months before investigating or taking action may mean a permanent loss of business. Admittedly, signals sometimes get mixed, and complete information may be lacking, but procrastination is not easily defended.

Just as problems should be quickly recognized, the causes of these problems—the "why" of the unexpected results—must be determined as quickly as possible. It is premature, and rash, to take action before knowing where the problems really lie. Returning to the previous example, the loss of competitive position in one or a few markets may reflect circumstances beyond the firm's immediate control, such as an aggressive new competitor who is drastically cutting prices to "buy sales." In this situation, all competing firms will likely lose market share, and little can be done except to stay as competitive as possible with prices and servicing. However, closer investigation may reveal that the erosion of business was due to unreliable deliveries, poor quality control, uncompetitive prices, or incompetent sales staff.

With the cause(s) of the problem defined, various alternatives for dealing with it should be identified and evaluated. This may require further research, such as obtaining feedback from customers and from field personnel. Finally, the decision to correct the situation should be made as objectively as possible. If drastic action is needed, there usually is little rationale for delaying. Serious problems do not go away by themselves: They tend to fester and become worse.

Finally, some learning experience should result from the misadventure. A vice president of one successful firm told me,

> I try to give my subordinates as much decision-making experience as possible. Perhaps I err on the side of delegating too much. In any case, I expect some mistakes to be made, some decisions that were not for the best. I don't come down too hard usually. This is part of the learning experience. But God help them if they make the same mistake again. There has been no learning experience, and I question their competence for higher executive positions.

Analyzing Successes

Successes deserve as much analysis as mistakes, although admittedly the urgency is less than with an emerging problem that requires quick remedial action. Any analysis of success should seek answers to at least the following questions:

Why Were Such Actions Successful?

- Was it because of the nature of the environment, and if so, how?
- Was it because of particular research, and if so, what and how?
- Was it because of particular engineering and/or production efforts, and if so, can these be adapted to other operations?
- Was it because of any particular element of the strategy—such as service, promotional activities, or distribution methods—and if so, how?
- Was it because of the specific elements of the strategy meshing well together, and if so, how was this achieved?

Was the Situation Unique and Unlikely to be Encountered Again?

- If the situation was not unique, how can these successful techniques be used in the future or in other operations at the present time?

ORGANIZATION OF THIS BOOK

In this tenth edition we have modified the classification of cases somewhat from earlier editions. As mentioned before, Part I on Marketing Wars examines the actions and countermoves of archrivals in a hotly competitive arena. In Part II, we study three firms that faced major changes and crises and mishandled them. Part III, Competitive Uncertainties, a new section, considers four firms that face an uncertain future and how they are trying to cope. Next are grouped cases of traditional marketing mistakes and then cases of notable marketing successes. Finally, we have brought back Entrepreneurial Adventures and follow the progress of two entrepreneurs we first encountered in an earlier edition. Let us briefly describe the cases that follow.

Marketing Wars

McDonald's had long dominated the fast food restaurant market. Then it began to falter, and hungry competitors, such as Burger King, Wendy's, and more recently Yum, made inroads into its competitive position. As it fought to regain its momentum, it explored diversifications and ever more store openings, while profitability plummeted. Then it found a new formula for profitable growth.

Pepsi and Coca-Cola for decades competed in the lucrative international arena. Usually Coca-Cola won out, but it could never let its guard down, and it recently did so in Europe. Now a trend toward noncarbonated beverages along with Pepsi's non-drink diversifications is swinging the momentum to Pepsi.

Boeing long dominated the worldwide commercial aircraft market, with the European Airbus only a minor player. A series of Boeing blunders, however, coupled with an aggressive Airbus, brought market shares close to parity, but now the momentum was with Airbus, and it finally wrested the number one position from Boeing.

Reebok and Nike are major competitors in the athletic footwear and apparel market. Nike was overtaken by Reebok in the late 1980s, but then Nike surged far ahead. How did this happen?

Managing Change and Crises

Albert Dunlap had a well-deserved reputation as the premier hatchet man, the one who would come into a sick organization and fire enough people to make it temporarily profitable—he was known as "Chainsaw Al." Somehow, with Sunbeam this seemingly proven downsizing strategy did not work, and Dunlap himself was fired by the board of directors. Later investigations brought fraud suits for accounting misdeeds.

Product safety lapses that result in injuries and even loss of life are among the worst abuses any company can make. Worse, however, is when such risks are allowed to continue for years. Ford Explorers equipped with Firestone tires were involved in more than two hundred deaths from tire failures and vehicle rollovers. After news of the accidents began surfacing, Ford and Firestone blamed the other for the deaths. Eventually, inept crisis management brought a host of lawsuits resulting in massive recalls and billions in damages.

Perrier, the bottled water firm, encountered adversity when traces of benzene were found in some of its product. Responsibly, it ordered a sweeping recall of all bottles in North America and, a few days later, in the rest of the world while it tried to correct the problem. For five months, Perrier kept the product off the market, thereby allowing competitors an unparalleled windfall. Worse was the realization by the public that claims regarding the purity of its product were false.

Competitive Uncertainties

Two faltering retail chains, Kmart and Sears, merged under the auspices of a hedge fund manager. Whether two weaklings can become one strong operation to compete with the likes of Wal-Mart and Target is uncertain at this time, though investors bid both stocks up to extravagant levels in anticipation. The real estate could be worth quite a bit if the retail business does not succeed, though this would hardly warrant the present stock prices. A crap shoot, or a calculated gamble by a very savvy turn-around expert? We will have to see.

In July 1999, Hewlett-Packard (H-P), the world's second biggest computer maker, chose Carly Fiorina to be its CEO. Thus she became the first outsider to take the reins in H-P's sixty-year history. Three years later, she engineered the biggest merger in the high-tech industry, with Compaq Computer. A year later, H-P boasted that this merger had become a model of effectively assimilating two giant organizations. But growth in profitability did not follow, and early in 2005, the board fired Fiorina.

Toys "R" Us for decades had been the category killer of the toy industry. In recent years, Kmart and Target began entering the toy industry and used toys as loss leaders to draw customers into their stores at Christmas time. Soon Wal-Mart was the biggest toy retailer, and Toys "R" Us was faltering. It became so desperate, it even seriously considered getting out of toys altogether and trying to survive in its Kids "R" Us stores. The issue and decision is still in doubt as of this publication date.

Gateway's situation was similar to Toys "R" Us. It was unable to compete with the low prices of Dell Computer, as it desperately sought ways to bring its costs down and still survive in the PC industry. It finally sold all of its Gateway stores and was attempting to develop relationships with hi-tech retailers. Its viability still remains in doubt.

Marketing Management Mistakes

The problems of Maytag's Hoover subsidiary in the United Kingdom almost defy reason. The subsidiary planned a promotional campaign so generous that the company was overwhelmed with takers; it could neither supply the products nor grant the prizes. In a miscue of multimillion-dollar consequences, Maytag had to foot the bill while trying to appease irate customers.

Merck, the pharmaceutical giant, learned that its blockbuster arthritis drug, Vioxx, doubled the risk of getting a heart attack or stroke. Over five years and $500 million in advertising, it had gained 20 million users in the United States, at the time it recalled the drug September 30, 2004. Critics and tort lawyers assailed the company for waiting so long to recall this "dangerous" drug, since research studies, as much as five years before, had raised questions about the safety of Vioxx. Others wondered whether Merck had recalled Vioxx too soon, whether the benefits outweighed the risks. A committee called together by the FDA, on February 18, 2005, by a narrow vote favored reintroduction of Vioxx. Now tort lawyers and their billions in damage suits had a temporary setback. But the situation is still fluid.

Snapple, a marketer of noncarbonated fruit-flavored and iced tea drinks, was acquired by Quaker Oats in late 1994 for $1.7 billion. As sales declined and losses mounted, it soon became apparent to all but the president of Quaker that far too much had been paid for this acquisition. No strategy changes could turn Snapple around. In 1997, Quaker sold Snapple for $300 million, a loss of $1.4 billion in less than three years.

Newell, a consumer-products firm, had successfully geared its operations to meeting the demands of giant retailers, particularly Wal-Mart. Rubbermaid had in recent years been unable to meet those stringent requirements. In 1999, Newell acquired Rubbermaid, confident of turning its operation around, only to find that Rubbermaid's problems were not easily corrected and had a negative impact on the fortunes of Newell as well.

In April 1992, just outside Paris, Disney opened its first theme park in Europe. It had high expectations and supreme self-confidence (critics later called it arrogance). The earlier Disney parks in California, Florida, and more recently Japan, were all spectacular successes. But rosy expectations became a delusion as marketing miscues finally showed Disney that Europeans, and particularly the French, were not carbon copies of visitors elsewhere.

Notable Marketing Successes

In the early 1960s, Harley-Davidson dominated a static motorcycle industry. Suddenly, Honda burst on the scene, and Harley's market share dropped from 70 percent to 5 percent in only a few years. It took Harley nearly three decades to revive, but now it had created a mystique for its heavy motorcycles and gained a cult following almost unique in American business.

Vanguard, the second largest mutual fund company, is rapidly closing on Fidelity, the largest. Vanguard's strategy is to downplay marketing, shunning the heavy advertising and overhead of its competitors. It provides investors with better returns through far lower expense ratios and relies mostly on word of mouth and unpaid publicity to gain new customers, while old customers continue to pour money in.

In somewhat similar fashion, Southwest Airlines found a strategic window of opportunity as the lowest cost and lowest price carrier between certain cities. And how it milked this opportunity! Now it threatened major airlines in many of their domestic routes.

Our last success in this section is also about a firm that dominates its industry through offering customers lowest prices. Wal-Mart is by far the largest retailer in the world and reflects the genius of its founder, Sam Walton, who did this in his lifetime. But size can bring coercive power, especially of smaller suppliers. It can also destroy business competitors and even change the social structure of small towns. Some are questioning whether Wal-Mart has gotten too big.

Entrepreneurial Adventures

Boston Beer burst on the microbrewery scene with Samuel Adams beers, higher priced even than most imports. Notwithstanding this—or maybe because of it—Boston Beer became the largest microbrewer. It showed that a small entrepreneur can compete successfully against the giants in the industry, and do this on a national scale.

OfficeMax, an office-supply category-killer chain, grew to $2.5 billion in sales in only a few years. The dedication and creative efforts of its founder serve as a model for any world-be entrepreneur who aspires to make it big. Yet it was number three in its industry with the heady years of profitable growth seemingly over. In October 2003, Michael Feuer, the founder, agreed for his firm to be acquired by Boise Cascade, a giant lumber firm.

GENERAL WRAP-UP

Where possible, the text depicts major personalities involved in these cases. Imagine yourself in their positions, confronting the problems and facing choices at their points of crisis or just-recognized opportunities. What would you have done differently, and why? We invite you to participate in the discussion questions, the hands-on exercises, the debates appearing at the ends of chapters, and the occasional Devil's Advocate invitation (a Devil's Advocate is one who argues an opposing position for the sake of testing the decision). There are also discussion questions for the various boxes within chapters.

While doing these activities, you may feel the excitement and challenge of decision making under conditions of uncertainty. Perhaps you may even become a better future executive and decision maker.

QUESTIONS

1. Do you agree that it is impossible for a firm to avoid mistakes? Why or why not?

2. How can a firm speed up its awareness of emerging problems so that it can take corrective action? Be as specific as you can.

3. Large firms tend to err on the side of conservatism and are slower to take corrective action than smaller ones. Why do you suppose this is?

4. Which do you think is likely to be more costly to a firm, errors of omission or errors of commission? Why?

5. So often we see the successful firm eventually losing its pattern of success. Why is success not more enduring?

MARKETING WARS

CHAPTER TWO

Burger Wars: McDonald's vs. Burger King, Yum et al.

*F*ew business firms anywhere in the world have been able to match the sustained growth of McDonald's. Initially, it grew with one simple product, a hamburger; while it has broadened its product mix today, it still remains uniquely undiversified. The foundation for the success has always been the most rigid standards and controls to be found anywhere. McDonald's insisted these be adhered to by all outlets, company owned as well as franchised, and therein was an enduring marketing strategy.

For decades, no competitor could match the standards of quality, service, and cleanliness that made McDonald's unique. In recent years, however, these standards and controls have slipped, while competitors countered its former advantage and became ever more aggressive. The ball game had changed, and McDonald's was struggling to keep the growth mode. One McDonald's CEO went on a new-store binge, but these new stores often cannibalized older outlets; another CEO embarked on a crusade to acquire other fast-food restaurants, but these proved a drain on profits. Then Jim Cantalupo took the company back to basics, and the company's fortunes turned around.

An ill wind now seemed to beset McDonald's. Cantalupo, 60, the savior, died suddenly of a heart attack. His successor was diagnosed with colon cancer shortly after taking office.

But before we get into that, let's see how McDonald's got started and the glorious decades that were to come as it dominated the fast-food industry.

RAY KROC'S DREAM

Ray Kroc faced a serious dilemma. He was 57 years old and all his life had dreamed of becoming rich, and worked hard at it, but real success eluded him. He had played piano with dance bands, then turned to selling paper cups for a firm called Lily-Tulip. He also moonlighted by working for a Chicago radio station, accompanying singers and arranging the music programs. Then he thought he might make his fortune by selling land in a Florida land boom. But that did not work out, and a year later he returned to Chicago almost broke. Lily-Tulip gave him back his old job, and he stayed there more than ten years.

In 1937, Kroc became intrigued with a new gadget, a simple electrical appliance that could mix six milkshakes at the same time. He quit Lily-Tulip again and made a deal with the inventor. He soon became the world's exclusive agent for the Prince Castle Multi-Mixer and for the next 20 years traveled all over the country peddling it. Though he didn't yet know it, at long last he was on the threshold of his dream.

In 1954, Kroc received an order for eight of the Multi-Mixers from a small hamburger stand in San Bernardino, California. He wondered what wild kind of business sold so many milkshakes. He decided to go and see for himself the operation of Maurice and Richard McDonald that needed to make 48 milkshakes at the same time.

When Ray Kroc arrived, he was amazed. It was a self-service hamburger stand, and he saw crowds of people waiting in line under golden arches. He was even more impressed with the speed of service and the cleanliness. Kroc badly wanted in on this business and hounded the McDonald brothers until they allowed him to start selling franchises. By 1960, he had sold some 200 franchises.

Kroc bought out the McDonald brothers, though he kept their name, and they took their money and quietly retired to their hometown of Bedford, New Hampshire. Once in control, it took Kroc only 17 years to reach the billion-dollar milestone. It gave him great satisfaction to think that IBM had needed 40 years to do this. Kroc would boast in his autobiography that the company was responsible for making more than 1,000 millionaires—the franchise holders.[1]

When Kroc retired in 1968, the company had more than 1,200 restaurants, and sales were $400 million. He had laid the foundation for great growth; by 1972, the number of outlets had climbed to 2,272, and sales were accelerating beyond $1 billion.

THE McDONALD'S GROWTH MACHINE

In its *1995 Annual Report*, McDonald's management was justifiably proud. Sales and profits had continued the long trend upward and even seemed to be accelerating. See Table 2.1 for sales and profits through 1998. Far from reaching a saturation point, the firm was opening more restaurants than ever, some 2,400 around the world in 1995, up from 1,800 the year before. "We plan to add between 2,500 and 3,200 restaurants in both 1996 and 1997, with about two thirds outside the United States. In other words, we opened more than six restaurants per day in 1995; over the next two years, we plan to open eight a day."[2] And, "Our growth opportunities remain significant: on any given day, 99 percent of the world's population does not eat at McDonald's ... yet."[3]

---

[1] Ray Kroc and Robert Anderson, *Grinding It Out: The Making of McDonald's* (New York: Berkley Publishing, 1977), p. 200.

[2] *McDonald's 1995 Annual Report*, p. 8.

[3] Ibid, p. 7.

TABLE 2.1   Growth in System-wide Sales and Profits, 1985–1998

	Sales (millions)	Percentage Gain	Income (millions)	Percentage Gain
1985	$11,011		$ 433	
1986	12,432	12.9	480	12.2
1987	14,330	15.3	549	14.4
1988	16,064	12.1	646	17.7
1989	17,333	7.9	727	12.5
1990	18,759	8.2	802	10.3
1991	19,928	6.2	860	7.2
1992	21,885	9.8	959	11.5
1993	23,587	7.8	1,083	12.9
1994	25,987	10.2	1,224	13.0
1995	29,914	15.1	1,427	16.6
1996	31,812	6.3	1,573	10.2
1997	33,638	5.7	1,642	4.3
1998	35,979	6.9	1,550	–5.6

Source: 1998 McDonald's Annual Report

Note: Systemwide sales include sales by all restaurants, whether operated by the Company, franchisees, or by affiliates operating under joint-venture agreements.

Commentary: Of particular interest is how the new expansion policies brought a burst of revenues and profits in the mid-1990s. But after 1995, growth in sales and earnings slowed. Note the first decline in profit gain in 1998, a harbinger of things to come.

Company management extolled the power of the McDonald's brand overseas, and how on opening days lines were sometimes "miles" long. "Often our challenge is to keep up with demand. In China, for example, there are only 62 McDonald's to serve a population of 1.2 billion."[4] By the end of 1995, the company had 7,012 outlets in 89 countries of the world, with Japan alone having 1,482. Table 2.2 shows the top-ten countries in 1999 in number of McDonald's units.

Sometimes in marketing its products in different cultures, adjustments had to be made. Nowhere was this more necessary than in Yugoslavia during the NATO bombings in the Kosovo confrontation. The following Information Box describes the changes McDonald's made there for these turbulent times.

Growth Prospects in the United States

In 1995, with 11,368 of its restaurants in the United States, wasn't McDonald's reaching saturation in its domestic market? Top management vehemently disputed this conclusion. Rather, it offered a startling statistical phenomenon to support accelerating expansion. Called "Greenberg's Law," after newly appointed McDonald's U.S. chairman Jack Greenberg, it maintained that the more stores

[4] Ibid.

TABLE 2.2 Top Ten Foreign Markets in
Number of Units as of Beginning of 1999

Japan	2,852 restaurants
Canada	1,085
Germany	931
England	810
France	708
Brazil	672
Australia	666
Taiwan	292
China	220
Italy	201

Source: McDonald's 1998 Annual Report
Commentary: Is the popularity in Japan a surprise?

INFORMATION BOX

McDONALD'S SUCCESSFUL ADVENTURES IN SERBIA, 1999

The NATO air war against Yugoslavia lasted 78 days. At first, the fifteen McDonald's restaurants in Yugoslavia were closed due to angry mobs bent on vandalizing. Fanned by media attacks on "NATO criminals and aggressors," mobs of youth smashed windows and painted insults. But the restaurants soon reopened, downplaying the U. S. citizenship and presenting McDonald's as a Yugoslav company.

They promoted the McCountry, a domestic pork burger with paprika garnish. (Pork is considered the most Serbian of meats.) To cater to Serbian identity and pride, they brought out posters and lapel buttons showing the golden arches topped with a traditional Serbian cap called the *sajkaca.* Dragoljub Jakic, the 47-year-old managing director of McDonald's in Yugoslavia, noted that the cap "is a strong, unique Serbian symbol. By adding this symbol of our cultural heritage, we hoped to denote our pride in being a local company."[5] They also handed out free cheeseburgers at anti-NATO rallies. One restaurant's basement in Belgrade even became a bomb shelter.

The result? In spite of falling wages, rising prices, and lingering anger at the United States, the McDonald's restaurants were thronged with Serbs.

Still, McDonald's globally is a prominent symbol of American culture and attracts outbursts of anti-American sentiment. For example, in August 1999, a McDonald's in Belgium was burned down by suspected animal-rights activists. And India has seen militant critics: "They (McDonald's) are the chief killers of cows in the world. We don't need cow killers in India."[6]

---

[5] Robert Block, "How Big Mac Kept From Becoming a Serb Archenemy," *Wall Street Journal,* September 3, 1999, p. B3.

[6] "Delhi Delights in McMutton Burgers," *Cleveland Plain Dealer,* November 6, 1999, p. D3

Do you think McDonald's in Serbia went too far in downplaying—some would say even denying—its American roots? Did it have any other reasonable option if it were to keep operating?

If militant activists become more violent about McDonald's "conducting a global conspiracy against cows," do you think McDonald's should abandon the India market? Why or why not?

McDonald's put in a city, the more per-capita transactions will result. Thus, with two stores in a city there might be sixteen transactions per capita per year. Add two or four more stores and the transactions will not only double, or quadruple, but may even do better than that. The hypothesized explanation for this amazing phenomenon seemingly rested on two factors: convenience and market share. With more outlets, McDonald's increased its convenience to consumers and added to its market share at the expense of competitors. Hence, the justification for the expansion binge.

Aiding this domestic expansion, the company had been able to reduce the cost of building a new U. S. traditional restaurant by 26 percent through standardizing building materials and equipment and global sourcing, as well as improving construction methods and building designs. It had also found abundant market opportunities in satellite restaurants. These were smaller, had lower sales volume, and served simplified menus. This format proved cost-efficient in such nontraditional places as zoos, hospitals, airports, museums, military bases, and in retail stores such as Wal-Mart, Home Depot, and other major stores. For example, such satellite restaurants were in some 800 Wal-Mart stores by the end of 1995, with more planned. In October 1996, a McDonald's Express opened in an office building in Lansing, Michigan, perhaps a harbinger of more such sites to come.

In its eager search for more outlets, McDonald's did something it had never done before. It took over stores from weak competitors. In late summer 1996, it bought 184 company-owned Roy Rogers outlets. "Here was an opportunity that was maybe once in a lifetime," Greenberg stated.[7] Earlier the same year, it acquired Burghy's, an 80-store fast-food chain in Italy. In New Zealand, it added seventeen restaurants with the Georgie Pie chain.

The new stores being opened were seldom like the old ones. The drive-through windows generated 55 percent of U. S. sales and made fewer seats needed inside. This left more space available for gas stations or for indoor playgrounds—Ronald's Playplaces—to attract families. McDonald's made joint ventures with Chevron and Amoco to codevelop properties. It also signed an exclusive marketing deal with Disney for promoting each other's brands.

[7] Gary Samuels, "Golden Arches Galore," *Forbes*, November 4, 1996, p. 48.

McDonald's has always been a big spender for advertising, and this has been effective. Even back in the 1970s, a survey of schoolchildren found 96 percent identifying Ronald McDonald, ranking him second only to Santa Claus.[8] In 1995, advertising and promotional expenditures totaled $1.8 billion, or 6 percent of sales.[9]

Factors in the Invincibility of McDonald's

Through the third quarter of 1996, McDonald's could proudly claim 126 consecutive quarters of record earnings. Since its earliest days, the ingredients of success were simple, but few competitors were able to effectively emulate them. The basic aspects were

- a brief menu, but having consistent quality over thousands of outlets
- strictly enforced and rigorous operational standards controlling service, cleanliness, and all other aspects of the operation
- friendly employees, despite a high turnover of personnel because of the monotony of automated food handling
- heavy mass media advertising directed mostly at families and children
- identification of a fertile target market—the family—and directing the marketing strategy to satisfying it with product, price, promotional efforts, and site locations (at least in the early years this meant the suburban locations with their high density of families)

However, by the end of 1996, international operations were the real vehicle of growth, providing 47 percent of the company's $30 billion sales and 54 percent of profits. Of no small concern, the domestic operation had not blossomed accordingly.

STORM CLOUDS FOR THE DOMESTIC OPERATION

Souring Franchisee Relations

In the market-share game, in which McDonald's dominated all its competitors, corporate management concluded that the firm with the most outlets in a given community wins. But as McDonald's unprecedented expansion continued, many franchisees were skeptical of headquarters' claim that no one loses when the company opens more outlets in a community because market share rises proportionately. Still, the franchise holder wondered how much his or her sales would diminish when another McDonald's opened down the street.

The 7,000-member American Franchisee Association, an organization formed to look after franchisees' rights, claimed that McDonald's operators were joining in

---

[8] "The Burger That Conquered the Country," *Time*, September 17, 1973, pp. 84–92.
[9] *McDonald's 1995 Annual Report*, p. 9.

INFORMATION BOX

THE CONTENTMENT OF TWO McDONALD'S FRANCHISEES

In 1980, Wayne Kilburn and his wife, Mary Jane, took over the only McDonald's in Ridgecrest, California, a town of 26,000. The Kilburns prospered in the years to come. Then McDonald's instituted its "market-share plan" for Ridgecrest. Late in 1995, it put a company-owned restaurant inside the Wal-Mart. A few months later, it built another outlet inside the China Lake Naval Weapons Center. A third company-owned store went up just outside the naval base. "Basically, they killed me," *Forbes* reported Kilburn saying. And he claimed his volume dropped 30 percent.[10]

In its *1995 Annual Report*, corporate headquarters offered another view concerning franchisee contentment. Tom Wolf was a McDonald's franchisee with 15 restaurants in the Huntington, West Virginia, and Ashland, Kentucky, markets. He opened his first McDonald's in 1974, had eight by the end of 1993, and opened seven more in the next two years, including two in Wal-Mart stores and another in an alliance with an oil company; in addition he added indoor Playplaces to two existing restaurants.

Did all this investment in growth make a difference? The *Annual Report* quoted Tom: "I wouldn't change a thing. Sales are up. I'm serving more customers, my market share is up and I'm confident about the future. Customers say that the Playplaces and Wal-Mart units are 'a great idea.' The business is out there. We've got to take these opportunities now, or leave them for someone else to take."[11]

"The high growth, market-share policy should not bother any franchisee. It simply creates opportunities to invest in more restaurants." Evaluate this statement.

---

[10] Samuels, p. 48.
[11] *McDonald's 1995 Annual Report*, p. 32.

---

record numbers.[12] Other franchisees formed a clandestine group called the Consortium, representing dissidents who felt present management was unresponsive to their concerns. They remembered a kinder and gentler company. See the above Information Box for contrasting franchisee views on the high-growth market-share policy.

Other concerns of franchisees were a new set of business practices developed by corporate headquarters, known as Franchising 2000. The company claimed it instituted this as a way to improve standards for quality, service, cleanliness, and value by giving franchisees better "tools." But some saw this as a blatant attempt to gain more power over the franchised operations. One provision revived a controversial A, B, C, and F grading system, with only franchisees who received A's and B's eligible for more

---

[12] Richard Gibson, "Some Franchisees say Moves by McDonald's Hurt Their Operations," *Wall Street Journal*, April 17, 1996, pp. A1, A8.

TABLE 2.3   Percentage of Franchised to Total Traditional Restaurants, Selected Years, 1985–1998

	1985	1992	1995	1998
Traditional restaurants				
Total	8,901	13,093	16,809	24,800
Operated by franchisees	6,150	9,237	11,240	15,281
Percentage franchised to total	69.1%	70.5	66.9	61.3

Source: Calculated from *1998 Annual Report*

Commentary: While by 1998, the ratio of franchised to total restaurants had dropped, still more than 60% were still operated by franchisees. This suggests the desirability of heeding franchisee concerns by corporate headquarters.

restaurants. Furthermore, McDonald's began using Franchising 2000 to enforce a single pricing strategy throughout the chain, so that a Big Mac, for example, would cost the same everywhere. The corporation maintained that such uniformity was necessary for the discounting needed to build market share. Those not complying risked losing their franchise.

Franchise relations should not be a matter of small concern to McDonald's. Table 2.3 shows the ratio of franchised restaurants to total restaurants up to 1998. As can be seen, franchises comprised, by far, the largest proportion of restaurants.

Menu Problems

In 1993, domestic per-store sales were increasing at a 4 percent annual rate. By the third quarter of 1996, sales had slumped to a 3 percent decrease, this being the fifth quarter in a row of declining sales. In part, this decline was thought to be attributable to older customers drifting away: "Huge numbers of baby-boomers ... want less of the cheap, fattening foods at places like McDonald's. As soon as their kids are old enough, they go elsewhere."[13]

In an attempt to win more business from this customer segment, McDonald's, with a $200 million promotional blitz, launched its first "grownup taste" sandwich, the Arch Deluxe line of beef, fish, and chicken burgers. It forecast that this would become a $1 billion brand in only its first year. But before long, some were calling this a McFlop. In September 1996, Edward Rensi, head of U. S. operations, tried to minimize the stake in the new sandwich and sent a memo to 2,700 concerned franchisees, "the Arch Deluxe was never intended to be a silver bullet."[14] On October 8, Rensi was replaced by Jack Greenberg.

McDonald's domestic troubles were not entirely new. As far back as the late 1980s, competitors, including Pizza Hut and Taco Bell, were nibbling at McDonald's

---

[13] Shelly Branch, "McDonald's Strikes Out With Grownups," *Fortune,* November 11, 1996, p. 158.
[14] Ibid.

market share, and Burger King was more than holding its own. Even the great traditional strength of McDonald's of unsurpassed controlled standards over food, service, and cleanliness seemed to be waning: A *1995 Restaurants and Institutions Choice in Chains* survey of 2,849 adults gave McDonald's low marks on food quality, value, service, and cleanliness. Top honors instead went to Wendy's.[15]

In 1991, McDonald's reluctantly tried discounting, with "Extra Value Meals," largely to keep up with Taco Bell's value pricing. But by 1995, price promotions were no longer attracting customers, and per-store sales began slumping. The new, adult-oriented Deluxe line was not only aimed at older adults, but with its prices 20 percent more than regular items, it was expected to parry the discounting.

The company previously had problems in expanding its menu. The McDLT was notably unsuccessful despite heavy promotion. Later, the low-fat McLean, an effort to attract weight-conscious adults, was a complete disaster. In fact, this beef-and-sea-weed concoction sold so badly that some operators kept only a few frozen patties on hand, while others, as revealed in an embarrassing TV expose, sold fully fatted burgers in McLean boxes to the few customers asking for them.

Some years before, the company had tried, but failed, to develop an acceptable pizza product. It was also unable to create a dinner menu that would attract evening-hour traffic. Two other experiments were also abandoned: a 1950s-style cafe and a family-type concept called Hearth Express that served chicken, ham, and meatloaf.

THE SITUATION IN THE NEW MILLENNIUM

Jack Greenberg was promoted to CEO of McDonald's in August 1998, and then to chairman of the board in May 1999. There was hope that he would improve the alienation felt by many franchisees. He quickly began diversifying within the fast-food industry, buying Donatos Pizza, a midwestern chain of 143 restaurants, proclaiming: "We would like to make this a growth opportunity for our franchisees."[16] Imitating some of its competitors, particularly Wendy's, McDonald's also installed a new cooking system to deliver sandwiches to order, "Made for You," which meant fresher with less waste compared with the old system of holding bins. "You don't grow this business by having clean washrooms" Greenberg said. "We will grow this business through food."[17]

Despite Greenberg's leadership, McDonald's domestic operations continued to falter. By 2001, it was averaging only 1 percent same-store sales growth, far behind the 4 percent average of Burger King and Wendy. After 44 years as one of America's premier growth companies, market saturation seemed imminent. The main reason was thought to be a stale menu, but that was hardly a new insight.

Of perhaps just as much concern was the deterioration of the stringent controls that for decades had marked McDonald's as the paragon among all firms. A 2001

---

[15] Ibid.

[16] James P. Miller and Richard Gibson, "Did Somebody Say Pizza?" *Wall Street Journal,* May 1, 1999, p. A4.

[17] Kevin Helliker and Richard Gibson, "The New Chief is Ordering Up Changes at McDonald's," *Wall Street Journal,* August 24, 1998, p. B4.

University of Michigan study on customer satisfaction showed that conditions had worsened from the 1995 survey that had given it low marks on food, service, and cleanliness. This 2001 study also ranked McDonald's among the poorest-performing fast-food chains, with 11 percent of customers dissatisfied because of slow service, wrong orders, dirty stores, and rude, uncaring employees. Estimates were that unhappy customers could mean an average of $60,000 in lost sales per year per store. In efforts to improve customer satisfaction, "customer recovery teams" were planned, along with better education of store managers and franchisees in handling complaints.[18]

Undoubtedly, such problems reflected the difficulty many businesses were having in hiring good help in the low unemployment of the late 1990s. But other fast-food chains were doing better in this regard than McDonald's. Perhaps another factor contributed to the quality control problems. In recognition of franchisee complaints, Greenberg threw out the Franchise 2000 rulebook with its 80 pages of onerous regulations and gave franchisees more say in their local menus.

The frenetic growth in outlets of the mid-1990s was over, as many angry franchisees had seen their sales decline as much as 30 percent due to cannibalization by nearby McDonald's outlets. In 1999, only 150 new outlets were added, down sharply from the 1,100 of a few years before.

Increasingly, Greenberg turned his attention to food diversifications. He planned to grow the 143-store Donatos Pizza regional chain to a national one of a thousand stores. He bought into Chipotle Mexican Grill, a popular Denver-based chain of Mexican restaurants. The purchase of Aroma, a coffee-and-sandwich bar in London, England, showed perhaps the most promise. In the UK, the cold-sandwich market was almost double the size of the burger market and growing twice as fast, appealing to a mostly single, health-conscious, and female customer base that had practically no overlap with the burger crowd—therefore, no cannibalization. Some 150 Aroma stores were planned by 2002. In another major acquisition, McDonald's acquired the faltering Boston Market chain on May 26, 2000. About 100 underperforming Boston Market restaurants were closed, and others were converted to McDonald's, Chipotle Mexican Grill, and Donatos Pizza. This still left more than 750 Boston restaurants that could challenge McDonald's management in achieving profitability.

In a major menu thrust beyond burgers, more new products were coming out of McDonald's test kitchens than ever before, many of these appealing regionally rather than nationally. For example, the McBrat, a $1.99 sandwich with sauerkraut and onion on a bratwurst, a big hit in Minnesota and Wisconsin; the McLobster Roll in New England; the Homestyle Burger with hot mustard in Texas; the Brutus Buckeye Burger for Ohioans; and even bagel breakfast sandwiches, were already doing well in 6,000 stores.[19]

Still, U.S. sales grew just 3 percent in 2000, while fourth-quarter net earnings declined 7 percent. McDonald's responded with the "New Tastes Menu," a collection of 44 items to be rotated four at a time. An analyst noted, however, that these were

---

[18] Richard Gibson, Dow Jones News, as reported in "McDonald's Leaders Finding Rudeness, Slowness Are Costing Company Business," *Cleveland Plain Dealer,* July 16, 2001, p. C6.

[19] Bruce Upbin, "Beyond Burgers," *Forbes,* November 1, 1999, pp. 218–223.

mostly "tired old products with such startling innovations like a strip of bacon or a dollop of ranch dressing."[20]

The Situation in the Rest of the World

In Europe, mad-cow hysteria and currency woes were playing havoc, and McDonald's stock was at a two-year low. But non-U.S. restaurants continued to offer the best opportunities, and by the end of 2000, foreign restaurants outnumbered U.S. outlets by 15,900 to 12,408. International business contributed 52 percent of total operating income by 2000. (Company public information.) The success of the international operations partly reflected McDonald's adaptations in foreign environments. (We saw an example of this earlier in the Serbian Information Box.)

Japan, especially, was a lucrative foreign market, and by 2001 the almost 3,600 McDonald's had changed the eating habits of the nation, making fast food a part of everyday life. McDonald's—*Maku* in Japanese shorthand—controlled about 65 percent of the fast-food burger market, serving 1.3 billion customers a year. The mad-cow scare, that had so severely affected demand in Europe, was at first largely averted in Japan, which used beef from Australia where there had been no disease. Later, the stigma also began to affect Japanese demand.

LATER DEVELOPMENTS

CEO Jack Greenberg, now 60, stepped down at the end of 2002, well ahead of his planned 2005 retirement. His had been a frustrating four-year effort to reinvent the firm and start it on a new growth pattern.

Greenberg's reinvention efforts included starting a fierce price war by selling two of McDonald's biggest sandwiches for $1 each, introducing some forty menu items, spending $151 million to overhaul the company's U.S. kitchens in order to make food hotter and fresher, and acquiring other restaurant chains. In November 2002, customers were even given the option of paying with credit cards and earning frequent flyer miles. Still, sales had remained lackluster, and profits fell in seven of the past eight quarters, while the stock price had sunk to a seven-year low.

Aside from the acquisitions, customer response to most of these efforts was poor. The price war mostly resulted in all burger chains facing lower profits with little increase in sales. The new "Made for You" kitchens sacrificed speed and service. And Greenberg could never bring customer service up to historic levels, despite sending mystery shoppers to evaluate service. The mad-cow scare in Europe in 2000 dragged down profits as well, but profitability was not regained with the end of mad-cow concerns.[21]

The foreign markets that had long sustained the growth mode were also faltering now. Germany was the largest European market, but McDonald's growth there stagnated as competition grew from Burger King, which expanded in Germany from

---

[20] Brandon Copple, "Same Old, Same Old," *Forbes,* February 19, 2001, p. 60.

[21] Shirley Leung and Ron Lieber, "The New Menu Option at McDonald's: Plastic," *Wall Street Journal,* November 26, 2002, pp. D1–2; Shirley Leung, "McDonald's Chief Plans to Leave," *Wall Street Journal,* December 6, 2002, pp. A3, A6.

268 stores in 2000 to 390 in 2002, and from local retailers such as gas-station food marts and traditional mom-and-pop bakeries. In the UK, McDonald's problems with service, cleanliness, and changes in consumer tastes now throttled its expansion efforts. In Japan, long the crown jewel in McDonald's foreign operations, the chain's 3,800 stores faced a saturated market, with its core customers—families with children—shrinking from a declining birthrate, while local competitors became stronger. Same-store sales in Japan fell 12.1 percent in 2002 and were expected to fall an additional 3.5 percent in 2003.

Domestically, even the restaurant chains that Greenberg acquired in his diversification efforts were not producing the expected profits. Boston Market and its partner brands, as a group, lost $67 million on sales of $1.07 billion in 2002. Some of these could face divestiture by a top management that is less growth minded.

James R. Cantalupo

Cantalupo succeeded Greenberg as CEO in January 2003. Recently retired as CEO of McDonald's International, his job now was to restore sales and profit growth company-wide. With his arrival, the company announced its first quarterly loss since going public in 1965, almost forty years before.

When the board brought him back to replace Greenberg, Cantalupo acted quickly to undo some of the high-profile projects of his predecessor. He killed a $1 billion technology effort, code named Innovate, that had been envisioned to be a global digital network linking 30,000 McDonald's restaurants to headquarters and vendors. "We know we need to make changes," Cantalupo said, but "We don't intend to throw capital at problems."[22] In his letter to shareholders for the *2002 McDonald's Annual Report,* Cantalupo announced

> We are targeting a lower earnings growth rate. Given the nature and size of our business, the prior earnings per share growth target in the 10 percent to 15 percent range is no longer realistic … in short, McDonald's is in transition from a company that emphasizes *adding restaurants to customers* to one that emphasizes *adding customers to restaurants.*[23]

He made investors happy by slashing capital spending by 40 percent, largely, through closing poorer performing restaurants and adding fewer new restaurants. He also raised the dividend 70 percent.

Cantalupo and his team addressed mounting customer complaints about slow drive-through service and surly employees. Efforts were made to improve the taste of burgers and promote salad entrees, while eliminating "super size" french fries and soft drinks—these latter two menu moves designed to placate critics blaming obese consumers on burger sellers.

---

[22] Richard Gibson and Steven Gray, "Death of Chief Leaves McDonald's Facing Challenges," *Wall Street Journal,* April 20, 2004, p. A16.

[23] *McDonald's 2002 Annual Report,* p. 3.

The attractiveness of the new low-growth policy of Cantalupo was fully evident in the summer and fall of 2003 when the stock price rose from $18 to over $24 by early October.

On April 19, 2004, a calamity of no small moment occurred. At a global convention of McDonald's franchisees in Orlando, Florida, just before he was to make the opening remarks about his successful 16-month campaign to restore sales and profit growth, Jim Cantalupo collapsed and died of an apparent heart attack. McDonald's board quickly named 43-year-old Charlie Bell to the top job. Bell was an obvious choice, having been president and chief operating officer since late 2002.

Then the company faced an almost unbelievable double whammy, when soon after Bell was named CEO, he was diagnosed with colon cancer and had to resign in November to focus on battling the disease.

RESURGING COMPETITORS

By 2003, McDonald's faced increased competitive pressure, although it still dominated the fast-food industry. One firm in particular, Yum Brands, had become a major factor in the fast-food industry. Table 2.4 shows the relative competitive positions of McDonald's and its major competitors as of 2003. Burger King had long been the closest competitor in size, but now Yum had more restaurants than McDonald's, although McDonald's still was the big leader in total revenues.

Burger King

Interestingly, the origins of Burger King and McDonald's were almost the same year. Burger King was founded in 1954, in Miami, by James McLamore and David Edgerton. Ray Kroc founded McDonald's one year later. As can be seen from Table 2.5, Burger King grew far slower than McDonald's, despite being a little older. In 1967, it had 8,000 employees in 274 restaurants when Pillsbury Company acquired it for $18 million.

TABLE 2.4 Competitive Positions of McDonald's and Major Competitors 2003[a]

	System-wide Sales	Net Income	No. of Stores
McDonald's	41.5	1.5	31,129
Yum	8.9	.7	33,000
Burger King	11.1	N.D.	11,223
Wendy's	3.1	.24	9,291

[a] In billions of dollars.

Sources: Company annual reports; N.D. not disclosed,

Commentary: You can see the still commanding position of McDonald's despite its lessening growth mode. At this point, the consolidation of five restaurant brands—four of these, KFC, Pizza Hut, Taco Bell, and Long John Silver's, being the global leaders of the chicken, pizza, Mexican-style food, and quick-service seafood categories—under the Yum umbrella, makes rapidly growing Yum perhaps the major competitor of McDonald's, even though Burger King still has the second place in sales.

TABLE 2.5 Competitive Position of Burger King and McDonald's in Total Sales and Restaurants, 1993–1998

	Total Sales (billions of $)					
	1993	1994	1995	1996	1997	1998
McDonald's	23.6	26.0	29.9	31.8	33.6	36.0
Burger King	6.7	7.5	8.4	9.0	9.8	10.3
Percentage of McDonald's	28.4%	28.0	28.1	28.3	29.2	28.0
	Total Restaurants (hundreds)					
McDonald's	14.2	15.9	18.4	21.0	23.1	24.8
Burger King	7.1	7.5	8.0	8.7	9.4	9.8
Percentage of McDonald's	50.0%	47.1	43.5	40.0	40.7	39.5

Sources: Calculated from company reports.

Commentary: You can see in these years that Burger King was unable to gain any ground on McDonald's except one year, 1997, in total sales. In number of restaurants, it steadily lost ground as McDonald's opened far more restaurants than ever before. This suggests the power position of the firm with greater size and resources.

Despite slower growth, Burger King was the first in the industry to introduce dining rooms where patrons could sit inside to devour their burgers and fries. In 1975, it was the first to introduce drive-through service, and this came to account for 50 percent of Burger King's business. McDonald's and other fast foods were quick to adopt these concepts.

In 1988, Grand Metropolitan PLC, an English firm, acquired Pillsbury and its Burger King. In 1997, Grand Metropolitan merged with Guinness to create Diageo, which in addition to owning Burger King also had such well-known consumer brands as Guinness Beer, Pillsbury, Green Giant, Haagen-Dazs, Smirnoff Vodka, and J & B Scotch Whiskey. As of April 1999, Burger King had 10,506 company-owned and franchised restaurants in all 50 states and 54 countries around the world, with sales of $10.3 billion. In December 2002, Diageo sold Burger King for $1.5 billion to a venture capital consortium led by Texas Pacific Group. In fiscal year 2003, Burger King had systemwide sales of $11.1 billion, and 11,223 total worldwide outlets.

Yum Brands

PepsiCo had spun this organization off in 1997, and it was now the world's largest restaurant operator in units, with 33,000 restaurants in five major chains: Pizza Hut, Taco Bell, KFC (Kentucky Fried Chicken), Long John Silver's, and A&W All-American Food. Yum CEO, David Novak, blamed the problems that led to the spin-off on PepsiCo's mismanagement and emphasis on marketing to the neglect of quality, service, and atmosphere. In 2002, the company changed its name to Yum Brands, from Tricon Global Restaurants, to reflect its expanding portfolio of brands and its ticket symbol on the New York Stock Exchange. Four of the company's restaurant brands—KFC, Pizza Hut, Taco Bell, and Long John Silver's—were the global leaders of the chicken, pizza, Mexican-style food, and quick-service seafood categories.

Wendy's

Wendy's worldwide sales were $3.1 billion in 2003, and it had 9,291 restaurants. It was founded in 1969 by Dave Thomas, well known from being the spokesman in TV commercials, until his death. Recently, the company began bringing back some of his old commercials. Wendy's has invested in Tim Hortons, the largest coffee and fresh baked goods restaurant chain in Canada; Baja Fresh Mexican Grill; Café Express, a bistro-style restaurant; and Pasta Pomodoro Italian style restaurants.

ANALYSIS

After decades of uninterrupted growth in sales, profits, and number of stores opened, McDonald's faced diminished prospects, domestically and foreign, by the latter 1990s. Though no one wanted to admit it then, the evidence was rather compelling that the company life cycle was reaching maturity without major policy changes. Pouring more efforts into additional outlets seemed ill advised, although it took a new CEO to recognize and come to grips with this. But the siren call of growth is difficult to subdue.

Relations with franchisees, formerly best in the industry, had deteriorated as corporate management pursued policies more dictatorial and selfish than ever before, policies that signaled the end of the kinder and gentler stance franchisees remembered. In particular, the new expansion policy aimed at increased market share, regardless of its effect on established franchisees, portended worsening relations and the start of an adversarial instead of supportive climate.

The cost-benefit consequences of an aggressive expansion policy were rationalized as in the company's best interest, especially as recent store construction became more cost-efficient. If total market share could be substantially increased, despite same-store sales declining, the accounting analyses supported more stores. But how much should the franchisee be considered in this aggressive strategy of McDonald's outlets competing, not so much with Wendy's, Burger King, and Taco Bell, as with other McDonald's outlets? And couldn't profitability be improved by more carefully selecting fewer new store sites and, at the same time, identifying marginal stores that perhaps should be closed?

A major domestic challenge for the growth-oriented McDonald's was the menu: how to appeal to adults and expand market potential. This offered another growth alternative, even more so, if the dinner market could be tapped. But the last successful menu expansion had been the breakfast menu, and that was decades ago.

What menu changes should be made? Installing a salad bar—would this be the menu breakthrough needed? With a history of past failures, expectations could hardly be robust. Yet McDonald's, as any chain organization whether fast food or otherwise, can test different prices and strategies or different menus and atmospheres in just a few outlets and, only if results are favorable, expand further. A few stores then can provide a powerful research tool.

A major trouble spot was McDonald's seeming inability to enforce tighter controls over product quality and service. The rigid standards and controls imposed in the days of Ray Kroc, that made McDonald's unique, had somehow eroded. Admittedly, as more and more outlets were added, enforcing tight controls became more difficult. Yet competitors, meantime, were doing a better job of matching, and surpassing, McDonald's former high standards. And the profit picture and shareholder attitudes were ever worsening. The glory days seemed only a pleasant memory.

Into this breach came a white knight. In less than 16 months, Jim Cantalupo, with an espoused low-growth strategy, had turned things around. But then he died suddenly of a heart attack. The new CEO, a month after assuming the office, was diagnosed with colon cancer and a few months later had to resign.

WHAT CAN BE LEARNED?

It is Possible to Have Strong and Enduring Growth Without Diversification

For more than four decades, since 1955, McDonald's had grown continuously and substantially. In all this time, the product was essentially the hamburger in its various trappings and accompaniments. Almost all other firms, in their quest for growth, have diversified, sometimes wisely and synergistically, at other times imprudently and even recklessly.

For such an undeviating focus, the product should have universal appeal, be frequently consumed, and have almost unlimited potential. The hamburger probably meets these criteria better than practically any other product, along with beer, soft drinks, and tobacco. And soft drinks, of course, are a natural accompaniment of the hamburger.

Eventually, even the hamburger began to fall short in providing continued strong growth, as the international market reached saturation and the domestic market oversaturation. McDonald's may be forced to seek judicious diversifications or lose the growth mode. There is risk: Firms in pursuit of growth often jump into acquisitions far too hastily and are faced with massive debt and overhead. And most of McDonald's present diversifications have not met their expectations.

Beware the Reckless Drive for Market Share

A firm can usually "buy" market share, if it is willing to sacrifice profits to do so. It can step up advertising and sales promotions. It can reduce prices, assuming that lower prices would bring more demand. It can increase sales staff and motivate them to be more aggressive. Sales and competitive position then will usually rise. But costs may increase disproportionately. In other words, the benefits to be gained may not be worth the costs.

As we saw, McDonald's aggressively increased market share in the mid-1990s by opening thousands of new domestic units. As long as developmental costs could be kept sufficiently low for these new units to be profitable and not cannibalize business from other McDonald's restaurants, then the strategy was defensible. Still, the costs of damaged franchisee relations resulting in lowered morale, cooperation, and festering resentments could be real indeed. Interestingly, this market share growth strategy was toned down by early 2000.

Maintaining the Highest Standards Requires Constant Monitoring

McDonald's heritage and its competitive advantage had long been associated with the highest standards and controls for cleanliness, fast service, dependable quality of food, and friendly and well-groomed employees. The following Information Box discusses strategy countering by competitors and the great difficulty in matching nonprice strengths.

Alas, in the last few years McDonald's has apparently let its control of operational standards slip. We have seen that surveys of customer satisfaction in 1995 and 2001 gave McDonald's low marks on food quality, value, service, and cleanliness, with its competitors showing up considerably better. Why this lapse? Without a doubt, maintaining high standards among thousands of units, company owned as well as franchised, requires constant monitoring and exhortation. But this was successfully done for over four decades. How was this lapse allowed to happen? We can only speculate that such standards became taken for granted, not emphasized as much. Then it became difficult to resurrect them.

Controls Can Be Too Stringent

In a belated attempt to improve standards and tighten corporate control, McDonald's instituted the controversial Franchising 2000. Among other things,

---

INFORMATION BOX

MATCHING A COMPETITOR'S STRATEGY

Some strategies are easily countered or duplicated by competitors. Price cutting is the most easily countered. A price cut can often be matched within minutes. Similarly, a different package or a warranty is easily imitated by competitors.

But some strategies are not so easily duplicated. Most of these involve service, a strong and positive company image, or both. A reputation for quality and dependability is not easily countered, at least in the short run. A good company or brand image is hard to match because it usually results from years of good service and satisfied customers. The great controls of McDonald's, with its high standards, would seem to be easily imitated, but they proved not to be, as no other firm fully matched them until recent years.

The strategies and operations most difficult to imitate often are not the wildly innovative ones, nor the ones that are complex and well researched. Rather they seem to be the simple ones: doing a better job in servicing and satisfying customers and in performing even mundane operations cheerfully and efficiently.

What explanation can you give for competitors' inability, for so long, to match the standards of McDonald's?

this called for grading franchisees, with those receiving the lower grades being penalized. McDonald's also wanted to take away any pricing flexibility for its franchisees: All restaurants now had to charge the same prices or risk losing their franchise. Not surprising, some franchisees were concerned about this new "get tough" management.

Can controls be too stringent? As with most things, extremes are seldom desirable. All firms need tight controls over far-flung outlets to keep corporate management alert to emerging problems and opportunities and maintain a desired image and standard of performance. In a franchise operation, this is all the more necessary since the company is dealing with independent entrepreneurs rather than hired managers. However, controls can be so rigid that no room is left for special circumstances and opportunities. If the enforcement is too punitive, the climate becomes more that of a police state than a teamwork relationship with both parties cooperating to their mutual advantages.

This brings us to the next insight for discussion.

There is Room for a Kinder, Gentler Firm in Today's Hotly Competitive Environment

Many longtime McDonald's franchisees remembered with sadness a kinder, gentler company, an atmosphere nurtured by founder Ray Kroc. To be sure, Kroc insisted that customers be assured of a clean, family atmosphere with quick and cheerful service. To Kroc, this meant strict standards, not only in food preparation but also in care and maintenance of facilities, including toilets. Company auditors closely checked that the standards were adhered to, under Kroc's belief that a weakness in one restaurant could have a detrimental effect on other units in the system. Still, the atmosphere was helpful—the inspectors were "consultants"— rather than adversarial. Kroc was proud that he was responsible for making more than 1,000 millionaires, the franchise holders.

Many franchisees traced the deterioration of franchiser-franchisee relations to the 1992 death of Gerald Newman, McDonald's chief accounting officer. He spent much time interacting with franchisees, sometimes encouraging them—he had a reputation for a sympathetic ear—sometimes even giving them a financial break.[24]

So, is it possible and desirable to be a kind and gentle company? With franchisees? Employees? Suppliers? Customers? Of course it is. Organizations, and the people who run them, often forget this in the arrogance of power. They excuse a "get tough" mind-set on the exigencies of competition and the need to be faithful to their stockholders.

Kind and gentle—is this an anachronism, a throwback to a quieter time, a nostalgia long past its usefulness? Let us hope not.

---

[24] Gibson, p. A8.

Any Firm Needs Contingency Planning, Especially with Regard to Succession

The improbable catastrophe that beset McDonald's—losing two CEOs to death and severe illness in only a few months—graphically shows the need for successor planning in developing understudies who can step in quickly, if necessary, to continue the momentum and successful policies. It also should raise a caution: Since accidents do happen, company policies should prohibit top executives all flying on the same plane—perhaps a corporate jet—or being in the same car. Insurance policies also can offer some protection against financial loss should major executives be unexpectedly incapacitated.

CONSIDER

Can you add other learning insights?

QUESTIONS

1. How do you account for the reluctance of competitors to imitate the successful efforts of another firm in their industry? Under what circumstances is imitation likely to be embraced?

2. To date, McDonald's has shunned diversification into unrelated food retailing operations as well as nonfood options. Discuss the desirability of such diversification efforts.

3. "Eventually—and this may come sooner than most think—there will no longer be any choice locations anywhere in the world for new hamburger outlets. As a McDonald's stockholder, I'm getting worried." Discuss.

4. Does the size of McDonald's give it a powerful advantage over its competitors? Why or why not?

5. What do you think is McDonald's near-term and long-term potential? What makes you think this?

6. Is it likely that McDonald's has really found a saturated market for its hamburgers?

7. Discuss the importance of market share in the fast-food industry.

8. Discuss the desirability of McDonald's efforts to insist on the same price in all domestic restaurants.

9. Do you think McDonald's "adaptability" in such countries as Yugoslavia went too far in repudiating U. S. values? Why or why not?

HANDS-ON EXERCISES

1. You have been given the assignment by Edward Rensi in 1993 to instill a recommitment to improved customer service in all domestic operations.

Discuss in as much detail as you can how you would go about fostering this among the 10,000 domestic outlets.

2. As a McDonald's senior executive, what long-term expansion mode would you recommend for your company?

3. As a Burger King senior executive, what long-term expansion mode would you recommend for your company to combat a McDonald's growth machine that has maybe grown a bit vulnerable?

4. Be a Devil's Advocate (and argue a dissenting view). Develop all the persuasive arguments you can that Cantalupo's limited expansion policies will doom the company's growth and invite competitive inroads.

TEAM DEBATE EXERCISES

1. Debate this issue: McDonald's is reaching the limits of its ability to grow without drastic change. (Note: The side that espouses drastic change should give some attention to the most likely directions for such, and be prepared to defend these expansion possibilities.)

2. Debate the issue of a "get-tough" attitude of corporate management toward franchisees even if it riles some, versus involving them more in future directions of the company. In particular, be prepared to address the challenge of bringing customer satisfaction up to traditional standards.

3. Debate this contention: Market share is overemphasized in this industry. (Both sides in their debate may want to consider whether this assertion may or may not apply to other industries.)

INVITATION TO RESEARCH

How have Cantalupo's slower growth policies fared since he is no longer with the company? Has growth in profitability continued? How about the company stock market valuation? Has McDonald's made any major acquisitions recently? Has Yum continued creeping up on McDonald's?

Cola Wars:
Coca-Cola vs. PepsiCo

*I*ntense competition between Pepsi and Coca-Cola has characterized the soft-drink industry for decades. In this chess game of giant firms, Coca-Cola ruled the soft-drink market throughout the 1950s, 1960s, and early 1970s. It outsold Pepsi two to one. But this was to change. Then the chess game, or "war," switched to the international arena, and it became a "world war."

EARLY BATTLES, LEADING TO NEW COKE FIASCO

Pepsi Inroads, 1970s and 1980s

By the mid-1970s, the Coca-Cola Company was a lumbering giant. Performance reflected this. Between 1976 and 1978, the growth rate of Coca-Cola soft drinks dropped from 13 percent annually to a meager 2 percent. As the giant stumbled, Pepsi Cola was finding heady triumphs. First came the "Pepsi Generation." This advertising campaign captured the imagination of the baby boomers with its idealism and youth. This association with youth and vitality greatly enhanced the image of Pepsi and firmly associated it with the largest consumer market for soft drinks.

Then came another management coup, the "Pepsi Challenge," in which comparative taste tests with consumers showed a clear preference for Pepsi. This campaign led to a rapid increase in Pepsi's market share, from 6 to 14 percent of total U.S. soft-drink sales.

Coca-Cola, in defense, conducted its own taste tests. Alas, these tests had the same result—people liked the taste of Pepsi better, and market-share changes reflected this. As Table 3.1 shows, by 1979, Pepsi was closing the gap on Coca-Cola, having 17.9 percent of the soft-drink market, to Coke's 23.9 percent. By the end of 1984, Coke had only a 2.9 percent lead, while in the grocery store market it was now trailing by 1.7 percent. Further indication of the diminishing position of Coke relative to Pepsi was a study done by Coca-Cola's own marketing research department. The study showed that in 1972, 18 percent of soft-drink users drank Coke exclusively, while only 4 percent drank only Pepsi. In 10 years the picture had changed greatly:

TABLE 3.1 Coke and Pepsi Shares of Total Soft-Drink Market, 1950s–1984

	Mid-1950s Lead	1975		1979		1984	
		% of Market	Lead	% of Market	Lead	% of Market	Lead
Coke	Better than 2 to 1	24.2	6.8	23.9	6.0	21.7	2.9
Pepsi		17.4		17.9		18.8	

Source: Thomas Oliver, *The Real Coke. The Real Story* (New York: Random House, 1986), pp. 21, 50; "Two Cokes Really Are Better Than One—For Now," *Business Week*, 9 September 1985, p. 38.

Only 12 percent now claimed loyalty to Coke, while the number of exclusive Pepsi drinkers almost matched, with 11 percent. Figure 3.1 shows this change graphically.

What made the deteriorating comparative performance of Coke all the more worrisome and frustrating to Coca-Cola was that it was outspending Pepsi in advertising by $100 million. It had twice as many vending machines, dominated fountains, had more shelf space, and was competitively priced. Why was it losing market share? The advertising undoubtedly was not as effective as that of Pepsi, despite vastly more money spent. And this raises the question: How can we measure the effectiveness of advertising? See the following Information Box for a discussion.

Coca-Cola Tries to Battle Back

The Changing of the Guard at Coke

J. Paul Austin, chairman of Coca-Cola, was nearing retirement in 1980. Donald Keough, president for the American group, was expected to succeed him. But a new name, Roberto Goizueta, suddenly emerged. Goizueta's background was far different

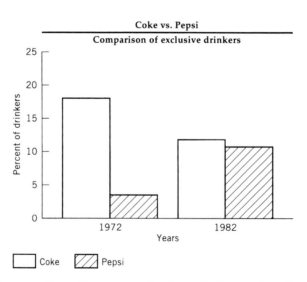

Figure 3.1 Coke versus Pepsi: Comparison of exclusive drinkers, 1972 and 1982.

INFORMATION BOX

HOW DO WE MEASURE THE
EFFECTIVENESS OF ADVERTISING?

A firm can spend millions of dollars for advertising, and it is only natural to want some feedback on the results of such an expenditure: To what extent did the advertising really pay off? Yet many problems confront the firm trying to measure this.

Most methods for measuring effectiveness focus not on sales changes, but on how well the communication is remembered, recognized, or recalled. Most evaluative methods simply tell which ad is the best among those being appraised. But even though one ad may be found to be more memorable or to create more attention than another, that fact alone gives no assurance of relationship to sales success. A classic example of the dire consequences that can befall advertising people as a result of the inability to directly measure the impact of ads on sales occurred in December 1970.

In 1970, the Doyle Dane Bernbach advertising agency created memorable TV commercials for Alka-Seltzer, such as the "spicy meatball man," and the "poached oyster bride." These won professional awards as the best commercials of the year and received high marks for humor and audience recall. But in December, the $22 million account was abruptly switched to another agency. The reason? Alka-Seltzer's sales had dropped somewhat. Of course, no one will ever know whether the drop might have been much worse without these notable commercials.

So, how do we measure the value of millions of dollars spent for advertising? Not well; nor can we determine what is the right amount to spend, what is too much, or too little.

Can a business succeed without advertising? Why or why not?

---

from that of the typical Coca-Cola executive. He was not from Georgia (the company is headquartered in Atlanta) and was not even southern. Rather, he was the son of a wealthy Havana sugar plantation owner. He came to the United States at age sixteen, speaking virtually no English. By using the dictionary and watching movies, he quickly learned the language and graduated from Yale in 1955 with a degree in chemical engineering. Returning to Cuba, he went to work in Coke's Cuban research lab.

Goizueta's complacent life was to change in 1959 when Fidel Castro seized power. With his wife and three children he fled to the United States, arriving with $20. At Coca-Cola, he became known as a brilliant administrator and in 1968 was brought to company headquarters; he became chairman of the board thirteen years later, in 1981. Donald Keough had to settle for being president.

In the new era of change, the sacredness of the commitment to the original Coke formula became tenuous, and the ground was laid for the first flavor change in ninety-nine years.

Introducing a New Flavor for Coke

With the market-share erosion of the late 1970s and early 1980s, despite strong advertising and superior distribution, the company began to look at the soft-drink product itself. Taste was suspected as the chief culprit in Coke's decline, and marketing research seemed to confirm this. In September 1984, the technical division developed a sweeter flavor. In perhaps the biggest taste test ever, costing $4 million, 55 percent of 191,000 people approved it over Pepsi and the original formula of Coke. Top executives unanimously agreed to change the taste and take the old Coke off the market.

But the results flabbergasted company executives. While some protests were expected, they quickly mushroomed; by mid-May 1985 calls were coming in at the rate of 5,000 a day, in addition to a barrage of angry letters. People were speaking of Coke as an American symbol and as a long-time friend who had suddenly betrayed them.

Anger spread across the country, fueled by media publicity. Fiddling with the formula for the 99-year-old beverage became an affront to patriotic pride. Even Goizueta's father spoke out against the switch and jokingly threatened to disown his son. By now the company began to worry about a consumer boycott against the product.

On July 11th company officials capitulated to the outcry. They apologized to the public and brought back the original taste of Coke.

Roger Enrico, president of Pepsi-Cola, USA, gloated, "Clearly this is the Edsel of the '80s. This was a terrible mistake. Coke's got a lemon on its hand and now they're trying to make lemonade." Other critics labeled this the "marketing blunder of the decade."[1]

Unfortunately for Pepsi, the euphoria of a major blunder by Coca-Cola was short lived. The two-cola strategy of Coca-Cola—it kept the new flavor in addition to bringing back the old classic—seemed to be stimulating sales far more than ever expected. While Coke Classic was outselling New Coke by better than two to one nationwide, for the full year of 1985, sales from all operations rose 10 percent and profits 9 percent. Coca-Cola's fortunes continued to improve steadily. By 1988, it was producing five of the top-ten selling soft drinks in the country and now had a total 40 percent of the domestic market to 31 percent for Pepsi.[2]

BATTLE SHIFTS TO INTERNATIONAL ARENA

Pepsi's Troubles in Brazil

Early in 1994, PepsiCo began an ambitious assault on the soft-drink market in Brazil. Making this invasion even more tempting was the opportunity to combat arch-rival Coca-Cola, already entrenched in this third largest soft-drink market in the world, behind only the United States and Mexico.

The robust market of Brazil had attracted Pepsi before. Its hot weather and a growing teen population positioned Brazil to become one of the world's fastest-growing soft-drink markets, along with China, India, and Southeast Asia. But the potential still had barely been tapped. Brazilian consumers averaged only 264 eight-ounce servings of soft drinks a year, far below the U. S. average of about 800.[3]

---

[1] John Greenwald, "Coca-Cola's Big Fizzle," *Time,* July 22, 1985, pp. 48–49.

[2] "Some Things Don't Go Better with Coke," *Forbes,* March 21, 1988, pp. 34–35.

[3] Robert Frank and Jonathan Friedland, "How Pepsi's Charge into Brazil Fell Short of Its Ambitious Goals," *Wall Street Journal,* August 30, 1996, p. A1.

Three times during the previous twenty-five years, Pepsi had attempted to enter the Brazilian market with splashy promotional campaigns and different bottlers. Each of these efforts proved disappointing, and Pepsi quickly dropped them and retreated from the field. In 1994, it planned a much more aggressive and enduring push.

A Super Bottler, Baesa, and Charles Beach

Buenos Aires Embotelladora SA, or Baesa, was to be the key to Pepsi's rejuvenated entry into Brazil. Baesa would be Pepsi's "superbottler," one that would buy small bottlers across Latin America, expand their marketing and distribution, and be the fulcrum in the drive against Coca-Cola. Charles Beach, the CEO of Baesa, was the person around whom Pepsi planned its strategy.

Beach, 61, was a passionate, driven man, a veteran of the cola wars, but his was a checkered past. A Coca-Cola bottler in Virginia, he was indicted by a federal grand jury on charges of price fixing and received a $100,000 fine and a suspended prison sentence. He then bought Pepsi's small Puerto Rican franchise in 1987. Then, in 1989, Beach acquired the exclusive Pepsi franchise for Buenos Aires, Argentina— one of the most important bottling franchises outside the United States. By discounting and launching new products and packages, he caught Coke by surprise. In only three years, he had increased Pepsi's market share in the Buenos Aires metro area from almost zero to 34 percent.[4]

With Pepsi's blessing, Beach expanded vigorously, borrowing heavily to do so. He bought major Pepsi franchises in Chile, Uruguay, and most importantly, Brazil, where he built four giant bottling plants. Pepsi worked closely with Baesa's expansion, providing funds to facilitate it.

However, they underestimated the aggressiveness of Coca-Cola. Their rival spent heavily on marketing and cold-drink equipment for its choice customers. As a result Baesa was shut out of small retail outlets, those most profitable for bottlers. Goizueta, CEO of Coca-Cola, used his Latin American background to influence the Argentine president to reduce an onerous 24 percent tax on cola to 4 percent. This move strengthened Coke's position against Baesa, which in contrast to Coca-Cola was earning most of its profits from non-cola drinks.

By early 1996, Baesa's expansion plans—and Pepsi's dream—were floundering. The new Brazilian plants were running at only a third of capacity. Baesa lost $300 million for the first half of 1996, and PepsiCo injected another $40 million into Baesa.

On May 9, Beach was relieved of his position. Allegations now surfaced that Beach might have tampered with Baesa's books.[5] But PepsiCo's troubles did not end with the debacle in Brazil.

Intrigue in Venezuela

Brazil was only symptomatic of other overseas problems for Pepsi. Roger Enrico, now CEO, had reasons to shake his head and wonder at how the gods seemed against him.

---

[4] Patrica Sellers, "How Coke Is Kicking Pepsi's Can," *Fortune,* October 28, 1996, p. 78.

[5] Ibid, p. 79.

But it was not the gods, it was Coca-Cola. Enrico had been on Coke's blacklist since he had gloated a decade before about the New Coke debacle in his memoir, *The Other Guy Blinked: How Pepsi Won the Cola Wars*. Goizueta was soon to gloat, "It appears that the company that claimed to have won the cola wars is now raising the white flag."[6]

The person Enrico thought was his close friend, Oswaldo Cisneros, head of one of Pepsi's oldest and largest foreign bottling franchises, suddenly abandoned Pepsi for Coca-Cola. Essentially, this took Pepsi out of the Venezuelan market.

Despite close ties of the Cisneroses with the Enricos, little things led to the chasm. The closeness had developed when Enrico headed the international operations of PepsiCo. After Enrico left this position for higher offices at corporate headquarters, Oswaldo Cisneros felt that Pepsi management paid scant attention to Venezuela: "That showed I wasn't an important player in their future," he said.[7] Because Cisneros was growing older, he wanted to sell the bottling operation, but Pepsi was only willing to acquire 10 percent.

Coca-Cola wooed the Cisneroses with red-carpet treatment and frequent meetings with its highest executives. Eventually, Coca-Cola agreed to pay an estimated $500 million to buy 50 percent of the business.

Pepsi's Problems Elsewhere in the International Arena

Pepsi's problems in South America mirrored its problems worldwide. It had lost its initial lead in Russia, Eastern Europe, and parts of Southeast Asia. While it had a head start in India, this was being eroded by a hard-driving Coca-Cola. Even in Mexico, its main bottler reported a loss of $15 million in 1995.

The contrast with Coca-Cola was significant. Pepsi still generated more than 70 percent of its beverage profits from the United States; Coca-Cola got 80 percent from overseas.[8]

Table 3.2 shows the top-ten markets for Coke and Pepsi in 1996 in the total world market. Coke had a 49 percent market share while Pepsi had only 17 percent, despite its investment of more than $2 billion since 1990 to straighten out its overseas bottling operations and improve its image.[9] With its careful investment in bottlers and increased financial resources to plow into marketing, Coke continued to gain greater control of the global soft-drink industry.

If there was any consolation for PepsiCo, it was that its overseas business had always been far less important to it than to Coca-Cola, but this was slim comfort in view of the huge potential this market represented. Most of Pepsi's revenues were in the U. S. beverage, snack food, and restaurant businesses, with such well-known brands as Frito-Lay, Taco Bell, Pizza Hut, and KFC (Kentucky Fried Chicken) restaurants. But as a former Pepsi CEO was fond of stating, "We're proud of the U. S.

---

[6] Ibid, p. 72.

[7] Ibid, p. 75.

[8] Frank and Friedland, p. A1.

[9] Robert Frank, "Pepsi Losing Overseas Fizz to Coca-Cola," *Wall Street Journal,* August 22, 1996, p. C2.

TABLE 3.2 Coke and Pepsi Shares of Total Soft-Drink Sales, Top Ten Markets, 1996

Markets	*Market Shares*	
	Coke	Pepsi
United States	42%	31%
Mexico	61	21
Japan	34	5
Brazil	51	10
East-Central Europe	40	21
Germany	56	5
Canada	37	34
Middle East	23	38
China	20	10
Britain	32	12

Source: Company annual reports, and Patricia Sellers, "How Coke Is Kicking Pepsi's Can," *Fortune,* 28 October 1996, p. 82.

Commentary: These market share comparisons show the extent of Pepsi's ineptitude in its international markets. In only one of these top 10 overseas markets is it ahead of Coke, and in some, such as Japan, Germany, and Brazil, it is practically a nonplayer.

business. But 95 percent of the world doesn't live here."[10] And Pepsi seemed unable to hold its own against Coke in this world market.

COKE TRAVAILS IN EUROPE, 1999

The Trials of Douglas Ivester

In early 1998, Douglas Ivester took over as chairman and chief executive of Coca-Cola. He had a tough act to follow, being the successor to the legendary Goizuerta. Things seemed to go downhill from then on, but it was not entirely his fault. The first quarter of 1999 witnessed a sharp slowdown in Coca-Cola's North American business, at least partly due to price increases designed to overcome weakness resulting from overseas economic woes. While most analysts thought the sticker shock of higher prices would be temporary, some thought the company needed to be more innovative, needed to do more than offer super-size drinks.[11] Other problems emanated from a racial discrimination lawsuit, as well as Mr. Ivester's "brassy"

[10] Frank, p. C2.
[11] Nikhil Deogun, "Coke's Slower Sales Are Blamed on Price Increases," *Wall Street Journal,* March 31, 1999, pp. A3, A4.

attempts to make acquisitions such as Orangina and Cadbury Schweppes, angering overseas regulators and perhaps motivating them to make life difficult for Coca-Cola.

Such concerns paled before what was to come.

Contamination Scares

On June 8th, a few dozen Belgian schoolchildren began throwing up after drinking Cokes. This was to result in one of the most serious crises in Coca-Cola's 113-year history. An early warning had seemingly been ignored when in mid-May the owner of a pub near Antwerp complained of four people becoming sick from drinking bad-smelling Coke. The company claimed to have investigated but found no problems.

The contamination news could not have hit at a worse time. Belgium was still reeling from a dioxin-contamination food scare in Belgian poultry and other foods, and European agencies were coming under fire for a breakdown in their watchdog responsibilities. Officials were inclined to be overzealous in their dealings with this big U. S. firm.

The problems worsened. Coca-Cola officials were meeting with Belgium's health minister, seeking to placate him, telling him that their analyses "show that it is about a deviation in taste and color" that might cause headaches and other symptoms but "does not threaten the health of your child." In the middle of this meeting, news came that another fifteen students at another school had gotten sick.[12]

It was thought that the contamination came from bottling plants in Antwerp, Ghent, and Dunkirk that produced cans for the Belgium market. European newspapers were speculating that Coke cans were contaminated with rat poison.

Soon hundreds of sick people in France were blaming their illnesses on Coke, and France banned products from the Dunkirk plant. France and Belgium rebuffed Coca-Cola's urgent efforts to lift the ban and scolded the company for not supplying enough information as to the cause of the problem. The setback left Coke out of the market in parts of Europe because the company had badly underestimated how much explanation governments would demand before letting it back in business.

Not until June 17 did Belgium and France lift restrictions, and then only on some products; the bans were continued on Coca-Cola's Coke, Sprite, and Fanta. Then the Netherlands, Luxembourg, and Switzerland also imposed selective bans until health risks could be evaluated. Some 14 million cases of Coke products eventually were recalled in the five countries, and estimates were that Coke was losing $3.4 million per day in revenues. Case volume for the European division was expected to fall 6 to 7 percent from the year earlier.[13] The peak soft-drink summer season had arrived, and the timing of the scare could not have been worse.

The European Union requested further study as the health scare spread. At the same time, Coca-Cola and its local distributors launched an advertising campaign

---

[12] "Anatomy of a Recall: How Coke's Controls Fizzled Out in Europe," *Wall Street Journal,* June 29, 1999, p. A6.

[13] Will Edwards, "Coke Chairman Tries to Assure Europeans," *Cleveland Plain Dealer,* June 19, 1999, pp. C1, C3; and Nikhil Deogun, "Coke Estimates European Volume Plunged 6% to 7% in 2nd Quarter," *Wall Street Journal,* July 1, 1999, p. A4.

defending the quality of their products. The company blamed defective carbon dioxide, used for fizz, for problems at Antwerp. It also said the outsides of cans made in Dunkirk were contaminated with a wood preservative during shipping. One company-commissioned study suggested that health problems were in the victims' heads. Meanwhile, the Ivory Coast seized 50,000 cans of Coke imported from Europe as a precautionary measure, though there was no evidence that anyone in the Ivory Coast had become ill by drinking imported Coke.

Problems continued to spread. All glass bottles of Bonaqua, a bottled water brand of Coca-Cola, were recalled in Poland because about 1,500 bottles were found to contain mold. This recall in Poland soon spread to glass bottles of Coke. Company officials believed the mold was caused by inadequate washing of returnable bottles. Barely a week later, the company recalled 180,000 plastic bottles of Bonaqua after discovering nonhazardous bacteria. Coca-Cola also had to recall some soft drinks in Portugal after small bits of charcoal from a filtration system were found in some cans.

Coca-Cola Finally Acts Aggressively

In the initial contamination episodes, Coca-Cola was accused of dragging its feet. Part of the problem in ameliorating the situation was the absence of an explanation by any top Coca-Cola officials. Ivester was criticized for this delay when he finally made an appearance in Brussels on June 18, ten days after the initial scare. He visited Brussels again four days later, meeting with the prime minister. Strenuous efforts to improve the company's image and public relations then began.

Ivester, in a major advertising campaign, apologized to Belgian consumers and explained "how the company allowed two breakdowns to occur." The ads showed his photograph along with these opening remarks, "My apologies to the consumers of Belgium; I should have spoken with you earlier." Ivester further promised to buy every Belgian household a Coke. A special consumer hotline was established, and fifty officials including several top executives were temporarily shifted from the Atlanta headquarters to Brussels.

Five thousand delivery people then fanned out across the country, offering a free 1.5-liter bottle of Coke's main brands to 4.37 million households. Around Belgium, Coke trucks and displays proclaimed, "Your Coca-Cola is coming back." In newspaper ads, the company explained its problems, noted it was destroying old products and using fresh ingredients for new drinks. A similar marketing strategy was planned for Poland, where 2 million free beverages were distributed to consumers.

Pepsi's Competitive Maneuvers Near the Millennium

Pepsi's Role in Coke's European Problems

Some thought that Coca-Cola's problems should have been Pepsi's gain. Yet Pepsi did nothing to capitalize on the situation, did not gloat, and did not increase advertising for its brand. Worldwide, Pepsi experienced some temporary gains in sales, most surprisingly in countries far removed from the scare—such as China. A Pepsi bottler in Eastern Europe probably expressed the prevailing company attitude when he observed that people were buying bottled water and juices, instead of soda pop:

"That's why we don't wish this stuff on anyone," he said, referring to the health scare.[14]

But Pepsi was not idle in Europe.

Pepsi's Antitrust Initiatives Against Coca-Cola

In late July 1999, European Union officials raided offices of Coca-Cola and its bottlers in four countries in Europe—Germany, Austria, Denmark, and Britain—on suspicions that the company used its dominant market position to shut out competitors. Coming at a time when Coca-Cola was still trying to recover from the contamination problems, this was a cruel blow. All the more so since such alleged noncompetitive activities affected its plans to acquire some additional businesses in Europe.

The raids were expected to lead to a full-blown antitrust action against Coke. The major suspicion was that Coke was illegally using rebates to enhance its market share. The several types of rebates under investigation were rebates on sales that boosted Coke's market share at the expense of rivals, and rebates given to distributors who agreed to sell the full range of Coke products or to stop buying from competitors.

Coca-Cola's huge market share in most countries of Europe fed the concern. See Table 3.3 for Coke's market shares of the total soft-drink market in selected countries in Europe.

While the market share of Coke was being scrutinized by European antitrust officials, the investigation was sparked by a complaint—filed by Pepsi—that Coke was illegally trying to force competitors out of the market.

Pepsi also filed a complaint with Italian regulators, and they were quicker to act. A preliminary report found that Coca-Cola and its bottlers violated antitrust laws by

TABLE 3.3   Coca-Cola's Market Share of Soft-Drink Market in Selected European Countries, 1998

France	59%
Spain	58
Germany	55
Central Europe	47
Italy	45
Nordic and Northern Eurasia	41
Great Britain	35

Source: Company published reports.

Commentary: The dominance of Coke in almost all countries of Europe, not surprisingly, makes it vulnerable to antitrust scrutiny.

---

[14] Nikhil Deogun and James R. Hagerty, "Coke Scandal Could Boost Rivals, But Also Could Hurt Soft Drinks," *Wall Street Journal,* June 23, 1999, p. A4.

abusing a dominant market position through practices such as discounts, bonuses, and exclusive deals with wholesalers and retailers. The Italian regulators also said there was evidence that Coke had a "strategic plan" to remove Pepsi from the Italian market, one of the biggest in Europe, by paying wholesalers to remove Pepsi fountain equipment and replace it with Coke. At about this time, Australian and Chilean officials also began conducting informal inquiries in their markets.

Coca-Cola officials responded to the Italian report as follows: "We believe this is a baseless allegation by Pepsi and we believe that Pepsi's poor performance in Italy is due to their lack of commitment and investment there. As a result, they are attempting to compete with us in the courtroom instead of the marketplace."[15]

COKE FINDS TOUGH GOING IN NEW CENTURY WHILE PEPSI SURGES

For decades, Coca-Cola was a premier growth company with some of the best-known brands in the world, and management seemed well positioned to take advantage of the global economy. But we have just seen lapses in the late 1990s, particularly in handling contamination problems in Europe and in dealing with antitrust charges there. Going into the new century, the new millennium, problems seemed more subtle but with longer lasting concerns. Not that the old esteemed company was withering away, but rather that it faced a slowing growth trend. For example, Coke generated average annual earnings growth of 18 percent between 1990 and 1997. In recent years, its net income grew at just a 4 percent average. Share prices had fallen hard, in 2004 trading at less than half their 1998 peak. At the same time, PepsiCo, while it never quite caught Coke in the cola wars, outdid its rival in overall business growth. The following comparative statistics show the slipping performance of Coca-Cola to PepsiCo over the five years to 2004.

	Coke	Pepsi
Sales 2003	$21 billion	$27 billion
Sales growth (5-year average)	2%	4%
Earnings	$4.3 billion	$3.6 billion
Earnings growth (5-year average)	4%	12%
Stock price (5 years ending 12/3/04)	– 40%	38%

Source: Bloomberg Financial Markets as reported in Dean Foust, "Gone Flat," *Business Week*, December 20, 2004, p. 82.

Part of the problem facing Coke was an industry problem, but with its heavy emphasis on carbonated soft drinks, it became worse for Coke than for Pepsi. Consumers, more concerned with health and obesity, were seeking new kinds of

[15] Betsy McKay, "Coke, Bottlers Violated Antitrust Laws in Italy, a Preliminary Report States," *Wall Street Journal*, August 13, 1999, p. A4.

beverages such as gourmet coffees, New Age teas, sports drinks, and waters. Carbonated beverages were no longer a growth sector of the market. One consultant said, "The carbonated soft-drink model is 30 years old and out of date."[16] Pepsi had pushed into the noncarb market with Tropicana juice, Gatorade sports drink, and Aquafina water, and these were billion-dollar beverage brands. Coca-Cola remained fixated on its flagship Coke brand, with sodas accounting for 82 percent of its world-wide beverage sales, far more than Pepsi. On the other hand, Pepsi not only had more strongly diversified into other non-carb beverages but also had its Frito-Lay Division with snack foods such as Lays, Doritos, and Baked Crunchy Cheetos; and then there was Quaker Oats that it acquired August 2001. (In 1997, PepsiCo had spun off its restaurant operations.) The following shows the breakdown of sales and profits for Pepsi's four major businesses as of 2004:

Percentage of Company Sales and Operating Profits		
Frito-Lay	34	41
PepsiCo Beverages	29	30
Quaker Foods	5	9
PepsiCo Int'l. (snacks and beverages)	32	20

Source: Public information as of 2004

Coke's Reluctance to Diversify

Critics blamed Coke's stubborn commitment to its four hallowed soda-pop brands—Coca-Cola, Diet Coke, Sprite, and Fanta—as going back to the sixteen-year reign of Roberto Goizueta, who guided Coke stock to a 3,500 percent gain in those years. Goizueta was the first CEO ever to break the $1 billion compensation barrier. After he died of lung cancer in 1997, he was almost deified, and his cola-centric philosophy became the gospel of the executives who followed and also of the aging board of directors.

The reluctance to diversify was evident when Coca-Cola decided against acquiring South Beach Beverage Company after negotiating two years. Pepsi made an offer and in weeks acquired the SoBe brand New Age juice company, which gave Pepsi access to a market completely bypassed by soda pop. Neville Isdell came out of retirement to head the company in May 2004, after earlier building distribution networks in India, Russia, and Eastern Europe. He showed the same conservative mind-set of his predecessors and passed on the chance to acquire Red Bull, a promising energy drink. Isdell still believed in the growth potential of carbonated soft drinks and their 30 percent profit margins. Because of this conservatism, Coke now lacked a popular entry in the highly profitable energy-drink category to compete with what had become the market leader, Red Bull. Some analysts saw this reluctance to diver-

---

[16] Tom Pirko, president of Bev Mark LLC, as quoted in Dean Foust, "Gone Flat," *Business Week*, December 20, 2004, p. 76.

sify as reflecting a corporate mind-set that still saw Coca-Cola as only a soda company, while Pepsi viewed itself as a beverage-and-snack company.[17]

Still, Coke had joined Pepsi and other firms in moving into bottled water by 2003, as this became the fastest growing sector of the beverage industry. Pepsi's Aquafina became the leading brand and was enhanced by a multimillion-dollar promotional campaign, while Coke, through acquisitions, amassed such brands as Dannon, Evian, and Dasani. However, Coke was less aggressive than its competitors in pursuing this market, and problems with Dasani further cooled the enthusiasm.

Other Problems

Ivester, CEO successor to Goizueta in the late '90s, in a desperate effort to try to sustain the profitability of the Goizueta era, imposed a 7.6 percent price hike on the concentrate it sold its bottlers. For decades, Coke had sold its beverage concentrate to U.S. bottlers at a constant price, no matter what price the soft drinks would later command at retail. Not surprisingly, these bottlers were now incensed and complained bitterly to the board and succeeded in pushing the already embattled Ivester to resign in late 1999. His successor, Douglas Daft, tried to work with them, but relations steadily deteriorated. Bottlers began fighting back with sharp increases in their retail prices of Coke. These hikes dampened sales of Coke but increased bottlers' profits. Some also refused to carry the company's new noncarbonated niche offerings, Mad River teas and Planet Java coffee; these flopped, and the company phased them out in 2003. Going into 2005, Isdell faced contentious bottler relations that needed to be addressed.

The C2 Disappointment

In the summer of 2003, Coca-Cola launched C2, a reduced-calorie, reduced-carb cola, with a $50 million promotional campaign. This was Coke's biggest product introduction since Diet Coke more than twenty years before. The company had expected this new beverage would help win back a critical consumer group—20- to 40-year-olds who were concerned about weight—and priced it at a 15 percent premium in the quest to achieve higher profits on its drinks. But sales of C2 fell nearly 60 percent a few weeks after the product introduction.

Isdell halted the premium pricing strategy to try to salvage the product, but still sales languished. The pricing strategy had been botched, as C2 at times retailed for 50 percent and more than regular Coke, especially on weekends when sodas were often discounted. Adding to the dissatisfaction with the higher prices, many consumers were critical of the taste, either too flat or with an aftertaste.

Advertising Miscues

Spending for advertising had become conservative during the reign of Ivester. He believed that the Coke brand could largely sell itself without a major commitment to

---

[17] Foust, p. 80; Leslie Chang, Chad Terhune, and Betsy McKay, "Coke's Big Gamble in Asia," *Wall Street Journal,* August 11, 2004, pp. A1, A6; "Behind Coke's CEO Travails: A Long Struggle Over Strategy," *Wall Street Journal,* May 4, 2004, pp. A1, A10.

advertising. The result of a reduced ad budget was lackluster ads that failed to attract the important youth market. Instead, Ivester shifted resources into more vending machines, refrigerated coolers, and delivery trucks—"growth through distribution." But some of these expanded distribution sites, such as auto part stores, did not pay off.

Global Problems

Even Coke's global strength was becoming tarnished. Ivester's slowness in responding to the contamination scare in Belgium and France in 1999 was but the first misstep. Coke's plans to make Dasani bottled water into a global brand were slowed by an aborted launch in Europe after elevated levels of bromate, a cancer-causing substance, were detected in bottles in Britain. Declining sales in Germany and Mexico, two very important markets, put more pressure on developing such markets as China and India. Yet these looked years away from contributing significantly to Coke's profitability. The distribution and capacity that Isdell built in Eastern Europe in the 1980s and 1990s proved to be extravagant, and write downs eventually exceeded $1 billion.[18]

Meantime, Pepsi was nibbling away at Coke's international markets. Its antitrust case against Coke in the European Union was eventually settled years later, in October 2004, with Coke having to drop its controversial incentive discounts to retailers, and agreeing to share display space with rivals such as PepsiCo. So, the playing field was more leveled to Pepsi's benefit.

Coke's Board of Directors

Few firms could boast as prestigious a board of directors as Coke. Warren Buffett, one of the world's richest and most influential investors, was a major presence on the board. Ten of the 14 directors dated back to the Goizueta era and still espoused his policies of concentrating on the basic core of carbonated soft drinks with less emphasis on diversifying. Critics of the board accused it of micromanaging and being too conservative and blamed it for the difficulty in recruiting highly regarded candidates for top management jobs and not retaining the ones it had.[19]

The board played a major part in vetoing the acquisition of Quaker Oats, the maker of Gatorade. CEO Douglas Daft had reached an agreement to buy Quaker for $15.75 billion in stock. But the board overruled him, calling the price too expensive. PepsiCo snapped up the company instead. Daft was left to contemplate his lack of support by the board, and his loss of faith among his peers. He tenure was short lived, and Isdell replaced him.

ANALYSIS

Coke's Outlook at the New Millennium

The situation by 2005 did not come about suddenly. It gradually crept up until a deteriorating stock price confronted investors, managers, and analysts. Yet the company

---

[18] Terhune and McKay, p. A6.
[19] For example, see Dean Foust, pp. 79, 82; and "Behind Coke's CEO Travails," pp. A1, A6.

was still healthy and profitable, but somehow the Coke name had lost its cachet and critics abounded. Then there was PepsiCo becoming more formidable all the time.

Proposals for dealing with the situation went to two extremes: (1) stick with the basics and simply do things better, or (2) vigorously diversify, even to non-drink areas as Pepsi had seemingly done successfully. The two approaches could be categorized as a mission of being a soda company versus an expanded mission of being a beverage-and-snack company. Coke's board, hearkening back to the glory days of Goizueta, was negative toward mergers and strongly favored doing a better job with the basic core, such as with advertising, distribution, and tapping international markets more aggressively. Critics, however, saw Coke as too wedded to the status quo and missing growth opportunities. Of course, there is a third option between the two extremes. This would look for suitable diversifications within the non-cola drink market, and even fortuitous and compatible non-drink additions, but without any mandate to go on a merger binge.

Several factors affect whatever direction the company eventually takes. One is the recent trend toward healthy lifestyles, and the foods and drinks that affect this either negatively or positively. Worrisome omens were appearing. Some schools were removing colas from their vending machines and school lunches. Advertisements and other publicity were trumpeting the health risks of fast foods and soft drinks. Was this the wave of the future, or merely a short-term phenomenon?

Then Coke needs to confront whether its days as a growth firm are over and if it is in the mature stage of its life cycle. The long-term consequences of this decision will hardly be inconsequential. In Chapter 2, McDonald's was facing some of the same issues and concerns as Coke. Disavowing aggressive growth—recognizing a mature life cycle—can be beneficial to investors, at least in the short run, since more profits are available for dividends. But the search for breakthrough diversifications should not be abandoned. The right one(s) might well put a mature firm on the growth path again.

What Went Wrong with the New Coke Decision?

The most convenient scapegoat was the marketing research that preceded the decision. Yet Coca-Cola spent about $4 million and devoted two years to the marketing research. About 200,000 consumers were contacted during this time. The error in judgment was surely not from want of trying. But when we dig deeper into the research, some flaws become apparent.

Flawed Marketing Research

The major design of the marketing research involved taste tests by representative consumers. After all, the decision point was whether to go with a different-flavored Coke, so what could be more logical than to conduct taste tests to determine acceptability of the new flavor, not only versus the old Coke but also versus Pepsi? The results were strongly positive for the new formula, even among Pepsi drinkers. This was a clear "go" signal.

With benefit of hindsight, however, some deficiencies in the research design merited concern. Research participants were not told that by picking one cola, they would lose the other. This proved to be a significant distortion: Any addition to the product line would naturally be far more acceptable than completely eliminating the traditional product.

While three to four new tastes were tested with almost 200,000 people, only 30,000 to 40,000 of these testers tried the specific formula for the new Coke. Research was geared more to the idea of a new, sweeter cola than that used in the final formula. In general, a sweeter flavor tends to be preferred in blind taste tests. This is particularly true with youths, the largest drinkers of sugared colas and the very group drinking more Pepsi in recent years. Interestingly, preference for sweeter tasting products tends to diminish with use.[20]

Consumers were asked whether they favored change as a concept, and whether they would likely drink more, less, or the same amount of Coke if there were a change. But such questions could hardly prove the depth of feelings and emotional ties to the product.

Symbolic Value

The symbolic value of Coke was the sleeper. Perhaps this should have been foreseen. Perhaps the marketing research should have considered this possibility and designed the research to map it and determine the strength and durability of these values— that is, would they have a major effect on any substitution of a new flavor?

Admittedly, when we get into symbolic value and emotional involvement, any researcher is dealing with vague attitudes. But various attitudinal measures have been developed that can measure the strength or degree of emotional involvement.

Herd Instinct

Here we see a natural human phenomenon, the herd instinct, the tendency of people to follow an idea, a slogan, a concept, to "jump on the bandwagon." At first, acceptance of new Coke appeared to be reasonably satisfactory. But as more and more outcries were raised—fanned by the media—about the betrayal of the old tradition (somehow this became identified with motherhood, apple pie, and the flag), public attitudes shifted strongly against the perceived unworthy substitute. The bandwagon syndrome was fully activated. It is doubtful that by July 1985 Coca-Cola could have done anything to reverse the unfavorable tide. To wait for it to die down was fraught with danger—for who would be brave enough to predict the durability and possible heights of such a protest movement?

Could, or should, such a tide have been predicted? Perhaps not, at least regarding the full strength of the movement. Coca-Cola expected some protests. But perhaps it should have been more cautious by considering a worst-case scenario in addition to what seemed the more probable, and by being better prepared to react to such a contingency.

---

[20] "New Cola Wins Round 1, But Can It Go the Distance?" *Business Week,* June 24, 1985, p. 48.

Pepsi, and Later Coca-Cola's, International Problems

Pepsi's Defeats in South America

With hindsight, we can identify many of the mistakes Pepsi made. It tried to expand too quickly in Argentina and Brazil, imprudently putting all its chips on a distributor with a checkered past, instead of building up relationships slower and more carefully. It did not monitor foreign operations closely enough or soon enough to prevent rash expansion of facilities and burdensome debt accumulations by affiliates. It did not listen closely enough to old distributors and their changing wants, and so lost Venezuela to Coca-Cola. Pepsi apparently did not learn from its past mistakes: For example, three times before, it had tried to enter Brazil and had failed. Why the failures? Why was it not more careful to prevent failure the next time?

Finally, we can speculate that maybe Pepsi was not so bad, but rather that its major competitor was so good. Coca-Cola had slowly built up close relationships with foreign bottlers over decades. It was aggressive in defending its turf. Perhaps not the least of its strengths, at least in the lucrative Latin American markets, was a CEO who was also a Latino, could speak Spanish and share the concerns, and build on the egos of its local bottlers. In selling, this is known as a dyadic relationship, and it is discussed further in the following Information Box. After all, why can't a CEO do a selling job on a distributor and capitalize on a dyadic relationship?

Coca-Cola's Problems in Europe

Could Coca-Cola have handled the Belgian crisis better? With hindsight, we see a flawed initial reaction. Still, the first incident of 24 schoolchildren getting ill and throwing up after drinking Coke seemed hardly a major crisis at the time. But crises

---

INFORMATION BOX

THE DYADIC RELATIONSHIP

Sellers are now recognizing the importance of the buyer-seller interaction, *a dyadic relationship*. A transaction, negotiation, or relationship can often be helped by certain characteristics of the buyer and seller in the particular encounter. Research suggests that salespeople tend to be more successful if they have characteristics similar to their customers in age, size, and other demographic, social, and ethnic variables.

Of course, in the selling situation, this suggests that selecting and hiring sales applicants most likely to be successful might require careful study of the characteristics of the firm's customers. Turning to the Pepsi/Coke confrontation in Brazil and Venezuela, the same concepts should apply and give a decided advantage to Coca-Cola and Roberto Goizueta in influencing government officials and local distributors. After all, in interacting with customers and affiliates, even a CEO needs to be persuasive in presenting ideas as well as handling problems and objections.

Can you think of any situations where the dyadic theory may not work?

often start slowly with only minor indications and then mushroom to even cata-strophic proportions. Eventually, hundreds of people reported real or imagined ill-nesses from drinking the various Coca-Cola products.

The mistakes of Coca-Cola in handling the situation were (1) not taking the ini-tial episodes seriously enough; (2) not realizing the intense involvement and skepti-cism of governmental officials, who demanded complete explanations of the cause(s) and were reluctant to lift bans; and (3) not involving Coke Chairman Douglas Ivester and other high-level executives soon enough. Allowing ten days to go by before his personal intervention was a long time for Ivester to let problems fester. Added to that, the quality-control lapses should not have been allowed to occur in the first place. Eventually, Ivester and Coke acted aggressively in restoring Coca-Cola but lost rev-enues could not be fully recovered.

Of interest in this environment of cola wars was Pepsi's restraint in not trying to take advantage of Coke's problems. This was not altruism but fear that the whole soft-drink industry would face decreased demand, so Pepsi did not want to aggravate the situation. Anyway, Pepsi saved its competitive thrusts for antitrust challenges.

With its great size and market-dominance visibility in country after country, Coca-Cola was vulnerable to regulatory scrutiny and antitrust allegations, especially when stimulated by its No. 1 competitor, PepsiCo. Does this mean that it is danger-ous for a firm to become too big? In certain environments, such as facing a foreign competitor in some European countries, this may well be the case. The firm then needs to tread carefully, tone down inclinations toward arrogance, and be subtle and patient in seeking acquisitions on foreign turf.

WHAT CAN BE LEARNED?

Consumer Taste is Fickle

Taste tests are commonly used in marketing research, but I have always been skepti-cal of their validity. Take beer, for example. I know of few people—despite their strenuous claims—who can, in blind taste tests, unerringly identify which is which among three or four disguised brands of beer. We know that people tend to favor the sweeter in taste tests. But does this mean that a sweeter flavor will always win out in the marketplace? Hardly; something else is operating with consumer preference other than the fleeting essence of a taste—unless the flavor difference is extreme.

Brand image usually is a more powerful sales stimulant. Advertisers consis-tently have been more successful in cultivating a desirable image or personality for their brands, or the types of people who use them, than by such vague statements as "better tasting."

Don't Tamper with Tradition

Not many firms have a hundred-year-old tradition to be concerned with—or even twenty-five years, or ten years. Most products have much shorter life cycles. No other product has been so widely used and so deeply entrenched in societal values and culture as Coke.

The psychological components of the great Coke protest make interesting speculation. Perhaps in an era of rapid change, many people wish to hang on to the one symbol of security or constancy in their lives—even if it's only the traditional Coke flavor. Perhaps many people found this protest to be an interesting way to escape the humdrum, by making waves in a rather harmless way, in the process of seeing if a big corporation might be forced to cry "uncle."

One is left to wonder how many consumers would even have been aware of any change in flavor had the new formula been quietly introduced without fanfare. But, of course, the advertising siren call of "New" would have been muted.

So, do we dare tamper with tradition? In Coke's case the answer is probably not, unless done very quietly, but then Coke is unique.

Don't Try to Fix Something That Isn't Broken

Conventional wisdom may advocate that changes are best made in response to problems, that when things are going smoothly the success pattern or strategy should not be tampered with. Perhaps. But perhaps not.

Actually, things were not going all that well for Coke by early 1985. Market share had steadily been lost to Pepsi for some years. So it was certainly worth considering a change, and the obvious one was a different flavor. I do not subscribe to the philosophy of "don't rock the boat." But Coke had another option.

Don't Burn Your Bridges

Coke could have introduced the new Coke but kept the old one. Goizueta was concerned about dealer resentment at having to stock an additional product in the same limited space. Furthermore, he feared Pepsi emerging as the No. 1 soft drink due to two competing Cokes. This rationale was flawed, as events soon proved.

Consider the Power of the Media

Press and broadcast media are powerful influencers of public opinion. With new Coke, the media exacerbated the herd instinct by publicizing the protests. News seems to be spiciest when someone or something can be criticized or found wanting. We saw this fanning of protests in Coke's contamination problems in Europe, to the extent that some people came up with psychosomatic illnesses after drinking Coca-Cola products. The power of the media should not only be recognized but also be a factor in making decisions that may affect an organization's public image.

International Growth Requires Tight Controls

In Pepsi's problems with Baesa, we saw the risks of placing too much trust in a distributor. One could question the selection of Charles Beach to spearhead the Pepsi invasion of Coke strongholds in South America. Prudence would dictate close monitoring of plans and performance, with major changes—in expansion planning, marketing strategy, financial commitments—approved by corporate headquarters. In international dealings, the tendency is rather to loosen controls due to the distances, different customs and bureaucratic procedures, and unfamiliar cultures. We will see an extreme example of this later in the Maytag case.

The Human Factor May Be More Important in International Dealings

Rapport with associates and customers may be even more important in the international environment than domestically. The distances involved usually necessitate more decentralization and, therefore, more autonomy. If confidence and trust in foreign associates are misplaced, serious problems can result. Customers and affiliates may need a closer relationship with corporate management if they are not to be wooed away. Furthermore, in some countries the political climate is such that the major people in power must be catered to by the large firm wanting to do business in that country.

Sound Crisis Management Requires Prompt Attention by Top Management

The chief executive is an expediter and a public relations figure in crises, particularly in foreign environments. Ivester's delay in rushing to Belgium may have held up resolution of the crisis for several weeks, and it cost Coca-Cola millions in lost revenues. No other person is as well suited as the CEO to handle serious crises. Some sensitive foreign officials see an affront to their country without top management involvement and are likely to express their displeasure in regulatory delays, calls for more investigations, and bad publicity toward a foreign firm. In the case of Coca-Cola, even though Ivester eventually made a conciliatory appearance, by that time some countries were receptive to antitrust allegations made by Pepsi against Coca-Cola.

Beware of High-Margin Insistence to the Neglect of Other Worthy Products

It is natural for executives to want to push the higher margin goods. After all, profitability deserves priority, everything else being equal. But often, lower margin goods may yield more total profits because of greater sales volume. Similarly, raising prices will produce higher margin per item, but lower volume may adversely affect total profits. In recent years, Coca-Cola hurt itself by concentrating on the higher margin cola drinks, to the neglect of other growth opportunities, and by injudiciously raising prices of its concentrate to bottlers, thus jeopardizing bottler relations.

CONSIDER

Can you think of other learning insights?

QUESTIONS

1. In the new Coke fiasco, how could Coca-Cola's marketing research have been improved? Be a specific as you can.

2. When a firm faces a negative press—as Coca-Cola did with the new Coke, and almost 15 years later in Europe—what recourse does a firm have? Support your conclusions.

3. "If it's not broken, don't fix it." Evaluate this statement.

4. Do you think Coca-Cola engineered the whole scenario with the new Coke, including fanning initial protests, in order to get a bonanza of free publicity? Defend your position.

5. Critique Pepsi's handling of Baesa. Could it have prevented the South American disaster? If so, how?

6. With hindsight, how might Enrico, CEO of PepsiCo, have kept Cisneros, his principal bottler in Venezuela, in the fold instead of defecting to Coke?

7. How could Coca-Cola have lessened the chances of antitrust and regulatory scrutiny in Europe?

8. Do you think Pepsi can ever make big inroads in Coke's market share in Europe? Why or why not?

9. A big stockholder complains, "All this fuss over a few kids getting sick to their stomach. The media have blown this all out of proportion." Discuss.

10. Do you think Coca-Cola is still a growth company? Why or why not? Defend your reasoning.

HANDS-ON EXERCISES

1. Assume that you are Robert Goizueta and that you are facing increased pressure in early July 1985 to abandon the new Coke and bring back the old formula. However, your latest marketing research suggests that only a small group of agitators are making all the fuss. Evaluate your options and support your recommendations to the board. (Do not be swayed by what actually happened—maybe the protests could have been contained.)

2. As a market analyst for PepsiCo, you have been asked to present recommendations to CEO Roger Enrico and the executive board, for the invasion of Brazil's soft-drink market. The major bottler, Baesa, is already in place and waiting for Pepsi's final plans and objectives. You are to design a planning blueprint for the "invasion," complete with an estimated timetable.

3. You are a staff assistant to Ivester. It is 1998, and he has just assumed the top executive job with Coca-Cola. One of his first major decisions concerns raising soft-drink prices over 7 percent to improve operating margins and make up for diminished revenues in a depressed European market. He wants you to provide pro and con information on this important decision.

TEAM-DEBATE EXERCISES

1. Debate the issue of whether Coke is in a mature stage of the life cycle or whether it is still in a growth stage. In the course of the debate, each side should consider how best to maximize its performance.

2. Debate Ivester's plan to distribute millions of free bottles of Coke products to people in Belgium and Poland. In particular, debate the costs versus benefits of this recovery strategy. Are the benefits likely to be worth the substantial cost?

INVITATION TO RESEARCH

What are the newest developments in the Cola wars? Has Coke lost market share in Europe? Has Pepsi been able to make any inroads in Latin America? How do the two firms stack up in profitability? Have there been any innovations in this arena? How has the bottled water battleground gone for the two rivals? How are their stock prices faring?

CHAPTER FOUR

Airliner Wars: Boeing vs. Airbus

The commercial jet business had long been subject to booms and busts: major demand for new aircraft and then years of little demand. By the second half of the 1990s, demand burgeoned as never before. Boeing, the world's leading producer of commercial airplanes, seemed in the catbird seat amid the worldwide surge of orders. This was an unexpected windfall, spurred by markets greatly expanding in Asia and Latin America at the same time as domestic demand, helped by deregulation and prosperity, boomed. In the midst of these good times, Boeing, in 1997, incurred its first loss in fifty years.

During this same period, Airbus (Airbus Industrie), a European aerospace consortium, an underdog, began climbing toward its long-stated goal of winning 50 percent of the over-100-seat airplane market. The battle was all-out, no-holds-barred, and Boeing was vulnerable.

BOEING

Background of the Company

Boeing's is a fabled past. The company was a major factor in the World War II effort and, in the late 1950s, led the way in producing innovative, state-of-the-art commercial aircraft. It introduced the 707, the world's first commercially viable jetliner. In the late 1960s, it almost bankrupted itself to build a jetliner twice the size of any other then in service, while the critics predicted it could never fly profitably. But the 747 dramatically lowered costs and airfares and brought passenger comfort previously undreamed of in flying. In the mid-1990s, Boeing introduced the high technology 777, the first commercial aircraft designed entirely with the use of computers.

In efforts to reduce the feast-or-famine cycles of the commercial aircraft business, Boeing acquired Rockwell International's defense business in 1996 and, in 1997, purchased McDonnell Douglas for $16.3 billion.

In 1997, Boeing's commercial aircraft segment contributed 57 percent of total revenues. This segment ranged from 125-passenger 737s to giant 450–500-seat 747s.

In 1997, Boeing delivered 374 aircraft, up from 269 in 1996. The potential seemed enormous: Over the next 20 years, air passenger traffic worldwide was projected to rise 4.9 percent a year and airlines were predicted to order 16,160 aircraft to expand their fleets and replace aging planes.[1] As the industry leader, Boeing had 60 percent of this market. At the end of 1997, its order backlog was $94 billion.

Defense and space operations made up 41 percent of 1997 revenues. This included airborne warning and control systems (AWACS), helicopters, B-2 bomber subcontract work, and the F-22 fighter, among other products and systems.

Problems with the Commercial Aircraft Business Segment

Production Problems

Boeing proved to be poorly positioned to meet the surge in aircraft orders. Part of this resulted from its drastic layoffs of experienced workers during the industry's last slump, in the early 1990s. Though Boeing hired 32,000 new workers over 18 months, starting in 1995, the experience gap upped the risk of costly mistakes. Boeing had also cut back its suppliers in strenuous efforts to slash parts inventories and increase cost-efficiency.

But Boeing had other problems. Its production systems were a mess. It had somehow evolved some 400 separate computer systems, and these were not linked. Its design system was labor intensive, paper dependent, and very expensive as it tried to cater to customer choices. A $1 billion program had been launched in 1996 to modernize and computerize the production process. But this was too late: The onslaught of orders had already started. (It is something of an anomaly that a firm that had the sophistication to design the 777 entirely by computers was so antiquated in its use of computers otherwise.)

Demands for increased production were further aggravated by unreasonable production goals and too many plane models. Problems first hit with the 747 Jumbo, and then with a new version of the top-selling 737, the so-called next-generation 737NG. Before long, every program was affected: also the 757, 767, and 777. While Boeing released over 320 planes to customers in 1997 for a 50 percent increase over 1996, this was far short of the planned completion rate. For example, by early 1998 a dozen 737NGs had been delivered to airlines, but this was less than one-third of the 40 supposed to have been delivered by then. Yet, the company maintained through September 1997 that everything was going well, that there was only a month's delay in the delivery of some planes.

Soon it became apparent that problems were much greater. In October, the 747 and 737 assembly lines were shut down for nearly a month to allow workers to catch up and ease part shortages. The *Wall Street Journal* reported horror stories of parts being rushed in by taxicab, of executives spending weekends trying to chase down needed parts, and of parts needed for new planes being shipped out to replace defective parts on an in-service plane. Overtime pay brought some

---

[1] *Boeing 1997 Annual Report.*

TABLE 4.1   Boeing's Trend of Revenues and Income, 1988–1998

	Revenue	Net Income
	(million $)	
1988	16,962	614
1989	20,276	675
1990	27,595	1,385
1991	29,314	1,567
1992	30,184	1,554
1993	25,438	1,244
1994	21,924	856
1995	19,515	393
1996	22,681	1,095
1997	45,800	– 177
1998	56,100	1,100

Source: Boeing Annual Reports

Commentary: Note the severity of the decline in revenues and profits during the industry downturn in 1993, 1994, and 1995. It is little wonder that Boeing was so ill prepared for the deluge of orders starting in 1995. Then in an unbelievable anomaly, the tremendous increase in revenues in 1997 to the highest ever—partly reflecting the acquisitions—was accompanied by a huge loss.

assembly-line workers incomes over $100,000, while rookie workers muddled by on the line.[2]

Despite its huge order backlog, Boeing took a loss for 1997, the first in over 50 years. See Table 4.1 for the trend in revenues and net income from 1988 to 1998. The loss mostly resulted from two massive write-downs. One, for $1.4 billion, arose from the McDonnell Douglas acquisition and, in particular, from its ailing commercial aircraft operation at Long Beach, California. The bigger write-off, $1.6 billion, reflected production problems, particularly on the new 737NG. Severe price competition with Airbus resulted in not enough profits on existing business to bring the company into the black. Production delays continued, with more write-downs on the horizon.

As Boeing moved into 1998, analysts wondered how much longer it would take to clear up the production snafus. This would be longer than anyone had been led to believe. Unexpectedly, a new problem arose for Boeing. Disastrous economic conditions in Asia now brought major order cancellations.

---

[2] Frederic M. Biddle and John Helyar, "Behind Boeing's Woes: Clunky Assembly Line, Price War with Airbus," *Wall Street Journal,* April 24, 1998, p. A16.

Customer Relations

Not surprisingly, Boeing's production problems resulting in delayed shipments had a serious impact on customer relations. For example, Southwest Airlines had to temporarily cancel adding service to another city because the ordered planes were not ready. Boeing paid Southwest millions of dollars of compensation for the delayed deliveries. Continental also had to wait for five overdue 737s.

Other customers switched to Boeing's only major competitor, Airbus Industrie, of Toulouse, France.

AIRBUS INDUSTRIE

Airbus had to salivate at Boeing's troubles. It had been a distant second in market share to the 60 percent of Boeing. Now this was changing and Airbus could see achieving a sustainable 50 percent market share. See the Information Box: Importance of Market Share for a discussion of market share.

Background of Airbus

Airbus was founded in 1970 as a consortium that came to include four countries: British Aerospace, DaimlerChrysler Aerospace (Germany), France's Aerospatiale,

---

INFORMATION BOX

IMPORTANCE OF MARKET SHARE

The desire to surpass a competitor is a common human tendency, whether in sports or business. A measurement of performance relative to competitors encourages this desire and can be highly motivating for management and employees alike. Furthermore, market-share performance is a key indicator in ascertaining how well a firm is doing, in spotting emerging problems, and sometimes allaying blame. As an example of the latter, declining sales over the preceding year, along with a constant and improving market share, can suggest that the firm is doing a good job, even though certain factors adversely affected the whole industry.

Market share is usually measured by (1) share of overall sales and/or (2) share relative to certain competitors, usually the top one or several in the industry. Of particular importance is trend data: Are things getting better or worse? If worse, why is this, and what needs to be done to improve the situation?

Since Boeing and Airbus were the only real competitors in this major industry, relative market shares became critical. The perceived importance of gaining, or not losing, market share led to severe price competition that cut into the profits of both firms, as will be discussed later.

How would you respond to the objection that market share data is not all that useful, since "it doesn't tell us what the problem really is?"

Can emphasizing market share be counterproductive? If so, why?

and Spain's Casa. Each of the partners supplied components such as wings and fuse-lages; the partners also underwrote the consortium's capital expenses (sometimes with government loans) and were prepared to cover its operating losses.

The organizational structure seemed seriously flawed. It was politicized, with the partners voting on major issues in proportion to their country's ownership stakes. From this fragmented leadership, public squabbles frequently arose, some very serious. For example, plans to produce a new 107-seat A318 were held up by the French, who thought they were not getting their fair share of the production. Finances were also tangled with components supplied by the various countries charged to Airbus at suspiciously high prices.

The result was that in 1998, Boeing made $1.1 billion on sales of $56.1 billion, while Airbus was losing $204 million on sales of $13.3 billion. Boeing accused Airbus of selling below cost in order to steal business from Boeing, and Airbus blamed Boeing for the low bids.

The competition between the two companies became increasingly bitter after 1996. In that year, Boeing and several Airbus partners discussed a joint development of a superjumbo. The talks ended when they could not agree on a single design. But Airbus suspected Boeing was not sincerely interested in this collaboration, that its main purpose in the talks was to stall Airbus's plans.

Airbus went ahead with its plans, while Boeing pooh-poohed the idea of such a huge plane.

Airbus Chairman Noel Forgeard

A slight Frenchman with a cheery disposition, Noel Forgeard, 52, joined the consortium in 1998 from Matra, a French aerospace manufacturer. He came with several major goals: to centralize decision making, to impose sensible bookkeeping, and to make Airbus consistently profitable. The task was not easy. For example, plans to build the world's largest airplane, code-named A3XX, were even threatened by disagreements over where it would be assembled. France and Germany thought it should be produced in their country. Forgeard stated, "The need for a single corporate entity is well recognized. Everybody here is focused on it."[3] Still, while the need for reorganizing into something like a modern corporation was evident to most executives, the major partners were divided over how to proceed.

The World's Largest Plane

The A3XX was designed as a double-decker plane that could carry 555 passengers comfortably—137 more than a Boeing 747-400 (it could even carry 750 people on routes around Asia, where people did not care as much about seating comfort). It was expected to fly by 2004, with prices starting somewhat over $200 million. Development costs could reach $15 billion, so essentially the A3XX was a bet-the-company project with an uncertain outlook, much as was Boeing's 747 30 years before. To pay for these costs, Airbus expected to get 40 percent from suppliers such

---

[3] Alex Taylor II, "Blue Skies for Airbus," *Fortune*, August 2, 1999, p. 103.

as Sweden's Saab, 30 percent from government loans arranged by its partners, and the rest from its own resources.

The huge financing needed for this venture could hardly be obtained without a corporate reorganization, one that would provide a mechanism for handling internal disputes among the various partner countries, not the least of which was where the plane would be assembled. So, Forgeard had necessity on his side for reorganizing. But the A3XX faced other issues and concerns.

Should a Plane Like the A3XX Even Be Built?

Boeing's publicly expressed opinion was that such a plane would never be profitable. "Let them launch it," said one Boeing official, with a hint of malice.[4] Boeing took the position that consumers want frequent, nonstop flights, such as Southwest Airlines had brought to prominence with its saturation of city-pair routes with frequent flights. An ultralarge aircraft would mean far less frequency.[5]

Airbus, meantime, surveyed big airlines and discerned enough interest in a superjumbo to proceed. It also consulted with more than 60 airports around the world to determine whether such a big plane would be able to take off and land easily. Weight is critical to these maneuvers, and Airbus pledged that the A3XX would be able to use the same runways as the 747 because of a new lightweight material. Instead of regular aluminum, the planes would use a product called Glare, made of aluminum alloy and glass-fiber tape.

Airbus promised ambitious plans for passenger comfort in this behemoth. It built a full-size 237-foot mockup of the interior to show prospective customers and enlisted 1,200 frequent flyers to critique the cabin mockup. To reduce claustrophobia, the designers added a wide staircase between upper and lower decks. Early plans also included exercise rooms and sleeping quarters fitted with bunk beds.

Airbus claimed that the 555-seat A3XX would be 15 percent cheaper to operate per seat-mile than Boeing's 747. Boeing maintained this was wildly optimistic. United Airlines Frederick Brace, vice president of finance, also expressed doubts: "The risk for Airbus is whether there's a market for A3XX. The risk for an airline is: Can we fill it up? We have to be prudent in how we purchase it."[6]

Competitive Position of Airbus

Airbus was well positioned to supply planes to airlines whose needs Boeing couldn't meet near term. Some thought it was even producing better planes than Boeing.

United Airlines chose Airbus's A320 twinjets over Boeing's 737s, saying passengers preferred the Airbus product. Several South American carriers also chose A320s over the 737, placing a $4 billion order with Airbus. For 1997, Airbus hacked out a 45 percent market share, the first time Boeing's 60 percent market share had eroded.

The situation worsened drastically for Boeing in 1998. US Air, which had previously ordered 400 Airbus jets, announced in July that it would buy 30 more. But the

[4] Steve Wilhelm, "Plane Speaking," *Puget Sound Business Journal,* June 18, 1999, p. 112.
[5] Ibid.
[6] Taylor, p. 108.

biggest defection came in August, when British Airlines announced plans to buy 59 Airbus jetliners and take options for 200 more. This broke its long record as a Boeing-loyal customer. The order, worth as much as $11 billion, would be the biggest victory of Airbus over Boeing.[7]

Beyond the production delays of Boeing, Airbus had other competitive strengths. While it had less total production capability than Boeing (235 planes vs. Boeing's 550), the Airbus production line was efficient, and the company had done better in trimming its costs. This meant it could go head to head with Boeing on price. And price seemed to be the name of the game in the late 1990s. This contrasted with earlier days when Boeing rose to world leadership with performance, delivery, and technology more important than cost. "They [the customers] do not care what it costs us to make the planes," Boeing chairman and chief executive Philip Condit admitted. With airline design stabilized, he saw the airlines buying planes today as chiefly interested in how much carrying capacity they could buy for a buck.[8]

Increasingly, passengers were grousing about the cramped interiors of planes designed for coast-to-coast trips, and the dearth of lavatories to accommodate 126 to 189 passengers on long flights. Passenger rage appeared to be cropping up more and more. *Forbes* magazine editorialized that "the first carrier that makes an all-out effort to treat passengers as people rather than oversized sardines will be an immense money-maker."[9]

Boeing's new 737–700s and 737–800s were notorious for giving customer comfort low priority. Airbus differentiated itself from Boeing by designing its A320 150-seat workhorse with a fuselage 7 1/2 inches wider than Boeing's, thus adding an inch to every seat in a typical six-across configuration.

In the first four months of 1999, Airbus won an amazing 78 percent of orders. US Airways chairman Stephen Wolf, whose airline had ordered 430 Airbus planes since 1996, said, "Airbus aircraft offer greater flexibility for wider seats, more overhead bin space, and more aisle space—all important in a consumer-conscious business."[10]

A Donnybrook

An interesting marketing brawl occurred in mid-1999 that was indicative of the intensity of this airliner war. Boeing won a $1.9 billion order for ten of its 777 jetliners from Singapore Airlines. This in itself would not have raised eyebrows, but there was more to it. As a condition, Boeing agreed to purchase for resale 17 competing Airbus A340-300 jets from Singapore Airlines, which would allow the airline to phase out these Airbus planes.

Airbus officials claimed that Boeing had agreed to unprofitable terms out of desperation to close a 777 sale agreement and that this signaled a new price war involving trade-ins to provide a discount rather than direct price cutting. Boeing crowed

---

[7] "British to Order Airbus Airliners," *Cleveland Plain Dealer,* August 25, 1998, p. C6.

[8] Howard Banks, "Slow Learner," *Forbes,* May 4, 1998, p. 54.

[9] "Plane Discomfort," *Forbes,* September 6, 1999, p. 32.

[10] Taylor, p. 104.

that the carrier's decision to eliminate the competing version of the A340 from its fleet was a victory.[11]

A month later, still stung by the marketing move of Boeing, and in an effort to thwart it, Airbus announced that it would not provide its standard support services for the jets it sold to Singapore Airlines if Boeing buys and resells them. Such a countermove could prove costly to Boeing. On the other hand, Boeing was likely to offer the jets first to airlines with fleets of the same planes, several of whom had already expressed interest. Refusing to provide support service would put Airbus in the position of denying support for a small number of planes within the fleet of a major customer. Move and countermove, this.[12]

WHO CAN WE BLAME FOR BOEING'S TROUBLES?

Was it CEO Philip Condit?

Philip Condit became chief executive in 1996, just in time for the emerging problems. He had hardly assumed office before he was deeply involved in the defense industry's merger mania, first buying Rockwell's aerospace operation and then McDonnell Douglas. Condit later admitted that he probably spent too much time on these acquisitions, and not enough time on watching the commercial part of the operation.[13]

Condit's credentials were good. His association with Boeing began in 1965 when he joined the firm as an aerodynamics engineer. The same year, he obtained a design patent for a flexible wing called the sailwing. Moving through the company's engineering and managerial ranks, he was named CEO in 1996 and chairman in 1997. Along the way, he earned a master's degree in management from the Massachusetts Institute of Technology in 1975, and in 1997 a doctorate in engineering from Science University of Tokyo, where he was the first Westerner to earn such a degree.

Was Condit's pursuit of the Rockwell and McDonnell Douglas mergers a major blunder? Although analysts did not agree on this, prevailing opinion was more positive than negative, mostly because these businesses could smooth the cyclical nature of the commercial sector.

Interestingly, in the face of severe adversity, no heads rolled, as they might have in other firms. See the Issue Box: Management Climate during Adversity.

Were the Problems Mostly Due to Internal Factors?

The airlines' unexpected buying binge, which was brought about by worldwide prosperity fueling air travel, maybe should have been anticipated. However, even the most prescient decision maker probably would have missed the full extent of this boom. For example, orders jumped from 124 in 1994 to 754 in 1996. With hindsight,

---

[11] Jeff Cole, "Airbus Industrie Charges Boeing Is Inciting Price War in Asian Deal," *Wall Street Journal*, June 21, 1999, p. A4.

[12] Daniel Michaels, "Airbus Won't Provide Support Service for Jets It Sold to Singapore Air if Boeing Resells Them," *Wall Street Journal*, July 28, 1999, p. A17.

[13] Banks, p. 56.

ISSUE BOX

MANAGEMENT CLIMATE DURING ADVERSITY: WHAT IS BEST FOR MAXIMUM EFFECTIVENESS

Management shake-ups during adversity can range from practically none to widespread head-rolling. In the first scenario, a cooperative board is usually necessary, and it helps if the top executive(s) controls a lot of stock. But the company's problems will probably continue. In the second scenario, at the extreme, wielding a mean ax with excessive worker and management layoffs can wreck havoc on a company's morale and longer-term prospects.

In general, neither extreme—complacency or upheaval—is good. A sick company usually needs drastic changes, but not necessarily widespread bloodletting that leaves the entire organization cringing and sending out resumes. But we need to further define *sick.* At what point is a company so bad off it needs a drastic overhaul? Was Boeing such a sick company? Would a drastic overhaul have quickly changed things? Certainly, Boeing management had made some miscalculations, mostly in the area of too much optimism and too much complacency, but these were finally recognized.

Major competitor Airbus was finally aggressively attacking, and that certainly had something to do with Boeing's problems. Major executive changes and resignations might not have helped.

How do you personally feel about the continuity of management at Boeing during these difficult times? Should some heads have rolled? What criteria would you use in your judgment of whether to roll heads or not?

we know that Boeing made a grievous management mistake in trying to bite off too much, by promising expanded production and deliveries that were wholly unrealistic. We know what triggered such extravagant promises: trying to keep ahead of archrival Airbus.

Huge layoffs in the early l990s contributed to the problems of gearing up for new business. An early-retirement plan had been taken up by 9,000 of 13,000 eligible people. This was twice as many as Boeing expected, and it removed a core of production-line workers and managers who had kept a dilapidated system working. New people could not be trained or assimilated quickly enough to match those lost.

Boeing had begun switching to the Japanese practice of lean inventory management that delivers parts and tools to workers precisely as needed, so that production costs could be reduced. Partly due to this change, and to the early 1990s downturn, Boeing's supplier base changed significantly. Some suppliers quit the aviation business; others had suffered so badly in the slump, that their credit was affected and they were unable to boost capacity for the suddenly increased business. The result was serious parts shortages.

Complicating production problems was Boeing's long-standing practice of customizing. Because it permitted customers to choose from a host of options, Boeing was fine-tuning not only for every airline but also for every order. For example, it offered the 747's customers 38 different pilot clipboards and 109 shades of the color white.[14] Such tailoring added significantly to costs and production time. This perhaps was acceptable when these costs could be easily passed on to customers in a more leisurely production cycle, but it was far from maximizing efficiency. With deregulation, fare wars made extreme customizing archaic. Boeing apparently got the message with the wide-bodied 777, designed entirely by computers. Here, choices of parts were narrowed to standard options, such as carmakers offer in their transmissions, engines, and comfort packages.

Cut-rate pricing between Boeing and Airbus epitomized the situation by the mid-1990s. Then, costs became critical if a firm was to be profitable. In that climate, Boeing was so obsessed with maintaining its 60 percent market share that it fought for each order with whatever price it took. Commercial airline production had somehow become a commodity business, with neither Boeing nor Airbus having products all that unique to sell. Innovation seemed disregarded, and price was the only factor in getting an order. So, every order became a battleground, and prices might be slashed 20 percent off list in order to grab all the business possible.[15] And Boeing did not have the low-cost advantage over Airbus.

Such price competition worked to the advantage of the airlines, and they grew skillful at gaining big discounts from Boeing and Airbus by holding out huge contracts and negotiating hard.

The cumbersome production systems of Boeing—cost-inefficient—became a burden in this cost-conscious environment. While some of the problems could be attributed to computer technology not well applied to the assembly process, others involved organizational myopia regarding even such simple things as a streamlined organization and common parts. For example, before recent changes the commercial group had five wing-design groups, one for each aircraft program. It now has one. Another example cited in *Forbes* tells of different tools needed in the various plane models to open their wing access hatches.[16] Why not use the same tool?

There is a paradox in Boeing's dilemma. Its 777 was the epitome of high technology, computer design, and efficient production planning. Yet much of the other production was mired in a morass with supplies, parts management, and production inefficiency.

Harry Stonecipher, former CEO of McDonnell Douglas before the acquisition and then president and chief operating officer of Boeing, cited arrogance as the mind-set behind Boeing's problems. He saw this as coming from a belief that the company could do no wrong, that all its problems came from outside, and that business as usual would solve them.[17]

---

[14] John Greenwald, "Is Boeing Out of Its Spin?" *Time*, July 13, 1998, p. 68.

[15] Biddle and Helyar, pp. A1, A16.

[16] Banks, p. 60.

[17] Bill Sweetman, "Stonecipher's Boeing Shakeup," *Interavia Business & Technology*, September 1998, p. 15.

The Role of External Factors

Adding to the production and cost-containment difficulties of Boeing were increased regulatory demands. These came not only from the U.S. Federal Aviation Administration but also from the European Joint Airworthiness Authority (a loose grouping of regulators from more than 20 European countries). The first major consequence of this increased regulatory climate concerned the new 730NG. Boeing apparently thought it could use the same over-the-wings emergency exits as it had on the older 737. But the European regulators wanted a redesign. They were concerned that the older type of emergency exits would not permit passengers in the larger version of the plane to evacuate quickly enough. So Boeing had to design two new over-the-wing exits on each side. This was no simple modification since it involved rebuilding the most crucial aspect of the plane. The costly refitting accounted for a major part of the $1.6 billion write-down Boeing took in 1997.

Europe's Airbus Industrie had made no secret of its desire to achieve parity with Boeing and have 50 percent of the international market for commercial jets. This mindset-led to the severe price competition of the latter 1990s as Boeing stubbornly tried to maintain its 60 percent market share even at the expense of profits. While its total production capacity was somewhat below that of Boeing, Airbus had already overhauled its manufacturing process and was better positioned to compete on price. Airbus's competitive advantage seemed stronger with single-aisle planes, those in the 120–200 seat category, mostly 737s of Boeing and A320s of Airbus. But this accounted for 43 percent of the $40 billion expected to be spent on airliners in 1998.[18]

The future was something else. Airbus placed high stakes on a superjumbo successor to the 747, with seating capacity well beyond that of the 747. Such a huge plane would operate from hub airports such as New York City's JFK. Meantime, Boeing staked its future on its own 767s and 777s, which could connect smaller cities around the world without the need for passenger concentration at a few hubs.

Have you ever heard of a firm complaining of too much business? Probably not, but then we're confronted with Boeing's immersion in red ink, caused by trying to cope with too many orders. However, Boeing's feast of too much business abruptly ended. Financial problems in Asia brought cancellations and postponements of orders and deliveries.

In October 1998, Boeing disclosed that 36 completed aircraft were sitting in company storage areas in the desert, largely because of canceled orders. By December 1998, Boeing warned that its operations could be hurt by the Asian situation for as long as five years, and it announced that an additional 20,000 jobs would be eliminated and production cut 25 percent.[19] Of course, it didn't help that Airbus was capitalizing on Boeing's production difficulties by wresting orders from the stable of Boeing's long-term customers, nor that Airbus planned a 30 percent production increase for 1999.

---

[18] Banks, p. 60.

[19] Frederick M. Biddle and Andy Pasztor, "Boeing May Be Hurt Up to 5 Years by Asia," *Wall Street Journal*, December 3, 1998, p. A3.

LATER DEVELOPMENTS

By 2001, the competition between Airbus and Boeing continued unabated. Airbus had gone ahead with its superjumbo A-380, the world's largest passenger jet, with delivery to start in 2006 for a list price of $239 million. In its standard configuration, it would carry 555 passengers between airport hubs. With delivery still five years away, Airbus already had orders for 72 of the jumbos and expected to reach the 100 milestone early in 2002. It would break even with 250 of the wide bodies.

In March 2001, Boeing scrapped plans for an updated, but still smaller, 747-X project. Instead, it announced plans for a revolutionary delta-winged "Sonic Cruiser," carrying 150 to 250 passengers higher and faster than conventional planes. The savings in time would amount to 50 minutes from New York City to London, and almost 2 hours between Singapore and London. Further time savings would come from the plane flying to point-to-point destinations, bypassing layovers at such congested hubs as London and Hong Kong. Delivery was expected in 2007 or 2008.

Both companies had undergone major organizational changes. As of January 1, 2001, Airbus was no longer a four-nation consortium but now an integrated company with centralized purchasing and management systems. Operations were streamlined toward bottom-line responsibilities.

Boeing had previously diversified itself away from so much dependence on commercial aircraft through its acquisitions of Rockwell's aerospace and defense business, McDonnell Douglas, Hughes Space & Communications, and several smaller companies. Boeing expected that within five years more than half its revenues would come from new business lines, including financing aircraft sales, providing high-speed Internet access, and managing air-traffic problems.[20]

Everything changed with 9/11.

The airline industry's woes that began with 9/11 intensified in 2002. By late that year two major carriers, U. S. Air and United, were in bankruptcy, but other airlines, with the exception of a few discount carriers, notably Southwest and JetBlue, were experiencing horrific losses. Airlines were placing no new orders and even reneging on accepting delivery of previously ordered planes. Boeing's jet production fell to half of what it had been a year earlier, and forecasts for 2003 and 2004 were little better.

In this environment, the competition between Airbus and Boeing for winning the few customers still buying became even more fierce and was influenced almost entirely by price. The biggest prize was capturing the 120-plane order from British budget carrier, easyJet, and this customer milked its power position to the utmost, repeatedly sending Boeing and Airbus back to improve their offers.

During the aviation slump in the early 1990s, Boeing had beefed up its order backlog by selling at steep discounts—only to find itself in a serious bind in 1997 when it could not keep up with the built-up demand, and production costs skyrocketed. Now, Boeing refused to follow Airbus into unprofitable terrain, and Airbus got

---

[20] Compiled from such sources as David J. Lynch, "Airbus Comes of Age with A-380," *USA Today,* June 21, 2001, pp. 1B, 2B; J. Lynn Lunsford, Daniel Michaels, and Andy Pasztor, "At Paris Air Show, Boeing-Airbus Duel Has New Twist," *Wall Street Journal,* June 15, 2001, p. B4.

the easyJet order. Though Airbus claimed it was not selling its planes at a loss, many people in the industry thought otherwise.

In late December 2002, Boeing announced it was shelving the ambitious development program for its high-speed Sonic Cruiser. In talks with potential customers to gauge interest in such a plane in this post-9/11 environment, few expressed any interest; most wanted a replacement plane that would be cheaper to operate than existing ones. So, Boeing began changing its focus to developing a new 250-seat plane that would be 20 percent cheaper to operate than existing jetliners.[21]

The Situation in 2003

The competition between Boeing and Airbus grew ever more fierce in 2003. For the first time, Airbus delivered more planes than Boeing. It already had 95 orders for its A380 superjumbo jet seating 550 passengers that should enter service in 2006, very close to its declared milestone of 100. Furthermore, Airbus thought it detected an opening for it to sell to the U.S. military. A $20 billion deal for Boeing to supply the U.S. Air Force with 100 modified 767 jetliners for midair refueling was in jeopardy as politicians criticized the agreement as being unfavorable to U.S. taxpayers and smacking of corporate welfare because of no competitive bidding.

Meanwhile, Boeing announced that it would stop making its twin-engine 757 because of waning interest. It was in preliminary planning for a new model, called the 7E7, a long-range jet that would seat 200–250 and be 20 percent cheaper to own and operate than other planes. This could enter service around 2008.

Boeing had not had a new model since 1995 and badly needed a success with the new plane. While military business had been booming, the company suffered serious setbacks elsewhere. It had to take write-offs on its slow-selling single-aisle 717, and also some $2.4 billion of its commercial satellite and launch business.

But Boeing achieved profitability by revamping assembly lines, contracting out fabrication of parts, and laying off 32,000 workers since 9/11. Union leaders claimed the result was an aging skilled workforce and rock-bottom morale.[22]

Boeing's Continuing Problems in 2004

In early 2004, Airbus captured a $7 billion, 110-plane order from Air Berlin, a discount airline that was Germany's No. 2 carrier. What made the situation all the more galling to Boeing Chairman and CEO Harry Stonecipher was that Air Berlin had

---

[21] *Sources:* J. Lynn Lunsford, "Boeing to Drop Sonic Cruiser, Build Plane Cheaper to Operate," *Wall Street Journal,* December 19, 2002, p. B4; Daniel Michaels and J. Lynn Lunsford, "Airbus Is Awarded easyJet Order for 120 New Planes Over Boeing," *Wall Street Journal,* October 15, 2002, pp. A3 and A6; and Scott McCartney and J. Lynn Lunsford, "Skies Darken for Boeing, AMR and UAL as Aviation Woes Grow," *Wall Street Journal,* October 17, 2002, pp. A1, A9.

[22] J. Lynn Lunsford, "Boeing, Losing Ground to Airbus, Faces Key Choice," *Wall Street Journal,* April 21, 2003, pp. A1, A8; J. Lynn Lunsford, "Boeing May Risk Building New Jet," *Wall Street Journal,* October 15, 2003, pp. A1, A13; and Daniel Michaels, "Airbus Sees Military-Sales Opening," *Wall Street Journal,* September 15, 2003, p. A8.

always flown Boeing 737s. A debate brewed among executives and customers over why the once-dominant Boeing was losing order after order.

Stonecipher blamed the company's sales force for not doing a better job of nurturing relationships. But some in the industry blamed Boeing's failures on poor pricing strategy, an unwillingness to bend, and a distorted notion that quality was still more important to airlines than price—all this at a time when airlines were struggling mightily to reduce costs.

Compounding the situation, Boeing was trying to gain commitments for its new 7E7 widebody, and Airbus was countering with its A350, which would be derived from its current A330 model. While Japan Airlines, late in 2004, agreed to order 30 7E7s from Boeing and take options for 20 more, this brought total orders and commitments for the plane to 112, but this was still well short of the goal of 200 by the end of 2004.

Boeing continued to attribute Airbus's success in the marketplace as due to billions of dollars of European subsidies that allowed it to underbid Boeing. Airbus maintained its success was planes that could be built more quickly and cheaply than Boeing's.[23]

In December 2004, Boeing had one source of satisfaction. Airbus disclosed that its flagship A380 superjumbo jetliner had cost overruns approaching $2 billion or about 12 percent in excess of the plane's original budget. The first flight of the huge A380 was expected in March 2005. Airbus saw no problem with this budget overage and said it will have "no impact on the overall profitability of the program.[24]

Late-Breaking News 2005

The corporate scandals that came to light in 2003, and began the tortuous climb to trial in late 2004 and 2005, have brought new diligence to directors of major corporations, since some are also under fire for their lack of controls and objective oversight over their CEOs. Jury verdicts—the most recent one as we go to production—was a guilty verdict on March 15, 2005 against Bernard Ebbers, CEO of the WorldCom meltdown. Character and integrity are becoming major criteria in board selections of CEOs and of their evaluations of present ones.

Harry Stonecipher had been brought back from retirement at Boeing in early 2004 to bolster ethical standards, following a string of scandals at Boeing, mostly involving conflicts of interest on government interactions. After fifteen months, Stonecipher himself was dismissed for unethical conduct after directors learned about his explicit e-mail to a female employee with whom he was having an affair. In a strange twist, he was asked to leave because he had violated the very code of conduct he had helped draft, which prohibited any behavior that may embarrass the company.

---

[23] Compiled from J. Lynn Lunsford, "Behind Slide in Boeing Orders: Weak Sales Team or Firm Prices?" *Wall Street Journal,* December 23, 2004, pp. A1, A6; Daniel Michaels, "Airbus Firms Up Plans for a New Jet," *Wall Street Journal,* September 30, 2004, p. A3.

[24] David Gauthier-Villars, Pierre Briancon, and Daniel Michaels, "Airbus Discloses Cost Overruns on Big A380 Jet," *Wall Street Journal,* December 16, 2004, pp. A3, A10.

Most firms no longer prohibit consensual romances between employees, single or married, as long as neither person reports to the other. Even Stonecipher's acknowledging that he erred in writing explicit e-mail on the company's computers would have been overlooked at most retail and entertainment companies. But, "one of the rules of doing business with Boeing's biggest customer—the government—is being discrete."[25]

WHAT CAN BE LEARNED?

Beware the "King-of-the-Hill" Three C's Mind-Set

Firms that have been well entrenched in their industry and that have dominated for years tend to fall into a particular mind-set that leaves them vulnerable to aggressive and innovative competitors.

These "three C's" are detrimental to a frontrunner's continued success:

complacency

conservatism

conceit

Complacency is smugness—a complacent firm is self-satisfied, content with the status quo, no longer hungry and eager for innovative growth. Conservatism, when excessive, characterizes a management that is wedded to the past, to the traditional, to the way things have always been done. Conservative managers see no need to change because they believe nothing is different today (e.g., "Our 747 jumbo jet is the largest that can be profitably used"). Finally, conceit further reinforces the myopia of the mind-set: conceit regarding current and potential competitors. The beliefs that "we are the best" and "no one else can touch us" can easily permeate an organization that has dominated its industry for years. Usually the three C's insidiously move in at the highest levels and readily filter down to the rest of the organization.

Stonecipher, former CEO of McDonnell Douglas and then president of Boeing, admitted to company self-confidence bordering on arrogance. The current problems of Boeing should have destroyed any vestiges of the three C's mind-set. But the former "king-of-the hill" position may be lost.

Growth Must Be Manageable

Boeing certainly demonstrated the fallacy of attempting growth beyond immediate capabilities in a growth-at-any-cost mind-set. The rationale for embracing great growth is that firms "need to run with the ball" if they ever get that rare

---

[25] Carol Hymowitz, "The Perils of Picking CEOs," *Wall Street Journal,* March 15, 2005, pp. B1, B4.

opportunity to suddenly double or triple sales. But there are times when a slower, more controlled growth is prudent.

Risks lie on both sides as businesses reach for these opportunities. When a market begins to boom and a firm is unable to keep up with demand without greatly increasing capacity and resources, it faces a dilemma: (1) stay conservative in fear that the opportunity will be short lived, but thereby abdicate some of the growing market to competitors or (2) expand vigorously to take full advantage of the opportunity, but risk being overextended and vulnerable should the potential suddenly fade. Regardless of the commitment to a vision of great growth, a firm must develop an organization and systems and controls to handle it or find itself in the same morass as Boeing, with quality control problems, inability to meet production targets, alienated customers, and costs far out of line. And not the least, having its stock price savaged by Wall Street investors while its market share tumbles. Growth must not be beyond the firm's ability to manage it.

Downsizing Has Its Perils

Boeing presents a sobering example of the risks of downsizing in this era when downsizing is so much in fashion. With incredibly bad timing, Boeing encouraged many of its most experienced and skilled workers and supervisors to take early retirement, just a few years before the boom began. Boeing found out the hard way that it could replace bodies, but not the skills needed to produce the highly complex planes under severe deadlines for output. The company would have been better off maintaining a core of experienced workers during the downturn rather than lose them forever. It would have been better suffering higher labor costs during the lean times and disregarding management's typical attitude of paring costs to the bone during such times. Yet when we look at Table 4.1 and see the severe decreases of revenues and income in 1993, 1994, and lasting well into 1995, we can understand the mind-set of Boeing's management.

Problems of Competing Entirely on Price

Price competition almost invariably leads to price cutting and even price wars to win market share. In such an environment, the lowest cost, most-efficient producer wins.

More often, all firms in an industry have rather similar cost structures, and severe price competition hurts the profits of all competitors without bringing much additional business. Any initial pricing advantage is quickly matched by competitors unwilling to lose market share. In this situation, competing on nonprice bases has much to recommend it. Nonprice competition emphasizes uniqueness, perhaps in some aspects of product features and quality, perhaps through service and quicker deliveries or maybe better quality control. A firm's reputation, if good, is a powerful nonprice advantage.

Usually, new and rapidly growing industries face price competition as marginal firms are weeded out, and more economies of operation are developed. The more mature an industry, the greater likelihood of nonprice competition, since cutthroat pricing causes too much hardship to all competitors.

Certainly the commercial aircraft industry was mature, and much has been made of airlines being chiefly interested in how much passenger-carrying capacity they can buy for the same buck, and of their pitting Airbus and Boeing against each other in bidding wars.[26] Nonprice competition badly needed to be reinstated in this industry. At that point, Airbus appeared to be doing a better job of finding uniqueness, with its passenger-friendly planes and its charting new horizons with the superjumbo.

The Synergy of Mergers and Acquisitions is Suspect

The concept of synergy says that a new whole is better than the sum of its parts. In other words, a well-planned merger or acquisition should result in a better enterprise than the two separate entities. Theoretically, this seems possible with operations streamlined for more efficiency and greater management and staff competence achieved as more financial and other resources are tapped—or in Boeing's case, with the peaks and valleys of commercial demand countered by defense and space business.

Unfortunately, as we will see in other cases, such synergy often is absent, at least in the short and intermediate term. More often such concentrations incur severe digestive problems—problems with people, systems, and procedures—that take time to resolve. Furthermore, greater size does not always beget economies of scale. The opposite may in fact occur: an unwieldy organization, slow to act, and vulnerable to more aggressive, innovative, and agile smaller competitors. The siren call of synergy is often an illusion.

The assimilation of the McDonnell Douglas and Rockwell acquisitions came at a most troubling time for Boeing. The Long Beach plant of McDonnell Douglas alone led to a massive $1.4 billion write-off and contributed significantly to the losses of 1997. Less easily calculated, but certainly a factor, was the management time involved in coping with these new entities.

CONSIDER

Can you think of additional learning insights?

QUESTIONS

1. Do you think Boeing should have anticipated the impact of Asian economic difficulties long before it did?
2. If it had more quickly anticipated the drying up of the Asian market for planes, could Boeing have prevented most of the problems that confronted it? Discuss.

---

[26] For example, Banks, p. 54.

3. Do you think top management at Boeing should have been fired after the disastrous miscalculations in the late 1990s? Why or why not?

4. A major stockholder grumbles, "Management worries too much about Airbus, and to hell with the stockholders." Evaluate this statement. Do you think it is valid?

5. What do you see for Boeing three to five years down the road? For Airbus?

6. Do you think it likely that Boeing can regain its former market share dominance over Airbus? Why or why not?

7. Discuss synergy in mergers. Why does synergy so often seem to be lacking despite expectations?

8. You are a skilled machinist for Boeing and have always been quite proud of participating in the building of giant planes. You have just received notice of another lengthy layoff, the second in five years. Discuss your likely attitudes and actions.

9. How wise do you think it was for Airbus to "bet the company" on the superjumbo A-380, the world's largest jet?

10. Do you think Airbus's more passenger-friendly planes give it a significant competitive advantage? Why or why not? Discuss as many aspects of this as you can.

HANDS-ON EXERCISES

Before

1. You are a management consultant advising top management at Boeing. It is 1993 and the airline industry is in a slump, but early indications are that things will improve greatly in a few years. What would you advise that might have prevented the problems Boeing faced a few years later? Be as specific as you can and support your recommendations as to practicality and probable effectiveness.

After

2. It is late 1998, and Boeing has had to announce drastic cutbacks, with little improvement likely before five years. Boeing's stock has collapsed and Airbus is charging ahead. What do you recommend now? (You may need to make some assumptions; if so, state them clearly and keep them reasonable.)

3. It is 2005, and you have been brought in as vice president of sales. What do you propose to counter the aggressive and successful efforts of Airbus to win customers?

4. Be a Devil's Advocate (one who argues an opposing position to ensure that all aspects of a course of action are considered): Amass all the arguments

and rationale you can for Boeing to continue with the high-speed Sonic Cruiser.

5. Be a Devil's Advocate. You are a union leader and the 32,000 layoffs after 9/11 appall you. Array all the arguments you can muster for Boeing to reconsider such massive layoffs. Be as persuasive as you can.

TEAM DEBATE EXERCISES

1. A business columnist writes: Boeing could "have told customers 'no thanks' to more orders than its factories could handle ... It 'could have done itself a huge favor by simply building fewer planes and charging more for them.'"[27] Debate the merits of this suggestion.

2. Debate the controversy of Airbus chairman Forgeard's decision to go for broke with the A3XX superjumbo. Is the risk/reward probability worth such a mighty commitment? Debate as many pros and cons as you can, and also consider how much each should be weighted or given priority consideration.

INVITATION TO RESEARCH

What is the situation with Boeing today? Has it remained profitable? How is the competitive position with Airbus?

What is the situation with the A380 superjumbo of Airbus? Is it a success or dismal failure?

---

[27] Holman W. Jenkins Jr., "Boeing's Trouble: Not Enough Monopolistic Arrogance," *Wall Street Journal*, December 16, 1998, p. A23.

CHAPTER FIVE

Sneaker Wars:
Nike vs. Reebok

*B*y the late 1970s and early 1980s, Nike had wrested first place in the athletic shoe industry from Adidas, the firm that had been supreme since the 1936 Olympics when Jesse Owens, wearing Adidas shoes, won his medals in front of Hitler, the German nation, and the world.

In the early 1980s, Reebok emerged as Nike's major competitor, showing a tremendous growth and becoming No. 1 in this industry by 1987. But Nike fought back and, three years later, regained the top-dog position. By the latter 1990s and into the new millennium, Nike had decisively pulled away in revenues and profitability. How did Reebok fight its way to the top in the first place? Why did it permit Nike to dislodge it so soon? Or did Nike use some inspired marketing strategy to do so?

Unfortunately, Nike became bedeviled about using so-called sweatshops in poor countries of the world to make its shoes cheaper. Despite many other firms doing the same thing, *outsourcing*, Nike became the focal point for criticisms of all kinds. Was it truly an ogre? Was it acting unethically, as vocal critics maintained? Such critics also derided Nike's targeting ghetto youth with its expensive celebrity shoes.

REEBOK

History

The ancestor to Reebok goes back to the 1890s when Joseph William Foster made the first known running shoes with spikes. By 1895, he was hand-making shoes for top runners. Soon, the fledgling company, J. W. Foster and Sons, was furnishing shoes for distinguished athletes around the world.

In 1958, two of the founder's grandsons started a companion company, which they named—fittingly they thought—after an African gazelle: Reebok. This company eventually absorbed J. W. Foster and Sons.

In 1979, Paul Fireman, a partner in an outdoor sporting goods distributorship, saw Reebok shoes at an international trade show. He negotiated for the North American distribution license and introduced three running shoes in the United

States that year. It was the height of the running boom. These Reeboks were the most expensive running shoes on the market at the time, retailing for $60. But no matter, demand burgeoned, outpacing the plant's capacity, and production facilities were established in Korea.

In 1981, sales were $1.5 million. But a breakthrough came the next year. Reebok introduced the first athletic shoe designed especially for women. It was a shoe for aerobic dance exercise and was called the Freestyle. Whether accidentally or with brilliant foresight, Reebok anticipated three major trends that were to transform the athletic footwear industry: (1) the aerobic exercise movement, (2) the great embracing of women with sports and exercise, and (3) the transference of athletic footwear to street and casual wear.

Sales exploded from $13 million in 1983 to $307 million in 1985. Almost unbelievably, sales tripled in 1986 to $919 million and by 1991 reached $2.7 billion.

A company publication in 1993, said:

> For more than a decade, the semi-official corporate motto has called for the company, its products and its people to always strive to "make a difference"; and one of the company's business objectives is to become "the best, most innovative and exciting sporting goods company in the world."[1]

Shifting Competitive Picture for Reebok

In 1987, Reebok's share of the U.S. athletic footwear market surpassed archrival Nike's as it racked up sales of $1.4 billion against Nike's plateauing sales of $900 million. Somehow, Reebok's sales growth then slowed, and in 1990 Nike overtook it, with $2.25 billion in sales to Reebok's $2.16 billion. The margin widened as Reebok began to lose ground, not sporadically, but steadily. Its meteoric sales increases of a few years before were no more, and stock market valuations and investor enthusiasm reflected this decline in fortunes.

Part of the shift in competitive position could be attributed to Nike's savvy advertising and to its two well-paid athlete endorsers: Michael Jordan and Pete Sampras. But perhaps Reebok could blame itself more for the change in its fortunes. Certainly, as the 1990s moved toward mid-decade, the flaws of Reebok were becoming more obvious and self-destructing.

Paul Fireman had purchased Reebok in 1984 and led it to more than a tenfold increase in sales in only five years. But with such growth, directors felt they needed an executive with experience running a big operation. Fireman, who owned 20 percent of the company's stock, didn't object. He maintained that he was glad to give up day-to-day responsibilities. While retaining the titles of chairman and CEO, he turned his attentions to private pursuits, including building a golf course on Cape Cod.

The new management was to prove inept. Amid unimproving performance, Reebok went through three different top executives in the next five years, the last being John Duerden, formerly with Xerox. Nothing seemed to stem the tide; Reebok

---

[1] *Reebok International, Ltd. Corporate Background,* January 1993, pp. 13–14.

continued losing ground against Nike. Finally, in August 1992, Fireman again took active charge, and he wasted little time bringing in a new management team. At the same time, he introduced aggressive plans for the company to regain its competitive position.

Aggressive Thrusts of Reebok

Fireman first attacked Nike in the basketball arena. Nike's share of basketball shoes was almost 50 percent, against Reebok's 15 percent. But about this time, Michael Jordan retired from basketball to try baseball. "Nike's success has become their albatross," Fireman exaulted. "Jordan is no longer on the radar screen."[2] He signed up Shaquille O'Neal, "the next enduring superstar," and planned to destroy the market dominance of Nike.

The pressure was stepped up on Nike at the NBA All-Star game in February 1994, when Reebok launched a national ad campaign for its Instapump. This was a sneaker that had no laces but instead was inflated with CO_2 to fit the foot. It was pricey, retailing for $130, but seemed on the cutting edge. Fireman expected this innovation to account for 10 percent of all Reebok's sales in three years.

Reebok also attacked another Nike stronghold—the $250 million market for cleated shoes, of which Nike had 80 percent. In January 1993, Reebok introduced a new line of cleated shoes aimed at high-school athletes. Fireman predicted that these sales should triple by 1994 to $45 million. In 1994, he also aimed an offensive into the outdoor hiking and mountaineering market, with 12 new shoes that he predicted would produce $100 million in new sales.

During the years Fireman was not at the helm, Reebok had tried a number of advertising slogans, such as "UBU" and "Physics Behind Physique." None of them were notably effective compared to the Nike "Just Do It" theme. Fireman now approved a new unifying theme for all ads, "Planet Reebok."

Fireman also did an about-face with his endorsement promotions. Despite Nike's heavy use of endorsements in its advertising, Reebok always had been reluctant to do much, thinking the huge sums celebrity athletes demanded were unreasonable. Suddenly, Fireman signed O'Neal in 1992 for $3 million and then went on to sign endorsement deals with some 400 football, baseball, and soccer stars. The brand logo was also changed to an inverted "V" with a slash through it that he hoped consumers would identify with high performance. "We'll be the market leader by the end of 1995," Fireman predicted.[3]

Consequences

Unfortunately, the aggressive efforts of Fireman to rejuvenate the company and win back market leadership from Nike continued to sputter. Some flaws were coming to light. For example, with Shaquille O'Neal, the Shaq Attaq shoe seemed a sure thing for teens. But it bombed. The problems: the shoes were white with light blue trim,

---

[2] Geoffrey Smith, "Can Reebok Regain Its Balance?" *Business Week*, December 20, 1993, p. 109.
[3] Ibid, p. 108.

and they cost $130. But now black shoes were the hot look, and how many teens could afford $130? In the first six months of 1993, sales of Reebok basketball shoes fell 20 percent, despite Shaq's influence.

By 1995, operating costs were surging, up to 32.7 percent of sales compared with 24.4 percent in 1991. They also exceeded the industry average of 27 percent. Reebok admitted that the increased costs were partly due to its aggressive pursuit of endorsement contracts with athletes as well as sporting-event sponsorships. For example, the company had signed up 3,000 athletes to wear Reebok shoes and apparel at the 1996 Olympics in Atlanta, up from 400 four years before. It had also bought endorsements from the San Francisco 49ers and other NFL teams, as well as basketball star Rebecca Lobo, to wear its products.

Some of the prior endorsements had not worked out well: Tennis pro Michael Chang had a $15 million endorsement contract, but Sampras and Agassi, both Nike endorsers, had eclipsed Chang. And Shaquille O'Neal became unhappy with his $3 million Reebok contract and began looking around for bigger money.

Reebok's costs also were increased by investments aimed at fixing distribution snags and opening a new facility in Memphis.

Other Reebok problems stemmed from management turmoil, including the departures and resignations of top executives. Some shareholders questioned whether Fireman was too difficult a boss: "How do you attract first-rate talent when there's been a history of turnover at the top?"[4]

Adding to Reebok's difficulties were price-fixing charges brought by the Federal Trade Commission. The government contended that Reebok had told retailers their supplies would be cut off if they discounted Reebok shoes too much. In May 1995, Reebok agreed to pay $9.5 million to settle the price-fixing charges, saying that while no evidence of wrongdoing was established, still it settled to avoid costly litigation.

But the more serious Reebok problem was in its relations with the major retailer player in the athletic footwear industry—Foot Locker.

The Struggle to Win Foot Locker

By 1995, Woolworth's Foot Locker, a chain of some 2,800 stores, had become the biggest seller of athletic footwear. It and related Woolworth units accounted for $1.5 billion of the $6.5 billion U.S. sales, this being some 23 percent. Nike had a winning relationship with this behemoth customer. In 1993, Nike's sales in Foot Lockers were $300 million, while Reebok was slightly behind, with $228 million. Two years later, Nike's Foot Locker sales had risen to $750 million, while Reebok's dropped to $122 million.[5]

The decline of Reebok's fortunes with Foot Locker can be attributed to poor handling by top management of this important relationship. Fireman seemed to resent the demands of Foot Locker almost from the beginning. For example, in the 1980s, when Reebok's aerobics shoes were facing robust demand, Foot Locker

---

[4] Joseph Pereira, "In Reebok-Nike War, Big Woolworth Chain Is a Major Battlefield," *Wall Street Journal,* September 22, 1995, p. A6.

[5] Ibid., p. A1.

wanted exclusivity, that is, special lines only for itself. The retailer saw exclusive lines as one of its major weapons against discounters and was getting such protection from other manufacturers—but not from Reebok, which persisted in selling its shoes to anybody, including discounters near Foot Locker stores.

In contrast, Nike had been working with Foot Locker for some years and by 1995 had a dozen items sold only by the chain, including Flights 65 and 67, high-priced basketball shoes. While Fireman began belatedly trying to fix the relationship, little had apparently been accomplished by the end of 1995.[6]

Adding to Reebok's troubles in cracking this major chain, Foot Locker's customers were mainly teens and Generation-X customers willing to pay $80 to $90 for shoes. But Reebok had given up that high-end niche with most of its products. Reebok's primary customer base had become older people and preteens unwilling or unable to pay the high prices.

Aggravating the poor relationship with Foot Locker was Reebok's carelessness in providing samples on time to Foot Locker buyers. Because of the chain's size, buying decisions had to be made early in the season. Late-arriving samples, or no samples, virtually guaranteed that such new items would not be purchased in any appreciable quantity. See the following Information Box for a discussion of the importance of major customers.

INFORMATION BOX

IMPORTANCE OF MAJOR ACCOUNT MANAGEMENT

Recognizing the importance of major customers has come belatedly to some sellers, probably none more belatedly than Reebok. These very large customers often represent a major part of a firm's total sales volume, and satisfying them in an increasingly competitive environment requires special treatment. Major account management should be geared to developing long-term relationships. Service becomes increasingly important in cementing such relations. To this end, understanding and catering to customer needs and wants is a must. If this means giving such important customers exclusivity, and making them the absolute first to see new goods and samples, this ought to be done unhesitatingly.

Such account management has resulted in changes in many organizations. Separate sales forces are often developed, such as "account managers" who devote all their time to one or a few major customers, while the rest of the sales force calls on smaller customers in the normal fashion. For a customer the size of Foot Locker, senior executives, even company presidents, need to become part of this relationship.

Given that you think the demands of a major retailer are completely unreasonable, what would you do if you were Mr. Fireman: give in completely, hold to your principles, negotiate, or what?

---

[6] Ibid., p. A6.

NIKE

History

Phil Knight was a miler of modest accomplishments. His best time was a 4:13, hardly in the same class as the below-4:00 world-class runners. But he had trained under the renowned coach Bill Bowerman at the University of Oregon in the late 1950s. Bowerman had put Eugene, Oregon on the map when year after year he turned out world-record-setting long-distance runners. Bowerman was constantly experimenting with shoes: He had a theory that an ounce off a running shoe might make enough difference to win a race.

In the process of completing his MBA at Stanford University, Knight wrote a research paper based on the theory that the Japanese could do for athletic shoes what they were doing for cameras. After receiving his degree in 1960, Knight went to Japan to seek an American distributorship from the Onitsuka Company for Tiger shoes. Returning home, he took samples of the shoes to Bowerman.

In 1964, Knight and Bowerman went into business. They each put up $500 and formed the Blue Ribbon Shoe Company, sole distributor in the United States for Tiger running shoes. They put the inventory in Knight's father-in-law's basement, and they sold $8,000 worth of these imported shoes that first year. Knight worked by days as a Cooper & Lybrand accountant, while at night and on weekends, he peddled these shoes, mostly to high-school athletic teams.

Knight and Bowerman finally developed their own shoe in 1972 and decided to manufacture it themselves. They contracted the work out to Asian factories where labor was cheap. They named the shoe Nike after the Greek goddess of victory. At that time they also developed the "swoosh" logo, which was highly distinctive and subsequently was placed on every Nike product. The Nike shoe's first appearance in competition came during the 1972 Olympic trials in Eugene, Oregon. Marathon runners persuaded to wear the new shoes placed fourth through seventh, whereas Adidas wearers finished first, second, and third in the trials.

On a Sunday morning in 1975, Bowerman began tinkering with a waffle iron and some urethane rubber, and he fashioned a new type of sole, a "waffle" sole whose tiny rubber studs made it springier than those of other shoes currently on the market. This product improvement—seemingly so simple—gave Knight and Bowerman an initial impetus, helping to bring 1976 sales to $14 million, up from $8.3 million the year before, and from only $2 million in 1972.

Now Nike was off and running. It was to stay in the forefront of the industry with its careful research and development of new models. By the end of the decade, Nike was employing almost one hundred people in the research and development section of the company. Over 140 different shoe models were offered, many of these the most innovative and technologically advanced on the market. Such diversity came from models designed for different foot types, body weights, sexes, running speeds, training schedules, and skill levels. By 1981, Nike led all athletic shoemakers with approximately 50 percent of the total market. Adidas, the decades-long market leader, had seen its share of the market fall well below that of Nike.

In 1980, Nike went public, and Knight became an instant multimillionaire, reaching the coveted *Forbes* Richest Four Hundred Americans with a net worth estimated at just under $300 million.[7] Bowerman, at age 70, had sold most of his stock earlier and owned only 2 percent of the company, worth a mere $9.5 million.

In the January 4, 1982 edition of *Forbes* in the "Annual Report on American Industry," Nike was rated No. 1 in profitability over the previous five years, ahead of all other firms in all other industries.[8]

But by the latter 1980s, Reebok had emerged as Nike's greatest competitor and threatened its dynasty. A good part of the reason for this was Nike's underestimation of an opportunity. Consequently, it was late into the fast-growing market for shoes worn for the aerobic classes that were sweeping the country, fueled by best-selling books by Jane Fonda and others. Reebok was there with the first athletic shoe designed especially for women: a shoe for aerobic dance exercise.

Figure 5.1 shows the sales growth of Reebok and Nike from their beginnings to 1995. Of particular note is the great growth of Reebok in the mid-80s; in only a few years it had surpassed Nike, which had plateaued as it missed the new fitness opportunity. Then as can graphically be seen, Reebok began slowing down—a slowdown it was unable to turn around through the mid-1990s, while Nike again surged. Table 5.1

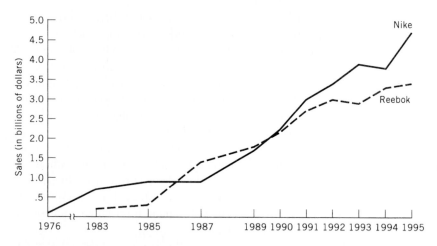

Figure 5.1 Sneaker Wars: Sales, Nike and Reebok 1976–1995 (billions of dollars)

Source: Company annual reports

Commentary: Here we can graphically see the charge of Reebok in the later 1980s that for a few years surpassed Nike but then faltered by 1990 as Nike surged even farther ahead.

---

[7] "The Richest People in America—The Forbes Four Hundred," *Forbes*, Fall 1983, p. 104.
[8] *Forbes*, January 4, 1982, p. 246.

TABLE 5.1   Sneaker Wars: Net Income Comparisons, Nike and Reebok 1985–1994 (billions of dollars)

	Nike	Reebok
1985	$10.3	$39.0
1986	59.2	132.1
1987	35.9	165.2
1988	101.7	137.0
1989	167.0	175.0
1990	243.0	176.6
1991	287.0	234.7
1992	329.2	114.8
1993	365.0	223.4
1994	298.8	254.5

Source: Company annual reports.

Commentary: Note how much more profitable Reebok was than Nike in the late 1980s. In one year, 1987, it was almost five times more profitable. But then in 1990, the tide swung strongly in Nike's favor. Note also that Nike's profitability was far steadier than Reebok's during this period.

shows the net income comparisons. Both firms had somewhat erratic incomes, but the early income growth promise of Reebok relative to Nike, as with sales, could not be sustained. This is confirmed with later revenue and income figures from 1995 to 1998, shown in Table 5.2.

Nike's Rejuvenation

The recharge of Nike, after letting its guard down to the wildly charging Reebok, has to be a significant success story. Usually, when a front runner loses momentum, the trend is difficult to reverse. But Phil Knight and Nike were not to be denied.

Still, in 1993, Nike did not look very much a winner, even though it had wrested market dominance from Reebok. From the high 80s in February of that year, share prices had plummeted to the mid-50s. The reason? Nike's sales were up only 15 percent and earnings just 11 percent, nothing outstanding for a once-hot stock. So Wall Street began questioning: How many pairs of sneakers does the world need? (Critics had once assailed McDonald's under the same rationale: How many hamburgers can the world eat?) Knight's response was that the Nike mystique could sell other kinds of goods: outdoor footwear, from sandals to hiking boots; apparel lines, such as uniforms, for top-ranked college football and basketball teams—from pants and jerseys to warm-up jackets and practice gear; even golf clothing and equipment. And these same products would be eagerly sought by the general public.

TABLE 5.2 Nike vs. Reebok Comparative Operating Statistics, 1995–1998

	Nike	Reebok	Nike % of Total
Revenues (million $):			
1995	$4,761	$3,481	57.8%
1996	6,471	3,478	65.0
1997	9,187	3,644	71.6
1998	9,553	3,225	74.8
Net Income (million $)			
1995	400	165	70.8
1996	553	139	79.9
1997	796	135	85.5
1998	400	24	82.2

Source: Calculated from company reports.

Commentary: In this comparative analysis, the further widening of the gap between Nike and Reebok is clearly evident. In revenues, Nike's market share against Reebok has grown from 57.8 percent to 74.8 percent in these four years—a truly awesome increase in market dominance. In net income, Nike's comparative performance is even more impressive, despite the poor 1998 profit performance partly due to poor economic conditions in the Asian markets. Nike's profits were down, but not nearly as much as Reebok's.

The greatest boost to the image of Nike in the years around the millennium was Tiger Woods. Phil Knight had given him a $40 million contract in 1996, just after he won his third straight U. S. Amateur championship and was about to turn pro. The next year Tiger won the prestigious Masters Golf Tournament by the biggest margin ever achieved, in the most watched golf finale in the history of television. In the golf tournaments, while wearing the conspicuous swoosh, Tiger focused attention on Nike as not even Michael Jordan had been able to do.

Could it be that an athletic shoe company could still face a growth industry? Apparently so, through wise diversifications within the larger athletic goods industry. See the following Issue Box for a discussion of how a business should define itself.

In his quest to remain the dominant player, Knight recalled what he learned from his old coach and Nike cofounder, Bill Bowerman: "Play by the rules, but be ferocious."[9]

But Knight and Nike were not ferocious to their customers. They pampered them, as we have seen in the relations with Foot Locker. And by the end of 1995, Nike's sales lead over Reebok was 38 percent. By 1999, it was 213 percent.

Handling Adversity

In the summer of 1996, Nike and many other U. S. manufacturers came under fire for farming production out to so-called sweatshops in poor countries of the world in

[9] Fleming Meeks, "Be Ferocious," *Forbes,* August 2, 1993, p. 41.

ISSUE BOX

HOW SHOULD WE DEFINE OUR BUSINESS?

Nike has developed its business horizons through the following sequence:

running shoes → athletic shoes → athletic clothing → athletic goods

In so doing, it has greatly expanded its growth potential. This idea of expanding perception of one's business was first put down on paper by Theodore Levitt in a seminal article, "Marketing Myopia" in the *Harvard Business Review* in July-August 1960. Levitt suggested that it was shortsighted for railroads to consider themselves only in the railroad business, and not in the much larger transportation business. Similarly, petroleum companies should consider themselves in the energy business and plan their strategies accordingly.

Can such expansion of a firm's business definition go too far? Even in Levitt's day, could a railroad really have the expertise to run an airline? Looking to Nike today, and its expanding views of tapping into the athletic goods market, do you think golf clubs and bags are a viable expansion opportunity? Football equipment? Fishing tackle?

order to reduce manufacturing costs. Nike became the major target for critics of these "abuses."

Then in April 1997 came another blow to Nike's image. Thirty-nine members of the Heaven's Gate cult committed suicide, all wearing Nikes with the swoosh logo readily visible. The "Just Do It" slogan of Nike was trumpeted as being entirely apt, and some even spoofed that Nike's slogan should be changed to "Just Did It."

Environmental factors, by no means unique to Nike, also tormented the firm. Demand in Asia was drastically reduced due to deep recession there. Another troubling portent was the public's growing disenchantment with athletes. Fan interest seemed to be dropping, perhaps reflecting a growing tide of resentment at overpriced athletes proving to be selfish, arrogant, and decadent—the very role models that Nike, Reebok, and other firms spent millions to enlist.

Knight had to wonder at another disturbing possibility: Had Nike grown too big? Was its logo, the swoosh, too pervasive, to the point that it turned some people off? Was even the tag line, "Just Do It," becoming counterproductive?

Concerned about such questions, Nike began reassessing. A new advertising campaign had the softer tag line, "I can." Nike began toning down its use of the swoosh, removing it from corporate letterheads and most advertising, and replacing it with a lowercase "nike."

Later Developments

At the beginning of the new millennium, Nike's dominant position continued to strengthen. Changing fashion trends, new products, cost cutting, and an Asian revival aided Nike. It found that with the public's growing disenchantment with many athlete endorsers it could shave its marketing budget by $100 million. Furthermore, prospects for 2000 were optimistic. Sales of athletic gear peak in Olympic years, and the expectations were reasonable that the summer games in Sydney, Australia, would stimulate a big buying spree in merchandise where Nike had a 35 percent share.[10]

Reebok turned out to benefit most by the Olympics; its shoes were seen on 2,500 pairs of feet. It had also scored a coup in sponsoring the CBS hit, *Survivor.* But after years of missteps, its market share was just 12 percent, although Paul Fireman was predicting this would rise to 25 percent within the next six years. The company was pursuing a smarter distribution strategy with less emphasis on discount chains and more on courting mall retailers, such as Foot Locker, for whom Fireman was now giving some exclusive rights. Reebok also was trying to win back teenage boys—who were spurning its conservative, even frumpy shoes—by new colorful designs endorsed by professional basketball player Allen Iverson, the latest endorser.

Nike continued to push its apparel lines that in 2001 accounted for about a third of the total $9 billion of sales, with particular attention given to women's wear. It opened NikeTown stores where shoppers could see the full range of products displayed in a hands-on environment. But it was also trying to boost its exposure in department stores, which were notorious for driving hard bargains.

See Table 5.3 for operating results of Nike and Reebok at the turn of the century. You can see from these statistics that Nike's dominance was increasing. Despite Reebok's improved showing in 2001, it still lagged far behind.

On November 19, 2004, Nike announced that Philip Knight, 66, was retiring from day-to-day management of his company, although he would remain chairman of the board. The announcement was not unexpected as he had two copresidents who were seen as possible successors. But he went outside the company to William Perez, the chief executive of family-controlled S.C.Johnson & Son, a consumer-products company, with such brands as Drano, Windex, and Glade air fresheners—rather tame compared to the big athletic endorsers. But Mr. Perez is a marathoner and a buyer of Nike shoes for 27 years and has "vast international experience that will help Nike expand further into markets abroad." Knight explained this choice of an outsider as preserving the leadership balance at the company, rather than upsetting it by elevating one of the company's executives.

Phil Knight tried to step back from active participation in daily operations in the late 1990s, but sales slipped, and he eventually came back to the helm. This management transition came at a time when performance was stronger than ever. Total sales in the previous year had climbed to $12 billion, and orders for the current year were up 9.9 percent.[11]

---

[10] Leigh Gallagher, "Rebound," *Forbes,* May 3, 1999, p. 60.

[11] Stephanie Kang and Joann S. Lublin, "Nike Taps Perez of S.C. Johnson to Follow Knight," *Wall Street Journal,* November 19, 2004, pp. A3, A6.

TABLE 5.3   Nike vs. Reebok Comparative Operating Statistics, 1999–2001

	Nike	Reebok	Nike % of Total
Revenues (million $):			
1999	$8,995	$2,872	75.8%
2000	9,449	2,865	76.7
2001	9,893	2,993	76.8
Net Income (million $)			
1999	579	11	98.1
2000	590	81	87.9
2001	663	103	86.6

Source: Calculated from company reports.

Commentary: In this latest comparative analysis, Nike dominance has grown well beyond that during 1995–1998 (see Table 5.2). In revenues, Nike's market share against Reebok averaged 76.4 percent in those three years, while Nike has over 90 percent of the combined profitability of the two firms.

ANALYSIS

The case shows the whipsawing of the two major competitors in what was once merely the athletic shoe industry, an industry now expanded far beyond its original focus. In its youth, Nike had outgunned the old entrenched Adidas, only to find Reebok surpassing it in the mid-1980s, as it failed to recognize soon enough a new opportunity. Somehow Nike came back stronger than ever. The explanation lies in the mistakes of Reebok and the luck and aggressiveness of Nike after its brief hiccup.

The most controllable factor in the divergent success patterns of these competitors had to be customer relations. Nike cultivated its customers, especially the larger dealers such as Foot Locker, while Reebok was surprisingly nonchalant and even arrogant in such relationships. A maker of even high-demand goods is myopic in being arbitrary and dictatorial toward dealers. This relationship should be viewed as symbiotic, with both parties benefiting from it, though the temptation is to capitalize on the perceived king-of-the-hill position. But the caprice of fashions and fads can quickly destroy this smugness, leaving the previous year's winner at the gate the next year, as was the case with the Shaq Attaq shoes and the expensive endorsements of Shaquille.

In other aspects of its comeback, Nike may have lucked out. It chose for its endorsing athletes, ones who grew to become the dominant figures in their sport, ones lionized by fans. The advertising theme of Nike caught on: "Just Do It" had great appeal to youth. But such home runs in advertising can never be guaranteed.

The success and visibility of Nike and its products brought with it critical public scrutiny. Was Nike—and other U.S. manufacturers as well—guilty of violations of accepted moral and ethical standards in farming out production to foreign subcontractors in Third World countries using child labor at low wages? Critics condemned this as exploitation to maximize profits. But others pointed out that while long hours in a smelly shoe or garment factory may be less than idyllic, it was superior to subsistence farming or laboring in even harsher workplaces.

Could Reebok rejuvenate itself as Nike had? That seems less likely today, with Nike's revenues four times greater than Reebok's and net income six times greater. Still, it could close the gap with a striking new product innovation—or if Nike becomes complacent. Remember the 3 C's of the last chapter as Boeing opened the gates for AirBus. And dare we forget, Nike vanquished the dominant Adidas in its early days.

WHAT CAN BE LEARNED?

No One Is Immune from Mistakes; Success Does Not Guarantee Continued Success

Some executives delude themselves into thinking success begets continued success. It is not so! No firm, market leader, or otherwise can afford to rest on its laurels, to disregard a changing environment and aggressive but smaller competitors. Adidas had as commanding a lead in its industry as IBM once had in computers. But it was overtaken and surpassed by Nike, a rank newcomer, and a domestic firm with few resources in an era when foreign brands (of beer, watches, cars) had a mystique and attraction for affluent Americans that few domestic brands could achieve. But Adidas let down its guard at a critical point. Similarly, but to a lesser degree, Nike then lagged against Reebok as it underestimated or was unaware of the growing interest among women in aerobic dancing and other physical activities.

Don't Underestimate the Importance of Catering to Major Customers

A firm should seek to satisfy all its customers, but for the larger ones, the major accounts, the need to satisfy their needs and wants is absolutely vital. In few cases is the stark contrast between effective and ineffective dealings with larger customers more obvious than between Nike and Reebok in their relations with the huge Foot Locker retail chain. Even though a manufacturer may resent the demands of a powerful retailer, the alternative is either meeting them or losing part or all of the business to someone else. However, a better course of action is to work closely with the large customer in a spirit of cooperation and mutual interest, not in an adversarial power struggle.

Consider the Power of Public Image

Granted that technological differences in running shoes have narrowed so that any tangible advantage of a brand is practically imperceptible, what makes Nike stand out? Isn't it the image and the Nike swoosh that identifies the brand? See the following Information Box for a discussion of the swoosh.

INFORMATION BOX

THE NIKE SWOOSH LOGO

The Nike swoosh is one of the world's best-recognized logos. In the very early days of Nike, a local design student at Portland State University was paid $35 for creating it. The curvy, speedy-looking blur turned out to be highly distinctive and has from then on been placed on all Nike products. Phil Knight even has the swoosh logo tattooed on his left calf. Because it has become so familiar, Nike no longer adds the name Nike to the logo. (Tiger Woods wears a cap and other clothing with the swoosh well visible.)

The power of such a well-known logo makes Nike's sponsorship of famous athletes unusually effective as they wear shoes and apparel displaying it in their sports exploits.

In your judgment, do you think Nike could have achieved its present success without this unique but simple logo? What do you think of the Reebok logo?

Items like running shoes, athletic equipment, and apparel have high visibility. For many youth, the sight of famous and admired athletes actively using the brand is an irresistible lure, feeding the desire to emulate them even if only through wearing the same brand … and maybe dreaming a little. The popularity of a brand becomes a further attraction: being cool, belonging to the in-group.

Is Nike's success in building its image transferable to other firms whose products cannot be identified with use by the famous? Do such firms have any possibilities for developing image-enhancing qualities for their brands? They certainly do.

Consider the long-advertised lonesome Maytag repairman. Maytag has been highly successful in building a reputation, an image for dependability and assured quality. In so doing, it has been able to sustain a higher price advantage over its competitors. A carefully nurtured image of good quality, dependability, reliable service, and being in the forefront of technology or fashion can bring a firm great success in its particular industry.

Is There a Point of Diminishing Returns with Celebrity Endorsements?

One would think so, and public attitudes today seem to bear this out. Athlete celebrities demand big bucks. Are their endorsements worth the price? Perhaps only in moderation and only with the best of the best. But one cannot always predict with certainty the future exploits of any athlete, even a Michael Jordan or Tiger Woods. Yet contracts are binding. While some would criticize Nike for too much emphasis on celebrity advertising, the right role models can play dividends. But the overkill of Reebok in seeking celebrity endorsements led to burgeoning costs and a mediocre payoff in sales. The message seems clear: Overuse of celebrity endorsements can be a financial drain. Added to this is the always-present risk that the athlete celebrity in contact sports may have a career-ending injury or be guilty of some nefarious activity that destroys his or her image.

Is a Great Executive the Key?

Was the rejuvenation of Nike and the decline of Reebok due mostly to the talents of a Phil Knight versus a Paul Fireman? Does the success of an enterprise depend almost entirely on the ability of its leader? Such questions have long baffled experts.

Several aspects of this issue are worth noting. The incompetent is usually clearly evident and identifiable. The great business leader may also be, but perhaps he or she simply lucked out. In most situations, competing executives are reasonably similar in competence. They have vision, the support of their organizations, and reasonable judgment and prudence. What then makes the difference? A good assessment of opportunities, an advertising slogan that really hits, a hunch of competitor vulnerability? Yes. But how much is due just to a fortuitous call, a gamble that paid off?

We know that Phil Knight had a history of great successes. After all, he beat Adidas and brought Nike from nowhere to the premier athletic footwear firm. Add to this his handling of a great challenge by moving Nike, for a second time, into the heady air of market leader. Was his ability as a top executive so much greater than that of Fireman? Would his absence have destroyed the promise of Nike?

Perhaps the basic question is: Can one person make a difference? Does that person have to be infallible? But Phil Knight was not infallible. He had a major perceptual lapse in the mid-1980s. But Fireman's lapses were more serious.

In the final analysis, Knight made a great difference for Nike. Certainly, we can identify other leaders who made great differences: Sam Walton of Wal-Mart, Herb Kelleher of Southwest Airlines, Lee Iacocca of Chrysler, Ray Kroc of McDonald's come readily to mind. Sometimes, one person can make a major difference, but they can still make bad decisions, misjudgments. Perhaps their success was in having a higher percentage of good decisions and, yes, having a little luck on their side. Since at the end of December 2004, Knight announced he was stepping down, and a new CEO chosen from outside the firm would be taking his place, we have a chance to see whether Knight left an enduring legacy, chose his successor wisely, or is irreplaceable.

CONSIDER

Can you think of additional learning insights?

QUESTIONS

1. "The success of Nike was strictly fortuitous and had little to do with great decision making." Evaluate this statement.

2. In recent years, Nike has moved strongly to develop markets for running shoes in the Far East, particularly in China. Discuss how Nike might go about stimulating such underdeveloped markets.

3. How could anyone criticize Fireman for signing up Shaquille O'Neal to a lucrative endorsement contract? Discuss.

4. Do you think the swoosh logo has become too widespread, that it is turning off many people?

5. Given that all decision makers will sometimes make bad calls, how might the batting averages of correct decision be improved? Can it really be improved?

6. Do you think the athletic goods industry has limited potential? Or is it still a growth industry? Your opinions, and rationale, please.

7. Is there a danger in catering too much to major customers? Discuss.

8. What do you think of the inverted V slash logo of Reebok? How would you evaluate it against Nike's swoosh?

9. Critics have condemned Nike's targeting ghetto youth with its expensive celebrity shoes. What is your opinion about this? Unethical? Shrewd marketing? A tempest in a teapot?

HANDS-ON EXERCISES

Before

1. It is 1985. Your production of shoes can hardly meet the burgeoning demand. The future seems unlimited. Design a program for Reebok to build stronger relations with its major customers, including Foot Locker.

After

2. It is 1995. Nike has again achieved market dominance, and its position seems unassailable. Some shareholders are calling for your resignation, Mr. Fireman. Design a strategy for again bringing Reebok to victory in this war against Nike. Be as specific as you can and defend your recommendations.

3. Be a Devil's Advocate (one who argues an opposing viewpoint to test the decision). Array all the rationale you can for *not* deemphasizing the swoosh. Be persuasive.

TEAM DEBATE EXERCISE

Debate the issue of endorsements for athletes. How much is too much? Where do we draw the line? Should we go only for the few famous? Or should we gamble on lesser-knowns eventually making it big and offer them long-term contracts? Argue the two sides of the issue: aggressive and conservative.

INVITATION TO RESEARCH

How has the battle gone between Reebok and Nike? Has Reebok been able to gain any ground? How are the two firms doing in overseas markets? What is your prognosis for their future competitive positions? Are there any "sleeper" competitors emerging, such as a newly energized Adidas? Has William Perez, the chosen successor of Phil Knight as CEO, proven a worthy successor, or was his choice a bad decision?

MANAGING CHANGE
AND CRISES

CHAPTER SIX

Al Dunlap Savages Scott Paper and Sunbeam

Al Dunlap was hired in July 1996 by two large Sunbeam investors to turn Sunbeam around. He had gained a reputation as a turnaround artist extraodinaire, most recently from his efforts at Scott Paper. His philosophy was to cut to the bone, and the press frequently called him "Chainsaw Al." But he met his comeuppance with Sunbeam. In the process, his philosophy came under bitter attack, as did his character. How far do you cut into an organization, and to the living, breathing people involved, before you cross the line? Opinions may differ on this, but the telling blow was "cooking the books" to make his performance look far better than it really was.

ALBERT J. DUNLAP

Dunlap wrote an autobiography, *Mean Business: How I Save Bad Companies and Make Good Companies,* describing his business philosophy and how it had evolved. The book became a best seller. Dunlap grew up in the slums of Hoboken, New Jersey, the son of a shipyard worker, and was imbued with the desire to make something of himself. He played football in high school and graduated from West Point. A former army paratrooper, he was known as a quick hitter, a ruthless cost cutter, a tough boss. But he got results, at least in the short term.

In 1983, Dunlap became chief executive of Lily Tulip Co., a maker of disposable cups that was heavily in debt after a buyout. He quickly exhibited the management philosophy that was to make him famous. He slashed costs by decimating the headquarters staff, closing plants, and selling the corporate jet. When he left in the mid-1980s, the company was healthy. In the latter 1980s, Dunlap became the No. 1 operations man for Sir James Goldsmith, a notorious raider of corporations. Dunlap was involved in restructuring Goldsmith's acquisitions of Crown-Zellerbach and International Diamond. In 1991, he worked on a heavily debt-laden Australian conglomerate, Consolidated Press Holdings. Two years later, after his "chainsaw approach," Consolidated Press was one hundred divisions lighter and virtually free of debt.

By then, Dunlap was a wealthy man, having made close to $100 million on his various restructurings. Still, at 56, he was hardly ready to retire. When the board of Scott Paper heard that he was available, they wooed him, even purchasing his $3.2 million house in Florida from him.

TABLE 6.1   Sales of Scott, 1990–1993 (billions)

1990	$3.9
1991	3.8
1992	3.9
1993	3.6
Total change, 1990–1993	(7.7%)

Source: Company annual reports.

Commentary: The company's deteriorating sales come at a time of great economic growth and advancing revenues for most firms.

SCOTT PAPER—A SICK COMPANY— AND DUNLAP'S RESULTS

An aged Scott Paper was reeling in the early 1990s. Per-share earnings had dropped 61 percent since 1989 on flat sales growth. In 1993, the company had a $277 million loss.

Part of the problem stemmed from Scott's commercial paper division, S.D. Warren. In 1990, the company spent to increase capacity at Warren. Unfortunately, the timing could not have been worse. One of the worst industry slumps since the Great Depression was just beginning. Three subsequent "restructurings" had little positive effect.

Table 6.1 shows the decline in sales from 1990 through 1993. Table 6.2 shows the net income and loss during these four years. Of even more concern, was Scott's performance relative to the major competitors, Procter & Gamble and Kimberly-Clark, during these four years. Table 6.3 shows the comparisons of profits as a percentage of sales, with Scott again showing up most poorly. Undoubtedly this was a company needing fixing.

In characteristic fashion, Dunlap acted quickly once he took over as CEO on April 19, 1994. That same day, to show his confidence and commitment, he invested $2 million of his own money in Scott. A few months later, after the stock had appreciated 30 percent, he invested another $2 million.

TABLE 6.2   Net Income of Scott and Percent of Sales, 1990–1993

	(millions)	% of sales
1990	$148	3.8
1991	(70)	(1.8)
1992	167	4.3
1993	(277)	(7.7)

Source: Company annual reports.

Commentary: The company's erratic profit picture, culminating in the serious loss of 1993, deserved deep concern, which it received.

TABLE 6.3   **Profit as a Percentage of Sales: Scott, Kimberly-Clark, and Procter & Gamble, 1990–1993**

	1990	1991	1992	1993
Scott	3.8%	(1.8)	4.3	(7.7)
P&G	6.6	6.6	6.4	(2.1)[a]
Kimberly-Clark	6.8	7.5	1.9	7.3

Source: Company annual reports.

[a] Extraordinary charges reflecting accounting changes.

Commentary: Scott again shows up badly against its major competitors, in the low percentage of earnings to sales and their severe fluctuations into earnings losses.

After only hours on the job, Dunlap offered three of his former associates top positions in the company. On the second day, he disbanded the powerful management committee. On the third day, he fired nine of the eleven highest-ranking executives. To complete his blitzkrieg, on the fourth day Dunlap destroyed four bookshelves crammed with strategic plans prepared by previous administrations.

ISSUE BOX

HOW SOON TO INTRODUCE DRASTIC CHANGE?

Some new administrators believe in instituting major changes as quickly as possible. They reason that an organization is expecting this and is better prepared to make the adjustments needed than it will ever be again. Such managers are often referred to as gunslingers—those who "shoot from the hip." Other managers believe in moving more slowly, gathering more information, and taking action only when all the pros and cons can be weighed. But sometimes, such delays can lull an organization into a sense of false calm and make for even more trauma when the changes eventually come.

Relevant to the issue of moving swiftly or slowly is the health of the entity. If a firm is sick, in drastic need of help, we would expect a new manager to move more quickly and decisively. A firm doing well, although perhaps not as well as desired, reasonably should not require such drastic and abrupt disruption.

It has always baffled me how a fast-acting executive can acquire sufficient information to make the crucial decisions of who to fire and who to retain, what operations need to be pruned and which supported, all within a few days. Of course, operating statistics can be studied before formally taking charge, but the causes of the problems or successes—the whys—can hardly be understood so soon.

Boards, investors, and creditors want a fast turnaround. Waiting months before taking action to fix a sick company is not acceptable. However, not all companies are easily fixable; some can defy the best efforts of past and new managers.

Do you think Dunlap acted too hastily in his initial sweeping changes? Playing the Devil's Advocate (one who takes an opposing view for the sake of debate), support a position that he did indeed act far too hastily.

Can such drastic and abrupt changes be overdone? Should change be introduced more slowly and with more reflection? See the Issue Box: How Soon to Introduce Drastic Changes? for a discussion of these questions.

At the annual meeting in June 1994, barely two months after assuming command, Dunlap announced four major goals for the first year. First, he vowed to divest the company of nonstrategic assets, most notably S.D. Warren, the printing and publishing papers subsidiary, that had received major expansion funding only a few years before. Second, he would develop a core team of accomplished senior managers. Third, Scott was to be brought to "fighting trim" through a one-time-only global restructuring. Last, Dunlap promised to develop new strategies for marketing Scott products around the world.

In one of the largest relative restructurings in corporate America, more than 11,000 positions out of a total of 25,900 worldwide were eliminated. This included 71 percent of the headquarters staff, 50 percent of the salaried employees, and 20 percent of the production workers. Such draconian measures certainly cut costs. But were they overdone? Might such cuts potentially have detrimental long-term consequences? Please see the Issue Box: How Deep to Cut? for a discussion of these topics.

In addition to cutting staff, Dunlap sought to reduce other costs, including outsourcing some operations and services. If these could be provided cheaper by other firms, then they should be farmed out. Dunlap announced that with the restructuring completed by year-end, pre-tax savings of $340 million were expected.[1]

By late fall of 1994, Dunlap's plans to divest the company of nonstrategic assets bore fruit. S.D. Warren was sold for $1.6 billion to an international investment group.

ISSUE BOX

HOW DEEP TO CUT?

Bloated bureaucratic organizations are the epitome of inefficiency and waste, whether in business corporations or in governmental bodies, including school systems. Administrative overhead might even exceed actual operating costs. But corrections can be overdone—they can go too far. In Scott's case, was the axing of 11,000 of 25,900 employees overdone?

Although we are not privy to the needed cost/productivity records, we can raise some concerns. Did the massive layoffs go well beyond fat and bloat into bone and muscle? If so, future operations might be jeopardized. Other concerns ought to be: Does an organization owe anything to its loyal and senior employees, or should they simply be considered pawns in the pursuit of maximizing profits. Where do we draw the line between efficiency and responsibility to faithful employees? And even to the community itself?

You may want to consider some of these questions and issues. They are current in today's downsizing mind-set.

---

[1] *The New Scott 1994 Annual Report*, p. 5.

Other asset sales generated more than $2 billion. Dunlap was able to lower debt by $1.5 billion and repurchase $300 million of Scott stock. This led to the credit rating being upgraded.

The results of Dunlap's efforts were impressive indeed. Second-quarter earnings rose 71 percent; third-quarter earnings increased 73 percent, the best quarterly performance for Scott in four years. Fourth-quarter earnings were 159 percent higher than in 1993, establishing an all-time record. For the whole year, net income increased 82 percent over the previous year, and the stock price performance, since Dunlap took over, stood at the top 1 percent of major companies traded on the New York Stock Exchange.[2]

Still, the cost slashing was not helping market share. In the fiscal year ending April 2, 1995, Scott's bath-tissue sales in key U.S. markets slipped 1 percent, and paper towels sales fell 5.2 percent.[3]

On July 17, 1995, Dunlap's efforts to make Scott an attractive acquisition candidate were capped by Kimberly-Clark's $7.38 billion offer for the firm. In the process, Dunlap himself would be suitably rewarded, leaving far richer than after any of his seven previous restructuring efforts. But Dunlap insisted , "I am still the best bargain in corporate America."[4]

THE SUNBEAM CHALLENGE

Sunbeam was a maker of blenders, electric blankets, and gas grills. These old-line products had shown little growth, and revenues and profits languished. After the well-publicized turnaround success of Dunlap at Scott, it was no surprise when he was courted for the top job at Sunbeam, and he entered the fray with gusto.

The day Dunlap was hired, Sunbeam stock rose 50 percent, "on faith." It eventually rose 300 percent. With his customary modus operandi, he terminated half of Sunbeam's 12,000 employees and cut back its product offerings. Gone were such items as furniture and bed linens, and efforts were concentrated on things like grills, humidifiers, and kitchen appliances. In 1996, he took massive write-offs amounting to $338 million, of which almost $100 million was inventory.

In 1997, it looked like Dunlap was accomplishing another of his patented "miracles." Sales were up 22 percent to $1.168 billion, while income had risen from a loss of $196 million the previous year to a gain of $123 million in 1997. For stockholders, this translated into earnings per share of $1.41 from a $2.37 loss in 1996. Table 6.4 shows the trend in revenues and income of Sunbeam through 1997.

In October 1997, after barely a year on the job, Dunlap announced that the turnaround was complete and that he was seeking a buyer for Sunbeam. Stockholders had much to be pleased about. From a low of $12 a share in 1996, the price had risen to $50. Unfortunately, there was a serious downside to this, as Dunlap was soon to find:

---

[2] Ibid., p. 6.

[3] Joseph Weber and Paula Dwyer, "Scott Rolls Out a Risky Strategy," *Business Week*, May 22, 1995, p. 45.

[4] Joann S. Lublin and Steven Lipin, "Scott Paper's 'Rambo in Pin Striper' Is on the Prowl for Another Company to Fix," *Wall Street Journal*, July 18, 1995, p. B1.

TABLE 6.4   Trend of Sunbeam Revenues and Income, 1991–1997

	1991	1992	1993	1994 (millions $)	1995	1996	1997
Revenues	886	967	1,066	1,198	1,203	964	1,168
Net Income	47.4	65.6	88.8	107	50.5	–196	123

Sources: Company annual reports.

Commentary: Dunlap came on the scene in July 1996, the year that Sunbeam incurred $196 million in losses. The $123 million profit for 1997 showed a remarkable and awesome recovery and would seemingly make Dunlap a hero with his slash-and-burn strategy. Unfortunately, a reaudit did not confirm these figures. The inaccurate figures were blamed on questionable accounting, including prebooking sales and incorrectly assigning costs to the restructuring. The auditors said the company overstated its loss for 1996, and overstated profits for 1997. The revised figures showed a loss of $6.4 million for 1997, instead of the $123 million profit. (Sources: Martha Brannigan, "Sunbeam Audit to Repudiate '97 Turnaround," *Wall Street Journal,* October 20, 1998, p. A3; and "Audit Shows Sunbeam's Turnaround Really a Bust," *Cleveland Plain Dealer,* October 21, 1998, pp. C1, C2.)

The high price for Sunbeam stock took it out of the range for any potential buyer; $50 gave a market capitalization of $4.6 billion, or four times revenues, a multiple reserved for only a few of the premier companies. So, for the time being, the stockholders were stuck with Dunlap.

Since he was not successful in selling the company, Dunlap went on a buying spree. He began talking about his "vision," in such words as "We have moved from constraining categories to expanding categories. Small kitchen appliances become kitchen appliances. We'll move from grills to outdoor cooking. Health care moves from just a few products to a broad range of products."[5]

So, Dunlap bought Coleman Company, Signature Brands and its Mr. Coffee, and First Alert for an aggregate of approximately $2.4 billion in cash and stock. Part of this was financed with $750 million of convertible debentures, and $60 million of accounts receivable that were sold to raise cash. Critics maintained he had paid too much for these, especially the $2.2 billion for money-losing Coleman. The effect of these acquisitions on Sunbeam's balance sheet was sobering if any stockholders had looked closely.

When Dunlap took over Sunbeam, though it was performing poorly, it had only $200 million in debt. By 1998, Sunbeam was over $2 billion in debt, and its net worth had dropped from $500 million to a negative $600 million.[6]

THE DEBACLE OF 1998, AND THE DEMISE OF DUNLAP

The first quarter of 1998 showed a complete reversal of fortunes. Revenues were down, and a first-quarter loss was posted of $44.6 million—all this far below expectations. Sunbeam's stock price plunged 50 percent, from $53 to $25. By midsummer, it was to reach a low of $4.62.

Dunlap conceded that he and top executives had concentrated their attention too much on "sealing" the acquisitions of Coleman and the two smaller companies, allow-

---

[5] As quoted in Holman W. Jenkins, Jr., "Untalented Al? The Sorrows of a One-Trick Pony," *Wall Street Journal,* June 24, 1998, p. A19.

[6] Matthew Schifrin, "The Unkindest Cuts," *Forbes,* May 4, 1998, p. 45.

ing underlings to offer "stupid, low-margin deals" on outdoor cooking grills. He pointed to glitches with new products, a costly recall, and even El Niño. "People don't think about buying outdoor grills during a storm," he said. "Faced with sluggish sales, a marketing executive offered excessive discounts," he further said. More job cuts were promised, through eliminating one-third of the jobs at the newly acquired companies.[7]

On Monday, June 15th, 1998, after deliberating over the weekend, Sunbeam's board abruptly fired Al Dunlap, having "lost confidence in his ability to carry out the long-term growth potential of the company."[8] Then a legal fight ensued as to what kind of severance package, if any, Dunlap deserved because of his firing. A severance package for Mr. Dunlap would be "obscene—an obscenity on top of an obscenity, capitalism gone crazy," said Michael Cavanaugh, union leader.[9] Other comments were reported in the media; a sampling is in the following Information Box.

INFORMATION BOX

THE POPULARITY OF "CHAINSAW" AL DUNLAP

Not surprising, the slashing policy of Dunlap did not bring him a lot of friends, even though he may have been admired in some circles. Here are some comments reported in the press, immediately after his firing:

> "He finally got what he's been doing to a lot of people. It was a taste of his own medicine." (union representative)
> "I'm happy the son-of-a-bitch is fired." (former supervisor)
> "Somebody at that company finally got some sense." (small-town mayor)
> "I couldn't think of a better person to deserve it. It tickled me to death. We may need to have a rejoicing ceremony." (small-town mayor)
> "I guess the house of cards came tumbling down … when you reduce your workforce by 50 percent, you lose your ability to manage." (former plant manager)

Is there a lesson to be learned from such comments as these? Perhaps it is that the human element in organizations and communities needs to be considered.

Taking a Devil's Advocate position (one who takes an opposing viewpoint for the sake of argument and full discussion), defend the philosophy of Dunlap.

Sources: Thomas W. Gerdel, "Workers at Glenwillow Plant Cheer Firing of 'Chainsaw' Al," *Cleveland Plain Dealer*, June 16, 1998, p. C2; and "No Tears for a Chainsaw," *Wall Street Journal*, June 16, 1998, p. B1.

---

[7] James R. Hagerty and Martha Brannigan, "Sunbeam Plans to Cut 5,100 Jobs as CEO Promises Rebound from Dismal Quarter," *Wall Street Journal*, May 12, 1998, pp. A3, A4.

[8] Martha Brannigan and James Hagerty, "Sunbeam, Its Prospects Looking Ever Worse, Fires CEO Dunlap," *Wall Street Journal*, June 15, 1998, pp. A1, A14.

[9] Martha Brannigan and Joann S. Lublin, "Dunlap Faces a Fight Over His Severance Pay," *Wall Street Journal*, June 16, 1998, p. B3.

Allegations of Fraud

At the end of a three-month audit after Dunlap's departure, auditors discovered accounting irregularities that struck down the amazingly high reported profits for 1997, the first full year of Dunlap's leadership. Rather than a turnaround, the good results came from improper accounting moves that adversely affected 1996 and 1998 results. The restated numbers showed that Sunbeam actually had a small operating loss in 1997, while 1996 showed a modest profit.

On May 15, 2001, the Securities and Exchange Commission (SEC) formally charged that Dunlap and some of his executives broke security laws to make Sunbeam look healthier and more attractive for a buyer. This was done by fraudulently shifting revenue to inflate losses under the old management and boosting income to create the false impression of the rapid turnaround in financial performance for 1997. Furthermore, revenue was increased in 1997 at the expense of future results by inducing retail customers to sell merchandise more quickly than normal, a practice known as *channel stuffing.* By the next year, the company was getting desperate to hide its mounting financial problems and misrepresented its performance and prospects in quarterly reports, bond offerings material, press releases, and statements to stock analysts. Dunlap denied any involvement or knowledge of such matters and said that any accounting changes by the auditors were "judgment calls" on matters subject to interpretation.[10]

The company was forced to restate financial results for 18 months, and it filed for bankruptcy protection in February 2001.

In early September 2002, Dunlap agreed to settle the SEC suit by paying $500,000 and agreeing never to be an officer or director of another public company. He neither admitted nor denied the SEC's claim that he masterminded the accounting fraud. A month earlier, Dunlap also paid $15 million in a settlement of a class-action suit filed by shareholders for their loses due to Sunbeam's fraudulent business practices.[11] All thoughts of a severance package for Dunlap after his firing were long forgotten.

The SEC also came to believe there was funny accounting at Scott Paper when Dunlap was running it. But this suspicion came at the height of the Enron furor, and the SEC had bigger game to pursue.[12]

A Ripple Effect

Dunlap's exploits brought turmoil to the executive-search industry. It seems major search firms checking his employment history prior to being hired by Sunbeam failed to uncover that he had been fired from two previous positions. He was terminated at

---

[10] Martha Brannigan, "Sunbeam Slashes Its 1997 Earnings in Restatement," *Wall Street Journal,* October 21, 1998, p. B23.

[11] Jill Barton, "Sunbeam's 'Chain Saw Al' to Pay $500,000 Judgment," Associated Press as reported in *Cleveland Plain Dealer,* September 5, 2002, p. C1.

[12] Floyd Norris, "Fraud Surrounded 'Chainsaw Al', Yet Little Was Done," *New York Times,* as reported in *Cleveland Plain Dealer,* September 8, 2002, p. G3.

Max Phillips & Sons in 1973, after only seven weeks. Three years later in 1976, he had been fired as president of Nitec Paper Corp. under circumstances of alleged fraud involving misstated profits, a situation not unlike his departure from Sunbeam.

While these episodes took place 20 years before the recruiting for Scott Paper and Sunbeam and were apparently overlooked because of his supposedly strong track record in recent years, significant and pertinent omissions in Dunlap's job history were not caught by search firms supposedly conducting thorough background checks. Along the way, Dunlap erased both jobs from his employment history, and no one who checked his background discovered the omissions.[13]

ANALYSIS

Was Dunlap's Management Style of "Slash and Burn" Appropriate?

We see conflicting evidence in the Scott and Sunbeam cases. Without doubt, he achieved his goal to make Scott an attractive acquisition candidate, and thus reward shareholders and himself (although suspicions later arose that the sterling results may have been tainted). That he did this so quickly seemed, at the time, a strong endorsement of his strategy for turning around sick companies—simply decimate the organization, sell off all ancillary units, cut costs to the bone, and virtually force the company into increased profitability.

The flaw with this reasoning is that it tends to boost short-term performance at the expense of the longer term. Morale and dedication of surviving employees are devastated. Vision and innovative thinking may be impaired since the depleted organization lacks time and commitment to deal effectively with more than day-to-day basic operations.

Dunlap's strategy backfired with Sunbeam. When he couldn't sell the company after manipulating the performance statistics for 1997, he was left with a longer-term management challenge that he was by no means equal to. It is ironic that the reputation for turning around sick companies acted against him with Sunbeam. Investors were so confident of his ability to quickly turn around the company that they bid the price up so high no other firm would buy it. And they were stuck with Dunlap.

Did the Adversity Require Such Drastic Changes?

Sales of Scott and Sunbeam were flat, with profit performance deteriorating. Stock prices were falling counter to a bull market, and investors were disillusioned. Did such situations call for draconian measures?

Neither company was in danger of going belly-up. True, they were off the growth path, but their brands continued to be well regarded by consumers. On the other hand, many firms become too bureaucratic, burdened with high overhead and chained to established policies and procedures. Such organizations desperately need

---

[13] Sources: Joann S. Lublin, "Search Firms Have Red Faces in Dunlap Flop," *Wall Street Journal*, July 17, 2001, pp. B1, B4, and Floyd Norris, "Uncovering Lost Years of Sunbeam's Fired Chief," *New York Times*, reported in *Cleveland Plain Dealer*, July 17, 2001, pp. C1, C4.

paring down, eliminating bloated staff and executive levels, and—not the least—curbing the red tape that destroys flexibility and creativity.

The best answer lies in moderation, cutting the deadwood, but not bone and muscle. The worst scenario is to cut with little investigation and reflection. This cost-cutting climate may degenerate to the extent that worthy operations and individuals are cut regardless of their merit and future promise. We would expect better long-term performance in an organization that is not decimated with shattered morale.

Dunlap quickly sold off the S.D. Warren unit of Scott, and this added $1.6 billion to Scott coffers. Previous Scott management had invested heavily in what seemed a reasonable diversification into commercial paper, only to encounter an unexpected industry downturn. How could this have been predicted? Was Warren worth keeping? Research and investigation might have found that it was.

Creeping Bureaucracy

Bureaucratic excesses often come about after years of reasonable success and viability. Bureaucracy seemed to have been rampant at pre-Dunlap Scott. After all, Dunlap eliminated 71 percent of the headquarters staff and four bookshelves crammed with strategic plans of previous administrations. Too many administrators and staff people bring higher overhead costs than leaner competitors, thus placing the firm at a competitive disadvantage. Some pruning needed to be done.

Was the same thing true with Sunbeam? Perhaps not to the same extent, although without more specific information we cannot know for sure. We can suspect, however, that Dunlap, caught up in his success at Scott, simply transferred his strategy to Sunbeam with no consideration of their differences. We might call this slashing by formula, and it suggests a rigid mind-set devoid of flexibility or compassion.

Paying too Much for Acquisitions

With Sunbeam, Dunlap made three questionable acquisitions and burdened the firm with several billions of dollars of debt. In particular, the $2.2 billion paid for money-losing Coleman, seemed another of Dunlap's shoot-from-the-hip decisions. Such questionable research in acquisitions decisions followed the pattern of his personnel-slashing decisions and the quick sale of S. D. Warren. Furthermore, the reckless accumulation of debt for these acquisitions almost suggests a masochistic mind-set. Or did Dunlap think that if the share price now dropped drastically, the firm would become attractive for an acquisition?

Detection of Fraud Destroys Any Perception of Management Competence

Dunlap apparently had a long history of manipulating records to make himself look better, as we will further see in the next section. While this fraud pales in comparison with the massive misdeeds of Enron, Tyco, WorldCom, and others—simply because Dunlap's were much smaller firms—it can no more be condoned than their fraudulent practices. Dunlap could yet face jail time, should the SEC decide to turn its attention to less publicized cases.

WHAT CAN BE LEARNED?

How to Jump-Start a Languid Organization

Can we find any keys to stimulating an organization not performing up to potential? Or maybe even to inspire it to perform beyond its potential? The challenge is similar to that of motivating a discouraged and downtrodden athletic team to rise up and have faith in itself and recommit itself to quality of performance.

In athletics and business, the common notion is that personnel changes have to be made. Dunlap introduced the idea of severe downsizing. But this is controversial, and in view of Dunlap's problems with Sunbeam, now almost discredited. So how much should be cut, how quickly should changes be made and how sweeping should they be, and what kind of information is most vital in making such decisions? Furthermore, there is the question of morale and its importance in any restoration.

We find more art than science in this mighty challenge of restoration. In particular, the right blend or degree of change is crucial. Let us look at some considerations:

- *How Much Do We Trim?* In most revival situations, some pruning of personnel and operations is necessary. But how much is too much, and how much is not enough? Is an ax always required for a successful turnaround? One would hope not. Certainly those personnel who are not willing to accept change may have to be let go. And weak persons and operations that show little probability of improvement need to be pruned, just as the athlete who can't seem to perform up to expectations may have to be let go. Still, it is often better to wait for sufficient information as to the "why" of poor performance, before assigning blame for the consequences.

- *How Long Do We Wait?* Mistakes can be made in taking action before all the facts are known, and in waiting too long. If the change maker procrastinates for weeks, an organization that at first was psychologically geared to major change might find it more traumatic and disruptive.

- *What Should Be the Role of Strategic Planning?* Major actions should hardly be taken without some research and planning, but strategic plans too often delay change implementation. They tend to be the products of a fumbling bureaucracy and of some abdication of responsibility. (Despite the popularity of strategic planning, it often is a vehicle for procrastination and blame dilution: e.g., "I simply followed the strategy recommendations of the consultants.") Dunlap had an aversion to strategic planning; he saw this as indicative of a top heavy bureaucratic organization. Perhaps he was right on this, when carried to an extreme. But going into an organization and heedlessly slashing positions without considering the individuals involved and their potential promise is akin to shooting from the hip, with little regard for careful aiming. Then there is the matter of morale.

• *Morale Considerations* Major restructuring usually is demoralizing to the organizations involved. The usual result is massive layoffs and forced retirements, complete reassignment of people, traumatic personnel and policy changes, and destruction of accustomed lines of communication and authority. This is hardly conducive to preserving stability and morale and any faint spark of teamwork.

Moderation is Usually Best

Much can be said for moderation, for choosing the middle position, for example, between heavy cost cutting and light cost cutting. Of course, the condition of the firm is a major consideration. One on the verge of bankruptcy, unable to meet its bills, needs drastic measures promptly. But the problems of Scott and Sunbeam were by means so serious. More moderate action could have been taken.

It is better to view the restoration challenge as a *time for building rather than tearing down.* This focuses attention more on the longer view than on short-term results that may come back to haunt the firm as well as the change maker, someone like Dunlap.

Periodic Housecleaning Produces Competitive Health

In order to minimize the buildup of deadwood, all aspects of an organization periodically ought to be objectively appraised. Weak products and operations should be pruned, unless solid justification exists for keeping them. Such justification might include good growth prospects or complementing other products and operations or even providing a desired customer service. In particular, staff and headquarters personnel and functions should be scrutinized, perhaps every five years, with the objective of weeding out the redundant and superfluous. Most important, these "axing" evaluations should be done objectively, with decisive actions taken where needed. While some layoffs may result, they might not be necessary if suitable transfers are possible.

Ethical Considerations Should be Involved in Downsizing

The impact severe downsizing has on people and communities is usually overlooked in these decisions. They are considered subordinate to the best interests of the firm (and its investors). Still, we intuitively wonder if at the extremes of downsizing some ethical issues do not arise. Perhaps such issues should pertain not alone to the severity of the job cuts but to how they are handled: For example, is the decision made with due research and reflection, or is it made quickly, ruthlessly, and perhaps by formula, such as cut 20 percent or 30 percent or, as was done, 50 percent of Sunbeam's employees? Is any attempt made to help fired employees find alternate employment or retraining? How fair is the severance package and/or the notice of termination?

In Dunlap's handling of Scott Paper and Sunbeam, we see an absence of any humanity. This doesn't necessarily make his actions unethical in the eyes of many people, provided that the greater good of the business is fostered. Later developments, however, even denied that business benefit, as fraudulent accounting led to reported profitability during the Dunlap years, when there was none.

CONSIDER

Can you add any other learning insights?

QUESTIONS

1. "Periodic evaluations of personnel and departments aimed at pruning cause far too much harm to the organization. Such 'axing' evaluations should themselves be pruned." Argue this position as persuasively as you can.

2. Now marshal the most persuasive arguments for such "axing" evaluations.

3. Describe a person's various stages of morale and dedication to the company as it goes through a restructuring, with massive layoffs expected and realized, but with the person finding himself or herself one of the survivors. How, in your opinion, would this affect productivity and loyalty?

4. Is it likely that any decades-old organization will be bloated with excessive bureaucracy and overhead? Why or why not?

5. What decision guides should be used to determine which divisions and subsidiaries are to be divested or sold?

6. What arguments would you make in a time of restructuring for keeping your particular business unit? Which are likely to be most persuasive to an administration committed to a program of heavy pruning?

7. Do you see any ethical problems in heavy downsizing of a sick company? How about one not so sick?

HANDS-ON EXERCISES

1. You are one of the nine high-ranking executives fired by Dunlap his third day on the job. Describe your feelings and your action plan at this point. (If you want to make some assumptions, state them specifically.)

2. You are one of the two high-level executives kept by Dunlap as he sweeps into office. Describe your feelings and your likely performance on the job.

3. You are one of the three outsiders brought into Scott vice-presidential jobs by Dunlap. You have worked for him before and must have impressed him. Describe your feelings and your likely performance. What specific problems, if any, do you foresee?

4. Devil's Advocate position. Several board members are concerned about the ethical aspects of Dunlap's downsizing plans. Argue as persuasively as you can that they essentially are at best of questionable ethics.

TEAM DEBATE EXERCISES

1. It is early 1996. The board of Sunbeam is considering bringing in a turn-around team. One is the team of Dunlap, which argues for major and rapid change. Another team under consideration is Clarence Ripley's, who advocates more modest immediate changes. Array your arguments and present your positions as persuasively as possible. Attack the recommendations of the other side as aggressively as possible. We are talking about millions of dollars in fees and compensation at stake for the winning team.

2. Debate the issue of the ethics of Dunlap in his severe downsizing. (For purpose of the debate, disregard the subsequent fraud charges from deceptive accounting.)

INVITATION TO RESEARCH

What is Dunlap up to after being fired by the Sunbeam board in mid-1998? Has he gracefully retired, or is he running scared pending legal charges? Is he still fighting for severance pay? Who replaced Dunlap, and how well is he doing? Are his policies much different from Dunlap's?

CHAPTER SEVEN

Ford Explorers with
Firestone Tires: Ill Handling
a Killer Scenario

$\mathbf{A}$ product defect that leads to customer injuries and deaths through manufacturer carelessness constitutes the most serious crisis that any firm should face. In addition to destroying brand reputation, ethical and social responsibility abuses are involved, and then legal and regulatory consequences. Managing such a crisis becomes far worse, however, when the manufacturer knew about the problems and concealed them or denied them.

This case is unique, in that two manufacturers were culpable, but each blamed the other. As a result, Firestone and Ford were savaged by the press, public opinion, the government, and a host of salivating lawyers. Massive tire recalls destroyed the bottom line and even endangered the viability of Bridgestone/Firestone, while sales of the Ford Explorer, the world's best-selling sport-utility vehicle (SUV), plummeted 22 percent in April 2001 from the year before, while domestic sales of SUVs overall climbed 9 percent.

A HORROR SCENARIO

Firestone tires mounted on Ford Explorers were linked to more than 200 deaths from rollovers in the United States, more than 60 in Venezuela, and a reported 14 in Saudi Arabia and neighboring countries. A widely publicized lawsuit took place in Texas in the summer of 2001. It had been expected that the jury would determine who was most to blame for the deaths and injuries from Explorers outfitted with Firestone tires.

Ford settled its portion of the suit for $6 million, one month before the trial began. While Firestone now became the sole defendant, jurors were also asked to assess Ford's responsibility for the accident.

The lawsuit was brought by the family of Marisa Rodriguez, a mother of three who was left brain damaged and paralyzed after the steel belt and tread of a Firestone tire tore apart during a trip to Mexico in March 2000. As a result, the Explorer rolled over three times, crushing the roof above Mrs. Rodriguez in the rear seat; her husband Joel, who was asleep in the front passenger seat, was also injured. The live pictures of Mrs. Rodriguez in a wheelchair received wide TV coverage.

After the federal court jury in the Texas border town of McAllen had been deadlocked for four days, a settlement was reached with Bridgestone/Firestone for $7.85 million. (The plaintiffs originally had asked for $1 billion.)

The out-of-court settlements with Ford and Firestone did not resolve the issue of who was most to blame for this and the hundreds of other injuries and deaths. But a lawyer for the Rodriguez family predicted that sooner or later a verdict would emerge: "There's going to be trials and there's going to be verdicts. We've got Marisa Rodriguezes all over the country."[1]

ANATOMY OF THE PROBLEM

The Ford/Firestone Relationship

Ford and Firestone had a long, intimate history. In 1895, Harvey Firestone sold tires to Henry Ford for his first automobile. In 1906, the Firestone Tire & Rubber Company won its first contract for Ford Motor Company's mass-produced vehicles, a commitment that continued through the decades.

Henry Ford and Harvey Firestone became business confederates and best friends who went on annual summer camping trips, riding around in Model T's along with Thomas Edison and naturalist John Burroughs. Further cementing the relationship, in 1947 Firestone's granddaughter, Martha, married Ford's grandson, William Clay Ford, in a dazzling ceremony in Akron, Ohio, that attracted a Who's Who of dignitaries and celebrities. Their son, William Clay Ford Jr., was to become Ford's chairman.

In 1988, Tokyo-based Bridgestone Corporation bought Firestone, twenty years after the Japanese company sold its first tires in the United States under the Bridgestone name. In 1990, Ford introduced the Explorer SUV to replace the Bronco II in the 1991 model year. It became the nation's top-selling SUV, and the Explorer generated huge profits for more than a decade. Bridgestone/Firestone was the sole supplier of the Explorer's tires.

The Relationship Worsens

The first intimation of trouble came in 1999 when, after 14 fatalities occurred, Ford began replacing tires of Explorers in Saudi Arabia and nearby countries. The tire failures were blamed on hot weather and underinflated tires. At the time, overseas fatalities did not have to be reported to U.S. regulators, so the accidents received scant attention in the media.

---

[1] "Firestone Agrees to Pay $7.5 Million in Tire Suit," *Cleveland Plain Dealer,* August 25, 2001, pp. A1, A13; and, Milo Geyelin and Timothy Aeppel, "For Firestone, Tire Trial Is Mixed Victory," *Wall Street Journal,* August 27, 2001, pp. A3, A4.

The media caught the scent in early 2000 when television reports in Houston revealed instances of tread separation on Firestone's ATX tires, and the National Highway Traffic Safety Administration (NHTSA) started an investigation. By May, four U.S. fatalities had been reported, and NHTSA expanded the investigation to 47 million ATX, ATXII, and Wilderness tires.

In August 2000, as mounting deaths led to increasing pressure from consumers and multiple lawsuits, Firestone voluntarily recalled 14.4 million 15-inch radial tires because of tread separation. The plant in Decatur, Illinois, was implicated in most of these accidents. Ford and Firestone agreed to replace the tires but estimated that 6.5 million were still on the road. Consumer groups sought a still wider recall, charging that Explorers with other Firestone tire models were also prone to separation leading to rollovers.

In December 2000, Firestone issued a report blaming Ford for the problems, claiming that the Explorer's design caused rollovers with any tread separations. On April 20, 2001, Ford gave NHTSA a report blaming Firestone for flawed manufacturing.

In May 2001, Ford announced that it was replacing all remaining 13 million Firestone Wilderness AT tires on its vehicles, saying that the move was necessary because Ford had no confidence in the tires' safety. "We feel it's our responsibility to act immediately," Ford CEO Jacques Nasser said. Ford said the move would cost the automaker $2.1 billion, although it hoped to get this money back from Firestone.

Firestone Chairman and CEO John Lampe defended his tires, saying "No one cares more about the safety of the people who travel on our tires than we do. When we have a problem, we admit it and we fix it."[2]

The Last Days

It is lamentable when a long-lasting close relationship is severed. But on May 21, 2001, Lampe abruptly ended the 95-year association, accusing Ford of refusing to acknowledge safety problems with its vehicles, thus putting all the blame on Firestone.

The crisis had been brewing for months. Many Firestone executives did not trust Ford, and even exchanging documents was done with rancor, with major disagreements in interpreting the data. Firestone argued that tread-separation claims occurred ten times more frequently on Ford Explorers than on Ranger pickups with the same tires, thus supporting their contention that the Explorer was mostly at fault. Ford rejected Firestone's charges about the Explorer, saying that for ten years the model "has ranked at or near the top in terms of safety among the twelve SUVs in its class." It stated that 2.9 million Goodyear tires mounted on more than 500,000 Explorers had "performed with industry-leading safety."[3]

[2] Ed Garsten, Associated Press, as reported in "Ford Tire Tab $2.1 Billion," *Cleveland Plain Dealer,* May 23, 2001, pp. C1, C4.

[3] Timothy Aeppel, Joseph B. White, and Stephen Power, "Firestone Quits as Tire Supplier to Ford," *Wall Street Journal,* May 22, 2001, pp. A3, A12.

The climax came in a May 21 meeting attended by Lampe and a contingent of Ford officials, during which both sides maintained that the other was to blame. Discussions broke down regarding any working together to examine Explorer's role in the accidents. At that point, Lampe ended their relationship. Each party then was left to defend itself before Congress, and the court of public opinion, and ultimately a siege of lawsuits. See the Information Box: How Emotion Influences Company Reputation for a discussion of how emotion drives consumers in their perception, good and bad, of companies.

Advantage to Competitors

Major competitors Goodyear and Michelin, as well as smaller competitors and private-label tire makers, predictably raised tire prices 3 to 5 percent. Goodyear then tried to increase production robustly to replace the millions of Firestone tires recalled or soon to be, but it was trying to avoid overtime pay to bolster profits. In a written statement, Goodyear said, "We are working very closely with Ford to jointly develop an aggressive plan to address consumers' needs as quickly as possible."[4]

INFORMATION BOX

HOW EMOTION INFLUENCES COMPANY REPUTATION

The second annual corporate-reputation survey conducted by the Harris market-research firm and the Reputation Institute, involving 26,011 respondents, found that emotional appeal—trust, admiration and respect, and generally good feelings toward—was the driving force in how people rated companies. The survey found that advertising did not necessarily change opinions. For example, despite a $100 million advertising campaign about what a good citizen Philip Morris Company was in feeding the hungry and helping victims of domestic violence, the company still received low marks on trust, respect, and admiration. But the most recent poll showed that Philip Morris no longer had the worst reputation in America. This distinction went to Bridgestone/Firestone, with Ford receiving the lowest reputation rating among auto companies.

Once lost, a company's reputation or public image is usually difficult to regain. For example, Exxon Mobil's reputation for environmental responsibility was still given low grades more than a decade after the destructive Alaskan oil spill involving the tanker *Exxon Valdez*.

Do you think Firestone's quest to improve its reputation should face the same problems as those occurring from the *Exxon Valdez*? Why or why not?

Source: Ronald Alsop, "Survey: Emotion Drives Public Perception of Companies," *Wall Street Journal*, February 11, 2001, p. 5H.

---

[4] Thomas W. Gerdel, "Goodyear, Michelin Raising Consumer Tire Prices," *Cleveland Plain Dealer*, May 23, 2001, pp. C1, C4.

The decrease in auto sales in the slowing economy that began in 2000 had led Goodyear to production cutbacks, including cutting 7,200 workers worldwide as it posted an 83 percent decline in profits in 2000. Now it was challenged to gear up to handle the windfall of the ending of the Ford/Firestone relationship.

WHEREIN LIES THE BLAME?

In years to come, courts and lawyers will sort out the culpability controversy. The outcome is in doubt, and the finger of blame points to a number of sources, though the weighting is uncertain. While Ford and Firestone should share major responsibility, NHTSA and the motoring public were hardly blameless.

Ford

The question whether the design of Ford's Explorer made it more prone to rollover than other SUVs will be decided in the courtroom. One thing seems clear: Ford recommended a low inflation level for its Firestone-equipped tires, and this would subject them to more flex in the sidewall and greater heat buildup. With high-speed driving in hot weather, such a high-profile vehicle would be more prone to roll over with any tire trouble, especially with inexperienced drivers. For example, Ford's recommended tire pressure was 26 pounds, and this would bring the car's center of gravity lower to the ground. This would seem good, but only at first look. Required by the government, the Uniform Tire Quality Grade (UTQG) provides comparative manufacturer information. Tires are subjected to a series of government-mandated tests that measure performance in treadwear, traction, and temperature resistance. All testing is done by the tire manufacturer. Ford was alone among SUV makers in equipping the Explorer with grade C tires rather than the more heat-resistant B tires that were the near universal standard on most SUVs. To make the C grade, tires had to withstand only two hours at 50 mph when properly inflated and loaded, plus another 90 minutes at speeds up to 85 mph. This standard dated back to 1968, when sustained highway speeds were much lower than today. Now, people drive hour after hour at speeds well above 70 mph.

The C-rated Firestones were used on millions of Ford pickup trucks without problems. However, in contrast with SUVs, most pickup trucks are not taken on long-haul, high-speed road trips filled with family and luggage.

Ford CEO Jacques Nasser justified replacing 13 million tires by claiming the Firestones were failing at a rate higher than Goodyears mounted on two million Explorers in the mid-1990s. But the Goodyears carried the B rating. The dangerous effect of heat buildup was shown by most Explorers' accidents taking place in hot Southern states and other hot-climate countries with high speed limits.

Ford engineers should have been aware of these dangers, if not immediately—certainly after a few years—and adapted the Explorer to customers who drive fast, pay little attention to tire maintenance, and are prone to panic with a blowout and flip the car. Unfortunately, the American legal environment, the tort system, makes the manufacturer vulnerable to lawsuits and massive damage claims should it acknowledge in retrospect that it had made a bad mistake in its tire selection and pressure recommendation. So the temptation was to blame the tiremaker and spend millions to turning it into a media monster.

Bridgetone/Firestone

Firestone tires were far from blameless. Early on, investigations of deadly vehicle accidents linked the causes to tire failure, notably due to shoddy manufacturing practices at the Firestone plant in Decatur, Illinois; the 6.5 million tire recall by Firestone was of the 15-inch radial ATX and ATX11 tires and Wilderness AT tires made in this plant. In June 27, 2001, the company announced the plant would be closed. But Firestone's poorly controlled manufacturing process proved not to be limited to this single operation. See the Information Box: A Whistle-Blower "Hero" about the whistle-blower who exposed another plant's careless disregard of safe tire production.

INFORMATION BOX

A WHISTLE-BLOWER "HERO"

Alan Hogan was honored in June 2001 by the Civil Justice Foundation for exposing how employees at a Bridgestone/Firestone plant in North Carolina routinely made defective tires. This consumer advocacy group, founded by the Association of Trial Lawyers of America, bestowed similar "community champion" awards on tobacco whistle-blower Jeffrey Wigand, and on Erin Brockovich, who exposed hazardous waste dangers and was the subject of a popular movie.

With his insider's knowledge of shoddy tire-building practices, Hogan was widely credited with bringing about the first recall. He testified at a wrongful death lawsuit in 1999 that he witnessed the crafting of countless bad tires built with dried-out rubber and wood bits, cigarette butts, screws, and other foreign materials mixed in. Hogan, who had quit the company and opened an auto-body shop in his hometown, became a pariah among many people for his revelations about the community's major employer, and company attorneys looked into his work and family life for anything they could use to discredit him. They tried to portray him as a disgruntled former employee. An anonymous fax accused him of spreading "vicious, malicious allegations" about the company. Employees were warned not to do business with car dealerships that dealt with his body shop.

But Hogan persevered and eventually won recognition and accolades. "I'm surprised it took this long," he said. "Maybe now people will see this is the way it's been since 1994, 1995, when they started covering this up." His whistle-blowing credentials were now in high demand as an expert witness in other lawsuits.

Do you see any reasons why Hogan may not have been completely objective in his whistle-blowing efforts?

Source: Dan Chapman, Cox News, as reported in "Firestone Ex-Worker Called Hero in Recall," *Cleveland Plain Dealer*, May 29, 2001, p. C1.

Still, there were contrary indications that the fault was not all Bridgestone/
Firestone's, that Ford shared the blame. General Motors had detected no problems
with Firestones it used as standard equipment in 14 of its models. In fact, in July 2001
GM named Firestone as its supplier of the year for the sixth consecutive time. Honda
of America was also loyal to Firestones, which it used on best-selling Civics and
Odysseys.[5]

On September 14, 2001, months after all Firestones had been recalled from
Ford Explorers, an apparently skilled driver, a deputy bailiff driving home from court,
was killed when he lost control of his Explorer, and it flipped over a guardrail, slid
down an embankment, and rolled over several times.[6]

Government

Public Citizen and other consumer groups were critical of the government, maintaining that it was too slow in completing its initial Firestone investigation and had
dragged its feet in any investigation of the Explorer. A Public Citizen study saw the
use of the specific Firestone tires as coming from cost- and weight-saving miscalculations and gambles by Ford, "making what was already a bad problem into a lethal
one." Not just the companies were at fault, but Federal regulators were lax in not
toughening standards on SUVs to prevent roofs from collapsing in rollover crashes.
"The human damage caused is barbaric and unnecessary," the study concluded.[7]

The Driver

There is no doubt that drivers contributed to accidents. They did so by neglecting tire
pressure so that it was often below even the low recommendations of Ford, by heavily loading vehicles, and by driving too fast over long periods so that heat could build
up to dangerous levels. Added to this, the lack of driving expertise to handle emergency blowouts was often the fatal blow. Yet, could a car maker, tire maker, or government really expect the average consumer to act with strict prudence? Precautions,
be they car standards or tire standards, needed to be imposed with worst scenarios in
mind as to consumer behavior.

CONSEQUENCES

Each company maneuvered to cast blame primarily on the other. Ford announced in
May 2001 it would triple the size of the Firestone recall—a $2.8 billion prospect, a
cost Ford wanted to shift to the tire maker. Firestone, at that point, severed its long
relationship with Ford by refusing to supply the company with more tires. CEO

[5] Garsten, pp, C1, C4; and Alison Grant, "Bridgestone/Firestone Faces Struggle to Survive," *Cleveland Plain Dealer*, August 5, 2001, pp. H1, H5.

[6] "SUV Flips, Killing Deputy Bailiff, 24," *Cleveland Plain Dealer*, September 15, 2001, p. B5.

[7] Alison Grant, "Government, Goodyear Still Navigating a Bumpy Road," *Cleveland Plain Dealer*, August 5, 2001, p. H5.

Lampe maintained Ford was trying to divert scrutiny of the rollover-prone Explorer by casting doubt on the safety of Firestone tires.

Both parties suffered in this name calling and buck passing. By Fall 2001, sales of Explorers were off sharply, as consumers wondered whether the hundreds of Explorer crashes were due to the SUV's design, or Firestone tires, or both. Ford lost market share to Toyota and other foreign rivals in the SUV market. In July 2001, it reported its first loss from operations since 1992. It also faced 200 product liability lawsuits involving Explorer rollovers. Still, Ford was big enough to absorb problems with one of its models.

Smaller Bridgestone/Firestone faced a more dangerous situation. In 2000, its earnings dropped 80 percent, reflecting the costs of recalling millions of tires as well as a special charge to cover legal expenses. The Firestone unit, which accounted for 40 percent of the parent company's revenue, posted a net loss of $510 million after it took a $750 million charge for legal expenses. Sales were forecast to plunge 20 percent in 2001, and costs of lawsuits could eventually reach billions of dollars, to the point where some analysts doubted Firestone as a brand could survive.[8]

Options Firestone Faced

The esteemed Firestone brand, launched more than a century ago, had been the exclusive tire supplier to the Indy 500. Now its future was in doubt, despite decades of brand loyalty. The brand faced three options:

Option #1

Some thought the company should try to deemphasize Firestone and push business to the Bridgestone label. This would likely result in some loss of market segmentation and the flexibility of having distinct low-end, mid-level, and premium tires. Others thought such a halfhearted approach would simply prolong the agony of hanging on to a besmirched brand.

Option #2

Obliterate the Firestone name, it being irretrievable. "Firestone should just give up," said one public relations analyst. "They've damaged themselves so severely." A University of Michigan Business School professor called the brand dead: "Can you imagine any jury claiming that somebody who's suspected of building bad tires is innocent?"[9]

Option #3

Try to salvage the brand. Some questioned the wisdom of abandoning the century-old Firestone name, with its rich tradition and millions of cumulative advertising dollars. They thought that with money, time, and creative advertising, Bridgestone/

---

[8] Akiko Kashiwagi, "Recalls Cost Bridgestone Dearly; Firestone's Parent's Profit Drops 80%," *Washington Post*, February 23, 2001, p. E03.

[9] Grant, p. H5.

Firestone should be able to restore its image. But to do so, Roger Blackwell of Ohio State University thought the company needed to make an admission of regret: "The lawyers will tell them not to admit blame ... But they need to do what Johnson & Johnson did when someone was killed by their product [cyanide-tainted Tylenol]. A credible spokesman got on TV and had tears in his eyes when he spoke." An independent tire dealer who lost $100,000 in sales in 2000, but was confident of a rebound, supported this option: "The American public is quick to forget," he said.[10]

POSTMORTEM

Buyers of Ford Explorers with Firestone tires for years faced far higher risks of deaths and injuries, in the United States and abroad, than they would have from other models. The *New York Times* reported that the tire defects, and their contribution to accidents, were known in 1996.[11] Not until August 1999 did Ford begin replacing tires on Explorers in Saudi Arabia, calling the step a "customer notification enhancement program." Fourteen fatalities had already been reported. Not until March 2000, after television reports of problems, did federal regulators and the two manufacturers take all this seriously.

Ford, in its concern with the bottom line, stubbornly refused to admit that anything was wrong with its SUV; meanwhile Firestone couldn't seem to clean up its act in the Decatur, Illinois, plant—and even some other plants, where carelessness and lack of customer concern prevailed. Minor ethical abuses became major when lives were lost, but the foot-dragging continued until lawyers came on the scene. Then these two tried to cover their mistakes with finger pointing, while a vulnerable public continued to be in jeopardy. Throughout this time, saving lives did not apparently have a very high priority. Eventually, the consequences came back to haunt the companies, with hundreds of lawsuits, millions of tire recalls, and denigration of their public images.

How could this have been permitted to happen? After all, those in top management were not deliberately vicious men. They were well intentioned, albeit badly misguided. Perhaps their worst sin was first to ignore and then refuse to admit and try to cover up increasingly apparent serious risk factors.

Part of the problem was the stubborn mind-set of top executives that nothing was wrong: a few accidents reflected driver carelessness, not a defective product. Neither company would assume the worst scenario: that this was a dangerous product used on a dangerous product that was killing people, and neither Ford nor Firestone could escape blame.

Forty years before, a somewhat similar situation occurred with the GM Corvair, a rear-engine car that exhibited instability under extreme cornering conditions, causing it to flip over. Ralph Nader gained his reputation as a consumer advocate in his condemnation of this "unsafe" car with a best-selling book, *Unsafe at Any Speed*. But

---

[10] Ibid.

[11] Keith Bradsher, "SUV Tire Defects Were Known in '96 But Not Reported; 190 Died in Next 4 Years," *New York Times*, June 24, 2001, p. 1N.

GM executives refused to admit there was any problem—until eventually the evidence was overwhelming, lawsuits flourished, and the federal government stepped in with the National Traffic and Motor Vehicle Safety Act of 1966. Among other things, this act required manufacturers to notify customers of any defects or flaws later discovered in their vehicles.

GM executives, like those of Ford and Firestone 40 years later, were honorable men. Yet something seems to happen to the conscience and the moral sensitivity of top executives. They commission actions in their corporate personas that they would hardly dream of doing in their private lives. John DeLorean, former GM executive, was one of the first to note this dichotomy:

> These were not immoral men who were bringing out this car [the Corvair]. These were warm, breathing men with families and children who as private individuals would never have approved [this project] for a minute if they were told, 'You are going to kill and injure people with this car.' But these same men, in a business atmosphere, where everything is reduced to terms of costs, corporate goals, and production deadlines, were able to approve a product most of them wouldn't have considered approving as individuals.[12]

We have to raise the question: Why this lockstep obsession with sales and profits at all costs? See the Information Box: The "Groupthink" Influence for a discussion of this issue.

LATER DEVELOPMENTS

On October 30, 2001, Ford Motor Company announced that Jacques Nasser would be replaced as CEO by William Clay Ford Jr., 44—the first Ford family member to be in charge since 1979. Ford is the son of William Clay Ford Sr., who is the grandson of founder Henry Ford and brother of Henry Ford II. Nasser had been under pressure for months for Ford's loss of market share and tumbling profitability and the adverse publicity of the Explorer.

In December 2001, the newly designed 2002 Ford Explorer received a top score in a crash test from the Insurance Institute for Highway Safety. Changes in the 2002 Explorer to improve passenger protection were part of the automaker's "commitment to continuous improvements," a Ford spokesperson said.[13]

Firestone also bounced back, despite dire predictions of the brand's demise, as U.S. operations suffered a $1.7 billion loss in 2001 on top of a $510 million loss in 2000. Some called this "the most unlikely brand resurrection in marketing history." Much of the credit for the survival was credited to Firestone CEO John Lampe, who crisscrossed the country giving pep talks to hundreds of Firestone's 10,000 dealers. These dealers became fiercely loyal at a time when 75 percent of tire buyers were influenced by dealers' recommendations, according to industry estimates. Several

---

[12] J. Patrick Wright, *On a Clear Day You Can See General Motors*, Grosse Point, Mich.: Wright Enterprises, 1979, pp. 5–6.

[13] Christopher Jensen, *Cleveland Plain Dealer*, December 12, 2001, pp. C1, C4.

INFORMATION BOX

THE "GROUPTHINK" INFLUENCE
ON UNETHICAL BEHAVIOR

The callousness about "killer" cars would, as John DeLorean theorized, probably never have prevailed if an individual was making the decision outside the corporate environment. But bring in *groupthink,* which is decision by committee, and add to this a high degree of organizational loyalty (vs. loyalty to the public interest), and such callousness can manifest itself. Why can the moral standards of groupthink be so much lower than individual moral standards?

Perhaps the answer lies in the "pack mentality" that characterizes certain committees or groups highly committed to organizational goals. All else then becomes subordinated to these goals, being a single-minded perspective. Within any committee, individual responsibility for decision is diluted since this is a committee decision. Furthermore, without the contrary arguments of a strong "Devil's Advocate" (i.e., one who argues the opposing viewpoint, sometimes simply to be sure that all sides of an issue are considered), a follow-the-leader syndrome can take place, with no one willing to oppose the majority views.

But there is more to it than that. Chester Barnard, a business executive, scholar, and philosopher, noted the paradox:

> People have a number of private moral codes that affect behavior in different situations, and these codes are not always compatible. Codes for private life, regarding family and religion, may be far different from codes for business life. Throughout the history of business, it has not been unusual to find that the scrupulous and God-fearing churchgoer is far different when he or she conducts business during the week: A far lower ethical standard prevails during the week than on the Sabbath. Nor has it been unusual to find that a person can be a paragon of love, understanding, and empathy with his or her family but be totally lacking in such qualities with employees or customers.[14] We might add that even tyrants guilty of the most extreme atrocities, such as Hitler and Saddam Hussein, have been known to exude great tenderness and consideration for their intimates.

What does it take for a person to resist and not accept the majority viewpoint? What do you think would be the characteristics of such a person? Do you see yourself as such a rebel?

[14] Chester I. Barnard, *The Functions of the Executive,* Cambridge, Mass.: Harvard University Press, 1938, p. 263.

splashy new tires were brought out, including the Firehawk Indy 500, which became a hit with racing fans. "We are selling as many Firestone tires as we've ever sold," one large dealer noted.

With communication improving between the two companies, Lampe could see signs that the rift with Ford was ending, and William Clay Ford even mentioned his great-grandfather Harvey Firestone in a Ford commercial. "It was a very honest thing to do. He didn't have to do that," Lampe observed.[15]

WHAT CAN BE LEARNED?

A Firm Today Must Zealously Guard Against Product Liability Suits

Any responsible executive needs to recognize that product liability suits, in today's litigious environment, can even bankrupt a firm. The business arena has become more risky, more fraught with peril for the unwary or the naively unconcerned. Consequently, any firm needs careful and objective testing of any product that can affect customer health and safety. Sometimes such testing may require that production be delayed, even if competition gains some advantage from this delay. The risks of putting an unsafe product on the market outweigh competitive concerns.

Suspicions and Complaints About Product Safety Must Be Thoroughly Investigated

We should learn from this case that immediate and thorough investigation of any suspicions or complaints must be undertaken, regardless of the confidence management may have in the product or of the glowing recommendations of persons whose objectivity could be suspect. To procrastinate or ignore complaints poses what should be unacceptable risks.

Sometimes the root of the problem is not obvious, or is more complex than first thought. In this Ford/Firestone case, objective research should have focused on both the Explorer and the Firestone tires, and how the situation could be remedied to minimize rollovers and save lives.

Health and Safety of Customers Is Entirely Compatible with the Firm's Well-Being

It is a lose/lose situation if this is ignored: The customer is jeopardized, but eventually the firm is, too, as lawsuits grow and damages increase. Why, then, the corporate mindset of "us versus them?" There should be no conflicting goals. Both win when customer welfare is maximized.

In the Worst Scenario, Go for a Conciliatory Salvage Strategy

Ford and Firestone faced a crossroads by late 1999 and early 2000. Reports of fatalities linked to Ford Explorers and Firestone tires were trickling in, the first occurring in the hot climate of Saudi Arabia, and these were in a matter of months to become a flood. How should a company react?

---

[15] Todd Zaun, "Defying Expectations, Bridgestone Embarks on a Turnaround, *Wall Street Journal,* March 12, 2002, p. A21; and Jonathan Fahey, "Flats Fixed," *Forbes,* May 27, 2002, pp. 40–41.

A salvage strategy can be attempted by toughing it out, trying to combat the bad press, denying culpability, blaming someone else, and resorting to the strongest possible legal defense. This essentially is what Ford opted to do, since it blamed Firestone for everything and spent millions advertising to promote this contention.

Firestone was more vulnerable since its shredded tires could hardly be denied, and it was forced to recall millions of tires, although it stoutly maintained that the cause of the shredding was underinflation and the wrong quality of tire, as well as the Explorer itself. At stake were company reputations, economic positions, viability for Firestone, and, most importantly, the lives of hundreds of users.

Conciliation usually is the better salvage strategy. This involves recognition and full admission of the problem and removal of the risk, even if this involved a full-market withdrawal until the source of the problem could be identified and correction made. Expensive, yes, but far less risky for the viability of the company and certainly for the health of those customers involved.

Neither strategy is without substantial costs. But the first course of action puts major cost consequences in the future, where they may turn out to be vastly greater as legal expenses and damage awards skyrocket. The second course of action poses an immediate impact on profitability, and will not avoid legal expenses, but may save the company and its reputation and return it to profitability in the near future.

Where Blame is Most Likely Shared, the Solution of the Problem Lies Not in Confrontation But in Cooperation

This is the most grievous component of the violations of the public trust by Ford and Firestone: denial and confrontation, rather than both parties working together to solve the problem of product safety.

CONSIDER

Can you think of additional learning insights?

QUESTIONS

1. Can a firm guarantee complete product safety? Discuss.
2. Based on the information presented, which company do you think is most to blame for the deaths and injuries? What led you to your conclusion?
3. "If an Explorer driver never checks the tire pressure and drives well above the speed limit, he has no one to blame but himself in an accident—not the vehicle and not the tires." Discuss.
4. Do you think the government should be blamed in the Explorer deaths and injuries? Why or why not?
5. Would you give credence to the "community champion" awards bestowed by a consumer advocacy group founded by the Association of Trial Lawyers,

and given to Alan Hogan in June 2001 for exposing careless tire production? Why or why not?

6. "Admittedly the groupthink mind-set may be responsible for a few unethical and bad decisions, but isn't this mind-set more likely to consider the consequences to the company of delivering unsafe products, and support aggressive corrective action?" Evaluate this.

7. Have you had any experience with a Ford Explorer? If so, what is your perception of its performance and safety?

8. Have you had any experience with Firestone tires? What is your perception of their performance and safety?

HANDS-ON EXERCISES

1. Place yourself in the position of John Lampe, CEO of Firestone, as the crisis worsens and accusations mount. Discuss how you would try to change the climate with Jacques Nasser of Ford from confrontational to cooperative. Be as specific as you can. Do you think you would be successful?

2. Firestone is on its knees after massive tire recalls and monstrous damage suits. You are a consultant brought in to help the firm recover. Be as specific as you can in recommendations, and in the priority of things to do. Make any assumptions you need to, but keep them reasonable. Defend your recommendations. (Do not be swayed by what actually happened. Maybe things could have been done better.)

3. You are a trusted aide of Nasser. Support his confrontational stance with Firestone before the Ford board of directors.

4. Be a Devil's Advocate. In a staff meeting the topic comes up that your SUVs have been involved in a number of deaths. The group passes this off as due to reckless drivers. Argue persuasively a contrary position.

TEAM DEBATE EXERCISES

1. Debate the issue of dropping or keeping the Firestone name. Defend your position and attack the other side.

2. Debate the issue of standing by Nasser at the height of the confrontation, or removing him. Be as persuasive as you can.

INVITATION TO RESEARCH

Can you find statistics about how competing tire companies, particularly Goodyear and Michelin, fared during and after the Firestone recall? Are Ford and Firestone friends again?

Is the Ford Explorer still the top SUV?

CHAPTER EIGHT

Perrier—Overresponding to a Crisis

On a Friday in early February 1990, the first news reached Perrier executive suites that traces of benzene had been found in its bottled water. Ronald Davis, president of the Perrier Group of America, ordered a sweeping recall of all bottles in North America. Just a few days later, Source Perrier S.A., the French parent, expanded the recall to the rest of the world while the company sought to identify the source of the problem and correct it.

Although, at first view, such a reaction to an unexpected crisis seemed zealous and the ultimate in customer concern and social responsibility, a deeper study revealed marketing mistakes of major proportions.

BEFORE

In late 1989, Ronald Davis, 43-year-old president of Perrier's U.S. operations, had reason to be pleased. During his 10-year tenure, Perrier's U.S. sales had risen from $40 million to more than $800 million at retail, which was a significant 25 percent of the company's worldwide sales. He was also proud of his firm being depicted in a May 1989 issue of *Fortune* as one of six companies that compete best. *Fortune* captioned: "These are companies you don't want to come up against in your worst nightmare. In the businesses they're in, they amass crushing market share."[1]

A company report in 1987 described the French source, a spring in Vergeze, as follows:

> One of Perrier's identifying qualities is its low mineral (particularly sodium) content. This is because the water spends only a short time filtering through minerals. While flowing underground, the water meets gas flowing vertically through porous volcanic rocks. This is how Perrier gets its fizz … the company assured us that production has never been limited by the source output. The company sells approximately one billion bottles of which 600 million are exported.[2]

---

[1] Bill Saporito, "Companies That Compete Best," *Fortune*, May 22, 1989, pp. 36ff

[2] B. Facon, *Source Perrier—Company Report*, November 13, 1987, p. 4.

TABLE 8.1   **Average Annual Growth of Beverage Sales, 1985–1989**

Beverage Type	Percent of Growth
Bottled water	+ 11.1
Soft drinks	+ 3.2
Milk	+ 1.5
Tea	+ 1.2
Beer	+ 0.4
Coffee	– 0.4
Wine	– 2.0
Distilled spirits	– 2.6

Source: Beverage Marketing Corporation, as reported in *Fortune,* April 23, 1990, p. 277.

Davis recognized that he was in two businesses, albeit both involved bottled water: (1) sparkling water, in the famous green bottle, which he had successfully positioned as an adult soft drink with a French mystique, an alternative to sodas or alcohol and (2) still water, a tap-water replacement, with the product delivered to homes and offices and dispensed through watercoolers. This latter business he saw as more resembling package delivery, such as UPS and Federal Express, and less akin to pushing soft drinks. Accordingly, he emphasized quality of professional service for his route drivers. While best known for the green-bottled Perrier, a mainstay of most restaurants and bars, the company owned nine other brands of bottled water, including Poland Spring, Great Bear, Calistoga, and Ozarka.

At a price of 300 to 1,200 times that of tap water, bottled water was the fastest growing segment of the U.S. beverage industry (see Table 8.1). Perrier controlled 24 percent of the total U.S. bottled-water business. Of the imported-bottled-water sector, the green bottle dominated with almost 50 percent of the market, although this market share had fallen when more competitors attempted to push into the rapidly growing market. In the 1980s, more than 20 firms had taken a run at the green bottle, but without notable success; these included such behemoths as Coca-Cola, PepsiCo, and Anheuser-Busch. Now, Davis was more concerned with expanding the category and was trying to shift the brand's image from chic to healthy, so as to make the brand more acceptable to the "masses."

THE CRISIS

The North American Recall

Davis, as he prepared his five-year plan in early 1990, wrote that competing in the 1990s would require not strategic planning, but "flexibility planning."[3] In retrospect, he seemed to be prophetic.

[3] Patricia Sellers, "Perrier Plots Its Comeback," *Fortune,* April 23, 1990, p. 277.

As Davis was fine-tuning his plan, the first news trickled in that a lab in North Carolina had discovered traces of benzene, a carcinogen, in some of the bottles. That same day, February 9, he ordered Perrier removed from distribution in North America.

Source Perrier officials were soon to inform reporters that the company believed the contamination occurred because an employee had mistakenly used cleaning fluid containing benzene to clean the production-line machinery that fills bottles for North America. Frederik Zimmer, managing director of Source Perrier, said that the machinery in question had been cleaned and repaired over the weekend. But in another news conference, Davis announced that he expected Perrier to be off the market for 2 to 3 months.

Such a long absence was seen by some marketing observers as potentially devastating to Perrier, despite its being the front-runner of the industry. Al Ries, chairman of a consulting firm and well-known business writer, was quoted in the *Wall Street Journal* as saying: "If I were Perrier, I would make a desperate effort to reduce that time as much as possible, even if I had to fly it in on 747s from France."[4]

Without doubt, competitors were salivating at a chance to pick up market share of the $2.2 billion annual U.S. sales. Major competitors included Evian and Saratoga, both owned by BSN of France, and San Peligrino, an Italian import. In 1989, PepsiCo had begun test marketing H2OH!, and in January 1990, Adolph Coors Company introduced Coors Rocky Mountain Sparkling Water. The Perrier absence was expected to accelerate their market entry.

Despite competitive glee at the misfortune of Perrier, some in the industry were concerned. They feared that consumers would forsake bottled water altogether, with its purity now being questioned. Would the public be as willing to pay a substantial premium for any bottled brand? See the following Information Box for a discussion of the relationship between *price* and *quality*.

Worldwide Recall

A few days later, the other shoe fell. After reports of benzene being found in Perrier bottles in Holland and Denmark on February 14, Source Perrier expanded its North American recall to the rest of the world and acknowledged that all production lines for its sparkling water had been contaminated in recent months by tiny amounts of benzene.

At a news conference in Paris, company officials acknowledged, for the first time, that benzene occurs naturally in Perrier water and that the current problem came about because workers failed to replace filters designed to remove it. This was a critical reversal of previous statements that the water was tainted only because an employee mistakenly used cleaning fluid containing benzene to clean machinery. Zimmer even went further, revealing that Perrier water naturally contains several gases, including benzene, that have to be filtered out.

---

[4] Alix M. Freedman and Thomas R. King, "Perrier's Strategy in the Wake of Recall," *Wall Street Journal*, February 12, 1990, p. B1.

The company insisted that its famous spring was unpolluted. But now, questions were being raised about this and other contradictory statements made about the problem. For example, how widespread was the contamination? Was benzene a naturally occurring phenomenon, or does it represent man-made pollution? Suspicions were tending toward the man-made origin. While benzene occurs naturally in certain foods, it is more commonly found as a petroleum-based distillate used in many manufacturing processes.

Particularly surprising was the rather nonchalant attitude of Perrier executives. Zimmer, the president, even suggested that "all this publicity helps build the brand's renown."[5]

Ronald Davis was quick to point out that the company did not have to recall its entire 70-million-bottle U.S. inventory. After all, health officials, in the U.S. and France, had noted that the benzene levels found in Perrier did not pose any significant health risk. The major risk really was to the image of Perrier: It had gone to great lengths to establish its water as naturally pure. And while not particularly dangerous, it was certainly not naturally pure—as all the world was finding out from the publicity about it. Add to this the undermining of the major attraction of bottled water that it was safer than ordinary tap water, and the recall and subsequent publicity assumed more ominous proportions.

INFORMATION BOX

IS QUALITY BEST JUDGED BY PRICE?

We as consumers today have difficulty in judging the quality of competing products. With their complex characteristics and hidden ingredients, we cannot rely on our own expertise to determine the best. So, what sources of information can we use? We can rely on our past experiences with the brand; we can be swayed by our friends and neighbors, we might be influenced by advertising and salespeople (but more and more we become skeptical of their claims); we can study *Consumer Reports* and other consumer information publications. But all of these sources are flawed in that the experience and information usually is dated, and is a limited sample—usually of one—so that we can seriously question how representative the experience is.

Most people judge quality by price: the higher the price, the better the quality. But such a price/quality perception sets us up. While it may be valid, it also may not be. With the publicity about the impurity of Perrier, we are brought to the realization that paying many times the price of tap water gives us no assurance of better quality, as measured by purity.

Is a price/quality misperception limited mostly to bottled water, do you think? How about liquor? Designer clothes? Perfume?

---

[5] Alix M. Freedman and Thomas R. King, "Perrier Expands North American Recall to Rest of Globe," *Wall Street Journal,* February 15, 1990, p. B1.

THE COMEBACK

It took until mid-July before Perrier was again widely available in the United States; this was 5 months rather than the expected 3 months. Still, Davis was confident that Perrier's sales would return to 85 percent of normal by the end of 1991. Actually, he was more worried about short supply than demand. He was not sure the one spring in Vergeze, France, would be able to replace the world's supply before the beginning of 1991.

Davis's confidence in the durability of the demand stemmed from his clout with retailers, where the brand does a majority of its business. He believed the brand's good reputation, coupled with the other brands marketed by Perrier that had replaced some of the supermarket space relinquished by Perrier, would bring quick renewal. To help this, he wrote letters to 550 CEOs of retail firms, pledging heavy promotional spending. The marketing budget was increased from $6 million to $25 million for 1990, with $16 million going into advertising and the rest into promotions and special events. A highly visible discount strategy was instituted, which included a buy-two, get-one-free offer. Supermarket prices had dropped, with bottles now going for $0.89 to $0.99, down from $1.09 to $1.19. To win back restaurant business, a new 52-member sales force supplemented distributor efforts. However, a setback of sorts was the Food and Drug Administration order to drop the words "naturally sparkling" from Perrier labels.

Still, a recent consumer survey indicated that 84 percent of Perrier's U.S. drinkers intended to buy the product again.[6] Davis could also take heart from the less-than-aggressive actions of his competitors during the hiatus. None appeared to have strongly reacted, although most improved their sales considerably. The smaller competitors proved to be short of marketing money and bottling capacity and apparently were fearful that a beleaguered Perrier would negatively affect the overall market. Big competitors, such as PepsiCo and Coors, who were introducing other bottled waters, somehow also appeared reluctant to move in aggressively.

CONSEQUENCES

By the end of 1990, however, it was clear that Perrier was not regaining market position as quickly and completely as Davis had hoped. Now more aggressive competitors were emerging. Some, such as Saratoga, La Croix, and Quibell, had experienced major windfalls in the wake of the recall. Evian, in particular, a nonsparkling water produced by the French firm BSN S.A., was the biggest winner. Through aggressive marketing and advertising it had replaced Perrier by the end of 1990 as the top-selling imported bottled water.

Perrier's sales had reached only 60 percent of prerecall levels, and its share of the imported bottled-water market had sunk to 20.7 percent from the 44.8 percent of 1 year earlier. While the Perrier Group of America expected to report a sales gain for

---

[6] Sellers, p. 278.

1990 of 3.7 percent, this was largely because of the strong performance of such domestic brands as Calistoga and Poland Spring.

Particularly worrisome for Davis was the slow return of Perrier to bars and restaurants, which had formerly accounted for about 35 percent of its sales. A sampling of comments of restaurant managers, as reported in such prestigious papers as *Wall Street Journal* and *Washington Post*, were far from encouraging. For example:

> The manager of the notable Four Seasons restaurant in New York City said his patrons had begun to shift to San Pellegrino: "I think Perrier is finished," he said. "We can write it off."[7]

> The general manager of Spago Restaurant in Los Angeles said: "Now consumers have decided that other brands are better or at least as good, so Perrier no longer holds the monopoly on water." And Spago no longer carries Perrier.[8]

> Le Pavillon restaurant in Washington, D.C., switched to Quibell during the recall and has not gone back to Perrier. "Customers still ask for Perrier, but it's a generic term like Kleenex, and customers aren't unhappy to get a substitute."[9]

Evian

David Daniel, 34, was Evian's U.S. CEO since June 1988. He joined the company in 1987 as the first director of marketing at a time when the American subsidiary was a two-person operation. By 1990, there were 100 employees.

Daniel came from PepsiCo, and his background was marketing. He saw Evian's sphere to be portable water that is good for you, a position well situated to capitalize on the health movement. He was particularly interested in broadening the distribution of Evian, and he sought out soft-drink and beer distributors, showing them that their basic industries were only growing at 1 to 3 percent a year, while bottled water was growing at over 10 percent per year. In 1989, Evian sales doubled to $65 million, with $100 million in sight for 1990. The attractiveness of such growth to these distributors was of no small moment.

Daniel made Evian the most expensive water on the market. He saw the price as helping Evian occupy a certain slot in the consumer's mind—remember the price/quality perception discussed earlier. For example, at a fancy grocery in New York's West Village, a 1-liter bottle of Evian sold for $2.50; the city charges a fraction of a penny for a gallon of tap water[10]—a lot of perceived quality in that. This type of pricing along with the packaging that made Evian portable—plastic nonbreakable bottles and reusable caps—were seen as keys in the selling of bottled water. See the following Issue Box for a discussion of Are Bottled Water Claims Bunk?

---

[7] Freedman and King, p. B3.

[8] Alix M. Freedman, "Perrier Finds Mystique Hard to Restore," *Wall Street Journal,* December 1, 1990, p. B1.

[9] Lori Silver, "Perrier Crowd Not Taking the Waters," *Washington Post,* July 4, 1990, p. 1.

[10] Seth Lubove, "Perched Between Perrier and Tap," *Forbes,* May 14, 1990, p. 120.

ISSUE BOX

ARE BOTTLED WATER CLAIMS BUNK?[11]

The bottled water industry came under serious attack in April 1991. As if the Perrier massive recall was not enough, now a congressional panel with wide media coverage accused the Food and Drug Administration of "inexcusably negligent and complacent oversight of the bottled-water industry." Despite its high price, the panel said, bottled water may be less safe than tap water. The panel noted that although consumers pay 300 to 1,200 times more for bottled water than for tap water, 25 percent of all bottled water comes from public drinking water sources. For example:

> Lithia Springs Water Company touts its "world's finest" bottled mineral water as "naturally pure" and recommends its special Love Water as an "invigorator" before bedtime. Yet, it was found to be tainted with bacteria.

> Artisia Waters, Inc., promotes its "100% pure sparkling Texas Natural Water." But it comes from the same underground source that San Antonio uses for its municipal water supply.

Furthermore, the FDA released a list of 22 bottled-water recalls because of contaminants such as kerosene and mold. For the most part, these went unnoticed by consumers, being overshadowed by the Perrier recall.

Critical studies still found the product no cleaner or safer than big-city tap water; a third of the bottles sampled were contaminated by synthetic chemicals, bacteria, and arsenic. Out of the average $1.50 spent for a bottle of water, 90 percent went for bottling, packaging, marketing, retailing, and other expenses. The industry in defense claimed that the federal Centers for Disease Control had never found a U.S. outbreak of disease or illness linked to bottled water.

At issue: Are we being hoodwinked? Debate two positions: (1) the bottled-water industry really is a throwback to the snake-oil charlatans of the last century and (2) a few unscrupulous or careless bottlers are denigrating the image of the entire industry, an industry that is primarily focused on health and purity.

---

[11] Examples are taken from Bruce Ingersoll, "FDA Finds Bunk in Bottled-Water Claims," *Wall Street Journal*, April 10, 1991, p. B1. Also, Lance Gay, "Bottlers Tap Profits from Designer Water," Scripps Howard reported in *Cleveland Plain Dealer*, September 11, 2001, pp. A1, A8.

Then, late in 1990, Evian benefited greatly from the Persian Gulf War, with free publicity from several newspapers and from all three national TV networks: GIs were shown gulping water from Evian bottles.

ANALYSIS

Was the massive recall overkill, or was it a prudent necessity? Did it show a concerned corporate citizen, or rather a panicked executive? Were consumers impressed with the responsibleness of the company, or were they more focused on its careless-ness? These questions are all directed at the basic impact of the recall and the subsequent actions and admissions: Was it to have favorable, neutral, or unfavorable public reactions?

Perrier did not have to recall its product. It was a North Carolina county laboratory that first noticed the excessive amounts of benzene in Perrier and reported its findings to the state authorities. The state agriculture and health departments did not believe that a recall was necessary, but they did insist on issuing a health advisory, warning that Perrier should not be consumed until further tests could be made. It was the state's plan to issue the health advisory that was reported to Davis on the afternoon of the critical day, February 9. He announced the recall later that same day.

We are left to wonder: Perhaps a full and complete recall was not needed. Perhaps things could have been worked out entirely satisfactorily with less drastic measures. Given that a recall meant a 3- to 5-month absence from the marketplace, should it not have been the action of last resort?

But let us consider Davis's thought process on that ill-fated afternoon in February. He did not know the source of the problem; he certainly had no reason to suspect that it emanated from the spring in southern France or that it was a world-wide problem. He probably considered it of less magnitude. Perhaps he thought of the total North American recall as a gesture showing the concerned thinking of the management of this product that had developed such a reputation of health and purity and, yes, status. Only after the fact do we know the error of this decision: that it was to bring a 5-month absence from the hotly competitive market; that it was to result in revelations far more serious than a simple employee error or even a natural occurrence largely beyond the company's control.

So, perhaps Davis's drastic decision was fully justified and prudent. But it was confounded by circumstances he did not envision.

A lengthy complete absence from the marketplace is a catastrophe of rather monumental proportions—all the more so for a product that is habitually and frequently consumed, in Perrier's case, sometimes several times daily. Such an absence forces even the most loyal customers to establish new behavior patterns, in this case switching brands. Once behavior becomes habituated, at least for some people, a change back becomes less likely. This is especially true if the competitive offerings are reasonably similar and acceptable. Anything that Perrier could have done to lessen the time away from the market would have been desirable—regardless of expense.

Perhaps the biggest problem for Perrier concerned the false impressions, and even outright deception, that the company had conveyed regarding the purity of its product. Now, in the wake of this total recall and the accompanying publicity, all was laid bare. Company officials in France had to own up that the contamination had occurred "in recent months," and not suddenly and unexpectedly on February 9.

But more than this, under intense pressure from the media to explain what caused the problem, Source Perrier ultimately conceded that its water does not bubble up pure, already carbonated and ready to drink, from its renowned spring in southern France. Instead, contrary to the image that it had spent tens of millions of dollars to promote, the company extracts the water and carbon dioxide gas separately and must pipe the gas through charcoal filters before combining it mechanically with the water to give the fizz. Without the filters, Perrier water would contain benzene and, even worse, would taste like rotten eggs.

Finally, the public relations efforts were flawed. Source Perrier officials issued a confusing series of public statements and clarifications. Early on, the company tried to maintain the mystique of Perrier by concealing information about the cause of the contamination and by blaming it on a mistake by cleaning personnel in using an oily rag, which could have contained some benzene, to wipe equipment used for bottles to be shipped to the United States. But the spokespeople knew the problem was more fundamental than that.

An aura of nonchalance was conveyed by corporate executives and reported in the press. This was hardly in keeping with a serious problem having to do with the possible safety of customers. Furthermore, Source Perrier relied mainly on media reports to convey information to consumers. Misinformation and rumors are more likely with this approach to public relations than in a more proactive strategy of direct company advertisement and statements.

The reputation of Perrier was on the ropes. And top management seemed unconcerned about the probability of severe public image damage. The following Information Box discusses the topic of ignoring possible image damage.

UPDATE

Despite occasional publicity about the rip-off accomplished by the bottled-water industry—charging exorbitant prices for water little better than tap water—public demand continued to grow. By 2003, bottled water had become the fastest growing sector of the beverage industry. Americans, for example, consumed 60 percent more bottled water in 2002 than they did 5 years before; the increase was even greater in India and China. Furthermore, bottled water carried hefty markups. Pepsi's Aquafina became the leading brand and was enhanced by a multimillion-dollar promotion campaign. Coke, through acquisitions, amassed such brands as Dannon, Evian, and Dasani, although plans to make Dasani into a global brand were slowed by an aborted launch in Europe after elevated levels of bromate, a cancer-causing substance, were detected in bottles in Britain. Nestlé was the industry leader with regional brands including Poland Spring and Deer Park. Perrier was only a minor player now. By summer 2003, competition among the major beverage companies became more intense as consumers leaned toward less-expensive private-label brands. The result? A water price war. Some would say it's about time that these exorbitant markups be curbed.[12]

---

[12] Sherri Day, *New York Times,* and reported in *Cleveland Plain Dealer,* Water War," May 13, 2003, p. C2.

INFORMATION BOX

IGNORING POSSIBLE NEGATIVE IMAGE CONSEQUENCES

We can identify several factors that induce a firm to ignore public image considerations until sometimes too late. First, a firm's public image often makes a nonspecific impact on company performance. The cause-and-effect relationship of a deteriorating image is virtually impossible to assess, at least until and unless image problems worsen. Image consequences may be downplayed because management is unable to single out the specific profit impact.

Second, an organization's image is not easily and definitively measured. Although some tools are available for tracking public opinion, they tend to be imprecise and of uncertain validity. Consequently, image studies are often spurned or given short shrift relative to more quantitative measures of performance.

Third, it is difficult to determine the effectiveness of image-building efforts. While firms may spend thousands, and even millions, of dollars for institutional and image-building advertising, measures of the effectiveness of such expenditures are inexact and also of questionable validity. For example, a survey may be taken of attitudes of a group of people before and after the image-building campaign is run. Presumably, if a few more people profess to be favorably disposed toward the company after the campaign than before, this is an indication of its success. But an executive can question how much this really translates into sales and profits.

Given the near impossibility of measuring the effectiveness of image-enhancing promotion, how do you account for the prevalence of institutional advertising, even among firms that have no image problems?

WHAT CAN BE LEARNED?

Beware Exiting a Market for Months, Particularly With a Regularly Consumed Product

Such absence allows new habits to be established and new loyalties to be created not only among consumers but also dealers and may be impossible to fully recover from. This is especially true if competing products are comparable, and if competitors are aggressive in seizing the proffered opportunity. Since a front-runner is a target anyway, abandoning the battlefield simply invites competitive conquest.

Deception Discovered Destroys a Mystique

No mystique is forever. Consumer preferences change, competitors become more skilled at countering, or perhaps a firm becomes complacent in its quality control or innovative technology. These conditions nibble away at a mystique and eventually destroy it. As in the case of Perrier, where long-believed healthfulness and purity of product are suddenly revealed to be false—with advertising less than candid and even deceptive—then any mystique comes tumbling down unlikely ever to be regained. This scenario can only be avoided if the publicity about the deception or misdeed is not widespread. But, with a popular product such as Perrier, publicity reaches beyond business journals to the popular press. Such is the fate of large, well-known firms.

Consumers Often Have a Price/Quality Misperception

Without doubt, most consumers judge quality by price: the higher the price, the higher the quality. Is a $2.50 liter of Evian better quality than a gallon of tap water costing a fraction of a cent? Perhaps. But is it a hundred times better? And yet many people embrace the misconception that price is the key indicator of quality, and are consequently taken advantage of every day.

A Few Unscrupulous Firms Can Damage an Industry Catering to Health

We, the general public, are particularly vulnerable to claims for better health, beauty, and youthfulness. We want to reach out, hopefully, for promises that are made about our important personal concerns. We become gullible in our desire to find ways to change our condition. And so we become victims of quacks and snake-oil charmers through the ages. Governmental agencies try to exercise strong monitoring in these areas, but budgets are limited, and all claims cannot be investigated. As congressional scrutiny has revealed, the bottled-water industry had long been overlooked by governmental watchdogs. Now hopefully this is changing, perhaps due at least partly to the Perrier recall.

Should an Organization Have a Crisis-Management Team?

Perrier did a poor job in its crisis management. Would a more formal organizational unit devoted to this have handled things better, instead of leaving it to top executives unskilled in handling catastrophes? The issue can hardly be answered simply and all inclusively. Crises occur rarely; and a serious crisis may never happen to a particular organization. A crisis team then would have to be composed of executives and staff who have other primary responsibilities. And their decisions and actions under fire may be no better than less formal arrangements. For severe crises—and Perrier's was certainly that—top executives who bear the ultimate responsibility therefore have to be the final decision makers. Some will be cooler under fire than others, but this usually cannot be fully ascertained until the crisis occurs. More desirable for most organizations would seem to be contingency plans, with plans formulated for various occurrences, including the worst scenarios. With such action plans drawn up under more normal conditions, better judgments are likely to result.

CONSIDER

Can you think of other learning insights from this case?

QUESTIONS

1. How could the public relations efforts of Perrier have been better handled?

2. Discuss the desirability of Perrier's price cutting during its comeback.

3. Whom do you see as the primary customers for Perrier? For Evian? For other bottled waters? Are these segments likely to be enduring in their commitment to bottled water?

4. Why do you think the big firms, such as Coca-Cola, PepsiCo, and Coors, were so slow in entering the bottled-water market?

5. Are you a regular user of bottled water? What is it that induces you to buy?

6. "The success of bottled water in the United States, unlike the situation in many countries of the world where bottled water is often essential for good health, attests to the power of advertising." Evaluate this statement.

7. Is the appeal of bottled water largely attributable to an image developed of sophistication and status?

HANDS-ON EXERCISES

1. Put yourself in the position of Ronald Davis on the afternoon of February 9, 1990. The first report of benzene found by a North Carolina lab has just come in. What would you do? Be as specific as you can, and describe the logic behind your decisions.

2. How would you attempt to build up or resurrect the mystique of Perrier after the recall?

TEAM DEBATE EXERCISES

1. Debate the issue of extreme measures (a massive recall) undertaken in a product safety situation versus more moderate reactions (a modest recall). Consider as many aspects of this issue as you can, and make educated judgments of various probable consumer and governmental reactions. (Do not be swayed by what actually happened; this extreme reaction may be criticized.)

2. Debate Ronald Davis's decision to discount prices as he sought to reestablish Perrier in the marketplace.

INVITATION TO RESEARCH

Assess the popularity of bottled water today. Has it increased or lessened since the events described? How prominent does Perrier seem to be in grocery stores, in restaurants, in sporting and outdoors events? From your observation, what are the characteristics of major customers for bottled water? Are they younger, more elderly, more athletic, more affluent?

PART THREE

COMPETITIVE UNCERTAINTIES

CHAPTER NINE

The Kmart/Sears Merger of Faltering Firms

On November 17, 2004, Kmart Holding Corp. chairman Edward Lampert and Sears chairman and CEO Alan Lacy announced the deal for Kmart to buy the once-dominant Sears department store chain for $11.5 billion. This merger of battered retail giants would propel the combination into the No. 3 position behind behemoth Wal-Mart, and Home Depot. This would be the second-largest retail merger ever. It would take the Sears name and be called Sears Holdings Corp.

Some analysts questioned the optimism of how such a merger of two faltering firms—both have long been hampered by weak management, outdated stores, and inefficient operations—could make one winner. However, investors thought otherwise and bid up the stocks of both companies. The name of the new company was to be Sears Holdings Corp. However, Kmart would be dominant. Part of the investor zeal was faith in Edward Lampert as a turnaround expert extraordinaire. That, and the suspected value of the combined company's real estate.

EDWARD LAMPERT

The 42-year-old Lampert had built a fortune buying struggling companies and turning them around. He had hitherto shunned publicity, though now this may be difficult to do in this highly visible merger. In 2003, any desire for secrecy was thwarted as he was kidnapped from the garage of his office building in Greenwich, Connecticut, with his captors demanding a $1 million ransom. This tested his persuasive skills, and they were not found wanting as he eventually convinced the kidnappers to let him go for $40,000.

The son of a lawyer in a comfortable New York City suburb, Lampert's life became more focused when his father died when he was 14. Interested in finance, he graduated from Yale and joined Goldman Sachs after graduating. There he found a mentor, Robert Rubin, who later became U.S. Secretary of Treasury. Lampert left the firm in 1988 at age 28 to start a hedge fund, ESL Investments, with about $25 million to invest. He had long been an admirer of Warren Buffett, second only to Bill Gates of Microsoft as the richest American. Buffett had gained his wealth by concentrating on undervalued, old-line companies that threw off lots of cash. And just as Buffett did in the 1960s with Berkshire, then just a declining textile mill in New Bedford, Massachusetts, Lampert did with bankrupt Kmart, gaining control in 2003 and turning it into a powerful investment vehicle. His investors today include the wealthy and famous, and he has made them even wealthier as his hedge fund's annual returns since 1988 have averaged almost 30 percent.

Unlike other hedge funds, ESL does not trade stocks actively but tends to take big positions and hold them long term. As an example of his investment style, Lampert, in 1997, bought an initial stake in AutoZone, a leading auto-parts retailer that was struggling. By 1999, he had a seat on the board , installed a new CEO, and boosted cash flow. To help profits, he raised prices, cut store-management budgets, and shifted to less-experienced staff, and the company's stock price surged from the low $20s in late 1999 to more than $100 in October 2003.[1]

Kmart had filed for Chapter 11 bankruptcy protection in January 2002, as it found itself unable to compete with the likes of Wal-Mart and Target. After the filing, more than 600 unprofitable stores were closed, 57,000 Kmart employees were terminated, and Kmart stockholders' common stock was wiped out. Lampert began buying Kmart debt after the filing, while a subsequent controversy over accounting and perks given to former executives had reduced the value of its bank debt to less than 70 cents on the dollar, and its bonds to about 35 cents on the dollar. He came to hold debt with a face value of about $1 billion. But bad news continued for Kmart, and Lampert faced paper losses of $100 million.

He demanded a seat on the court-sanctioned committee of holders of bank debt and bonds. There he argued against the slowness of the bankruptcy process and the "excessive" fees paid to lawyers and consultants. Lampert forced the resignation of Kmart's chief executive and installed Julian Day, a former Sears executive, as CEO. He pushed hard to get the company out of bankruptcy quickly. "He was absolutely confident that the business was worth something, despite an enormous amount of skepticism by most parties," said Henry Miller, a financial adviser to Kmart during its bankruptcy restructuring.[2]

But Lampert's hedge fund had to pour in more money to buy out Kmart's banks, and when the retailer emerged from bankruptcy in May 2003, he held more than 50 percent of Kmart's new stock through conversion of his debt holdings into equity. He then led an aggressive strategy of closing or selling another 600 stores. The proceeds from these, no longer having the burden of billions of dollars of debt, and severe cost cutting brought a speedy financial turnaround, with profits being posted in each of the last four quarters after Lampert took over. The stock price, meantime, increased sevenfold from its price of $15 a share when it emerged from bankruptcy, and the hedge fund had gained almost $4 billion from its Kmart holdings. ESL Investments now owned 43 million shares of Kmart and 31 million shares of Sears. In the wake of the merger news, in one day it recorded paper profits of nearly $600 million.

[1] Rachel Beck, "So, Does 2 + 2 = 5 for Kmart, Sears?" *Associated Press* as reported in *Cleveland Plain Dealer,* November 23, 2004, p. C5.

[2] Gregory Zuckerman and Mitchell Pacelle, "Sears Suitor Faces a Tough Bet," *Wall Street Journal,* November 18, 2004, p. C4.

THE EVOLUTION OF KMART

Kmart had been a newcomer to the discount scene. The early discounters started a few years after World War II, offering goods in barns, lofts, warehouses, abandoned factories, all places of low overhead. Shopping amenities were few. Goods were displayed on pipe racks, maybe jumbled on tables, and there were no services and hardly any employees except those at the checkouts. But prices were far lower than traditional retailers could offer. Most of the early discounters were ill managed, undercapitalized, and very vulnerable to the sophisticated management that S. S. Kresge Co. had developed in more than half a century of being the second largest variety chain behind only Woolworth. The name Kresge was changed to Kmart in 1977.

Kmart destroyed its weaker competitors and was second only to Sears in sales, until 1990. Sears, however, carried appliances, furniture, tools, some machinery, automobile accessories and tires, and other goods that Kmart and department stores did not carry, so that Sears' sales statistics were not entirely comparable with Kmart.

Sam Walton started Wal-Mart in 1969, and in the late 1970s, Wal-Mart sales were only 5 percent of Kmart's. It had 150 stores to Kmart's more than 1,000 that were mostly in urban locations. Wal-Mart stayed in rural small towns where it developed technology to have lean inventories, reduce overhead to the lowest in the industry, yet keep shelves well stocked and be able to offer lowest prices.

When Wal-Mart finally began invading Kmart's turf, it had a significant price advantage that Kmart never was able to overcome. In addition, the Wal-Mart stores were newer than the aging stores of Kmart. In 1990, Wal-Mart caught up with Kmart and then irresistibly surged ahead while Kmart faltered. In a desperate effort to win back customers, Kmart's management increased its inventory investment and tried to match Wal-Mart's prices. But with Wal-Mart's efficiency and low overhead , Kmart could not match its prices without going into the red. Unable to compete with Wal-Mart and an aggressive Target aimed at a slightly more affluent customer, Kmart became ripe for Lampert's takeover.

THE EVOLUTION OF SEARS

Sears spanned three centuries of being a dominant force in the retail industry. It started in the late 19th century when it sent thousands of rural Americans the Sears Roebuck catalog, quickly dubbed the "consumer's bible." This offered not only a great variety of goods but also far more cheaply than they could be bought elsewhere. It even advertised itself as the "Cheapest Supply House on Earth" and turned America into a consumer democracy, where everyone had equal access to the same goods at the same price.[3] Sears surpassed Montgomery Ward as the largest retailer in 1900, with sales of $10 million to Ward's $8.7 million. Never again would Ward surpass Sears. The catalog became a fixture in millions of American homes—and outhouses—and enabled farm families to keep up with changing fashions and the raft of manufactured goods becoming available.

---

[3] Cynthia Crossen and Kortney Stringer, "A Merchant's Evolution," *Wall Street Journal*, November 18, 2004, p. B1.

By the 1920s, with many of its customers migrating to the cities or else having cars and better roads, Sears' founding principle of bringing cheap merchandise to remote areas of the country was becoming obsolete. In a major strategic decision, it opened its first retail store in Chicago in 1925, and by 1933 had 400 stores. It launched its famous Kenmore and Craftsman brands in 1927, and started the Allstate Insurance Co. in 1931. In 1953, Sears issued its own credit card and started the Discovery Card in 1985. In 1981, it diversified, acquiring Dean Witter Reynolds and Coldwell Banker. In 1993, with much handwringing, Sears discontinued the catalog and sold its interests in its financial units. In 2002, it acquired Lands' End for $1.9 billion.

By the 1990s, Sears found itself squeezed by a changing retail environment. Its lower- and middle-class customers were flocking to the powerful and efficient Wal-Marts and Targets for low prices. Those wanting quality were drawn to Nordstrom or specialty retailers like Gap. Those looking for home improvement and building supplies were drawn to surging category-killer chains such as Home Depot and Lowe's.

At the time of the merger with Kmart, Sears had 870 mostly mall-based stores and 1,100 specialty stores, with net income for partial 2004 of $648 million; Kmart had 1,504 stores, almost all standing alone and not in malls, with net income for partial 2004 of $533 million, after Lampert had taken it out of bankruptcy and closed or sold about 600 losing stores.[4] With its sluggish sales in recent years, Sears had also lost favor with investors until the announced merger.

LAMPERT'S CHALLENGE

Possible Problems

In order to generate the most short-term profit possible after buying distressed Kmart and thus drive share prices up, Lampert put no money into improving its stores—though many were old and drab—in the 18 months after it came out of bankruptcy protection. He reduced inventories, avoided most discounting, and cut advertising and other expenses. He was able to sell some stores to chains such as Home Depot and also some to Sears. Other unsaleable money-losing stores were closed. But his cash flow shored up the balance sheet with a $3 billion cash hoard and dazzled investors in the planned merger.

As a result of no significant investments, same-store sales slid drastically, 13 percent in one recent quarter. In the highly competitive retail environment, such frazzled stores would likely be lodestones for the chain's efforts to revive itself without major rejuvenation. But any major investments would reduce profits.

One objective of mergers is to combine and coordinate operations and products wherever possible, to avoid redundancies, and strengthen existing product lines. Could some Sears' goods be readily sold in Kmart stores and vice versa? Sears had strong brands in its Kenmore appliances and Craftsman tools. Wal-Mart was not much of a factor with such goods. But would these bulky appliances be practical to

---

[4] WSJ Research, "Down the Aisles," *Wall Street Journal,* November 18, 2004, p. B1.

move into Kmarts? They would require considerable space, which would mean less room for groceries, paper goods, household staples and similar products. They would also require a much higher level of employee than typically found in a Kmart, and major remodeling to support such high-priced and bulky products. None of the three competitors—Sears, Kmart, and Wal-Mart—was strong in apparel, although Wal-Mart was improving its quality and had introduced a more stylish George line. In 2002, Sears bought the Lands' End apparel brand, and this had done well in upscale markets, but not so well in less-affluent ones.

It was doubtful that either Kmart or Sears had the merchandising/computer technology to match Wal-Mart in preventing out-of-stocks and overstocks of other goods. Anecdotal incidents of Kmart and Sears merchandising expertise were troubling. Visits to Kmart and Sears stores in Ohio, by retail consultants after the merger was announced, found Kmart depleted in some grocery items, while Sears still had baseball caps in November for faraway teams such as Oakland, Atlanta, and San Francisco.[5]

Kmart was not alone in having steadily declining same-store sales. Sears also had sliding sales almost every month for the previous four years before the merger. CEO Alan Lacy had tried. He had reorganized departments, dropped product lines, changed store signs, added clothing lines, and laid off thousands of employees. He sold the credit-card business in 2003 to Citigroup at about the same time as Kmart was beginning its credit card. The Lands' End acquisition brought more expertise in apparel. Still, same-store sales declined. Will Lampert do any better?

Lampert's Goals for the New Merger

Lampert had a reputation for keeping his cards close to his vest. So a plethora of analysts began speculating about how he would proceed, and how successful this would be. Investors seemed dazzled by his past successes in turning around distressed companies. At a news conference after the announced merger, Lampert and Lacy of Sears talked about potential synergies, a buzz word often used to support a merger decision. See the following Information Box for an analysis of the synergy of Lands' End in fitting in with the Kmart/Sears merger.

Lambert and Lacy talked of squeezing suppliers, thanks to the $40 billion a year in buying power of the two companies. They talked of streamlining back-office operations. They predicted annual savings of $500 million within three years. They would aim to synchronize such areas as merchandising and planning, with cross-selling between stores, bringing Craftsman tools, Diehard batteries, and possibly Kenmore appliances into Kmarts and Martha Stewart goods into Sears.

Most Sears stores were in traditional malls, but malls were losing some favor with consumers. Research recently found that 80 percent of consumer shopping dollars were now spent elsewhere than malls, compared to about 60 percent in 1995. Furthermore, six of the nation's largest retailers were not in malls, this being twice

[5] Amy Merrick and Ann Zimmerman, "Can Sears and Kmart Take on a Goliath Named Wal-Mart?" *Wall Street Journal*, November 19, 2004, p. B1.

INFORMATION BOX

LANDS' END: DOES IT FIT IN WITH THE NEW MERGER?

Lands' End was a longtime catalog seller that had built a strong following with its high-quality items such as cashmere sweaters, its wide range of sizes and assortments, and sporting a high level of customer service. It was based in a small Wisconsin town, and its most direct competitor was L.L. Bean, also from a small town, but in Maine.

Sears bought the company in 2002 for $1.9 billion, hoping it would be a cornerstone brand, beef up apparel sales, and draw customers who were buying appliances and other nonclothing items. Lands' End thought the exposure to potential customers in Sears' 870 locations would be healthy. The reverse was more the case. The wider exposure weakened Lands' End exclusivity, and it was often poorly positioned "in between men's suits, snow blowers, tools, denim and work clothes." Charlie O'Shea, an analyst for Moody's, said, "It hasn't done what I think Sears wanted it to do. The general idea was to take the higher-income demographic, the hard-line appliance shopper, and have them walk across the store and buy apparel." But this was not happening enough.

Kmart's takeover of Sears caused more consternation for Lands' End. The blue-collar image of Kmart seemed incompatible with the quality image Lands' End had built up over the years. Kmart had to wonder, too, whether Lands' End merchandise would sell at all in its stores, or simply take up precious space better used for other goods. Instead of the synergy effect to $2 + 2 = 5$, with the total result better than the two separate operations before, it seemed more a $2 + 2 = 3$, with the combined result worse than the two separate operations were before.

Do you think Lands' End goods will sell in Kmart stores? What would it take? How could Lands' End do better in Sears stores.?

Source: Aaron Nathans, "Sears-Kmart Union Puts Lands' End in Double Jeopardy," *New York Times*, as reported in *Cleveland Plain Dealer,* January 13, 2005, p. C6.

the number of the late 1990s.[6] Several hundred more Kmart stores could be converted into Sears stores, which would enable Sears to address the location problem in its business model and begin to adapt to a retailing environment that had shifted to stand-alone big box stores. Some of this adaptation would be to a new chain called Sears Grand, which is closer to the popular off-mall format of the Wal-Marts and Home Depots.

Sears Grand stores have a mix of appliances, lawn and garden goods, hardware, and clothing. Since these stores are bigger than regular Sears department stores, they can add products such as books and magazines, CDs and DVDs, as well as groceries and everyday necessities. Sears was testing such stores in different sizes and formats.

---

[6] Amy Merrick and Dennis K. Berman, "Kmart to Buy Sears for $11.5 Billion," *Wall Street Journal,* November 18, 2004, p. A8.

INFORMATION BOX

ADVANTAGES OF CHAINS: OPPORTUNITY
FOR EXPERIMENTATION

An organization with numerous similar outlets has an unparalleled opportunity for experimenting with new ideas in the quest for what might be most productive and compelling. Prospective strategy changes can be tested with a few stores, any promising modifications determined, and the success of the strategy ascertained from concrete sales and profit results.

All this can be done with relatively little risk since only a few outlets of the total chain are involved, and the strategy can be adopted throughout the organization only if results are favorable. Such experimentation is hardly possible for the firm with few comparable units, which usually is the case with manufacturers; but where it can be done, the risks in making major strategy changes are greatly reduced, and the arena for creative innovation is enhanced.

How would you design such an experiment for Sears Grand? Be as specific as you can, and make any assumptions needed.

See the above Information Box for a discussion of the advantage that chains offer of being able to test different marketing strategies in a few stores and hone their effectiveness before going larger scale. These stores were thought to be better able to compete in the home improvement market against the likes of Wal-Mart, Home Depot, Lowe's, and Best Buy.

What should be of concern to investors is whether Lampert can make this third largest retailer sufficiently competitive in today's hostile environment. This suggests some semblance of growth, with some new stores and rejuvenated ones—this might be called a patient turnaround strategy. But perhaps this is not what Lambert is expecting to do. Do Sears and Kmart need to grow, or would a status quo situation be acceptable as long as steady income is generated at least in the intermediate future?

If Lampert succeeds in the turnaround, and the stock of the combined companies rises accordingly, then he will be well armed to pull off more deals, to be well on the way to becoming another Warren Buffett. But maybe he doesn't need to be a hero. By squeezing cash out of every aspect of Kmart's operation over eighteen months he has already built a war chest of $3 billion. Sears also has a $2.7 billion cash reserve that can probably be increased as he wrings inefficiencies out of the aging firm. Kmart, furthermore, has $3.8 billion in tax credits carried over from previous losses that should shield profits for some years to come. Maybe simply continuing accumulating a cash hoard is enough to give Lampert the ammunition to pursue his goal of great wealth and invest in other promising distressed bargains.

Some analysts see Lampert's best course of action lies in liquidating the underlying real estate of Kmart and Sears. However, once the best locations have been sold off, then there would not be much left. In an economy of rising interest rates, this speculative hope that liquidating real estate would fuel ever-rising stock prices could be wistful thinking.[7]

ANALYSIS

Whether operational gains can be achieved from the Kmart/Sears merger is uncertain, especially against the might of competitors Wal-Mart, Target, and Home Depot. Adding to the competitive uncertainties is the length of time needed to assimilate the merger in the disparate organizations and operations. Such assimilation could take years before any synergies might be realized. This suggests that this third largest retailer may be particularly vulnerable for some years and probably lose market share never to win it back.

The great cash hoard that Lampert can generate from a stripped down Kmart and Sears operation, and the inflated stock prices influenced by all this cash and by the optimistic assessment of real estate values for liquidation, promises only a short-term reprieve. Perhaps long enough to get these two dinosaur retailers on the growth track again? Only maybe. A better expectation would be of a patient turnaround, and a modest one to boot.

How is the cash to be spent? If it is spent in seeking other acquisitions of declining businesses, and leaving Kmart and Sears to fend for themselves with deteriorated and underfunded stores in the arena of the world's greatest retailers, then their eventual survival is hardly promising. In ten years will there still be a Kmart and a Sears? But Lampert's cash may grow considerably. Then he may be left with the reputation of a raider who guts his acquisitions. I wonder whether he really would want that. I also wonder whether he can pull off a turnaround of even modest proportions. Such a turnaround would undoubtedly take all of the accumulated cash—and probably more, taking on debt again—to rejuvenate stores, increase inventories, advertising, perhaps new computer technology.

Another option might be to gradually close down the weaker chain, and pour resources into making the other stronger. This stronger entity would probably be Sears, and it appeals to a more affluent customer than Kmart's generally blue-collar customer. Some Kmarts, in more affluent neighborhoods, might be convertible to Sears. But still this is going to take major investment.

Will Lampert succeed with Sears and Kmart? This really depends on how he defines *succeed.* Does it mean becoming a bigger force in the marketplace? Or does it mean accumulating a cash bonanza? What do you think?

LATEST BREAKING NEWS

On March 24, 2005, with shareholders signing off, Kmart officially bought Sears for $12.3 billion. Lampert told reporters, "It's an opportunity to transform two companies that once were great—to transform them into a great company relative to the

---

[7] Jesse Eisinger, "Will Lampert Get It All to Fit?" *Wall Street Journal,* November 24, 2004, p. C1.

21st century. I think there's a presumption that you're going to see a lot of store closings. That's a wrong presumption. Our program is to keep as many stores open as we can." Lampert also denied the company had plans to get rid of Lands' End: "Land's End isn't for sale. It's a great American brand, and I think it's a brand that we could run very, very well."

Some layoffs would be forthcoming from among the 5,000 people working at the two firm's headquarters—the Kmart headquarters in Troy, Michigan, would be combined with Sears' headquarters in Hoffman Estates, Illinois—but the vast majority of the 400,000 work force would keep their jobs. Plans were to convert about 400 of the Kmart stores over the next 3 years to a new midsize "Sears Essentials" store format being launched outside its traditional malls.

Standard & Poor's analysts cautioned investors that "the combination of heightened business risk, intense competition and possible under-achievement in the company's off-mall strategy could lead to sales and margin problems, as well as deteriorating credit measures."[8]

Sixty-nine percent of Kmart shareholders voted to approve the deal in a sparsely attended session lasting five minutes. Two hours later, Sears shareholders also voted 69 percent in favor of the deal, but the scene was raucous, as retired and former Sears employees upset about the acquisition by Kmart clamored against the deal. "This is a sad and dark day for Sears Roebuck," a former auto center manager fumed at the meeting. "It is unbelievable that Kmart, two years out of bankruptcy, would be strong enough to purchase Sears, a company in business for over a century."[9]

WHAT CAN BE LEARNED?

Beware Optimistic Projections for Mergers

Optimistic assumptions have no place in merger decisions. Most mergers are consummated with rather high expectations of synergy and growth. Many of these do not work out as expected at least within the desired time frame of a year or two. And some never work out, and eventually the losing acquisitions are given up on, or hung on to while draining financial and managerial resources. We will see three such cases later in the book; in the next chapter, Hewlett-Packard, Carly Fiorina's vigorous selling the board on the merger with Compaq may have contributed to her downfall.

Will this great merger of Kmart and Sears become the country's third largest retailer, will it meet the declared expectations of Lampert, or will he flee from the scene with a hoard of cash and two gutted former retail empires?

[8] Andrew Leckey, "Analysts Rate Sears Stock as a 'Hold'," Tribune Media Services as reported in *Cleveland Plain Dealer,* March 30, 2005, p. C5.

[9] Dave Carpenter, "Sears Sale to Kmart Gets Blue, er, Green Light," Associated Press, as reported in *Cleveland Plain Dealer,* March 25, 2005, pp. C1, C3.

Assumptions Should Be Defended in Merger Decisions

Objectivity and conservative projections are called for in merger decisions. These are often the most important decisions these managers will ever have to make and deserve thorough investigation and research. Top management should insist that assumptions and their reasoning be defended, at least as much as possible in an uncertain future. It is prudent to consider a worst-cast scenario: "What if?" The use of a Devil's Advocate—one who takes an opposing position for the sake of bringing out all aspects of a particular course of action—can often be very worthwhile in such major decisions, yet is so seldom used.

Don't Depend on Stock Prices to Support a Risky Merger

The stock market is a volatile instrument. The get-rich motivation of some investors can foster wild and unreasonable speculations. It is not unusual for share prices of some firms to be bid up far beyond their fair value, with more and more investors living in a dream world and joining the bandwagon, only to have prices come tumbling down as more sobering realities become evident. Kmart's and Sears' prices seem to conform to this pattern: a gamble bid up to unrealistic levels.

What happens to Lampert's grand scheme if the inflated stock prices of Kmart and the new enterprise, Sears Holdings Corp., lose their lofty valuations? This would mean less financial assets for future acquisitions. If the loss of valuation is quite severe, sufficient capital to rejuvenate the aging stores of Sears and Kmart may be limited. We wonder how Lampert's hedge fund, ESL Investments, and its wealthy clients would tolerate sharply falling share prices of this major holding in the fund.

Use Same-Store Sales Instead of Total Sales Statistics in Evaluating Retail Performance

A key measure of how a retail chain is doing (aside from income statistics) is same-store sales. Total sales reflect new store openings and tell nothing about how existing stores are doing and may hide a deteriorating situation. For example, if existing stores are showing steadily declining sales—as both Kmart and Sears stores were at the time of the merger—this is a major indicator of how vulnerable these stores are. One wonders how many can be converted to a growth mode again. For decisions regarding which stores to close, the trend in same-store sales has to be a major input. This is especially true if different store managers have still been unable to turn things around. A further analysis should be made before any decision to cut: Why is the store not doing better? Is it incompetence, bad location, aggressive competitors, untrained or unmotivated staff … what? What would it take to correct these problems, and is this reasonable to undertake?

Old Facilities Are Vulnerable to Newer Competitors

Kmart and Sears have older stores than most of the Wal-Marts, Targets, Home Depots, and Lowe's. This presents a quandary in trying to compete without major investments to rejuvenate and open new state-of-the-art stores. Customers prefer to shop at nicer stores, it is easier to attract better employees, and even suppliers tend to give preferential treatment to those firms they see as growing rather than stagnant. This is a conundrum for the retailer with old stores trying to compete. Where is the money coming from for major rejuvenation of existing stores? Would it be better to spend the limited resources on new stores? What is this going to do to overhead and ability to compete against lowest prices?

Minimum Reinvestment May Be Desirable in Some Circumstances

Sometimes marginal property is not worth much additional investment. But it still may not be a candidate for closure, even though little or no growth is on the horizon. It depends on how much overhead it requires and whether it can generate some profit, even at low sales. If the store or operation is debt free—and debt is a major factor in overhead—then it may be worth keeping for a while at least. With Lampert's buying up the debt of Kmart in exchange for equity, the overhead was greatly reduced and these operations were grinding out a cash flow of $3 million in the first 18 months of his control. The problem from Lampert's perspective is whether stock prices will stabilize at a high level, once the no-growth future becomes evident.

CONSIDER

Can you think of other learning insights?

QUESTIONS

1. Do you think this merger will fly? Why or why not?
2. Explain why total sales information for a retail chain is insufficient in evaluating performance.
3. Visit a Kmart store and a Wal-Mart store. What was your overall impression as to strengths and weaknesses?
4. Visit a Sears and a Target store. What was your overall impression as to their strengths and weaknesses?
5. Do you think you would like to be a Kmart store manager?
6. Does the size of the Kmart/Sears entity after the merger give it a competitive advantage? Why or why not?
7. Is market share all that important in this case? Discuss.
8. "Kmart does not really have to match the low prices of Wal-Mart. It should not even try." Evaluate this statement by an analyst.

HANDS-ON EXERCISES

1. Be a Devil's Advocate (one who argues a contrary position). Lampert has about decided to limit any additional investment in Kmart either for rejuve-

nating stores or building up inventory. Argue as persuasively as you can against this draconian decision. (You maybe should be a little diplomatic; you don't want to antagonize him.)

2. You are an ambitious Sears store manager. Describe how you might design your career path to achieve a high executive position in Lambert's new retail behemoth. (Assume that Lambert is not going to abandon this enterprise.)

3. You are the principal adviser to Sears' Alan Lacy. He wants you to develop a plan for positioning the new Sears Grand stores. Develop a plan of action for these stores, identifying various options, and then persuasively presenting one. You might rather do the same thing with the Sears Essentials store format.

TEAM DEBATE EXERCISES

1. The controversy has developed regarding whether Kmart and Sears should continue as two separate entities, or whether one or the other should be phased out with resources directed to only one. Debate the two positions using all the salient arguments you can muster for your position. You should be prepared to attack the other side.

2. You represent one group of shareholders of Lambert's hedge fund, ESL. Your group is opposed to this merger and believes everybody would be better off if the over $3 billion cash hoard generated so far by Kmart is used for other growth opportunities. You will be debating another group of shareholders who stand solidly behind the merger with Sears.

INVITATION TO RESEARCH

How has the merger gone? Is it generally deemed to be successful? Has Lambert stayed with his initial plan to be instrumental in turning around the Kmart and Sears operations? Has the stock market continued to be kind to this endeavor?

CHAPTER TEN

Hewlett-Packard Under Carly Fiorina

*I*n July 1999, Hewlett-Packard, the world's second-largest computer maker, chose Carly Fiorina to be its CEO. Thus she became the first outsider to take the reins in H-P's 60-year history. Never before had the company ever filled any top jobs with outsiders, and now this. Fiorina now became one of only three women to head a *Fortune* 500 company.

Three years later in May 2002, Fiorina engineered the biggest merger in high-tech history, with Compaq Computer. To do so, she had to convince government regulators in the United States and Europe that this merger was not anticompetitive. She also had to get stockholder approval in the face of bitter opposition by Walter Hewlett, son of cofounder Bill Hewlett. She even had to survive a court challenge by Hewlett, who claimed she misled stockholders into voting for the merger.

By August 2003, it looked like the massive merger and the differing cultures were being well assimilated—unlike the problems of many mergers, including several in this book. Was H-P to be the model, a paragon, for bringing together two organizations?

CARLY FIORINA

Carleton (Carly) Fiorina disappointed her father, a federal court judge and law professor, by dropping out of law school after one semester at UCLA. (The name Carleton was a tradition started in the Civil War when her father's family lost all the men named Carleton. In remembrance, each descendant named either a son Carleton or a daughter Cara Carleton. Carly is the ninth Cara Carleton since the Civil War.)

Before dropping law, Fiorina earned a BA in medieval history and philosophy from Stanford University in 1976. She received a MBA in marketing from the University of Maryland in 1980 and a MS from MIT's Sloan School.

She was 44 years old when chosen for the CEO post at Hewlett-Packard, after nearly 20 years at AT&T and Lucent Technologies. At Lucent, she spearheaded the spin-off from AT&T in 1996, overseeing the company's initial public offering and the marketing campaign that positioned Lucent as an Internet company. In 1998, she became president of Lucent's global service-provider business, a $19 billion operation that sold equipment to the world's largest telephone companies.

Fiorina is known for having a "silver tongue and an iron will," being articulate and persuasive. She has a personal touch that inspires intense loyalty, even giving such things as balloons and flowers to employees who land big contracts. Her coddling of customers at Lucent was legendary, as were her sales and marketing skills.[1]

Still, how did a student of philosophy, medieval history, and marketing succeed in being the winning candidate for CEO by H-P's search committee? Each member of the committee listed 20 qualities they would like to see in the new CEO. Then they boiled these down to four essential criteria: the ability to conceptualize and communicate sweeping strategies, the operations savvy to deliver on quarterly financial goals, the power to bring urgency to an organization, and the management skills to drive a nascent Internet vision throughout the company. Carly was selected from 300 potential candidates.[2] She would be the first outsider in the company's history to be CEO; indeed, no other outsiders had even been high-level executives. See the following Issue Box for a discussion of promoting from within.

THE HEWLETT-PACKARD COMPANY (H-P)

H-P was founded by Stanford University classmates Bill Hewlett and Dave Packard in 1938. They invented their company's first product in a tiny Palo Alto, California,

---

ISSUE BOX

SHOULD WE PROMOTE FROM WITHIN?

A heavy commitment to promoting from within, as had long characterized H-P, is sometimes derisively called "inbreeding." The traditional argument against this stand maintains that an organization with such a policy is not alert to needed changes, that it is enamored with the status quo, "the way we have always done it." Proponents of promotion from within talk about the motivation and great loyalty, as well as team spirit, that it engenders, with every employee knowing that he or she has a chance of becoming a high-level executive.

The opposite course of action—that is, heavy commitment to placing outsiders in important executive positions—plays havoc with morale of trainees and lower-level executives and destroys the sense of continuity and loyalty. A middle ground seems preferable: filling many executive positions from within, promoting this idea to encourage the achievement of current executives and the recruiting of trainees, and at the same time bringing the strengths and experiences of outsiders into the organization.

Do you think there are particular circumstances in which one extreme or the other regarding promotion policy might be best? Discuss.

---

[1] Peter Burrows, with Peter Elstrom, "H-P's Carly Fiorina: The Boss," *Business Week Online*, August 2, 1999, pp. 1, 3.

[2] Ibid.

garage. It was an audio oscillator, an electronic test instrument used by sound engineers. One of their first customers was Walt Disney Studios, which purchased the oscillators to develop and test an innovative sound system for the movie *Fantasia*. From 1938 to 1978, Bill and Dave built a company that became a model for thousands of subsequent Silicon Valley enterprises. In so doing, they created an informal egalitarian culture where brilliant engineers could flourish. Their emphasis on teamwork and respect for coworkers was dubbed the "H-P Way."

From 1978 to 1992, John Young directed H-P into becoming a major computer company, something AT&T, Honeywell, RCA, and other first-generation electronics companies never were able to do. But Young's efforts to consolidate H-P's independent units bogged the company down in bureaucracy.

From 1992 to 1999, Lew Platt, a well-liked engineer who had joined the firm in 1966, guided H-P for its growth in the mid-1990s, but he encountered difficulties when PC prices and Asian sales plummeted in the late 1990s. By now, H-P had become a staid company, but one with deep engineering roots and old-fashioned dependability.

THE SITUATION WHEN CARLY FIORINA TOOK OVER

"Some might say we're stodgy, but no one would say this company doesn't have a shining soul," Fiorina said when she took over.[3] H-P had had no major breakthrough product since the inkjet printer in 1984. And the "H-P Way" had evolved into a bureaucratic, consensus-style culture, somehow not conducive to being in the forefront in a time of rapid technological innovations.

A bloated bureaucracy seems a concomitant of many old successful organizations. We have already encountered others in this book, such as Sunbeam, Scott Paper, and Boeing. Examples abound of the bureaucracy run amok that had developed at H-P. The company had 130 different product groups. When retailer Best Buy wanted to buy some computer products, 50 H-P salespeople showed up to push their units' goods. When a vice president at H-P wanted an operational change, 37 different internal committees had to approve it.[4]

The dearth of new products went along with the cumbersome bureaucracy and the many different product groups. Managers often were reluctant to invest in new ideas for fear of missing their sales goals. If the proposed new product did not seem assured of healthy profits or might cannibalize or take away business from existing products, it was not considered further.

The crown jewel of H-P's arsenal of products was its printer business, which it had dominated since the 1980s. Ink and toner refills brought H-P some $10 billion annually, 15 percent of total revenues. The profitability of these refills enabled the company to sell printers at low prices, much as Gillette sells its razors for bare-bones prices, but makes huge profits on the sales of blades.

---

[3] Burrows and Elstrom, p. 1.
[4] Examples cited in Burrows and Elstrom, pp. 4–5.

In 1998, with revenue growth slowing to the low single-digits, CEO Platt began to act more decisively in combating the malaise. He hired McKinsey & Co. consultants to explore restructuring, which led to the spin off of H-P's $8 billion test-and-measurement division, which had little relevance to the faster-growing computer and printer businesses. Platt put his own job on the line, suggesting the board hire a new CEO. This led to Fiorina's hiring.

FIORINA'S ACTIONS

The Merger with Compaq

Fiorina began searching for a big deal soon after becoming CEO. H-P and Compaq agreed to the rough outline of a merger in June 2001, then spent four months planning it before the formal announcement. But she could hardly have expected the controversy of the ensuing merger battle, in which Walter Hewlett, an H-P board member, first voted in favor of the deal and then waged a bitter and public campaign against it. He voted his family's 24 percent of the ballots against the merger, and it passed by only three percentage points. Not content with this defeat, Hewlett sued, charging that Fiorina and H-P had illegally manipulated the vote, but he was unsuccessful and the merger went ahead.

What might have led to serious divisiveness among the organization and particularly the higher executive staff, and made Fiorina's job difficult at best, had more of the opposite effect. While some had initially resented her as an outsider who didn't understand the "H-P Way," now most united behind their controversial new leader. "None of us anticipated the conflict. Carly was characterized as someone who destroyed the soul of H-P, and we were her willing accomplices," Susan Bowick, H-P's personnel chief said as she seethed.[5] Still, we would expect that many employees would resist change, knowing that Fiorina's arrival most likely heralded substantial changes and jobs lost. See the following Information Box for a discussion of resistance to change.

Forcing the Integration with Compaq

The planning and trade-offs that went into merging the two firms may prove to be a model for other successful mergers. One month after the merger announcement, and before it had been officially approved, executives and staff from both firms met to come up with decisions on thousands of matters that would be involved in bringing a smooth integration. This ranged from what product lines to keep to which pension plan to use. The group started with almost 100 employees and grew to 2,500 by the merger's completion. Of the 15 highest ranking executives, 10 were to come from H-P and 5 from Compaq.

When the books of both organizations were opened, striking contrasts became evident: H-P lost $100 million a quarter on an industry-standard product called NetServer but made money on a proprietary model; Compaq had the reverse prob-

---

[5] Quentin Hardy, "We Did It," *Forbes*, August 11, 2003, p. 80.

INFORMATION BOX

RESISTANCE TO CHANGE

People, and organizations, have a natural reluctance to embrace change. Change is disruptive. It can destroy accepted ways of doing things and familiar authority-responsibility relationships. It makes people uneasy because their routines will likely be disrupted, their interpersonal relationships with subordinates, coworkers, and superiors may well be modified. Positions that were deemed important before the change may be downgraded or even eliminated. And persons who view themselves as highly competent in a particular job may be forced to assume unfamiliar duties.

Resistance to change can be combated by good communication with participants about forthcoming changes. Without such communication, rumors and fears can assume massive proportions. Acceptance of change can be facilitated if managers involve employees as fully as possible in planning the changes, solicit and welcome their participation, and if they can be assured that their own positions will not be impaired, only changed. Gradual, rather than abrupt changes, also make a transition smoother, as participants can be initially exposed to the changes without drastic upheavals.

In the final analysis, however, needed changes should not be delayed or canceled because of their possible negative repercussions on the organization. If change is necessary, it should be initiated. Individuals and organizations can adapt to change, although it may take some time.

The worst change an employee may face is layoff. And when no one knows when the next layoff will occur or who will be affected, morale and productivity may be devastated. Discuss how managers might handle the necessity of upcoming layoffs.

lem. H-P's PC (personal computer) sales were mostly from retail, while Compaq had a profitable Web-based business. One company got a better deal from Microsoft on Windows, while the other did better with chips from Intel—these small percentage differences amounted to billions of dollars.

The decision was made early that only one of the two companies' practices in the various areas could be allowed to survive in the new organization, and these changes would not be delayed. The choices involved jobs; the more consolidation, the more jobs lost. For examples: the H-P Jornade handheld was dropped in favor of the Compaq iPAQ; the money-losing H-P NetServer was killed and Compaq's rival Proliant line kept; Compaq's consumer PC business was axed in favor of the H-P business; H-P's corporate PC business was killed and Compaq's kept. Table 10.1 shows how the various product categories of the two firms were meshed.

The companies' four incompatible e-mail systems were consolidated into one, connecting 215,000 PCs and 49,000 other devices. Before the merger, H-P and Compaq had more than a thousand locally set policies on such things as rebates for customers and dental coverage for employees. These were unified into a single set of rules for 160 countries.

TABLE 10.1   **How H-P and Compaq Meshed**

Servers

H-P servers made money on Unix, not Linus.

Compaq made money on Linus, not Unix.

Commercial PCs

Compaq made money. H-P lost.

Consumer PCs

H-P made money. Compaq lost. (In order to maximize retail shelf space, H-P closed the Compaq commercial line but kept the brand.)

Printers

H-P was the world leader. Compaq contracted it out.

Handhelds

Compaq's IPAQ won over H-P's money-losing Jornada.

Software

Compaq had software for individual servers to work harder. H-P had software to manage big groups of servers.

Direct sales over the Internet

Compaq had a $500 million engine. H-P needed one.

Headquarters

Compaq's Houston base was closed. H-P stayed in Palo Alto, California.

Sources: Company; and Quentin Hardy, "We Did It," *Forbes*, August 11, 2003, p. 80.

Commentary: We can see from this meshing of the various products and systems that there was not major duplication. In most areas, where one was weak, the other was strong. The weak one then was eliminated or absorbed. This probably accounted for the success of Fiorina in getting the merger approved by U.S. and European antitrust regulators.

Cost Cutting Through Greater Efficiencies

Opportunities for cost cutting abounded. For examples:

- The old H-P spent $140 million a year for printing documents, manuals, and brochures, with estimates that $50 million of these were unused; expenditures for the combined giant were now reduced to $130 million, with only $10 million of estimated waste.

- H-P's manufacturing costs in the first year of the merger were down 26 percent. All H-P vendors were organized into just five supply chains, and most suppliers were connected to H-P via the Internet and got consumption data and replenished orders automatically, for a saving of $1 billion. Inventory was sliced from 48 days' supply to 40 days, thereby freeing up $1.2 billion in working capital.

- Accounts receivable were shrunk by 4 days, and the faster customer payments freed up $800 million.

- 17,000 jobs were eliminated after the merger.

Through these and other cost savings from the complex merger, Fiorina was able to cut $3.5 billion in annual costs—a billion more and a year earlier than promised.[6]

New Products and New Business

In the first full year after the merger, the results were impressive. Some 3,000 new patents had been racked up and 367 new products introduced. The patents spanned every part of the technology complex, from print technology to molecular computing. H-P gained market share in key categories and won a 10-year $3 billion outsourcing deal with Procter & Gamble. Combined sales to Disney have more than doubled since 2001. H-P built technology for Walt Disney World's newest ride, Mission: Space, and wireless headsets that explained the theme park in five languages.

The sales and profit quarterly results for fiscal 2002 are shown in Table 10.2. The first two quarters reflect the figures for the two companies before the merger, the last two quarters are after the merger. The last quarter's figures, ending October 31, 2002, made Carly Fiorina particularly proud:

> During the fourth quarter of fiscal 2002, we returned to profitability after incurring nearly $3 billion in significant restructuring and other acquisition-related charges, which led to an overall operating loss of $2.5 billion in the third fiscal quarter. The charges were primarily for eliminating redundant positions and offices around the world, in-process research and development, and employee retention bonuses incurred in accordance with the acquisition-integration plans we drew up in the first half of the year.[7]

On the basis of H-P's apparent success in its merger with Compaq, Fiorina began pitching to corporate America that you have to consolidate and you have to cut, and we can help you do it because we have done it ourselves. H-P portrayed itself as The Greatest Case Study Ever Told. In merging its systems with Compaq's, H-P could boast that it had erected a single communications network linking more than a quar-

TABLE 10.2   Quarterly H-P Results Before and After the Merger[a]

	Before Merger		After Merger	
	January 31	April 30	July 31	October 31
Net revenue	$11,383	$10,621	$16,536	$18,048
Earnings (loss) from operations	625	414	(2,476)	425

[a] For fiscal year ended October 31, 2002 (millions).

Source: Hewlett-Packard Company Reports.

Commentary: You can see from this profit realized for the fourth quarter ended October 31, 2002 that Fiorina had reason to feel that the merger had been well orchestrated and the two firms rather quickly integrated. The big loss in the third quarter reflected the extraordinary expenses and write-offs due to the merger, and these were now behind the company as it looked to 2003 and beyond.

[6] Ibid, pp. 76–82.

[7] *H-P Annual Report, 2002*, CEO Carly Fiorina's Statement, January 31, 2003, p. 25.

ter million PCs and handhelds; it handled 26 million e-mails a day. It also cut the number of software applications used from 7,000 to 5,000 and of components bought from 250,000 to 25,000.

We can perform similar miracles for you, Fiorina and her colleagues told such clients as General Electric, the Department of Homeland Security, Walt Disney Company, and many smaller firms. H-P called its approach, "adaptive enterprise," which used new technology and smarter consulting to help organizations lower their overhead. H-P guaranteed in written contracts that its adaptive model would save 15–30 percent in operating costs. H-P claimed its own information technology budget fell 24 percent after the merger by making use of this adaptive approach.

The Threat of IBM

H-P's most awesome competitor to its services and consulting business was IBM. IBM called its approach "on-demand computing," and it was well equipped to dominate this market. While IBM's annual revenue was only $9 billion more than H-P's $72 billion, the market value of its stock at $142 billion was more than twice H-P's. IBM made huge profits, more than double H-P's, even though IBM employed more than twice as many people. IBM was already a major factor in higher-profit services, while H-P still got most of its revenue from such hardware as printers, servers, and PCs, many of these barely covering their costs. In a recent quarter, for example, H-P's $5 billion PC business had a profit margin of only .4 of 1 percent. Furthermore, IBM had several years up on H-P in promoting its Business Consulting Services, part of its $36.3 billion Global Services unit. And it could boast that it also recently slashed $3 billion in costs by selling off three factories, shifting manufacturing to cheaper locations such as China and Ireland, and simplifying product designs. In the process, it reduced inventories by a third, cut suppliers by half, and found other economies such as packaging PCs in cheaper cardboard boxes and recycling components from old mainframes.[8] Table 10.3 shows selected comparisons between IBM and H-P.

Still, H-P could claim one of the fastest and most effective mergers in all of business, and by far the biggest in the computer industry. It saw its adaptive model as a technology and strategy that could be sold to other firms contemplating mergers and strategic changes. The first big test was a $3 billion Procter & Gamble contract, for which the bidding specifications ran 10,000 pages. H-P was the underdog against the likes of IBM and Electronic Data Services. But it won the contract on the first round, selling the potential cost savings, data virtualization, and new across-the-company roles for 2,000 P&G technicians that it agreed to involve in the deal. IBM claimed that H-P took a big future loss on the P&G contract to get a trophy win. "It's good news to hear that," said H-P veteran Ann Livermore, who ran the services business. "They're still underestimating our capabilities."[9]

With this win, selling moved into high gear at H-P. See the following Information Box for a discussion of the importance of selling at all levels of an organization.

[8] Daniel Lyons, "Back on the Chain Gang," *Forbes*, October 13, 2003, pp. 114, 116.
[9] Hardy, p. 82.

TABLE 10.3   IBM and H-P Selected Comparisons, 2002

	IBM	H-P
Sales (000,000)	81,186	63,082
Profits (000,000)	8,060	(680)
Assets (000,000)	96,484	72,093
Annual Cash Flow	$13.8 bil.	$4.8 bil.
Annual R&D	about $5 bil.	about $4 bil.
Total patents	38,000	19,000
Patents in past year	3,288	3,000
Size of sales army	35,000	21,750

Sources: "The Top 500 Companies in America," *Forbes,* April 14, 2003, p. 144; and Quentin Hardy, "We Did It," *Forbes,* August 11, 2003, p. 82.

Commentary: H-P, with the Compaq merger, approaches the size of IBM in sales and in assets. The loss in income is hardly a true comparison with IBM because of the nonrecurring expenses of the merger. H-P shows surprising strength in R&D spending and in patents in the past year. But its much lower cash flow is an impediment against IBM, and the sales staff is far smaller.

INFORMATION BOX

IMPORTANCE OF SELLING AT ALL LEVELS

Whether you are working for a small or a large company, whether you are the lowest employee, a professional sales rep, a high-level corporate executive, or even the CEO, you should always be selling—to employees, customers, your bosses, Wall Street. Maybe you don't even realize it, but what you're really selling is yourself although it may more ostensibly be a product, the company, or an idea.

Carly Fiorina certainly sold herself, to those who could make her CEO—chosen from 300 other candidates. And she sold herself to the organization, if not to Walter Hewett, so that they accepted her and were motivated far beyond what they had been.

Including Fiorina, each of H-P's 15 highest-ranking executives became a seller, as well as a manager, calling on 7 to 15 major customer accounts. For example, Peter Blackmore, a former Compaq top executive, who ran the $11 billion-a-year large computer business, spent almost every weekday on a H-P jet calling on major accounts, and also managed sales reps who brought in as much as $400 million a year each. "The thing you have to learn is the sheer scale of all this. Wherever you are, you have to get each process implanted right, or it won't work. People watch you all the time, your body language—you can't have an off day," he said. But Blackmore further expounded, "It's worth the exhaustion. It took IBM eight years to get their act together. We're going to beat them in two or three."

Do you agree with this assessment of the importance of selling at all levels in an organization. Can you think of some exceptions?

Sources: Adapted from Carol Hymowitz, "Business Leaders List Books That Inspire and Inform Their Work," *Wall Street Journal,* October 14, 2003, p. B1; and Quentin Hardy, "We Did It," *Forbes,* August 11, 2003, pp. 80, 82.

WAS THE "SUCCESSFUL" MERGER TRULY SO?

Skeptics of the H-P merger with Compaq, for a while, appeared to be proven wrong. CEO Fiorina impressed analysts with cost cuts faster and deeper than they had ever imagined. She unveiled a host of new consumer products and new vision. Investors were willing to attribute anemic revenue growth to the deep recession in technological spending.

As the economy and stock market began to improve in 2003, H-P stock flirted with a 52-week high of $24 a share until August 20, the day after H-P announced it had missed its third-quarter earnings expectations because of slack European markets, which accounted for 40 percent of company sales, plus price cutting in personal computers and weakness in H-P's enterprise businesses. The stock slid 11 percent on this news.

Dell was the big culprit affecting H-P's computer sales, and it had turned in a strong quarter, by contrast. H-P failed to raise PC prices fast enough to keep pace with such components as computer memory. It also missed the boat in forecasting sales for flat-panel computer screens and had to use expensive air freight to meet the demand. Then Dell announced it was cutting prices of business computers by 22 percent.[10]

Fiorina planned to excite consumers, who had been steadier customers than corporate clients—consumer-related sales comprised 30 percent of total H-P sales—with 150 new products in time for the back-to-school and Christmas seasons 2003. H-P was also testing a "store-in-store" concept at consumer electronics retailers, such as Circuit City. The H-P area, within these larger retailers, would emphasize how all the H-P products can work together, with assortments well beyond just PCs and printers, for example, media-center PCs that link home entertainment and computers together. But adding to H-P's worries, Dell recently announced that it would cut prices on its personal computers and network servers. Sales for H-P's personal-systems division, which included notebooks and desktops, rose 4.5 percent in the third quarter, but the division remained unprofitable.

Printers and ink refills have long carried H-P, with rising sales and profits. Yet the enterprise-systems group that generated about 20 percent of total revenue remained the last of H-P's four main businesses to still be in the red as fiscal 2003 drew to a close. The turnaround of the systems group, which made server computers, storage devices, and related software used by large corporations and agencies, was plagued by competition from Dell and IBM, and slow tech spending by corporate customers. Unless this could quickly be turned around, it would represent a continuing black mark on the controversial $19 billion Compaq purchase, which was partly undertaken to repair the enterprise business.[11]

Whether the merger with Compaq was a model of how best to handle mergers remains controversial and questionable.

---

[10] Quentin Hardy, "HP Slips Up," *Forbes,* September 15, 2003, p. 42.

[11] For more details, see Amy Tsao, "Carly Fiorina's Next Big Challenge," *Business Week Online,* August 22, 2003; and Pui-Wing Tam, "Man on the Hot Seat at H-P's Struggling Enterprise Unit," *Wall Street Journal,* August 19, 2003, pp. B1, B5.

UPDATE 2005

The situation—and especially the stock price of H-P—had not improved by the beginning of 2005. The closing price by end of January was under $20 a share, which was 15 percent less than when the Compaq deal was announced in September 2001, and 50 percent less than when Fiorina was named CEO in July 1999. (Admittedly, the tech sector had not been robust in the previous four years, but H-P had fallen considerably more than its major competitors, IBM and Dell.) The H-P board began considering a reorganization that would distribute some key day-to-day responsibilities of Fiorina to other executives. "She has tremendous abilities" one person close to the situation said. "But she shouldn't be running everything every day. She is very hands on, and that slows things down."[12]

Other criticisms centered on the Compaq merger. This was Fiorina's "Get-Big" strategy to compete with IBM. But it seemed to have led to complex and myriad problems. H-P's PC unit was taking a beating from Dell. It found itself faltering against IBM in servicing big corporate clients and had been unable to come up with any big new consumer gadgets. A controversy was brewing whether H-P would be better off broken into pieces, rather than keeping the company whole. The example of IBM was given to support breaking up: "IBM had the courage recently to exit the bleak PC business. By contrast, H-P continued to hold fast."[13]

H-P's Board Ousts Fiorina

Abruptly on February 9, 2005, the board fired Fiorina, after she resisted the directors' plan for her to cede some day-to-day authority to the heads of H-P's key business units. This was just before she had been scheduled to attend a meeting at the White House with members of the Business Roundtable. Just a few weeks later, H-P reported a 10 percent increase in revenue for its first fiscal quarter, better than expected.

ANALYSIS

Unlike many other mergers such as Snapple in Chapter 15 and Newell Rubbermaid in Chapter 16 that quickly proved sour, H-P's merger with Compaq at first seemed a qualified success, even though the combined company still had profitability problems. After all, despite being larger now, it still faced the formidable competition of IBM and Dell Computer. The boom in corporate high-tech spending ended, and long-term growth prospects for the industry no longer seemed robust, while a number of marginal firms were on the ropes. With the merger, H-P would seem poised to take advantage of a revival of corporate interest and perhaps a regeneration of con-

[12] Pui Wing Tam, "Hewlett-Packard Board Considers a Reorganization," *Wall Street Journal*, January 24, 2005, pp. A1, A5.

[13] Jesse Eisinger, "Carly Fiorina Fails at Hewlett-Packard After Betting Badly," *Wall Street Journal*, January 26, 2005, pp. C1, C2; and, Ben Elgin, "Carly's Challenge," *Business Week*, December 13, 2004, pp. 98–108.

sumer interest from appealing new products. All the while, H-P still dominated the high-profit ink-refill market. We can identify these major factors that seemed to promise a successful merger:

- *First of all, it was not a hostile acquisition.* Both parties believed coming together would strengthen the resulting firm, making it a bigger power in the market, and bringing substantial cost savings.

- *Thorough and objective planning of the merger.* For four months before the merger was even announced, a top-level committee was studying the feasibility and planning for the integration of the two organizations. After the approval of the merger, months more of detailed preparation were involved. All conceivable problems or stumbling points were identified and resolved, with prompt implementation once the merger was officially approved.

- *Involvement of executives and staffs of both firms.* The study group began with not quite 100 employees and had 2,500 by the merger's completion. Top-level executives and staffs of both firms participated, in apparently a spirit of equality and objectivity, and many stayed with the new organization.

- *Redundancies were avoided at all costs.* Early disagreements or indecisions were curbed by H-P strategist Robert Napier. "Every business decision triggers an IT (information technology) event," he declared. Such would force the new H-P to reconfigure its systems, which would be costly and time consuming. So the commitment was made to pick just one of the two companies' products and practices and make it law. The new merger mantra became: "Adopt and go."[14]

- *Compatibility and congeniality were sought.* Fiorina joined the rather close-knit H-P as an outsider and had to strive to gain acceptance. The bitter merger battle with Walter Hewlett served to unite most of the organization behind Fiorina. The goodwill apparently carried over with the acceptance of Compaq employees as part of the H-P team, even though some 17,000 jobs were eliminated because of redundancies.

Fiorina admitted that one of the toughest aspects of the integration was the reduction of workforce through a combination of layoffs, early retirements, and attrition. "Although layoffs are never easy, we worked hard to conduct this process with dignity and compassion, recognizing the many contributions our employees had made during their careers."[15]

Monday-Morning Quarterbacking After the Ouster

Perhaps Fiorina could have been a better administrator. Heading a $56 billion firm, perhaps she needed to delegate more, not be too hands-on. This lack of delegation is not an uncommon fault of executives, but it can limit their effectiveness in higher

[14] Quentin Hardy, p. 81.
[15] *H-P's 2002 Annual Report*, p. 23.

positions. She resisted the idea of any assistant or vice chairman, and maybe this should have been reconsidered. She was in a difficult situation, with the might of Dell in PCs, and the powerful IBM at the other extreme of the industry. Add to this a resentful Walter Hewlett who was still influential with the board, and perhaps Fiorina's doom was sealed. (At the end of the chapter in the hands-on and debate exercises, we will invite students to address Fiorina's situation in 2005 before the abrupt termination decision, and also whether the company should be broken up as some experts think, perhaps into printing and nonprinting operations, or into consumer and corporate businesses.)

People were quick to judgment in the days following the ouster news. Shareholders blamed her for the sagging stock price. Long-term employees condemned her for upsetting the company's paternalistic culture. Industry analysts faulted her for H-P's sluggish computer business. While Fiorina was a dynamic and charismatic leader who was widely esteemed in the business world, yet inside H-P her rather autocratic management style stirred deep animosity from some employees, and several high-level executives had quit for other positions. Reports were that reactions to her ouster led to "jubilant" champagne toasts.[16]

Any analysis of the merits of the ouster of such a top executive, the highest profile woman CEO, would have to wait for the one who follows her and any resulting turnaround success.

WHAT CAN BE LEARNED?

Don't Rush Into the Merger or Acquisition

Major blunders occur when firms spend billions of dollars for acquisitions without careful research and reasoned judgment. Sometimes it seems that CEOs are throwing around shareholders' money for a crap shoot. Sometimes it seems they get so caught up in the acquisitions game, especially if another firm is also interested in the acquisition, that a bidding war drives up prices beyond the reasonable.

Enough time should be taken to ensure what is a fair price and where the limit should be. Enough research needs to be done to prevent surprises. Ideally, the investigation should go beyond the numbers and records—the quantitative data— and look for qualitative from employees, customers, and suppliers. For example, does the firm and its brands have a good reputation, a so-so one, or a negative one? Such information can hardly be gained in just a few weeks.

How Compatible Are the Two Organizations?

While complete compatibility is hardly possible, especially in hostile acquisitions, it should be a major factor in the decision. Compatibility encompasses not only

---

[16] Pui-Wing Tam, "Fallen Star: H-P's Board Ousts Fiorina as CEO," *Wall Street Journal*, February 10, 2005, pp. A1, A8.

personnel in the two organizations and any cultural differences that may make assimilation difficult, but products, distribution channels, ways of doing business, and a number of other factors. We will see in several other cases in this book the lack of compatibility and the nasty surprises that came from this.

Redundancies Should Be Identified and Decisions Made About Them

We saw in this case superb attention given to identifying redundant products and operations and the decisions to remove these duplications. Sometimes H-P's product or way of doing things was eliminated, other times Compaq's. The issues were already being decided before the merger was even announced. Such efforts brought profitable integration of the merger within a year.

One major argument for a merger is that two firms can thereby streamline separate operations by combining their various entities into one. For example, two separate sales forces might be combined into one; similarly with such staff departments as information technology, human resource departments, and the like. Therefore, total costs should be less than they would be with two separate firms. If the matter of redundancy is not quickly resolved, any cost benefits of the merger are delayed. Yet, sometimes the result of a poorly researched merger is an indigestible mess.

Assumptions Should Be Defended

It is easy when caught up in the merger game, especially in a bidding war, to assume all kinds of optimistic things, such as a synergy that does not exist, a compatibility that can never be achieved, a sales potential that is not to be realized. Optimistic assumptions have no place in merger decisions. So much money is involved, so much executive and staff time will be needed, that the bad merger decision can torment the firm and its shareholders for years to come. Objectivity and conservative projections seem called for.

Top management should insist that assumptions and their reasoning be defended, at least as much as possible in an uncertain future. It might be prudent to consider a worst-case scenario: What if? The use of a Devil's Advocate—one who takes an opposing position for the sake of bringing out all aspects of a particular course of action—can often be very worthwhile, yet is so seldom utilized.

The Power of a Charismatic Leader

Carly Fiorina was a charismatic leader. Even though new to the H-P organization, she seemed able to motivate employees and managers to jump-start the innovation machine, to escape the staid and bureaucratic culture that had crept into the organization in recent years. She appeared able to get key people in both firms to support the Compaq merger and to work together to make it work. Mergers can succeed without charisma, but it helps if enthusiasm and commitment can be instilled. Yet a charismatic leader can make enemies and can arouse jealousies that undermine and detract. One wonders if there was not some of this present in the H-P organization.

CONSIDER

Can you think of other learning insights?

QUESTIONS

1. We noted the four criteria the H-P search committee for the new CEO proposed. Do you think "human relations skills" should have been a fifth? Why or why not? Can you think of other criteria that might have been added?

2. "Tradition has no place in corporate thinking today." Discuss this statement.

3. Giant organizations are often plagued with cumbersome bureaucracies. Discuss how this tendency could be prevented as an organization grows to a large size over many years.

4. Playing a Devil's Advocate (one who takes an opposing position for the sake of examining all aspects of a decision), present the case against the Compaq merger. (You may want to research the arguments raised by Walter Hewlett in his aggressive campaign against the merger.)

5. "H-P is gouging the consumer in charging such high prices for its ink refill cartridges. Sure, it's a high profit item, but such profits cross the line and are obscene." Discuss.

6. Do you think the 17,000 jobs lost in the merger was laudatory, or should it be condemned? What would swing your opinion?

7. Should all redundancies be eliminated? Can you think of any that might be worth continuing?

HANDS-ON EXERCISES

1. You have been asked by Carly Fiorina to draw up a rationale for eliminating 17,000 jobs. She wants this to be as tactful and persuasive as possible.

2. Be a Devil's Advocate and argue against the elimination of 17,000 jobs.

3. Michael Dell, founder and CEO of Dell Computer, has his sights set on invading H-P's lucrative printer and ink refill business. As an advisor to Carly Fiorina, what action, if any, would you recommend H-P take to try to thwart Dell's incursion? Be prepared to support your recommendations.

4. Place yourself in the position of Carly Fiorina at the beginning of 2005 facing a critical board, skeptical stockholders, and a negative press. Lay out your strategy to protect your position. Do you think this would have saved her job? Why or why not?

TEAM DEBATE EXERCISES

1. The search committee for a new CEO is seriously considering Carly Fiorina. Based on the information in the case, debate the controversy: should we hire this woman who is an outsider, or look for someone else among our 300 candidates?

2. In the planning for the implementation of the merger, it has been proposed that all redundancies should be eliminated, that any commonalities of products and practices be resolved by axing one and combining into the other. Debate this draconian proposal.

3. Debate the controversy of breaking up H-P into two or three separate units. For the group proposing the breakup, you will need to specify which parts should be spun off, and why.

INVITATION TO RESEARCH

How has H-P's operating performance fared in 2005 and beyond? Has the stock price risen above the low to middle 20s?

Who succeeded Fiorina as chief executive? What is his or her background? Has a turnaround been achieved yet?

Whatever happened to Walter Hewlett?

What is Fiorina doing now?

CHAPTER ELEVEN

Toys "R" Us: Trying to Defend Against Wal-Mart

*C*harles Lazarus was generally regarded as a genius who originated the *category killer* concept with his Toys "R" Us stores. He pioneered offering a huge variety of toys at very good prices (even if service left something to be desired), and this spawned a host of imitators with other categories of goods. The concept was so potent that it wiped out most other toy stores and even department stores that had long featured toys at Christmastime. Department stores settled for only a few token and hoped-for best-selling items.

With such a powerful concept, how could any non-category killer stores compete? Yet times were changing.

THE HEADY YEARS

The Beginning

Charles Lazarus was 22 years old when he borrowed $2,000 to open a baby furniture store. World War II had ended, and a baby boom was beginning. His first store was barely 40 ft. by 60 ft. Later, the idea for a toy store came from a customer wanting to buy baby toys.

In 1957, he opened the first toy supermarket. Discount stores were just beginning to emerge on the retail scene, and Lazarus's stores brought the discount format to a new category of goods. In the late 1970s, Lazarus took Toys "R" Us public.

Toys "R" Us (TRU) became the largest and fastest-growing toy and children's specialty chain in the world. Its earnings grew an astonishing 40 percent each year between 1978 and 1983. Between 1985 and 1992, TRU opened an average of 43 toy stores each year in the United States, 17 more overseas, and 26 Kids "R" Us apparel stores. In so doing, it pushed some rivals into bankruptcy and then snapped up their best store sites.

See the following information box for more discussion of the category killer phenomenon.

INFORMATION BOX

CATEGORY KILLER STORES

A category killer store is the ultimate in specialty stores. It carries only a limited number of product categories but offers tremendous choice within those categories. Category killers get their name from the strategy of carrying such a huge assortment of merchandise at good prices in a particular category of goods that they destroy the competition.

For example, Sportmart, a Chicago-based sporting goods chain, offered customers a choice of 70 models of sleeping bags, 265 styles of socks, and 15,000 fishing lures. The big category killer bookstores of Borders and Barnes & Noble have some 100,000 book titles in stock, and a host of magazines. Table 11.1 lists major category specialists.

TABLE 11.1   Major Category Specialists, 1996

Company	Sales (millions)	Number of Stores
Home Furnishings		
Bed, Bath & Beyond	$ 601	80
Linens-n-Things	554	145
IKEA US	511	13
Crafts		
Michaels	1,295	442
Fabri-Centers	835	936
Books		
Barnes & Noble	1,349	358
Borders	684	116
Sporting Goods		
Sports Authority	1,046	136
Sports and Recreation	526	80
Pet Supply		
PETsMART	1,030	262
Office Supply		
Office Depot	5,300	504
Staples	3,068	443
Office Max	2,543	468
Computers		
CompUSA	2,813	96
Computer City	1,800	99
Consumer Electronics		
Best Buy	7,200	251
Circuit City	7,030	719

Sources: "DSN Top 200," *Discount Store News,* July 1, 1996, and "State of the Industry," *Chain Store Age Executive,* August 1996, Section 2.

Commentary: Why do you suppose there are no apparel category killer stores? Or are there?

Do you think the category killer superstores could result in overkill in that they offer customers too much variety? Do you see any negative implications for a bookstore offering 100,000 different titles, or a sporting goods store with 70 different sleeping bags?

The stores were usually built in uniform dimensions, with this standardization lowering architectural costs, purchasing of fixtures, and such other costs as inventory and manpower requirements. Company executives also believed such standardization minimized customer confusion. The stores stocked some 18,000 items throughout the year, in sharp contrast to most competitors who shrunk their toy departments right after Christmas.

The year-round commitment of TRU not only generated significant sales volume throughout the year but also had two further advantages: (1) It secured advantageous terms from toymakers who quickly saw TRU as the major factor in the market who also provided some leveling of the extreme seasonality and (2) TRU could determine which toys would be hot sellers in the coming peak Christmas selling season, and order accordingly. The competitive advantage over traditional toy retailers was awesome.

The company gained a whopping 25 percent share of toy retailing in the United States by 1990 and now turned its attention overseas. It pulled off a coup in 1991, breaking into the Japanese market, a market notorious for barriers to entry, especially to discount firms. Japanese consumers flocked to TRU, and in 1992 Michael Goldstein, then vice chairman, predicted that foreign sales would exceed $10 billion by 2000.[1]

The vast buying power of TRU brought prosperity to the major toy manufacturers, in particular, Mattel and Hasbro. For much of the past 15 years, these had grown together with TRU. They acquired smaller manufacturers but cut back on new toy development while funneling more money into movie and TV-licensed products. And they relied on TRU to be the sales engine. In the process, they spurned smaller toy departments and stores.

In these years it seemed that nothing could really compete against the category killer retailers.

As 1998 began, TRU operated or franchised 1,454 stores that emphasized products for children. The flagship TRU chain included 698 stores in the United States and 441 in overseas markets. Its Kids "R" Us clothing chain had 215 domestic units. In 1997, the company purchased a 77-store chain, Baby Superstores. It changed the name to Babies "R" Us and quickly grew this to 98 stores, making it the country's largest baby-store chain. It had also opened two megastores called KidsWorld. These combined a toy store, a baby store, a clothing store, a shoe store, a restaurant, a candy store, and a kids' hair salon—two acres of floorspace. But these stores were too big for most customers, and no new ones were opened.

Sales for 1997 (actually fiscal year ending January 31, 1998) reached $11 billion, which was an 11-percent increase over the previous year.

CLOUDS ON THE HORIZON

By the early 1990s, the environment for toys began to change, a change not recognized very quickly by TRU management.

---

[1] Paul Klebnikov, "Trouble in Toyland," *Forbes*, June 1, 1998, p. 60.

In 1994, Charles Lazarus, now 74, handed the reins to Michael Goldstein, but the facade of invincibility was beginning to crumble. Discount chains such as Wal-Mart, Kmart, and Target began using toys as loss leaders, pricing them at cost or below in order to attract customer traffic to purchase regular markup items. Warehouse clubs like Sam's Club, Costco, and BJ's Wholesale Club also were moving into the toy business. At the other end of the market, small chains emphasizing educational toys and interactive shopping for the smaller fry were growing fast; these included Zany Brainy and Noodle Kidoodle.

All of a sudden, TRU was being tormented by price competition more severe than it had ever seen. As a double whammy, it was also beset by competitors' service and decor—aimed at making shopping a desirable experience for parents and kids—beyond anything that its bare-bones boxy stores had ever considered. Its big competitive advantage, vast assortments, was still there. But customers began to be drawn by other shopping considerations, not the least of which was avoiding the long waits at TRU cash registers.

At a Wal-Mart, the merchandise assortment may be one 16-inch bicycle instead of the half dozen at TRU. But the bicycle is less expensive, the store is clean and pleasant, and the sales clerks courteous and usually far more knowledgeable than those at TRU, who often were strained to even direct a customer to the right aisle in the cavernous building.

In efforts not to be too badly outpriced by the discounters, the operating margins of TRU slipped from 12 percent to 8 percent over the 4 years from 1994 to 1998. But still it could not match the prices of Wal-Mart and other discounters.

Michael Goldstein tried to use his market clout to discourage the big toy manufacturers such as Mattel and Hasbro from selling to the warehouse clubs. This brought charges of anticompetitive practices by the Federal Trade Commission.

In 1996, Goldstein tried to react to the nicer decor of his new competitors. He instituted Concept 2000, a remodeling plan for the old utilitarian stores. As much as resources would allow, those stores selected were designed to be less cluttered, to be cleaner and brighter with nicer displays and fixtures, and to have better customer service. Books, videogames, Barbie dolls, and Legos were given separate departments. The cost of such rejuvenation averaged $1.5 million per store.

But the new concept didn't work. For the money spent, the return on investment was not positive, and most sales gains turned out to be disappointing. Eventually only 15 percent of the stores were remodeled; the rest remained the old warehouse-like boxes.

Even the international operations soured. The seeming coup in 1991 of breaking into the Japanese market, leading to the optimism of Goldstein for foreign sales exceeding $10 billion by 2000, was an acute disappointment. For 1997, foreign sales were only $3 billion. What went wrong?

For one thing, the TRU format needed cheap land and big parking lots, conditions seldom met in most foreign environments, whether Far East or Europe. Furthermore, labor laws and regulations were often stifling. TRU found that its operating margins suffered overseas: 6 percent compared to 8 percent in the United States. So this business proved less profitable than expected.[2]

2 Klebnikov, p. 60.

The Storm Descends

Things came to a head in March 1998. TRU announced earnings of $490 million, or $1.70 a share, for the year ended January 31, way below analysts' expectations. This reflected a loss in market share of toy retailing from 25 percent in 1990 to 20 percent. TRU soon announced inventory cutbacks, store closings, and work force cuts. In so doing, it took a $495 million charge. Efforts to reduce inventories involved another $500 million.[3]

Profitability problems continued. In the first half of the next fiscal year, operating profit fell more than 30 percent. In the third quarter, income fell 50 percent.

Losing the Clout

As the largest toy seller, TRU had enjoyed tremendous clout with its suppliers. It was their largest single customer by far. Now this was changing. With the inventory cutbacks announced in 1998, Hasbro and Mattel faced drastic cutbacks in profits themselves. For example, Mattel's second-quarter 1998 sales to TRU were off $72 million, contributing to an 11 percent fall in second-quarter earnings for Mattell.[4]

Not surprising, Mattel sought to reduce its dependency on TRU. For 1998, TRU was expected to account for 15 percent of Mattel's sales, down from 18 percent in 1997, and 22 percent in 1996. Sales to Wal-Mart, on the other hand, were up to 15 percent in 1997 from 12 percent in 1996.[5] Hasbro's sales to TRU were down even more: $125 million for the first half of 1998, and expected to be down as much as $200 million for the full year.[6]

Such drastic cutbacks brought on by TRU's weaknesses suggested continuing problems for the company as suppliers were driven into the camps of major competitors, most notably Wal-Mart. The deteriorating market share of TRU would hardly be easy to turn around for it had lost its momentum to this most aggressive of all competitors.

EFFORTS TO REVITALIZE

Two weeks into 1998, Michael Goldstein relinquished operating command to Robert Nakasone, 50, who had joined the firm in 1985.

Nakasone proposed a major revamping. Inventories would be streamlined and reduced with heavy markdowns to clear out slow-selling goods and overstocks. Some of the problems with inventories were a consequence of TRU stockrooms being a mess. The company averaged less than four inventory turns a year, compared with

---

[3] Joseph Pereira, "Hasbro to Buy Galook, Issues Earnings Warning," *Wall Street Journal*, September 29, 1998, p. B4.

[4] Lisa Bannon, "Mattel Cuts Forecast for Yearly Profit in Wake of Toys 'R' Us Restructuring," *Wall Street Journal*, September 25, 1998, p. B8.

[5] Ibid.

[6] Pereira, p. B4.

INFORMATION BOX

IMPACT OF MERCHANDISE TURNOVER ON PROFITABILITY

Let us compare a Toys "R" Us store with a Target store of the same sales volume. The TRU store has a turnover of 4, while Target has 8 turns.

Toys "R" Us:

Sales	$12,000,000
Net profit percentage	5%
Net profit dollars	$600,000
Stock turnover	4
Average stock investment	$\dfrac{12,000,000}{4} = 3,000,000$
Profitability as measured by return on investment, without considering investment in store and fixtures)	$\dfrac{600,000}{3,000,000} = 20\%$

Target:

Sales	$12,000,000
Net profit percent	5%
Net profit dollars	600,000
Stock turnover	8
Average stock investment	$\dfrac{12,000,000}{8} = 1,500,000$
Return on investment	$\dfrac{600,000}{1,500,000} = 40\%$

Therefore, the store with the higher stock turnover will be more profitable; it can also lower prices and still be as profitable or more so than its competitor with the lower turnover.

Note: To simplify this example, inventory investment is figured at retail price, rather than cost, which would technically be more correct. However, the significance of increasing turnover is more easily seen here.

Why does a store like Target (or Wal-Mart) have so much higher a merchandise turnover than TRU? What could TRU do to improve its turnover?

seven turns at Wal-Mart and eight turns at Target Stores.[7] The preceding Information Box shows the importance of high inventory turnover on profitability.

Nakasone also announced that the work force would be slashed by as much as 3,000 or 2.8 percent, and 50 underperforming toy stores, mostly in Germany and France, but also nine in the United States, would be closed. Also, 31 of the 214 Kids "R" Us clothing stores in the United States were to be closed and some distribution centers.

Nakasone pinned hopes for the future on TRU's new C-3 stores, with nine such stores being tested for the Christmas season in Georgia, Tennessee, and North Carolina. If results were encouraging, he planned in 1999 to upgrade 200 of the 697 U.S. toy stores to this format, with most of the rest in 2000. The conversion would cost about $500,000 per store, considerably less than the $1.5 million of the Concept 2000 redesign. Much was at stake in the nine test stores. (Pity the employees of these stores: We would expect home office executives to be underfoot during the Christmas season.)

The new C-3 stores included a reduction in the back room space by 18 percent and a reorganization of the store's layout to feature more departmental display of goods. They were touted as more customer friendly, cost-effective, and a concept with a long-term vision.[8]

To enhance shareholder value, the Board of Directors approved a $1 billion share repurchase program.

Following the company announcement of its charges to restructure its store base and reduce inventory levels, credit-rating agency Standard & Poor's on September 16, 1998, placed the debt of the company on a CreditWatch with negative implications for borrowing and interest rates.

Standard & Poor's was also concerned about the company's use of excess cash flow and short-term borrowing to aggressively repurchase shares.[9]

NEARING THE END?

During Christmas 2003, Wal-Mart, already the biggest toy retailer, having knocked TRU out of first place, moved to increase its market share even more. It drastically reduced prices on many of the hottest toys in late September, long before the peak selling season. This essentially denied TRU and its smaller competitors a profitable Christmas season as they were forced to match these low prices or lose more of their customers. As a result, two major toy chains, famed FAO Schwarz, along with its Zany Brainy and Right Start stores, and KB Toys filed for bankruptcy protection, unable to match Wal-Mart's prices. TRU also suffered, seeing its share of the U.S. retail toy market slip from 25 percent in the late 1980s to just 15 percent as Wal-Mart now commanded 25 percent of this market. TRU faced a major decision of whether it should even continue in the toy business.

---

[7] Klebnikov, p. 56.

[8] William M. Bulkeley, "Toys 'R' Us to Take Big Charge, Cut Jobs and Close 59 Stores," *Wall Street Journal,* September 17, 1998, p. A4; and Laura Liebeck, "Toys 'R' Us Shakes It Up," *Discount Store News,* October 5, 1998, p. 1.

[9] Bulkeley, p. A4.

In August 2004, the company announced that it was indeed exploring selling its core 1,200-store toy chain. At the very least, it was planning a possible spinoff of toys from its smaller but faster growing Babies "R" Us unit that was growing by 20 percent a year with very good profit margins.

Its first Babies "R" Us stores opened in 1997 and had the same effect on the established inefficient baby products retailers as TRU did in beating up small toy retailers several decades before. The Babies unit, by fiscal 2003, had grown to nearly 200 stores in the United States and had operating earnings of $202 million, up 16 percent from the year before. Its revenues were about 15 percent of the parent company's fiscal 2003 revenues of $11.4 billion.

Suppliers to the Rescue

As the 2004 Christmas peak selling season drew closer, some of TRU's key suppliers moved to help out. They gave TRU a number of their best toys for exclusive selling— that is Wal-Mart, Target, and the other major retailers would not have them to discount. Furthermore, the manufacturers would foot most of the costs of their TV commercials that would stress, "Available exclusively at Toys "R" Us."

Why would these toymakers volunteer to do this? After all, wouldn't they risk antagonizing the Wal-Mart behemoth? One toy-company executive said, "Toys 'R' Us is the industry's lifeblood. As Toys 'R' Us goes, so do we." A further-weakened TRU would mean an even more powerful Wal-Mart, a firm notorious among suppliers for driving down prices, while TRU historically had been more accommodating, and with its 10,000 products had by far the broadest merchandise assortment in the industry.[10]

Will this make a difference in TRU's stated plans to segregate its major businesses into separate companies in 2005?

ANALYSIS

Disregard for Market Changes

TRU never detected looming significant changes in the marketplace. This is an example of the unfortunate mind-set that success guarantees continued success, that nothing needs to change.

So, for a crucial decade and a half it changed neither its stores nor its way of doing business. Sure, it opened more stores, all the same boxy warehouses. Sure, it diversified into babies and kids apparel stores, again with the same type of store. And it reached for overseas markets, as most firms were wont to do. But its operational strategy remained basically the same.

In particular, TRU ignored changes in

- competition
- consumer tastes

[10] Compiled from Joseph Pereira, Bob Tomsho, and Ann Zimmerman, "Toys 'Were' Us?" *Wall Street Journal*, August 12, 2004, pp. B1, B2; Joseph Pereira and Ann Zimmerman, "Toys 'R' Us Suppliers Pitch In," *Wall Street Journal*, November 10, 2004, pp. B1, B2.

By the 1990s, new competitors were emerging. They were nothing like the small independents or the underfinanced imitators of TRU of the 1970s and 80s or the department stores for whom toys were only a seasonal sideline. Now TRU faced the might of a Wal-Mart, or a Target, or warehouse clubs enlarging their toy departments, as well as the creative merchandising of slick toy chains such as Zany Brainy. It had become a victim of its own success. The profits piling up at TRU brought all these rivals salivating to get a piece of the action. And TRU had become flabby and inefficient.

With more attractive shopping alternatives, more and more consumers were becoming dissatisfied with the poor service and the lack of amenities at TRU. In an era of prosperity, greater choice (which TRU still offered, the major competitive advantage it had managed to hold onto) became not as strong a patronage factor as better prices, nicer decor, better service, and excitement/entertainment.

Inability to Be Competitive with Prices

TRU's operating efficiency had worsened over the years. The caliber of employees in its stores was not particularly high, reflecting a misguided cost containment. Undoubtedly, operating procedures and computer technology were not on the cutting edge. As a result, TRU was vulnerable when aggressive, and very efficient competitors came on the scene. The inefficiency of TRU was most evident in inventory control and a much lower turnover than these new competitors. Many store stockrooms were a mess, and control inadequacies led to huge overstocks of some goods and stockouts of others. The efficient inventory control technology of firms like Wal-Mart enabled them to sell profitably at lower prices than TRU could match without straining profit margins.

The Burden of Older Facilities

Half of the TRU toy stores in the United States were built before 1989, and more than half of the Kids "R" Us stores.[11] Many of these were much older than 10 years. Its stores were consequently more dated than most of the newer competitors. In retrospect, we can criticize TRU management for not having established a systematic program for rejuvenating older facilities. But in the eagerness to open ever more new stores, it is easy to understand how older ones were given low priority for attention and funding. Still, this was a crucial flaw in the competitive struggle, and one that brought the need for a major catch-up program, but with it a dilemma in allocating scarce resources.

The Down Side of Buyback Programs

TRU instituted a major buyback program for its common stock. The motivation for buybacks of this kind is that profits can be distributed over fewer shares, thus making earnings per share higher to the benefit of investors. However, this is a temporary palliative at best. While it suggests that current stock market valuations of the firm

---

[11] *1998 Toys "R" Us Annual Report*, p. 2

are too low, it also raises the suspicion that management sees less payoff in investing for future growth, that it is indeed repudiating a growth strategy.

THE ANSWER TO TRU'S PROBLEMS

At this stage in the life cycle of TRU, it appeared to face three alternatives if it were to overcome a pervasive declining trend in market position and profits.

1. Stronger expansion abroad. It already had, as of the beginning of 1998, 441 stores overseas or 30 percent of all stores. This was a substantial overseas presence, but these stores had lower operating profits—6 percent vs. 8 percent—than the domestic stores, primarily because of labor and other regulations and land expenses. Furthermore, as the new millennium approached, the economic situation in many countries was less promising.

2. Meet discount stores on price. Given the relative inefficiencies of TRU compared to Wal-Mart and the other major competitors, this could hardly be achieved without a revolution in its inventory control and operating procedures. Even if it can do this, TRU will most likely only be matching the efficiency of competitors and not be gaining a competitive advantage. With major discount competitors using toys as loss leaders, at least during the peak Christmas selling season, a price advantage for TRU can probably never be achieved. But after the disaster of Christmas 2003, TRU needed to meet the prices of Wal-Mart and Target on the leader items. At the same time, it can seek to find as much exclusivity as possible.

3. Upscaling. This option on a large scale would have severe cost consequences. Profits would be drastically affected. But TRU may have no choice but to do some modest scaling up. It must consider getting away from the worst features of the drab warehouse box stores, and the poor service of low-paid employees.

TRU may have another option. Not every toy shopper during the hectic Christmas season is a fanatic about getting the absolutely lowest price. Convenience and a good assortment may be more important. Wal-Mart and Target typically are making loss leaders of only a few of what they think are the best-selling toys. Nothing says that TRU has to meet these killer prices. Sure, it will lose some sales, but it could salvage a profitable season.

Finally—TRU may have to recognize that its category killer concept was great in its time but now has become rusty as a vehicle for continued growth in toy retailing. Some moderation of extreme assortment may be more desirable today. Should this experience be sobering for other category killer stores?

But is giving up the toy business altogether the answer?

LATE-BREAKING NEWS

On St. Patrick's Day, 2005, a deal was announced for a $6.6 billion buyout of TRU by a group of two private-equity firms, Bain Capital and the famed buyout firm Kohlberg Kravis Roberts (KKR), as well as a real estate trust, Vornado. After a seven-month auction in which TRU wanted to sell off the faltering toy business from its more lucrative Babies "R" Us segment, KKR et al. wanted the whole firm. They would make TRU a privately-held company that would free executives from the pressure of quarterly earnings reports. "It will help them become a more streamlined operation with diverse products, not just toys, but lifestyle products," Chris Byrne, a toy consultant noted.

Still, part of the attractiveness of TRU to these well-heeled buyers was as a real-estate play. While the operating potential would not be neglected, "Real estate is always going to be in the forefront of our minds," said Steve Roth, chairman of Vornado. As many as 150 to 200 of the company's 975 stores were likely to be closed, and some of these were in attractive locations and would sell readily to other retailers. But this trimming would likely reduce sales and overall business by 25 percent.[12]

WHAT CAN BE LEARNED?

Vulnerability of Original Masters

We see this time and again. Success does not ensure continued success. McDonald's, Coca-Cola, and Boeing exhibited this in Part I, although these firms show promise in making comebacks. (Perhaps in another edition TRU may also make a great comeback, but it seems doubtful now.) The three C's mind-set of conservatism, complacency, and conceit appears to be as operative for TRU as for these other firms.

Now with its aging and unattractive stores, slumping efficiency that results in high overhead and higher prices, and poorer service than competitors, for many consumers it is no longer the first choice for toy shopping.

Often, organizational malaise confronts a long-established frontrunner, malaise not only of workers but also of management. It is difficult to detect such letting down, until a competitive position starts to crumble. In the case of TRU, the competitive position worsened, at first insidiously and then calamitously. At first, other toy category-killer chains had been vanquished by the stronger TRU. But the big general merchandise discounters gradually upped their toy assortments, finding toys to be great traffic builders at Christmastime.

How Can Frontrunners Stay Sharp?

TRU needed to keep in the forefront of the industry in its stores, in technology (primarily computers for information and inventory control), and in procedures for handling operations as efficiently as possible. Stores should have been refurbished and updated on a regular schedule. TRU should have led in the develop-

---

[12] Jeffrey Gold, "Private Partners to Buy Out Toys 'R' Us," Associated Press as reported in *Cleveland Plain Dealer*, March 18, 2005, pp. C1, C5; and Joseph Pereira and Ray A. Smith, "What's Next for Toys 'R' Us?" *Wall Street Journal*, March 18, 2005, p. B4.

ment of inventory control systems and efficient stockroom and warehouse handling and storage of goods to ensure lean and adequate stocks. Constant efforts should have been made to ensure that procedures were streamlined, that demands on suppliers were reasonable while extracting from them maximum efficiency in providing goods promptly at lowest prices. TRU had the clout to demand the same efficiency from suppliers as it did for itself.

Then there were the employees and management people. Higher caliber, more motivated people were sorely needed. To attract such people was perhaps the most difficult problem of all. Profit sharing, better advancement opportunities, incentive pay, a specific program to lure higher caliber people—such could have made TRU a more attractive place to work. To counter the argument that this would cost too much, we know that Wal-Mart and Target have achieved far better employees. At the least it would seem that TRU could have done a much better job of hiring, training, and motivating its people.

Can Consumers Have Too Much Choice?

The premise of category killer stores is that the more choice offered, the greater the appeal. This may be true for books. But is it true for toys and everything else? For many consumers, so much choice is confusing, makes decisions difficult, and is time-consuming. For those consumers not altogether thrilled at unlimited choice, the major competitive advantage of TRU is lost.

A New Concept of Value

The management guru, Peter Drucker, raised the challenge for managers to change their thinking from old assumptions of the past. One of his paradigms concerned the importance of value to a customer, and how this may differ drastically from what management thinks it is.[13] Take the reality of what value really is to a mother buying toys. Is a mind-boggling assortment to choose from really the value she is looking for? Especially when checkout lines are four and five deep. Or is ease of shopping, good prices, reasonable assortment, and some interactive things for her kids to do in the store of far more value?

CONSIDER

Can you think of additional learning insights that could be applicable to other firms in other situations?

QUESTIONS

1. Do you think a consumer can have too much choice in shopping? What might this depend on?

---

[13] Peter F. Drucker, "Management's New Paradigms," *Forbes,* October 5, 1998, pp. 169–170.

2. Do you think the absolute lowest price for an item is most important for many consumers? What percent would you say comparison shop for the lowest price? What implications, if any, do you see from your estimate?

3. Compare the future promise of Borders, the book superstore, and TRU. What in your judgment accounts for the difference in their prospects?

4. "Let's face it. TRU has seen its heyday. It will never come back again. It should be content with a smaller share of the market, and not worry so much about Wal-Mart, and making all kinds of drastic and expensive changes." Evaluate this statement from a stockholder.

5. Would you be content to work as a management trainee at TRU today? If not, what would it take to attract you?

6. In its early decades, TRU ran roughshod over all competitors. Yet today, bigger, with more resources and experience, it is faltering. How do you explain this?

7. In what way does inventory turnover affect profitability? How can inventory turnover be increased?

8. Would you characterize Wal-Mart as a category killer store? Why or why not?

9. Be a Devil's Advocate, one who argues an opposing position for full coverage of relevant aspects. Present all the points you can muster for why TRU should not give up its toy business. Be as persuasive as you can.

HANDS-ON EXERCISES

1. It is 1990 and you are a senior assistant to the general merchandise manager of TRU. You sense that the toy environment is changing and you are concerned that TRU is not changing. You have repeatedly told your boss about your concerns, but to no avail. What might you do at this point? Discuss your rationale for whatever decision or nondecision you take. Also consider the implications.

2. You are a staff assistant to the new CEO, R.C. Nakasone. He has assigned you to develop a proposal to improve the "shopability" of present TRU stores. He wants you to consider all aspects of this, from some remodeling—but probably not to exceed $500,000 per store—to better customer service, better employees, better layout, and what other aspects you may come up with. In addition to the recommendations, he wants you to consider the cost/benefit implications. (You may need to make some assumptions on costs.)

TEAM DEBATE EXERCISE

Debate the whole general issue of drastic change versus moderate change for TRU. In arguing the two sides, consider short-term and long-term aspects. Try to be as specific as you can be, including cost consequences, with the less-than-complete information that is available. Be as persuasive in presenting your position as possible, and attack the others' position. The extreme position would include abandoning the toy operation.

INVITATION TO RESEARCH

1. Try to find out as much about TRU's management development program as you can, such as educational and experiential requirements, starting pay and future expectations, most likely career path, etc.

2. How is TRU doing today after its big buyout? Since it is now a private company, operating statistics may be impossible to get, but you may still be able to get a feel for the situation from published articles.

CHAPTER TWELVE

Gateway's Efforts
to Stay Alive

*T*he mettle of a person, or a firm, is best tested and judged, not in the euphoria of prosperity and boom conditions, but in the bleakness of adversity. The several years before and after the millennium provided the testing ground in the marketing wars among PC makers.

By 2002, the lower-price PC market had narrowed to two main adversaries, the founders of their firms: Michael Dell of Dell Computer and Ted Waitt of Gateway. Both had started their ventures in the mid-1980s on a shoestring. One was 19 years old; the other 22. Both became billionaires. But by 2002, the personal computer (PC) boom was over, spending for technology was stagnant, and high-tech was in the vanguard of the stock market collapse. Once mighty and highly valued names, such as Lucent, Cisco Systems, and Compaq, were only grim reminders of lost chances to cash out in the heady days of 50 percent annual growth.

Some analysts saw the PC market as saturated, with everyone who needed and could afford a desktop or laptop already having one. Technological advances had slowed with the current generation of machines already fast enough for most uses, thus lessening incentive to replace or trade up. The economic downturn further supported tightened rather than extravagant spending. With the product life cycle for PCs lengthened, long-term growth prospects dimmed for computer makers. The high stock multiples of only a few years before were hardly sustainable in a low growth era. Furthermore, as the market became saturated, not all firms were likely to survive.

TED WAITT OF GATEWAY

In the fall of 2002, Ted Waitt, chairman and CEO of Gateway, had to be concerned. It would be bad enough if the computer collapse was affecting all firms equally, with market shares staying about the same. But this was not happening. While Gateway and most others were suffering, one firm—Dell—seemed somehow to be profiting and picking up great chunks of market share, much of it at Gateway's expense.

Waitt's thoughts went back to the beginning, to the farmhouse, where in 1985 he and friend Mike Hammond had put their dreams to the test with a used computer, a three-page business plan, and a loan of $10,000 guaranteed by his grandmother. Waitt had dropped out of the University of Iowa to devote full time to this fledging endeavor, to this dream. The business plan was simple and had not changed much even by 2002: offer products directly to customers and build them to their specifications, with the goal of providing the best value for the money by bypassing middlemen. The enterprise grossed $100,000 in its first year and was on the way to becoming a multibillion-dollar company.

Now Waitt's thoughts turned to the heady years of growth and unbelievable promise. In 1989, he began selling computers online, taking pride in being the first in the industry to do so. Even mighty Dell did not use the Internet for sales until 1996. In 1991, Waitt got the idea of introducing the cow-print boxes, which brought wide acclaim for Gateway and made its products distinctive. He was then on a roll and, in 1992, began offering customers a choice of software at no additional cost. It was with a great sense of achievement that he learned in 1993 that Gateway had become one of the *Fortune* 500 biggest firms, one year after Dell had joined these prestigious ranks. Not bad for an Iowa farmboy. But that same year, something even more momentous happened. Waitt took the firm public, and investor enthusiasm was so great that he became an instant multimillionaire, and not long after, a multibillionaire. A person can get used to these accomplishments. In 1996, Waitt introduced a nationwide network of what he called Gateway Country stores—after all, he was a country boy—where customers could try out his products, get advice from technical experts, and learn more about the technology in high-tech classrooms. With things going so well, he felt he could ease up a bit and confidently chose a successor.

He shrugged his shoulders in disgust. In 1999, his one-third share of the business was worth $9 billion. Now in 2002, it was worth $400 million, and still falling, an unbelievable personal loss of over $8.5 billion. He felt flummoxed.

At first Waitt blamed his handpicked successor, who was ousted when he returned as CEO. But his magic touch now seemed to elude him. He faced a battle for market share in a down market and a price war to boot with his nemesis Michael Dell. Dell had somehow gotten his costs so low that he could undersell all competitors and still make money. In desperation, Waitt slashed Gateway's workforce by ten percent. But it was not enough. Then he scaled back the company's international ambitions by exiting Europe and Asia and reduced the workforce by another twenty-five percent. But Gateway's U.S. market share dropped from 7.4 percent in 2001 to 5.6 percent in 2002.

Waitt turned his attention to Apple Computer. If he couldn't match Dell on price, maybe he could attack Apple. On August 26, 2002, he launched a nationwide TV brand battle against Apple, with a new computer, the Profile 4, which resembled Apple's iMacs but was $400 cheaper (albeit with fewer features). For years, Waitt had struggled to establish Gateway as a cult brand (hoping his rural Holstein theme with the black-and-white cow spots would convey an image of heartland honesty and dependability), one that would appeal to Apple's cultlike followers as well as others. But that had not happened, and he was thinking of putting the cow to rest. See the Information Box "Trying to Upgrade an Image, Maybe to a Mystique" for a report on Gateway's efforts to change its image, hopefully to one that might have more potential for a cult following than its cow spots.

INFORMATION BOX

TRYING TO UPGRADE AN IMAGE, MAYBE TO A MYSTIQUE

For years, the Gateway brand had been symbolized by a Holstein cow—its white boxes speckled with black cow spots—and the company carried over this theme to its Gateway Country stores. CEO Ted Waitt even appeared in television commercials with a bovine co-star. He had hoped such a homespun flavor might appeal to many buyers, perhaps conveying an image of integrity and frugality. But as the computer war intensified, with Gateway steadily losing market share, Waitt thought an upgrade was needed, and he killed his beloved cow. "I'm been calling it the de-prairiefication" of the company, he said. The change to sleek black-and-silver PCs and laptops went beyond the product to the stores and advertisements.

Analysts were divided in their endorsement of the shifting strategy. "I don't think consumers will hold it against them that they don't have the cow. Any campaign gets old after a while," said one.

Others disagreed: "The cow motif was one of those odd, quirky, counterintuitive trademarks that succeeded in spite of themselves."

"Odd and quirky" sounds like getting close to a mystique. Do you think Ted Waitt made a good decision in de-prairiefication? Why or why not?

Source: Adapted from Frank Ahrens, "Gateway Changing Its Spots to Create an Upscale Image," *Washington Post,* as reported in *Cleveland Plain Dealer,"* November 10, 2002, p. G3.

Apple had nourished its cult with magazines, chat groups, and a storied twenty-year battle against the standard PC. But could Gateway gain some of this following? Critics were not very complimentary, citing Profile 4's lack of a rewriteable DVD drive and upgraded graphics, its boxiness compared with Apple's sleek design, and a screen that did not swivel as smoothly. Well, critics be d____d; his model was still $400 cheaper.

But the price war with Dell could not be ignored. Trying to reduce costs was cutting into muscle, hurting market share, and still not yielding profits. The loss in the quarter ending June 30, 2002 tripled to $61 million on revenues of $1 billion. By contrast, Dell was prospering with a $501 million profit on sales of $9.5 billion, up 11 percent from the previous year. To add salt to the wounds, one of their executives gloated in a prominent business journal: "It hasn't been a tough market for us."[1]

Now analysts were picking at Gateway's bones, like jackals on the prowl. They were speculating that many of Gateway's 274 stores would have to be closed, and

---

[1] Arlene Weintraub, "Gateway: Picking Fights It Just Might Lose," *Business Week,* September 9, 2002, p. 52.

more production outsourced to foreign manufacturers, if there was any hope of returning to profitability.[2]

Doggedly, Waitt predicted as 2002 drew to a close that Gateway would show a quarterly profit at some point during 2003. But he was disconcerted to learn that both the Council of Institutional Investors and the huge Calfornia Public Employees Retirement System had added Gateway to their lists of underperformers.[3]

DELL COMPUTER

Michael Dell, a tall curly-haired youth of 19, started Dell Computer a year before Waitt in a dorm room at the University of Texas in 1984 with $1,000. He also had the idea that computer systems could be sold directly to customers rather than going through middlemen. He thought the manufacturer could better understand the needs of customers and provide them the most effective computing systems at lower prices. This direct marketing would also do away with retailers and their high margins.

Three years later in 1987, Dell began his international expansion by opening a subsidiary in the United Kingdom. The next year, Dell took his enterprise public, with an initial offering of 3.5 million shares at $8.50 each, and became an instant multimillionaire. By 1992, Dell was included in the *Fortune* 500 roster of largest companies. In 1997, the presplit price per share of the common stock reached $1,000, and Michael Dell was a multibillionaire.

With the bruising industry downturn, Dell's stock price fell along with all the rest, its shares by mid-2002 down 55 percent from the early 2001 peak of $59. So, Michael Dell bought 8.5 million shares of his company to add to the 300 million he already owned.

Competition in 2002

In this troubled environment, Dell's revenue in 2001 grew 2.6 percent while that of the PC industry fell 14 percent. For the quarter ending May 3, 2002, Dell reported $457 million in earnings on sales of $8 billion. These figures were flat from the year-earlier figures but far better than Dell's competitors.

Compaq, once the master of the PC business, found its stock collapsing from $50 to below $10 and was forced into a merger with Hewlett-Packard (H-P) since it could not compete profitably with Dell. Gateway was on the ropes, and even high-end manufacturers like Silicon Graphics and Sun Microsystems were losing sales to Dell. Only IBM seemed insulated from Dell's competitive strength, due to its huge mainframe and services businesses that were not directly in competition.

In Fall 2002, with the Christmas season looming, PC makers dropped prices to new lows. Big names like IBM and H-P, which usually catered to the higher-end mar-

---

[2] Ibid.

[3] Gary McWilliams, "Gateway's Loss Shrinks, but It Sees Gloomy Year," *Wall Street Journal,* October 18, 2002, p. A7.

ket, went squarely after low-price leader Dell. Other makers dropped their already-low prices even more. For example:

- H-P and eMachines had models starting at $399.
- Gateway announced its own $399 desktop.
- Microtel Computer Systems brought out a bare-bones machine for $199.
- H-P cut prices for its new H-P Compaq Evo to $899, from $1,100 a few months before.
- Even laptop prices plummeted: For example, IBM's ThinkPad notebooks were reduced to $950.

The severe industry price cutting soon extended beyond PCs. H-P reduced operating costs by $800 million by consolidating suppliers and shutting factories. It sought to increase selling efforts direct to customers, thus bypassing middlemen, and expected such direct methods to reach one-third of all sales by November 2003. To be competitive, H-P cut prices on computers aimed at business buyers by 10 percent to 15 percent. Dell entered the switch market (the technology linking computer networks) with prices one-half to two-thirds those of comparable models from 3Com and Cisco. 3Com promised "aggressive discounts to meet Dell pricing."[4]

To counter the severe price cutting of rivals, Dell started selling unbranded PCs through computer dealers that it had traditionally shunned. This program was aimed at small- and medium-size businesses.

THE SITUATION WORSENS FOR GATEWAY

By the end of the Christmas season 2002, Ted Waitt's hopes that this might be a turn-around year were dashed. He had stocked his 274 retail stores with cash-and-carry PCs and broadened the merchandise assortment to include hot sellers such as digital cameras and plasma TVs, and he spent dearly for advertising. Waitt tried to build PC sales by price matching, everyday low prices, and even daily specials, but all these only added to Gateway's losses. Now he had to contemplate restructuring again, with the retail chain foolishly created in the heady days of 1996 coming under close scrutiny for new cost cuts. The *Wall Street Journal* noted, however, that Waitt was in no danger of losing his job since he was the largest stockholder.[5]

The situation worsened in latter 2003, despite Waitt's dogged prediction of at least one profitable quarter for 2003. On October 24, its stock price plunged 24 percent after Gateway reported a third-quarter loss of $136.1 million and issued a dour forecast for the fourth quarter. Waitt's push into consumer electronics had failed to offset PC woes. Still, a few analysts saw hope for the company in its having no debt

---

[4] Pui-Wing Tam, Gary McWilliams, and Scott Thurm, "As Alliances Fade, Computer Firms Toss Out Playbook," *Wall Street Journal,* October 15, 2002, p. A8.

[5] Gary McWilliams, "Under Gateway's Tree, Another Shake-up," *Wall Street Journal,* January 6, 2003, pp. A13, A15; and "Slaughterhouse," *Forbes,* January 20, 2003, p. 34.

and $1 billion in cash and securities (most of the current assets came from big income tax refunds, but these ended in the first quarter of 2003). But even a good-sized cash horde would not long endure with over $100 million quarterly losses.

Dell, meantime, in August 2003 again slashed PC prices, this time aiming more specifically at H-P, which had just reported that its PC unit had slipped into the red in its fiscal third quarter ended July 31 because of overly aggressive price cutting. Dell had a monstrous advantage in its low-cost structure: Dell's overhead in the second quarter of 2003 was 9.6 cents, while H-P's was 21.3 cents per dollar of sales.[6] Ted Waitt could take some perverse satisfaction in seeing that Gateway was not alone in being savaged by Dell: even much larger H-P was just as vulnerable.

Still, Gateway was Dell's most direct competitor. Both firms sold PCs directly to customers by phone or on the Internet, thereby bypassing dealers. A point of difference was the several hundred Gateway Country stores in which customers could "test

TABLE 12.1   Market Shares of Top Three Competitors (million $), 1994–2003

	2003	2001	2000	1998	1996	1994
Dell						
Revenue	41,440	31,168	31,888	18,243	7,759	3,475
Mkt. Share	35.1%	37.8	35.3	25.1	15.2	11.2
Gateway						
Revenue	3,402	6,080	9,601	7,468	5,035	2,701
Mkt. Share	2.9%	7.4	10.6	10.3	9.8	8.7
Hewlett-Packard						
Revenue	73,061	45,226	48,782	47,061	38,420	24,991
Mkt. Share	62.0%	54.8	41.5	64.6	75.0	80.1

Sources: Company annual reports.

Note 1: The market shares are computed as the relative revenue to the total of these three leading competitors. For example, in 2001 the total revenues of Dell, Gateway, and H-P were $82,474 (millions). Dell's market share then was its own revenues divided by the total revenues for the year:

$$\frac{31,168}{82,474} = 37.8\%$$

Note 2: The three competitors had slightly different fiscal years. I have adjusted them all to the same calendar years.

Note 3: 2003 figures for H-P reflect the merger with Compaq. H-P is also more diversified than Dell and Gateway, especially with its printer and ink division. Hence, its market share is biased upward for PCs.

Commentary: The trend information of these statistics is the major significance. It shows over these nine years that Dell has increased its market share relative to its major competitors from 11.2 percent to 35.1 percent, a major feat in a competitive market. In the same years, H-P has had a steady decline in market share from 80.1 percent to 54.8 percent in 2001, then a spike after the acquisition of Compaq to 62.0 percent in 2003. Gateway, after gaining market share steadily up to 1999, had a precipitous decline in its competitive position.

[6] Gary McWilliams and Ann Zimmerman, "Dell Price Cut Put a Squeeze on Rival H-P," *Wall Street Journal*, August 21, 2003, pp. B1, B7.

TABLE 12.2 Net Income Comparisons of Gateway and Its Major Competitors (million $), 1994–2003

	2003	2001	2000	1998	1996	1994
Dell						
Net income	$2,645	1,246	2,236	1,460	531	149
% of three competitors	51.0%	66.6	37.0	30.9	15.8	8.1
Gateway						
Net income	(515)	(1,014)	253	346	251	96
% of competitors	NM	NM	4.2	7.3	7.5	5.2
H-P						
Net income	2,539	624	3,561	2,946	2,586	1,589
% of competitors	49.0	33.4	58.8	61.8	76.7	86.7

Sources: Company annual reports.

Note 1: The net income percentage of competition is computed similarly to Note 1 in Table 12.1. Instead of relative market share based on revenues, we have compared individual net incomes as a percent of the total of the three firms.

Note 2: See Note 2 and Note 3 in Table 12.1. NM means not meaningful, in this case because of the net loss.

Commentary: Here again, trend information is very revealing of the shifting competitive strengths in this market. Dell's profitability compared to its two main rivals shows steady gains, with a huge jump in 2001. H-P's relative profitability has been steadily declining since 1994 and took a real hit in 2001. Even in 2003 after the major costs of the Compaq acquisition should have been out of the way, H-P's profitability was less than Dell's on greater than 40% more revenue. Gateway's profitability, which had a nice trend in the boom days of the industry, suffered badly in the industry downturn, and with the huge loss in 2001 and a half-a-billion-dollar loss even in 2003 has to be considered in extreme difficulty. Its viability as a separate entity may be in doubt.

drive" PCs in the store. Both companies geared their offerings to the low end of the price range, but Gateway was having serious problems competing with Dell on price. Gateway had lost $1 billion on $6 billion in revenues in 2001, and the company was on the ropes. See Table 12.1 for the trend in operating results from 1994 through 2003 for Dell, Gateway, and H-P, and the relative shifts in market shares for these three major PC competitors. Table 12.2 shows net income comparisons and the trends for these same three competitors.

A NEW STRATEGY FOR GATEWAY

The Acquisition of eMachines

In early 2004, Gateway acquired privately held eMachines for $290 million in stock and cash. At the time of the acquisition, eMachines employed only 138 workers to achieve its $1 billion in annual sales. And it was consistently profitable. Along with the acquisition, Gateway got Wayne R. Inouye who agreed to serve as CEO of Gateway, while Waitt would remain chairman.

Wayne Inouye

Inouye, 51, had a reputation for frugality. For example, he never spent more than $6 for lunch, bought the cheapest gas for his car, and was known to be a coupon clipper for even such staples as soap. Not surprising, he came from modest means, the son of a tomato and peach farmer in the Central Valley of California. He had dropped out of the University of California at Berkeley in the 1970s and, for a time, sold guitars to rock musicians. Then he switched to selling electronic goods to dealers and built close relationships with such key PC retailers as Best Buy, CompUSA, Circuit City, Wal-Mart, Sam's Club, Costco, and Office Depot among others in the United States, as well as key dealers in the UK and Japan.

Inouye planned to turnaround Gateway by employing the same strategy he had used with eMachines. There he slashed expenses by eliminating waste and consolidating suppliers. At the same time, he made eMachines attractive to dealers by improving quality and providing prompt order filling—all this with some of the lowest prices in the industry.

A Turnaround?

At Gateway, Inouye announced plans to return to the firm's original mission of marketing personal computers. He would do away with most of the consumer electronics—such as big-screen TVs, DVD recorders, and digital cameras—that Waite had plunged into only four years before. "Our first objective is to fix our core business. People talk about multitasking, but in real life you have to focus on one thing at a time," he said.[7]

Inouye closed the last 188 of the original 274 Gateway Country stores across the United States, Europe, and Japan—a diversification that Waitt had never been able to bring into profitability. Paradoxically, these closings came just after Gateway had spent some $35 million to remodel the stores and reposition them as one-stop shops for all sorts of consumer electronics.

Inouye moved to outsource manufacturing and customer service. The firm would continue to directly market PCs and related products via the Internet and telephone sales. But it would also market through the big retailers that Inouye had so successfully courted in his years with eMachines.

By the end of 2004, Inouye expected to reduce overhead costs that had been the highest in the industry at 26 percent of revenues, to below Dell's 9.6 percent. Much of this would come from closing the Country Stores. By the end of October, the number of employees would be reduced from 7,500 to 1,800. With this restructuring, Inouye expected Gateway to return to profitability even with thin PC margins of about 8 percent.

Boldly he announced 3- to 5-year goals to unseat Hewlett-Packard as the leading seller of home PCs after its merger with Compaq, and to become a $10 billion busi-

---

[7] Gary McWilliams, "Gateway CEO Presses Restart: Back to PCs," *Wall Street Journal*, September 13, 2004, B5.

ness by expanding U.S. and overseas sales to at least one million PC sales a quarter, up from 795,000. "I don't think it's a big stretch," he insisted.[8]

Still, critics questioned Inouye's abandonment of the higher markup consumer electronics that contributed 75 percent of the company's gross margin (i.e., the profit margin before expenses) even though these generated just 22 percent of revenue. (Compared with consumer electronics, PCs produced 78 percent of total company revenues but only 25 percent of gross margin.) They also questioned Inouye's prediction of besting H-P's share of the home PC market. "We're going to vigorously protect our market position," H-P said.[9]

ANALYSIS

Were the Gateway Stores the Crucial Mistake?

With hindsight, this issue seems hardly controversial. The stores created a massive overhead that led to unremitting losses, despite their contributing 75 percent of the firm's gross margin. But the expenses of the stores could not be brought down enough to yield a net profit. We can see three options that Gateway faced in dealing with these stores: (1) increase sales substantially, (2) reduce expenses drastically, (3) get rid of the stores. Let us briefly examine these three possibilities.

1. *Increase store sales substantially.* Waitt and Gateway had no real experience in retailing. Furthermore, with the Gateway stores they were up against such seasoned and well-heeled competitors as Office Depot, Best Buy, Wal-Mart, Circuit City, and the like. The effort to increase sales substantially would seem doomed from the start. Adding more stores would only make the drain on profits worse.

2. *Reduce expenses significantly.* This possibility seems even more remote than increasing sales substantially. Perhaps some operations could have been made more efficient so that expenses would be reduced. But it is doubtful that substantial expense reduction would be possible in an environment of aggressive and highly efficient competitors.

3. *Get rid of the stores.* Why did it take Waitt so long to recognize the futility of this store operation? Then in desperation he even poured another $35 million into rejuvenating the stores, just before Inouye came on board and then got rid of them.

Expanding the Product Line?

This issue goes hand in hand with the Gateway Stores dilemma. Gateway's expanding the product line beyond PCs in order to make the stores more attractive compounded an untenable situation, lacking as it did the resources to compete with the

[8] Ibid, B1.
[9] Ibid., B5.

likes of other electronics and appliance competitors. While the possibility of higher markups for such goods seemed attractive, any firm's priority has to be net profit and not gross margin. Higher profit margins for some goods must be weighed against the increase in overhead required to sell them.

Is There Any Defense Against a Master Price Cutter Such as Dell?

A firm has only two real defenses in competing on a price basis: (1) If it is able to build on an image of higher quality or service, this would allow a price premium or (2) If it can cut its expenses and perhaps be willing to accept a lower profit margin, it may be able to match the price cutter's prices.

Waitt could hardly change Gateway's image to one of higher quality or service, especially as the industry was becoming more mature with technological break-throughs unlikely. If he could have developed a mystique and cult following for his Gateway brand, such might have permitted a price premium. But few firms are able to do this, and such cult followings are more fortuitous than planned.

Still, he might have come close to matching Dell's low overhead by strenuous efforts at streamlining and a willingness to accept less profit. Certainly, Waitt could hardly do this saddled with the millstone of the stores.

One other possibility remains: Don't try to match the lowest prices in the industry. While many customers will be lost to the lower-price competitors, enough may be interested in something more than lowest prices, and even perceive that higher prices denote higher quality.

Can Gateway Be Salvaged?

The acquisition of eMachines and Wayne Inouye, the frugal CEO, may be the last best hope for Gateway to be a viable factor in the hotly competitive PC market. Inouye's quick disposal of the Gateway stores and the more gradual phasing out of the consumer electronics business are steps in the right direction. Now, can he make good on his promises to provide the big consumer electronics retailers with better customer service as well as competitively low prices? We will see in the next few years whether the competitive uncertainties facing Gateway will be eased.

WHAT CAN BE LEARNED?

A Firm Ignores Its Basic Core Business at Its Peril

Every reasonably successful firm has a basic core of its operation that is unchanging, that should be the final bastion to fall back on for regrouping, if necessary. This is often, but not always, the product or strategy with which the firm got its successful start. In an age of diversification, mergers, and acquisitions, this core is often ignored in the quest for greater growth opportunities. But sometimes the diversifications do not work out or become vulnerable. Sometimes a firm finds itself in a crisis situation, and viability may depend on retrenchment back to the core.

This retrenchment back to the core may save Gateway. We shall have to wait to see.

Cut Your Losers and Those Operations Where Your Competence Does Not Match Competitors'

The Gateway retail stores certainly fall into this situation. Probably no amount of time and training would make Gateway stores competitive with the powerful Best Buys, Circuit Citys, and Wal-Marts. While the decision to venture into retail stores seemed reasonable in the early growth stage of marketing PCs to consumers—where the computers could be demonstrated and customers given hands-on training and service—the decision should have been reexamined years before it was. Waitt stayed too long with a losing operation having little likelihood of ever succeeding.

A Price War Can Be Disastrous

A price war developed toward the end of 2002. An economic downturn and disinterested customers were background factors, but Dell initiated it. Generally, a price war is detrimental to all participants because of its effect on profitability and is shunned by mature industries (though gasoline wars do flare up from time to time). Most firms in a mature industry have similar costs, and innovations are scarce. So all firms suffer from such price wars, even though revenue may increase some because of the lower prices.

For new industries, price wars are more common as technology advances and production economies develop, and as inefficient firms are weeded out. But the computer industry has matured, and most marginal firms are long gone. Dell, alone among its competitors, stood to gain from a price war, and Michael Dell had no qualms about starting one.

Survival of the Fittest—Power of Lower Costs

If a firm has managed to reduce its operating costs and overhead significantly below its competitors, and if they are not able to quickly match these cost reductions, then a price war can be a shrewd marketing strategy. While it may reduce profits somewhat, market share gains could be significant, and such gains may be lasting. In two later cases, Southwest Airlines and Vanguard, we find similar instances of firms having significantly lower costs than the rest of the industry; their advantage has barely been matched, as few firms could cut costs sufficiently to meet their prices and still be profitable. The power of lower costs can make for a survival of the fittest environment and result in greater efficiency and price benefits to customers.

It Is Difficult But not Impossible to Match the Price Cutter's Low Prices

The key to matching a competitor's low prices lies with reducing your overhead to nearly that of the competitor. This may be achieved by severe cost cutting, by weeding out inefficient and cost-draining operations (sometimes referred to as running a tight ship), or, as is becoming more prevalent albeit controversial today, out-sourcing some operations to foreign countries where labor costs are much cheaper.

If our firm is burdened with heavy fixed costs, such as mortgages and other borrowings that reflect profligate expansion efforts in the past, then overhead can never be reduced to be competitive with leaner competitors. The best course of action in this scenario is to divest the poor profit-performing operations, even if this must be done at a loss. Such overhead loads may also come from a cumbersome organization, such as too much bureaucracy, too many layers of management, too many staff people, and the like. Some weeding may well need to be done.

Matching an aggressive competitor's low prices may mean being willing to accept less profit at least in the near term.

A Firm May Not Need to Match a Competitor's Low Prices, If It Has a Unique Product and/or Marketing Strategy

Such differentiation may come from an unique product; it may also come from a good reputation, perhaps of quality and service, with this usually fostered by advertising and branding over the years. Such nonprice competition insulates a firm from the worst of price competition. Certainly if Gateway could come up with such uniqueness, it could worry less about a price war with Dell. But in the mature PC market, such distinctiveness and/or innovation may not be achievable.

Is It Possible to Develop a Cult Following?

A cult following usually depends on a company or brand developing (or acquiring) a sort of mystique. Few brands have been able to do this. Coors beer did back in the 1960s when it became the brew of celebrities and the emblem of the purity and freshness of the West. Marlboro rose to become the top seller on a somewhat similar image, the Marlboro man. The Ford Mustang had a mystique at one time, and Apple also had its devoted followers. But no one has beat Harley-Davidson in capitalizing on the mystique of its big motorcycles, and we will describe this feat in Chapter 18.

How does a firm develop a mystique? There is no simple answer, no guaran-tee. Certainly a company's product has to be distinctive, even if only psychologi-cally. But it takes more than a distinctive product—many firms strive for this, and few achieve a mystique. Image-building advertising, focusing on the type of per-son the firm is targeting, may help. Even better is image-building advertising of people who customers might wish to emulate—like Nike did so well with athletes.

Perhaps in the final analysis, acquiring a mystique is more fortuitous than delib-erate. Two lessons, however, can be learned about mystiques. First, they seldom last forever. Second, once gained, the company may be able to exploit them by extending the name or logo to other goods, even unrelated ones, through licensing.

The Prescription for Great Wealth

Great wealth can come from going public with a successful format. We saw in this case how Michael Dell and Ted Waitt became, not only millionaires but also billionaires, when they took their enterprises public. They had prior examples and inspirers: Bill Gates of Microsoft and Steve Jobs of Apple.

While these are extraordinary success stories, on smaller scales many small businesses can find themselves attractive to investors seeking growth companies that may offer better potential than existing firms. If the founder of the business keeps a substantial block of the company's stock, the payoff from investors' positive appraisal of the enterprise can be mind boggling.

CONSIDER

Can you identify additional learning insights that could be applicable to other firms in other situations?

QUESTIONS

1. "Tradition has no place in corporate thinking today." Discuss this statement.

2. Discuss the pros and cons involved in Dell's decision to start a price war as the downturn worsened in 2000.

3. Discuss the options Gateway faced with an industry price war.

4. "The computer industry—and most high tech as well—is saturated. This is no longer a growth area, and investors should look elsewhere for growth." Evaluate this statement.

5. "Gateway, with its Holstein cow image, was on the verge of developing a cult following. Now they're doing away with it. I'm selling my Gateway stock." Evaluate this attitude.

6. "I see no one in this foreseeable market who can compete with Dell." Evaluate.

7. How do you judge the quality of a product, computer or otherwise? Is it mostly on price? Discuss your perception of price and quality, as well as any ramifications.

8. Do you think Gateway will still be around in five years? Give the rationale for your prediction?

HANDS-ON EXERCISES

1. Be a Devil's Advocate (one who argues against a proposed decision to test its merits). Argue against Ted Waitt's decision to abandon the cow. Be as persuasive as you can.

Before

2. You are Ted Waitt of Gateway just before the slide of the high-tech industry. What might you have done to prevent the profit collapse and market-share erosion that occurred? Defend your position.

After

3. You are Ted Waitt of Gateway near the end of 2002, with your firm on the ropes. What restorative program do you propose? Defend your ideas.

TEAM DEBATE EXERCISES

1. Debate Mr. Inouye's strategy to shift away from higher-margin consumer electronics and concentrate all efforts on PCs and related items.

   I would suggest dividing into two groups, with one being as persuasive as possible in arguing for the drastic cutback, while the other strongly contests this and proposes a more conservative approach to regaining profitability. Be prepared to attack your opponents' arguments and defend your own.

2. "There is no need to be unduly concerned with Dell's price war. Our products are higher quality than Dell's and consumers and business customers alike will quickly recognize that they get what they pay for." Debate this statement, with one group supporting it, the other contesting it.

INVITATION TO RESEARCH

What is the situation in the PC industry today? Is Dell still muscling all its competitors? Has Gateway turned profitable without its Gateway Stores? Is Inouye still CEO of Gateway?

PART FOUR

MARKETING MANAGEMENT MISTAKES

CHAPTER THIRTEEN

Maytag: An Incredible Sales Promotion in England

*T*he atmosphere at the annual meeting in the little Iowa town of Newton had turned contentious. As Leonard Hadley faced increasingly angry questions from disgruntled shareholders the thought crossed his mind: "I don't deserve this!" After all, he had only been CEO of Maytag Corporation for a few months, and this was his first chairing of an annual meeting. But the earnings of the company had been declining every year since 1988, and in 1992, Maytag had had a $315.4 million loss. No wonder the stockholders in the packed Newton High School auditorium were bitter and critical of their management. But there was more. Just the month before, the company had the public embarrassment and costly atonement resulting from a monumental blunder in the promotional planning of its United Kingdom subsidiary.

Hadley doggedly saw the meeting to its close and limply concluded: "Hopefully, both sales and earnings will improve this year."[1]

THE FIASCO

In August 1992, Hoover Limited, Maytag's British subsidiary, launched this travel promotion: Anyone in the United Kingdom buying more than 100 U.K. pounds worth of Hoover products (about $150 in American dollars) before the end of January 1993 would get two free round-trip tickets to selected European destinations. For 250 U.K. pounds worth of Hoover products, they would get two free round-trip tickets to New York or Orlando.

A buying frenzy resulted. Consumers had figured out quickly that the value of the tickets easily exceeded the cost of the appliances necessary to be eligible for them. By the tens of thousands, Britishers rushed out to buy just enough Hoover products to qualify. Appliance stores were emptied of vacuum cleaners. The Hoover factory in Cambuslang, Scotland, that had been making vacuum cleaners only three

---

[1] Richard Gibson, "Maytag's CEO Goes Through Wringer at Annual Meeting," *Wall Street Journal*, April 28, 1993, p. A5.

days a week was suddenly placed on a 24-hour, seven days a week production sched-ule—an overtime bonanza for the workers. What a resounding success for a promo-tion! Hoover managers, however, were unhappy.

Hoover had never ever expected more than 50,000 people to respond. And of those responding, it expected far less would go through all the steps necessary to qualify for the free trip and really take it. But more than 200,000 not only responded but also qualified for the free tickets. The company was overwhelmed. The volume of paperwork created such a bottleneck that by the middle of April only 6,000 peo-ple had flown. Thousands of others either never got their tickets, were not able to get the dates requested, or waited for months without hearing the results of their appli-cations. Hoover established a special hot line to process customer complaints, and these were coming in at 2,000 calls a day. But the complaints quickly spread, and the ensuing publicity brought charges of fraud and demands for restitution. This raises the issue of loss leaders–how much should we use loss leaders as a promotional device?—discussed in the following Issue Box.

Maytag dispatched a task force to try to resolve the situation without jeopardiz-ing customer relations any further. But it acknowledged that it's "not 100% clear" that all eligible buyers will receive their free flights.[2] The ill-fated promotion was a stag-

ISSUE BOX

SHOULD WE USE LOSS LEADERS?

Leader pricing is a type of promotion with certain items advertised at a very low price—sometimes even below cost, in which case they are known as loss leaders—in order to attract more customers. The rationale for this is that such customers are likely to pur-chase other regular-price items as well with the result that total sales and profits will be increased. If customers do not purchase enough other goods at regular prices to more than cover the losses incurred from the attractively priced bargains, then the loss leader promotion is ill advised. Some critics maintain that the whole idea of using loss leaders is absurd: The firm is just "buying sales" with no regard for profits.

While UK Hoover did not think of their promotion as a loss leader, in reality it was: They stood to lose money on every sale if the promotional offer was taken advantage of. Unfortunately for its effectiveness as a loss leader, the likelihood of customers purchas-ing other Hoover products at regular prices was remote, and the level of acceptance was not capped, so that losses were permitted to multiply. The conclusion has to be that this was an ill-conceived idea from the beginning. It violated these two conditions of loss leaders: They should stimulate sales of other products, and their losses should be limited.

Do you think loss leaders really are desirable under certain circumstances? Why or why not?

[2] James P. Miller, "Maytag U.K. Unit Find a Promotion Is Too Successful," *Wall Street Journal,* March 31, 1993, p. A9.

gering blow to Maytag financially. It took a $30 million charge in the first quarter of 1993 to cover unexpected additional costs linked to the promotion. Final costs were expected to exceed $50 million, which would be 10 percent of UK Hoover's total revenues. This for a subsidiary acquired only four years before that had yet to produce a profit.

Adding to the costs were problems with the two travel agencies involved. The agencies were to obtain low-cost space available tickets and would earn commissions selling "packages," including hotels, rental cars, and insurance. If consumers bought a package, Hoover would get a cut. However, despite the overwhelming demand for tickets, most consumers declined to purchase the package, thus greatly reducing support money for the promotional venture. So, Hoover greatly underestimated the likely response and overestimated the amount it would earn from commission payments.

If these cost overruns added greatly to Maytag and Hoover's customer relations and public image, the expenditures would have seemed more palatable. But with all the problems, the best that could be expected would be to lessen the worst of the agitation and charges of deception. And this was proving to be impossible. The media, of course, salivated at the problems and were quick to sensationalize them:

> One disgruntled customer, who took aggressive action on his own, received the widest press coverage, and even became a folk hero. Dave Dixon, claiming he was cheated out of a free vacation by Hoover, seized one of the company's repair vans in retaliation. Police were sympathetic: they took him home, and did not charge him, claiming it was a civil matter.[3]

Heads rolled also. Initially, Maytag fired three UK Hoover executives involved, including the president of Hoover Europe. Mr. Hadley, at the annual meeting, also indicated that others might lose their jobs before the cleanup was complete. He likened the promotion to "a bad accident ... and you can't determine what was in the driver's mind."[4]

The issue, receiving somewhat less publicity, was why corporate headquarters allowed executives of a subsidiary such wide latitude that they could saddle parent Maytag with tens of millions in unexpected costs. Did top corporate executives not have to approve ambitious plans? A company spokesman said that operating divisions were "primarily responsible" for planning promotional expenses. While the parent may review such outlays, "if they're within parameters, it goes through."[5] This raises the issue, discussed in the following Issue Box, of how loose a rein foreign subsidiaries should be allowed.

---

[3] "Unhappy Brit Holds Hoover Van Hostage," *Cleveland Plain Dealer*, June 1, 1993, p. D1; and Simon Reeve and John Harlow, "Hoover Is Sued Over Flights Deal," *London Sunday Times*, June 6, 1993.

[4] Gibson, p. A5.

[5] Miller, p. A9.

ISSUE BOX

HOW LOOSE A REIN FOR A FOREIGN SUBSIDIARY?

In a decentralized organization, top management delegates considerable decision-making authority to subordinates. Such decentralization—often called a "loose rein"—tends to be more marked with foreign subsidiaries, such as UK Hoover. Corporate management in the United States understandably feels less familiar with the foreign environment and more willing to let the native executives operate with less constraints than it might with a domestic subsidiary. In the Maytag/Hoover situation, decision-making authority by British executives was evidently extensive, and corporate Maytag exercised little operational control, being content to judge performance by ultimate results achieved. Major deviations from expected performance goals, or widespread traumatic happenings—all of which happened to UK Hoover—finally gained corporate management attention.

Major advantages of extensive decentralization or a loose rein are: (1) top management effectiveness can be improved since time and attention is freed for presumably more important matters; (2) subordinates are permitted more self-management, which should improve their competence and motivation; and (3) in foreign environments, native managers presumably better understand their unique problems and opportunities than corporate management, located thousands of miles away, possibly can. But the drawbacks are as we have seen: Parameters within which subordinate managers operate can be so wide that serious miscalculations may not be stopped in time. Since top management is ultimately responsible for all performance, including actions of subordinates, it faces greater risks with extensive decentralization and giving a free rein.

"Since the manager is ultimately accountable for whatever is delegated to subordinates, then a free rein reflects great confidence in subordinates." Discuss.

BACKGROUND ON MAYTAG

Maytag is a century-old company. The original business, formed in 1893, manufactured feeder attachments for threshing machines. In 1907, the company moved to Newton, Iowa, a small town thirty miles east of Des Moines, the capital. Manufacturing emphasis turned to home-laundry equipment, and wringer-type washers.

A natural expansion of this emphasis occurred with the commercial laundromat business in the 1930s, when coin meters were attached to Maytag washers. Rapid growth of these coin-operated laundries took place in the United States during the late 1950s and early 1960s. The 1970s hurt laundromats with increased competition and soaring energy costs. In 1975, Maytag introduced new energy-efficient machines, and "Home Style" stores that rejuvenated the business.

The Lonely Maytag Repairman

For years Maytag reveled in a coup, with its washers and dryers enjoying a top-quality image, thanks to decades-long ads in which a repairman laments his loneliness because of Maytag's trouble-free products. (The actor who portrayed this repairman

TABLE 13.1   Maytag Operating Results, 1974–1981 (millions)

	Net Sales	Net Income	Percentage of Sales
1974	$229	$21.1	9.2%
1975	238	25.9	10.9
1976	275	33.1	12.0
1977	299	34.5	11.5
1978	325	36.7	11.3
1979	369	45.3	12.3
1980	346	35.6	10.2
1981	409	37.4	9.1

Average net income percentage of sales: 10.8%

Source: Company operating statistics.

Commentary: These years show a steady, though not spectacular growth in revenues, and a generally rising net income, except for 1980. Of particular interest is the high net income percentage of sales, with this averaging 10.8 percent over the eight-year period, with a high of 12.3 percent.

died in early 1997.) The result of this dependability and quality image was that Maytag could command a price premium: "Their machines cost the same to make, break down as much as ours—but they get $100 more because of the reputation," grumbled a competitor.[6]

During the 1970s and into the 1980s, Maytag continued to capture 15 percent of the washing machine market and enjoyed profit margins about twice that of competitors. Table 13.1 shows operating results for the period 1974–1981. Whirlpool was the largest factor in the laundry equipment market, with a 45 percent share, but this was largely because of sales to Sears under the Sears' brand.

Acquisitions

For many years, until his retirement December 31, 1992, Daniel J. Krumm had influenced Maytag's destinies. He had been CEO for 18 years and chairman since 1986, and his tenure with the company encompassed 40 years. In that time, the home-appliance business encountered some drastic changes. The most ominous occurred in the late 1980s with the merger mania, in which the threat of takeovers by hostile raiders often motivated heretofore conservative executives to greatly increase corporate indebtedness, thereby decreasing the attractiveness of their firms. Daniel Krumm was one of these running-scared executives, as rumors persisted that the company was a takeover candidate.

Largely as a defensive move, Krumm pushed through a deal for a $1 billion buyout of Chicago Pacific Corporation (CPC), a maker of vacuum cleaners and other appliances with $1.4 billion in sales. As a result, Maytag was burdened with $500 mil-

---

[6] Brian Bremmer, "Can Maytag Clean Up Around the World?" *Business Week,* January 30, 1989, p. 89.

TABLE 13.2   Maytag Operating Results, 1989–1992

	Revenue (000,000)	Net Income	Percent of Revenue
1989	$3,089	131.0	4.3
1990	3,057	98.9	3.2
1991	2,971	79.0	2.7
1992	3,041	(315.4)	(10.4)

Source: Company annual reports.

Commentary: Note the steady erosion of profitability, while sales remained virtually static. For a comparison with profit performance of earlier years, see Table 13.1 and the net income to sales percentages of this more "golden" period.

lion in new debt. Krumm defended the acquisition as giving Maytag a strong foothold in a growing overseas market. CPC was best known for the Hoover vacuums it sold in the United States and Europe. Indeed, so dominant was the Hoover brand in England that many people did not vacuum their carpets but "hoovered the carpet." CPC also made washers, dryers, and other appliances under the Hoover brand, selling them exclusively in Europe and Australia. In addition, it had six furniture companies, but Maytag sold these shortly after the acquisition.

Krumm had been instrumental in transforming Maytag, the number-four U.S. appliance manufacturer—behind General Electric, Whirlpool, and Electrolux—from a niche laundry-equipment maker into a full-line manufacturer. He had led an earlier acquisition spree in which Maytag had expanded into microwave ovens, electric ranges, refrigerators, and freezers. Its brands now included Magic Chef, Jenn-Air, Norge, and Admiral. The last years of Krumm's reign, however, were not marked by great operating results. As shown in Table 13.2, revenues showed no gain in the 1989–1992 period, while income steadily declined.

Trouble

Although the rationale for internationalizing seemed inescapable, especially in view of a recent wave of joint ventures between U.S. and European appliance makers, still the Hoover acquisition was troublesome. While it was a major brand in England and in Australia, Hoover had only a small presence in Europe. Yet this was where the bulk of the market was, with some 320 million potential appliance buyers.

The probabilities of the Hoover subsidiary being able to capture much of the European market were hardly promising. Whirlpool was strong, having ten plants there in contrast to Hoover's two plants. Furthermore, Maytag faced entrenched European competitors such as Sweden's Electrolux, the world's largest appliance maker; Germany's Bosch-Siemens; and Italy's Merloni Group. General Electric had also entered the market with joint ventures. The fierce loyalty of European to domestic brands raised further questions as to the ability of Maytag's Hoover to penetrate the European market without massive promotional efforts, and maybe not even then.

Australia was something else. Hoover had a good competitive position there, and its refrigerator plant in Melbourne could easily be expanded to include Maytag's washers and dryers. Unfortunately, the small population of Australia limited the market to only about $250 million for major appliances.

Britain accounted for half of Hoover's European sales. But, at the time of the acquisition, its major appliance business was only marginally profitable. This was to change: After the acquisition it became downright unprofitable, as shown in Table 13.3 for the years 1990 through 1992, as it struggled to expand in a recession-plagued Europe. The results for 1993, of course, reflected the huge loss from the promotional debacle. Hardly an acquisition made in heaven.

Maytag's earlier acquisitions also were becoming soured. Its acquisitions of Magic Chef and Admiral were diversifications into lower-priced appliances, and these did not meet expectations. But they left Maytag's balance sheet and its cash flow weakened (see Table 13.4). Perhaps more serious, Maytag's reputation as the nation's premier appliance maker became tarnished. Meanwhile, General Electric and Whirlpool were attacking the top end of its product line. As a result, Maytag found itself in the No. 3 or 4 position in most of its brand lines.

ANALYSIS

Flawed Acquisition Decisions

The long decline in profits after 1989 should have triggered strong concern and corrective action. Perhaps it did, but the action was not effectual as the decline continued, culminating in a large deficit in 1992 and serious problems in 1993. As shown in Table 13.2, the acquisitions brought neither revenue gains nor profitability. One suspects that in the rush to fend off potential raiders in the late 1980s, the company bought busi-

TABLE 13.3 Operating Results of Maytag's Principal Business Components, 1990–1992

	Revenue (000,000)	Income[a] (000)
1990		
North American Appliances	$2,212	$221,165
Vending	191	25,018
European Sales	497	(22,863)
1991		
North American Appliances	2,183	186,322
Vending	150	4,498
European Sales	486	(865)
1992		
North American Appliances	2,242	129,680
Vending	165	16,311
European Sales	502	(67,061)

Source: Company annual reports.

[a] This is operating income, that is, income before depreciation and other adjustments.

Commentary: While these years had not been particularly good for Maytag in growth of revenues and income, the continuing, and even intensifying, losses in the Hoover European operation had to be troublesome. And this is before the ill-fated early 1993 promotional results.

TABLE 13.4   Long-Term Debt As a Percentage of Capital from Maytag's Balance Sheets, 1986–1991

Year	Long-Term Debt/Capital
1986	7.2%
1987	23.3
1988	48.3
1989	46.8
1990	44.1
1991	42.7

Source: Company annual reports.

Commentary: The effect of acquisitions, in particular that of the Chicago Pacific Corporation, can be clearly seen in the buildup of long-term debt: in 1986, Maytag was virtually free of such commitments; two years later its long-term debt ratio had increased almost sevenfold.

nesses it might never have under more sober times, and that it also paid too much for these businesses. Further, they cheapened the proud image of quality for Maytag.

Who Can We Blame in the U.K. Promotional Debacle?

Corporate Maytag management was guilty of a common fault in their acquisitions: It gave newly acquired divisions a loose rein, letting them continue to operate independently with few constraints: "After all, these executives should be more knowledgeable about their operations than corporate headquarters would be." Such confidence is sometimes misguided. In the U.K. promotion, Maytag management would seem as derelict as management in England. Planning guidelines or parameters were far too loose and under-controlled. The idea of subsidiary management being able to burden the parent with $50 million of unexpected charges, and to have such erupt with no warning, borders on the absurd.

Finally, the planning of the U.K. executives for this ill-conceived travel promotion defies all logic. They vastly underestimated the demand for the promotional offer and greatly overestimated paybacks from travel agencies on the package deals. Yet it took no brilliant insight to realize that the value of the travel offer exceeded the price of the appliance—indeed, 200,000 customers rapidly arrived at this conclusion—and that such a sweetheart of a deal would be irresistible to many, and that it could prove to be costly in the extreme to the company. A miscalculation, or complete naivete on the part of executives and their staffs who should have known better?

How Could the Promotion Have Avoided the Problems?

The great problem resulting from an offer too good could have been avoided, and this without scrapping the whole idea. A cost-benefit analysis would have provided at least a perspective as to how much the company should spend to achieve certain benefits, such as increased sales, greater consumer interest, and favorable publicity. See the following Information Box for a more detailed discussion of the important planning tool of a cost-benefit analysis.

A cost-benefit analysis should certainly have alerted management to the possible consequences of various acceptance levels and of the significant risks of high acceptance. However, the company could have set limits on the number of eligibles: perhaps the first 1,000 or the first 5,000. Doing this would have held or capped the costs

---

INFORMATION BOX

COST-BENEFIT ANALYSIS

A cost-benefit analysis is a systematic comparison of the costs and benefits of a proposed action. Only if the benefits exceed the costs would we normally have a "go" decision. The normal way to make such an analysis is to assign dollar values to all costs and benefits, thus providing a common basis for comparison.

Cost-benefit analyses have been widely used by the Defense Department in evaluating alternative weapons systems. In recent years, such analyses have been sporadically applied to environmental regulation and even to workplace safety standards. As an example of the former, a cost-benefit analysis can be used to determine if it is socially worth spending X million dollars to meet a certain standard of clean air or water.

Many business decisions lend themselves to a cost-benefit analysis. It provides a systematic way of analyzing the inputs and the probable outputs of particular major alternatives. While in the business setting some of the costs and benefits can be very quantitative, they often should be tempered by non-quantitative inputs to reach the broadest perspective. Schermerhorn suggests considering the following criteria in evaluating alternatives.[7]

Benefits: What are the "benefits" of using the alternatives to solve a performance deficiency or take advantage of an opportunity?

Costs: What are the "costs" to implement the alternatives, including direct resource investments as well as any potential negative side effects?

Timeliness: How fast will the benefits occur and a positive impact be achieved?

Acceptability: To what extent will the alternatives be accepted and supported by those who must work with them?

Ethical soundness: How well do the alternatives meet acceptable ethical criteria in the eyes of multiple stakeholders?

What numbers would you assign to a cost-benefit analysis for Maytag Hoover's plan to offer the free airline tickets, under an assumption of 5,000 takers? 20,000 takers? 100,000 takers? 500,000 takers? (Hint: We know that 200,000 people qualified for the free tickets, and that the final costs were expected to reach $50 million. If we assume that costs would have a straight-line relationship with number of takers, then costs for 5,000 takers would be 2-1/2% of $50 million, 20,000 takers would be 10% ... etc. Now you need to estimate the value of the benefits for the various levels of takers.) What would be your conclusions for these various acceptance rates? Is there a point of diminishing returns?

---

[7] John R. Schermerhorn, Jr., *Management, 6th ed.* (New York: John Wiley, 1999), p. 61.

to reasonably defined levels and avoided the greater risks. Or the company could have made the offer less generous, perhaps by upping the requirements or by lessening the premiums. Such more moderate alternatives would still have made an attractive promotion, but not the major uncontrolled catastrophe that happened.

Final Resolution?

Maytag's invasion of Europe proved a costly failure. In the summer of 1995, Maytag gave up. It sold its European operations to an Italian appliance maker, recording a $135 million loss.

Even by the end of 1996, the Hoover mess was still not cleaned up. Hoover had spent $72 million flying some 220,000 people and had hoped to end the matter. But the fight continued four years later, with disgruntled customers who never flew taking Hoover to court. Even though Maytag had sold this troubled division, it still could not escape emerging lawsuits.[8]

UPDATE—LEONARD HADLEY

In the summer of 1998, Leonard Hadley could look forward and backward with some satisfaction. He would retire the next summer when he turned 65, and he had already picked his successor. Since assuming the top position in Maytag in January 1993 and confronting the mess with the U.K. subsidiary his first few months on the job, he had turned Maytag completely around.

He knew no one expected much change from him, an accountant who had joined Maytag right out of college. He was known as a loyal but unimaginative lieutenant of his boss, Daniel Krumm, who died of cancer shortly after naming Hadley his successor. After all, he reflected, no one thought that major change could come to an organization from someone who had spent his whole life there, who was a clone so to speak, and an accountant to boot. Everyone thought that changemakers had to come from outside, like Al Dunlap of Scott Paper and Sunbeam (this was described in Chapter 6). Well, he had shown them, and given hope to all No. 2 executives who resented Wall Street's love affair with outsiders.

Within a few weeks of taking over, he'd fired a bunch of managers, especially those rascals in the U.K. who'd masterminded the great Hoover debacle. He determined to get rid of foreign operations, most of them newly acquired and unprofitable. He just did not see that appliances could be profitably made for every corner of the world, because of the variety of regional customs. Still, he knew that many disagreed with him about this, including some of the board members who thought globalization was the only way to go. Still, over the next 18 months he had prevailed.

He chuckled to himself as he reminisced. He had also overturned the decadeslong corporate mind-set not to be first to market with new technology because they

[8] "Hoover Can't Clean Up Mess from Free Flights," *Cleveland Plain Dealer,* December 12, 1996, p. C1; and Dirk Beveridge, "Hoover Loses Two Lawsuits Tied to Promotion," *Gannett Newspapers,* February 21, 1997, p. F4.

would "rather be right than be first." His "Galaxy Initiative" of nine top-secret new products was a repudiation of this old mind-set. One of them, the Neptune, a front-loading washer retailing at $1,100, certainly proved him right. Maytag had increased its production three times and raised its suggested retail price twice, and still it was selling like gangbusters. Perhaps the thing he was proudest of was getting Maytag products in Sears stores, the seller of one-third of all appliances in the United States. Sears' desire to have the Neptune was what swung the deal.

As an accountant, he probably should be focusing first on the numbers. Well, 1997 was certainly a banner year with sales up 10.9 percent over the previous year, while profitability, as measured by return on capital, was 16.7 percent, sales and profit gains leading the industry. And 1998, so far, was proving to be even better, with sales jumping 31 percent and earnings 88 percent.

He remembered the remarks of Lester Crown, a Maytag director: "Len Hadley has—quietly, softly—done a spectacular job. Obviously, we just lacked the ability to evaluate him [in the beginning]."[9]

Leonard Hadley retired August 12, 1999. He knew he had surprised everyone in the organization by going outside Maytag for his successor. He chose Lloyd Ward, 50, Maytag's first black executive, a marketing expert from PepsiCo, and before that Procter & Gamble, who had joined Maytag in 1996 and was currently president and chief operating officer.

However, with extreme regret, Hadley found his choice of successor was flawed, or maybe Ward was just a victim of circumstances mostly beyond his control. After 15 months, Ward left citing differences with Maytag's directors amid sorry operating results. Hadley came out of retirement to be interim president and CEO. Some 3,400 Maytag workers, a quarter of Newton's population, roared when they heard the news. They had feared the company would be moved to either Chicago or Dallas, or that it would be sold to Sweden's Electrolux. Hadley assured them that such things would never happen as long as he was at the helm.[10] Hadley retired again in June 2001 when Ralph F. Hake became his successor.

Hake came to Maytag from Fluor Corporation, an engineering and construction firm, where he had been executive vice president. Before that he spent 12 years in various executive positions with Maytag's chief rival, appliance manufacturer Whirlpool.

Hake kept headquarters in Newton, Iowa, but moved three plants to Reynosa, Mexico, intensifying fears that Maytag might export even more jobs to countries with cheap labor. However, Hake tried to allay such concerns: "I do not anticipate multiple plant shutdowns or restructuring here." However, some analysts cautioned that consumers were becoming increasingly cost conscious—and less concerned with whether a product is made in the United States or abroad.

---

[9] Carl Quintanilla, "Maytag's Top Officer, Expected to Do Little, Surprises His Board," *Wall Street Journal*, June 23, 1998, pp. A1, A8.

[10] "Maytag Chief Quits as Profits Plummet," *Cleveland Plain Dealer*, November 10, 2000, p. C3; and Emily Gersema, "Maytag Rehires Former CEO After Time of Internal Turmoil," *Wall Street Journal*, January 15, 2001, p. H3.

Hake also sought to move the company's product line beyond the traditional to more unusual products. He created a Strategic Initiatives Group with 10 to 12 members to introduce a premium-priced line of mixers, blenders, toasters, and coffee makers under the brand name Jenn-Air Attrezzi. The hope was that such a focus on creative thinking would move the company out of its slump.[11]

WHAT CAN BE LEARNED?

Again—Beware Overpaying For an Acquisition

Hoping to diversify its product line and gain overseas business, Maytag paid $1 billion for Chicago Pacific in 1989. As it turned out, this was far too much, and the debt burden was an albatross. Hadley conceded as much: "In the long view, it was correct to invest in these businesses. But the timing of the deal, and the price of the deal, made the debt a heavy burden to carry."[12]

Zeal to expand, and/or the desire to reduce the attractiveness of a firm's balance sheet with heavy debt and thus fend off potential raiders, do not excuse foolhardy management. The consequences of such bad decisions remain to haunt a company, and the ill-advised purchases often have to be eventually sold off at substantial losses (as we saw in Chapter 6 and will also see in Chapter 15). The analysis of potential acquisition candidates must be soberly and thoroughly done, and rosy projections questioned, even if this means the deal may be soured.

In Decision Planning, Consider a Worst-Case Scenario

There are those who preach the desirability of positive thinking, confidence, and optimism—whether it be in personal lives, athletics, or business practices. But expecting and preparing for the worst has much to commend it, since a person or a firm is then better able to cope with adversity, avoid being overwhelmed, and more likely to make prudent rather than rash decisions.

Apparently the avid acceptance of the promotional offer was a complete surprise; no one dreamed of such demand. Yet was it so unreasonable to think that a very attractive offer would meet wild acceptance?

In Using Loss Leaders, Put a Cap on Potential Losses

Loss leaders, as we noted earlier, are items promoted at such attractive prices that the firm loses money on every sale. The expectation, of course, is that the cus-

[11] David Pitt, Associated Press, as reported in "Maytag's Moves to Mexico Under Fire," *Cleveland Plain Dealer,* August 6, 2003, p. C2; and Fara Warner, *New York Times,* as reported in "Maytag Cookin' With New Twist on Tools for the Kitchen," *Cleveland Plain Dealer,* September 14, 2003, pp. G1, G6.

[12] Kenneth Labich, "Why Companies Fail," *Fortune,* November 14, 1994, p. 60

tomer traffic generated by such attractive promotions will increase sales of regular profit items so that total profits will be increased.

The risks of uncontrolled or uncapped loss leader promotions are vividly shown in this case. For a retailer who uses loss leaders, the loss is ultimately capped as the inventory is sold off. With UK Hoover there was no cap. The solution is clear: Attractive loss leader promotions should be capped, such as the first 100 or the first 1,000 or for one week only. Otherwise, the promotion should be made less attractive.

Beware Giving Too Loose a Rein, Thus Sacrificing Controls, Especially of Unproven Foreign Subsidiaries

Although decentralizing authority down to lower ranks is often desirable and results in better motivation and management development than centralization, it can be overdone. At the extreme, where divisional and subsidiary executives have almost unlimited decision-making authority and can run their operations as virtual dynasties, then corporate management essentially abdicates its authority. Such looseness in an organization endangers cohesiveness; it tends to obscure common standards and objectives; and it can even dilute unified ethical practices.

Such extreme looseness of controls is common with acquisitions, especially foreign ones. It is easy to make the assumption that these executives were operating successfully before the acquisition and have more firsthand knowledge of the environment than the corporate executives.

Still, there should be limits on how much freedom these executives should be permitted—especially when their operations have not been notably successful. In Maytag's case, the U.K. subsidiary had lost money every year since it was acquired. Accordingly, one would expect prudent corporate management to have condoned less decentralization and insisted on tighter controls that it might otherwise.

The Power of a Cost-Benefit Analysis

For major decisions, executives have much to gain from a cost-benefit analysis. It forces them to systematically tabulate and analyze the costs and benefits of particular courses of action. They may find that likely benefits are so uncertain as to not be worth the risk. If so, now is the time to realize this, rather than after substantial commitments have already been made.

Without doubt, regular use of cost-benefit analyses for major decisions improves executives' batting averages for good decisions. Even though some numbers may have to be judgmental, especially as to probable benefits, the process of making this analysis forces a careful look at alternatives and most likely consequences. For more important decisions, input from diverse staff people and executives will bring greater power to the analysis.

CONSIDER

What additional learning insights can you add?

QUESTIONS

1. How could the promotion of UK Hoover have been better designed? Be as specific as you can.

2. Given the fiasco that did occur, how do you think Maytag should have responded?

3. "Firing the three top executives of UK Hoover is unconscionable. It smacks of a vendetta against European managers by an American parent. After all, their only 'crime' was a promotion that was too successful." Comment on this statement.

4. Do you think Leonard Hadley, the Maytag CEO for only two months, should be soundly criticized for the U.K. situation? Why or why not?

5. Please speculate: Why do you think this UK Hoover fiasco happened in the first place? What went wrong?

6. Evaluate the decision to acquire Chicago Pacific Corporation (CPC). Do this for the time of the decision, and for now—after the fact—as a post mortem. Defend your overall conclusions.

7. Use your creativity: Can you devise a strategy for UK Hoover to become more of a major force in Europe?

8. Evaluate the reflections of Hadley in the summer of 1998. Do you agree with all of his convictions and actions? Why or why not?

HANDS-ON EXERCISES

1. You have been placed in charge of a task force sent by headquarters to England to coordinate the firefighting efforts in the aftermath of the ill-fated promotion. There is neither enough productive capacity nor enough airline seats available to handle the demand. How would you propose to handle this situation? Be as specific as you can and defend your recommendations.

2. As a staff vice president at corporate headquarters, you have been charged to develop company-wide policies and procedures that will prevent such a situation from ever occurring again. What would you recommend?

TEAM DEBATE EXERCISE

How tightly should you supervise and control a foreign operation? This Maytag example suggests very tightly. But is this an aberration, unlikely to be encountered again? Debate the issue of very tight controls versus relative freedom for foreign operations.

INVITATION TO RESEARCH

Is Maytag still independent or has it been acquired? Is Maytag's headquarters still in Newton, Iowa? Can you find further information on the effectiveness of the Strategic Initiatives Group in generating innovative new products? How is the company doing since Ralph Hake took over as CEO? Have any more plants been moved abroad?

CHAPTER FOURTEEN

Merck's Vioxx Catastrophe

Newton Acker, 71, was on a bicycling vacation with his wife in southern France. While he had some arthritis, he was otherwise exceptionally healthy, with low blood pressure and cholesterol. Indicative of his fitness, he bicycled 5,000 miles a year. Indicative of his longevity potential, his parents had lived to age ninety. Yet on September 3, 2004, this paragon of good health suddenly died of a stroke.

On September 30, four weeks later, Merck pulled Vioxx from the market after a study showed it doubled the risk of heart attacks and strokes. "That's the answer," Acker's son, a F-16 pilot, immediately thought, as his dad had been taking Vioxx for 14 months before his death. He blamed Merck for failing to act sooner and planned to sue.[1]

Vioxx was a $2.5-billion-a-year arthritis drug and provided well over ten percent of the $22 billion revenues of the pharmaceutical giant. Some 20 million Americans had taken Vioxx by the time of the recall. Tort lawyers salivated at the tens of thousands who may have had "major adverse events" attributable to the drug, and they rushed to set up toll-free numbers to solicit potential clients. The cost of settling the lawsuits could run well into the tens of billions of dollars, which would be the biggest legal onslaught the drug industry had ever seen. Merck's stock dropped $33 billion in value between September 30 and November 1.

Let us examine how Merck got into this mess, whether it was fully culpable and ethically a pariah, or whether it was the victim of tragic circumstances. What could it have done to prevent this catastrophe, and what could it do at this point?

CEO RAYMOND GILMARTIN WITH EDWARD SCOLNICK, AND MERCK

The 63-year-old Merck chairman, Raymond Gilmartin, was soft spoken, calm, and seemingly unruffled as he tried to defend the company. Merck had had a towering past. From its labs came major drugs to treat AIDS, osteoporosis, high cholesterol,

---

[1] Example cited in Matt Herper and Robert Langreth, "Merck's Mess," *Forbes,* November 1, 2004, p. 50.

and hypertension. The company had been in the vanguard in donating millions of dollars worth of medicines to fight infectious Third World diseases—an embracing of social responsibility dating from the 1940s. In *Fortune's* corporate reputation survey, Merck was the Most Admired Company in American business for seven straight years in the 1980s. Its stock was among the bluest of blue-chip stocks.[2]

Much of the research reputation of Merck came from Edward M. Scolnick, the president of Merck Research Labs, who was a physician and a world-class scientist. He motivated an uncommon burst of R&D productivity, that in a five-year period in the 1990s brought to market fifteen unique drugs, many becoming blockbusters. For a decade until he retired in 2003, he was the de facto No. 2 man at Merck, and the only inside director on the board besides CEO Gilmartin.

Scolnick's leadership and example permeated the research organization. He had graduated from Harvard Medical School and personally had authored some 200 scientific articles. His own drive for perfection stimulated his staff, and Merck scientists considered themselves the best in the industry. For two decades, Merck research published more scientific papers and patented more compounds than any of its competitors. The company was known for providing meticulous supporting documents for its Food and Drug Administration (FDA) submissions for approval. These, along with its superb reputation in science, brought faster approvals than any of its competitors. For example, between 1995 and 2001, Merck submitted 13 major new drugs, and all were approved with an average review time of less than eleven months—Vioxx actually won approval in just 6 months of review. Pfizer's submissions during the same period faced an average review time of over two years. Quick approval could mean hundreds of millions in sales.[3] The renown of Merck's Research Labs and of its scientists, however, also fostered a negative culture, one of arrogance and insularity.

Gilmartin was picked by the board in 1994 to return the company more to its roots and be more research driven. His predecessor, Roy Vagelos, had made a number of acquisitions in efforts to diversify Merck from its core drug-research business. Gilmartin was the first nonscientist to ever head the company, having been trained in electrical engineering, and had been CEO of Becton Dickinson where he gained a reputation for efficiency and as a turnaround expert.

Gilmartin sold off many of Merck's non-core businesses, including Medco, a $30-billion-a-year drug-distribution company that had been purchased just before Vagelos retired. The recommitment of Merck to its core research brought Gilmartin and Scolnick into a close alliance, with Gilmartin usually deferring to Scolnick. The drugs in the pipeline were Scolnick's babies—he took personal interest in them, not only in their medical utility but also even to their positioning in the marketplace—and many had phenomenal growth. Take the case of Fosamax.

---

[2] John Simons and David Stipp, "Will Merck Survive Vioxx?" *Fortune*, November 1, 2004, pp. 91–104.
[3] Ibid, pp. 96, 97.

Fosamax

Fosamax was an innovative drug for osteoporosis, the bone loss women often experience as they age. It was introduced in 1995 but attracted little public attention at the time. However, Scolnick envisioned a market much larger than ailing old ladies. He urged Merck to launch a public-awareness campaign, and the drug produced $280 million in sales in its first year.

Not long after its release for the market, the FDA threatened to revoke its approval when it was discovered that Fosamax caused some patients to experience erosion in the esophagus. Scolnick went on a vigorous letter-writing campaign, contacting doctors and sending more supporting data to the FDA. In the end, the FDA consented to keep Fosamax on the market with a warning label telling patients to sit upright for an hour after taking the drug. Scolnick had saved the drug, and by 2003 its sales were $2.7 billion.

Other blockbusters followed. In 1995, also came Cozaar, a $2.5-billion-a-year drug for hypertension. Crixivan, for HIV, was introduced the next year. In 1998, five medicines came out of Merck's labs, including the $2-billion-a-year asthma remedy, Singulair, and Propecia for baldness. But by 1999, it was becoming more difficult for all drug companies to find blockbusters—the easier ones had already been found, and more difficult science was needed for any more blockbusters, and these carried higher risks of failure or potential problems. Merck came into the new millennium facing patent expirations and few miracle drugs in the pipeline.

Vioxx

Vioxx was the last of Scolnick's blockbusters. It was discovered in a Merck lab in 1994 and was one of a new class of painkillers called Cox-2 inhibitors. These reduced pain and inflammation without the side effects of ulcers and gastrointestinal bleeding that could result from common painkillers like ibuprofen. Some estimated that drugs like ibuprofen, called nonsteroidal anti-inflammatory drugs (NSAIDs), killed more than 10,000 American a year due to intestinal bleeding.[4]

Vioxx worked wonders in clinical trials with arthritis patients, and the FDA approved it quickly in May 1999. Scolnick trumpeted to the press that he was taking Vioxx himself for back pain. On the cover of its 1999 annual report, Merck proclaimed that the drug was "its biggest, fastest, and best launch ever."

Over the next five years, Vioxx became one of the great triumphs of *direct-to-consumer* marketing. Merck spent more than $500 million on commercials proclaiming its virtues, and some 20 million Americans had taken it, and it was generating $2.5 billion in annual sales, second only to Celebrex, a $3 billion-a-year drug that Pfizer acquired when it bought Pharmacia in 2003. See the following Issue Box for a discussion of pharmaceutical advertising campaigns, one of the fastest-growing ad categories in recent years.

[4] Ibid, p. 100.

ISSUE BOX

DIRECT-TO-CONSUMER ADVERTISING— IS IT VASTLY OVERDONE?

Merck spent more than $500 million on commercials proclaiming the virtues of Vioxx, only to have it revealed to be a risky remedy for arthritis. The pharmaceutical industry had discovered the effectiveness of advertising prescription drugs directly to consumers instead of the medical profession. By barraging consumers with the benefits of such drugs, drug companies hoped that many would either demand these prescriptions or at least express strong interest to their doctors—and this proved to be very effective marketing. Often these heavily advertised brands became blockbusters, generating billions of dollars for their drug companies. Over the past decade, pharmaceutical advertising exploded to become the tenth largest advertising category in the United States. The ads had become increasingly aggressive as drug companies promoted their products as hip, using imagery similar to that for soda, sneakers, and cars—for example, having pert women pitching erectile-dysfunction drugs. The debate over whether such marketing was appropriate had raged for years, but nothing deterred the new order of things. In 2003, expenditures for prescription-drug ads jumped 24 percent to $3.21 billion. Meanwhile, ad spending on transportation and tourism rose only 0.2 percent.

Merck's removal of Vioxx from the marketplace reopened criticisms about the efficacy and tone of direct-to-consumer drug advertising. "The advertising and promotions played a major role in making people think Vioxx was safer and more effective than it is, and safer than other drugs and treatments for arthritis and pain," said Sidney Wolfe, director of Public Citizen's Health Research Group. Another cause for concern as advertising stimulated demand quickly for new drugs, was that millions of people would become users before any serious side effects could be discovered. Thereby, many more people would be exposed to risks, as they were with Vioxx. But it is doubtful that Merck's recall will induce drug makers to voluntarily retreat from their increasingly aggressive advertising stance.[5]

Do you think the aggressive drug advertising should be curtailed? Why or why not? If so, what limits would you impose?

Warning Signs

There were early warning signs about Vioxx. Even before the FDA had approved it, scientists at the University of Pennsylvania discovered that Cox-2 inhibitors interfered with enzymes believed to play key roles in warding off cardiovascular disease. The researchers reported this to the companies involved and then to the academic media that this was something that could lead to heart attacks and strokes.

---

[5] *Sources:* Brian Steinberg and Suzanne Vranica, "Not Such a 'Beautiful Morning'" *Wall Street Journal*, October 2, 2004, pp. B1, B4; and Anna Wilde Mathews and Barbara Martinez, "Celebrex Drama May Finally Prompt Changes at the FDA," *Wall Street Journal*, December 20, 2004, pp. B1, B4.

Merck thought the evidence of cardiovascular effects was inconclusive and even conflicting. Then in early 2000, Merck's own 8,000-person study found that arthritis patients taking Vioxx had three times as many serious cardiovascular problems as those on naproxen, sold under the Aleve brand. However, Merck dismissed the result, contending that the discrepancy was due to an extra heart benefit from the naproxen, thus making Vioxx look bad by comparison. Still, in April 2002, Merck updated the Vioxx label to include information about possible cardiovascular risk.

The company embarked on another long-term study of 2,600 patients, called APPROVe, aimed at seeing whether Vioxx would lead to a reduction of colon polyps. The researchers also compared Vioxx with a placebo, instead of another drug, to test definitively whether the arthritis drug increased cardiovascular risk. On September 23, 2004, Gilmartin was told that the APPROVe study indeed showed that patients using Vioxx had twice the risk of getting a heart attack or stroke as those on a placebo, but after only 18 months of regular use. At that point, Gilmartin and other executives made the decision to recall Vioxx. And the hornet's nest was unleashed.

THE CONTROVERSY

Arguments for Not Recalling Vioxx

Compelling arguments could be raised that Vioxx should not have been recalled, that it was doing far more good than harm. The company could go to the FDA and have the product information updated with the new findings. The majority of the outside clinicians Merck consulted suggested it do that, since there were clearly millions of people who were benefiting without getting heart attacks.

Merck thought the decision to recall Vioxx was an example of the company's high ethical standards. Gilmartin told *Fortune* that he never had any doubt about his course of action: "Withdrawing the drug was going to be the responsible thing to do. It's built into the principles of the company to think in this fashion. That's why the management team came to such an easy conclusion." Most employees felt the same way. Peter Kim, who succeeded Scolnick when he retired in 2002, said, "There has been an incredible outpouring of emotion that says, 'I'm proud that we did the right thing. And I'm proud to be part of an organization that would actually do the right thing.'"[6]

Critics of Merck's Delay

Despite the withdrawal, Merck faced a torrent of criticisms from scientists who believed that Merck largely ignored warning signs because it was so hungry for sales. Harvard researcher Daniel Solomon who had studied Cox-2 inhibitors observed, "If Merck were truly acting in the interest of the public, of course they should have done more studies on Vioxx's safety when doubts about it first surfaced." He also criticized the FDA for not pressuring Merck to resolve the doubts faster. William Castelli, former director of the Framingham Heart Study, an influential investigator of cardiac

---

[6] Simons and Stipp, p. 102.

risk factors, raised another issue. Since Cox-2 inhibitors reduce inflammation, which is a probable risk factor for heart disease, many researchers expected Vioxx to reduce the risk of heart attacks rather than raise it. When some studies "suggested the exact opposite, it should have rung everyone's bell that something was not right."[7]

Perhaps the most vocal critic was Eric Topol, chairman of cardiology at the Cleveland Clinic. He and a number of other researchers had raised questions about Vioxx in medical journals as far back as 2001. Shortly after Vioxx was withdrawn, he wrote a stinging rebuke in the *New England Journal of Medicine*. He wrote, "Had the company not valued sales over safety, a suitable trial could have been initiated rapidly [to pin down Vioxx's cardiovascular risk] at a fraction of the cost of Merck's direct-to-consumer advertising campaign."[8] Merck refused to accept the evidence of three early research studies that found Vioxx increasing heart attack risk. The company maintained that the studies were unreliable and were contradicted by several other studies that showed no risk.

Even if Merck would not accept these research findings of increased heart attack risk with Vioxx, it should have been alerted by more than 400 lawsuits that had been filed on behalf of Vioxx patients before the recall. This was the tip of the iceberg that was to rise to 3,000 calls in the week following the recall.

Defenders of Merck

While trial lawyers could see no reasonable justification for Merck's delay in recalling Vioxx, some other experts questioned the validity of the criticisms. They saw these criticisms aimed more at enriching lawyers and destroying the pharmaceutical industry through an excess of litigation and reactionary over-regulation. Did Merck and the FDA err so badly with a widely-used drug that draconian measures should have been taken by both?

We should recognize that all drugs have side effects, especially when taken in large doses and over the long term. More than 10,000 people die per year from gastrointestinal bleeding caused by drugs like naproxen and ibuprofen, and this was the side effect that newer drugs like Vioxx and Celebrex were designed to avoid. Do the possible side effects nullify the good that can come from these drugs? And who should be the right people to weigh the benefits against the risks—courts and regulators or doctors and patients?

The concept of *relative risk* has been posed as key to decisions on drug benefits and dangers. Take disabling arthritis for example. The study that led to the withdrawal of Vioxx in September found 7.5 events of cardiovascular problems per 1,000 in the placebo groups versus 15 per 1,000 among those taking Vioxx, and only after eighteen months at a high dose. This, of course, is a doubling of the risk factor with heavy and long-time use. But for our arthritis patient, disabled and in severe pain, would 15 chances out of 1,000 of getting a heart attack convince you to drop Vioxx?

[7] Simons and Stipp, p. 104.

[8] Ibid.

Indeed, Merck's decision to withdraw Vioxx would seem irresponsible to those patients who could not find relief elsewhere. Incidentally, the point could be raised that this irresponsibility in withdrawing the drug could also extend toward Merck's shareholders who were savaged by Merck's concession that the drug was a disaster and had no place in pharmacology, thus leaving the battleground to trial lawyers thirsting for such an admission. Of particular interest should be Pfizer's reaction with its own Celebrex, a Cox-2 inhibitor like Vioxx, which follows in the next section.[9]

Should Pfizer's Celebrex Also Be Withdrawn?

At $3 billion-a-year in sales, Celebrex was the best-selling Cox-2 inhibitor, with Vioxx number 2 at $2.5 billion. Yet when the news broke of Vioxx's recall September 30th, Pfizer stubbornly refused to take Celebrex off the market, as well as its Bextra, another Cox-2 inhibitor. Earlier research studies had involved only Vioxx and while Celebrex and Bextra were of the same family of drugs, they had mostly eluded the same implications of potential cardiovascular risks. At this point, Pfizer stood to gain big from Vioxx's troubles, with many people expected to switch to Celebrex.

The situation changed on a Thursday night in the middle of December. Pfizer CEO Henry McKinnell got an unexpected phone call at his home in Greenwich, Connecticut. He learned that a review of a cancer study had for the first time linked high doses of Celebrex to greater heart-attack risks, even greater than those associated with Vioxx.

McKinnell and his colleagues decided to keep the drug on the market. They bet that the medical community and consumers would decide there was a need for a Cox-2 inhibitor like Celebrex. They took a calculated risk with this decision. If more adverse information came to light, Pfizer would face an intense legal attack. Then there was a concern whether doctors would continue to prescribe the drug.

Also lurking in the wings was the FDA's eventual decision on Cox-2 inhibitors. Indicative of how serious the FDA was taking this matter, it asked Pfizer to suspend its use of direct-to-consumer advertising and alter its marketing to doctors while the company and regulators examined the data from the National Institutes of Health trial. "It was a desire not to have mixed messages going out to physicians and patients," said John Jenkins, director of the FDA's office of new drugs. "We thought it would be very strange for consumers to be watching the evening news and see a story about Celebrex's potential risk, and then see an ad with a contrasting message."[10]

See the Information Box on page 212 for the latest information on the FDA's changing stance regarding drugs already approved and in the marketplace.

With word of the study, new prescriptions dropped 56 percent in one week. A subsequent review of patient data by WellPoint, the nation's largest provider of health

---

[9] The reasoning in this section is influenced by "The Painkiller Panic," in the editorial of *Wall Street Journal*, December 23, 2004, p. A10.

[10] Scott Hensley, Ron Winslow, and Anna Wilde Mathews, "As Safety Issue Hit Celebrex, Pfizer Decides to Hang Tough," *Wall Street Journal*, December 20, 2004, p. A6.

INFORMATION BOX

FDA ESTABLISHES BOARD
TO REVIEW APPROVED DRUGS

Plans for a special monitoring board to keep checking on medicines once they are on the market were announced February 15, 2005, on the eve of a three-day scientific meeting on the safety of prescription painkillers like Vioxx and Celebrex that blossomed into a $5 billion-a-year business before potential killer side effects came to light. A medical journal questioned whether continued use of such products was justified. "Because there are well-established options for treatment of all the approved indications for these drugs, it is reasonable to ask whether the use of the drugs can now be justified," Dr. Jeffrey Drazen, editor of the *New England Journal of Medicine*, wrote.

The FDA said it wasn't currently planning to seek new regulatory authority, such as the ability to suspend the marketing of a drug when safety questions arise or prevent direct-to-consumer advertising of newly approved drugs. That would require changes in the law, but it said it could consider such a move in the future. Currently, the agency has the authority to force the removal of a drug from the market, but only if the product is an imminent health hazard, which might take years to go through the legal process. The board will be charged with making recommendations to the agency if it thinks action is needed but will lack the authority to pull drugs or change labeling. It also is to recommend when the agency should alert consumers about potentially problematic drugs at an early stage.

Does this sound like the new board will be the answer for drug safety? Why or why not?

Sources: Randolph E. Schmid, *Associated Press,* as reported in "New Panel to Check Ongoing Drug Risks, *Cleveland Plain Dealer,* February 16, 2005, p. A12; and Anna Wilde Mathews and Leila Abboud, "FDA Establishes Board to Review Approved Drugs," *Wall Street Journal,* February 16, 2005, pp. A1, A6.

---

benefits, found that both Vioxx and Celebrex increased patients' risk of heart attack and stroke about 20 percent, while Bextra increased the risk 50 percent.[11]

OUTLOOK FOR MERCK

How Bad Will the Lawsuits Get?

Given the millions who were taking Vioxx—potentially 80 million worldwide—it is a certainty that many thousands have suffered heart attacks. Of course, many of these would statistically have suffered heart attacks without having taken Vioxx. Surely

---

[11]"Painkiller Study Reinforces Cardiovascular Risk," *Wall Street Journal,* February 15, 2005, p. D4.

Vioxx cannot be blamed for the great majority of these. But plaintiffs' lawyers will have little difficulty finding medical experts who will testify as to a causal relationship, and jurors will be more inclined to make decisions favoring a grieving spouse rather than a large corporation. And the drug industry hardly has a sterling reputation these days of skyrocketing drug prices and its widely publicized pressures to prohibit cheaper Canadian drug imports. The cost of settling lawsuits could well be in the tens of billions.

Gilmartin conceded that withdrawing the blockbuster Vioxx would hurt short-term profits. But he insisted the company's financial position would carry it through: "We're fortunate to have been managed conservatively, because this is the kind of event that you want to be able to protect yourself against."[12] The company had more than $10 billion in liquid assets. Even after the Vioxx recall, Standard & Poor's and Moody's kept Merck's triple-A bond rating, for the time being

But adversity was not finished with Merck. In November 2003, the company was forced to cancel work on potential blockbuster drugs for depression and diabetes. The former didn't work in a pivotal clinical trial, and the diabetes drug was found to pose a cancer risk. Furthermore, anticholesterol Zocor and its $5 billion-a-year revenue goes off patent in 2006, and Merck urgently needs to replace those sales. The stock price of $95 in 2000 was under $30 by February 2005.

What is Merck's Best Strategy for the Future?

With Merck seemingly on the ropes, Wall Street and consultants were talking merger as a possible solution to Merck's difficulties. Much of the talk involved Schering-Plough—Merck had sales of $22.9 billion in 2004, while Schering-Plough's sales were $8.3 billion. The two companies had worked well together on a joint venture for two cholesterol-lowering medicines, Zetia and Vytorin. Schering's CEO, a turnaround specialist, would be a logical contender to succeed Gilmartin.

But Gilmartin was against a large-scale merger. He believed Merck should not shift from his strategy of reducing costs while entering partnerships with smaller, innovative companies and licensing promising compounds. Gilmartin admitted Merck's scientists had been arrogant and unwilling to work with others in the past but insisted this had changed, as witness 47 licensing deals in 2003, versus 10 in 1999.[13] The problem with licensing deals was that with so many big companies chasing the same deals, licensing was becoming ever more expensive. This left the option open for buying small biotech companies outright.[14] But with its share price down 35 percent since the Vioxx withdrawal, little likelihood that this price would go up anytime soon, and the threat of lawsuits hung over its head, Merck was hardly in a power position for attractive merger terms.

---

[12] Simons and Stipp, p. 92.

[13] Simons and Stipp, p. 104.

[14] Jeanne Whalen and Leila Abboud, "Big Pharma, Flush With Cash, Is Looking Acquisitive," *Wall Street Journal,* February 16, 2005, pp. C1, C4.

ANALYSIS

We find conflicting attitudes regarding Merck's removal of Vioxx from the market. Some well-known doctors thought Merck waited far too long in trying to protect its profitability. Others praised it for full disclosure of information and taking action only after contradictory research findings were sorted out and evaluated. Merck's biggest competitor, Pfizer, with a comparable drug, Celebrix, even refused to take it off the market. All the while, trial lawyers were readying their ammunition for a full assault on Merck, the likes of which the drug industry had never seen before. How are we to judge the culpability of Merck? And yes, perhaps the double culpability of Pfizer for standing pat with its hand? The full judgments of the relative culpabilities will probably be years away as the lawsuits wend their ways through the judicial system.

Did Merck Make a Monumental Marketing Mistake?

It can be argued that Merck made two monumental marketing mistakes. First, it should have been more receptive to the early indications that something might be amiss with Vioxx. It should not have been so blinded by skepticism that the early research studies were inconclusive and that the early lawsuits were rare exceptions and provided no cause-and-effect relationships. It should have undertaken intensive research studies to ascertain the truth. In those early days, it could well have involved Cleveland Clinic's Dr. Topol, a renowned heart specialist and researcher and the most vocal critic of Vioxx, and it should have kept in close touch with the FDA.

However, it is not difficult to understand Merck's procrastination. Holding back the marketing of this blockbuster drug would mean millions in profits lost. Additional research would perhaps have raised doubts that might have destroyed the future promise. Then the benefits in relieving severe arthritic pain seemed so great, and the number of heart attack and stroke risks so minor in comparison. Sure, the bottom line would be involved if the marketing were delayed or muted—and the critics pounced on this for the recall delay—but I suspect that with Merck's culture and the quick recall once the full measure of the side effects was established, that the bottom line took second place in the decision. (I'm not that sure about Pfizer.)

The second mistake that Merck made was to recall so quickly. The FDA, as a regulatory agency, should have been fully involved in this decision. The very real factor was whether the good outweighed the bad with this drug, and agreement was lacking here. Perhaps the FDA should have encouraged Merck to go ahead with Vioxx but with warnings prominently placed. If physicians and their patients felt the cardiovascular risk was too great, then they would not use it. Otherwise, accept the risk and, perhaps, closely monitor the possible risk factors in the individual patient. The advertising should probably be toned down, and full and prominent disclosure made.

As we noted in the Issue Box, pharmaceutical advertising is close to getting out of control, in the amount spent and in the claims and emotional images repeated time and time again. I do not believe the industry can regulate itself in toning down these marketing efforts, which suggests that government may need to do some regulating sometime in the future.

WHAT CAN BE LEARNED?

Always Be Ready for the Worst Scenario

Firms particularly involved with health and safety—but not limited to these—need to be prepared for a worst scenario, that something catastrophic might happen with their product(s). It is good to have contingency plans for coping with such extreme crises. For a drug firm, it is not unrealistic to think that a blockbuster drug could have ill effects not discovered in the early trials and even be deadly with long-term use. Here are sample questions that should be considered in any preparation for a worst scenario: How is this situation to be handled? What public relations efforts need to be planned? Should top executives be personally involved in such public relations? Should a total recall be made or will a partial one be sufficient? How are we to handle the millions, and even billions of costs emanating from this? How can we avoid the worst of litigation? What governmental bodies should we interact with? What changes in strategies ought to be considered, if any? How can we best insure against this worst scenario happening?

It is so much easier to make plans, and even brainstorm, in the calm setting of an office or committee room or boardroom, than in the frenzied panic of a situation suddenly gone bad. Also, while we're thinking about crisis situations, certain prudent policies should be followed for crisis avoidance. For example, don't allow key personnel to be on the same plane, or even in the same car. Understudies should be trained to take over key jobs, at least temporarily, in the event of such unexpected happenings as serious injury or death, or unexpected resignation. And what about a computer breakdown, or a fire, or another 9/11?

Be Alert to Early Hints of Trouble

Sometimes crises come suddenly and catastrophically. Other times they come on "little cat feet." These early hints of something amiss often go practically unnoticed until they mushroom into something much more serious. We saw in Chapter 3, in the Coca-Cola case, where a few Belgian schoolchildren getting sick after drinking Cokes led to a far worst contamination scare. There was even an earlier warning a month before when four people in an Antwerp pub became sick from drinking a bad-smelling Coke.

The early hints of trouble with Vioxx for the most part went unnoticed—a few lawsuits, questionable research findings, one or two scientists' and physicians' warning. It was so easy to find reasons not to be concerned about these, to excuse them as not valid, not representative, contradictory, even overzealous. It was also so easy to discredit their importance as the sporadic side effects that any drug will have. With millions and billions at stake for a blockbuster drug that had already been approved by the FDA and with all accompanying research data fully supportive, a delaying or withdrawal from the market at that time would have been almost heretical. Yet it would have been the right decision, to investigate the conflicting information and not release Vioxx until all questions were cleared up. If the early hints of problems had been investigated before the marketing was in full force, the trauma would have been more muted.

Eagerness to Sue Should Be Factored into Some Decisions

In today's litigious environment, a firm with any risk of lawsuits needs to factor in this very real consequence of doing business today. It should surely be a deterrent for actions that come close to crossing the line. Insurance and financial reserves may need to be established, rather than paying out dividends, if the risk of litigation is particularly high, as it would seem to be for pharmaceutical firms. When we consider the possibility of tens of billions in lawsuits for Merck, decisions should certainly be taken to try to avoid this possibility. Perhaps this is what influenced Merck to recall Vioxx so abruptly, and maybe too hastily. Especially, as some lawyers will see this as an admission of guilt. Unfortunately, the possibility of vulnerability to lawsuits seemed not to influence Merck's decisions to disregard early warning signs.

Particularly interesting in this case is the contrary decision by Pfizer not to withdraw its Celebrex from the market. How this will play out in the courts remains to be seen. In the meantime, Pfizer is reaping a harvest at Merck's expense, even though new prescriptions for Celebrex are drastically down.

The Pharmaceutical Industry Needs to Improve Its Public Image

Drug firms have reputations, despite recent advances in medicines, that are in the pits. They are seen as uncaring, profit-mongering makers of products not always better than existing products, sometimes less safe, and with huge advertising budgets, substantially higher priced. Anything negative receives widespread press coverage. This is not surprising in this time of high drug prices, and with the aggressive actions of major drug companies to curb importation of much cheaper drugs from Canada. Stories of massive lobbying by the industry in Washington have not gone unnoticed by many consumers. The power of special interest groups has affected the objectivity of the FDA, various members of Congress, and even the executive branch of the government—all to the detriment of the average consumer, so is the common belief. This negative image, which seems ignored by the industry, poses particularly grave consequences and dangers. Jury awards in damage suits consequently yield judgments out of proportion to actual injuries in many cases—the grieving spouse versus the huge uncaring drug firm, this is an unequal contest in the courtroom. This industry truly needs to be concerned about its public image and take strong measures to improve it.

CONSIDER

Can you add to these learning insights?

QUESTIONS

1. On balance, do you think Merck is an ethical and socially responsible company? Why or why not? How about Pfizer?

2. How could the disaster with Vioxx have been avoided in the first place?

3. What is your opinion of pharmaceutical advertising?

4. Discuss the idea of *relative risk*. What is the significance of it for the drug firm itself, for the FDA, for tort lawyers, and for the consumer?

5. Do you think Merck CEO Gilmartin acted wisely in recalling Vioxx? Why or why not?

6. "The more than $10 billion Merck has hoarded attests to the obscene profits these drug companies are making at our expense," a consumer advocate speaks up. Evaluate this statement.

7. "The FDA is in the pocket of the drug industry. What a travesty this is." Comment.

HANDS-ON EXERCISES

1. You have been a public relations consultant to Merck and know the company well. You have just been summoned to the office of CEO Gilmartin. His hands tremble as he tells you of the latest research finding that Vioxx doubles the incident of heart attacks and strokes. He wants you to lay out a public relations plan that would ease the repercussions of this catastrophe. Be as specific as you can. If you have to make some assumptions, state them clearly and keep them reasonable.

2. You are a staff assistant to Gilmartin. He wants you to analyze two courses of action for expanding the firm in 2005. Should this be through licensing, or should it be through merging with other companies? Or something else? Present all the factors bearing on this decision that you can, and discuss their relative merits and priorities.

3. Be a Devil's Advocate. Array all the arguments you can to Chief Executive Henry McKinnell of Pfizer that the company is making a big mistake in not pulling Celebrex off the market as Merck has done with Vioxx.

TEAM DEBATE EXERCISES

1. It is early 1999 and Vioxx has just been introduced to the market and a massive advertising campaign is planned for it. At the same time, several small research studies have indicated possible heart attack risks. Debate these two positions: (1) Abort the market introduction until the questionable research findings can be verified or disproved and (2) Continue with the marketing plans since these research studies are small and of questionable validity. (Don't be swayed by what actually happened. In 1999, there was little expectation that anything could go wrong with this great new breakthrough drug.)

2. It is 2004 and the latest research report confirms that Vioxx doubles the risk of heart attacks and strokes. Debate the decision to pull Vioxx off the

market. Array as many arguments as you can for either decision and be prepared to attack the arguments of the other side.

INVITATION TO RESEARCH

What is the situation with Merck and Vioxx today? Has Merck made any large acquisitions? Have some lawsuits been settled yet, and what sizes are the damage awards?

Is Pfizer's Celebrex still on the market, or has it been recalled?

Has the FDA's new oversight committee been effective in drug safety?

CHAPTER FIFTEEN

Snapple: Quaker's Reckless Acquisition

*I*n late 1994, Quaker Oats CEO William D. Smithburg bought Snapple Beverage Company for $1.7 billion. Many thought he had paid too much for this maker of non-carbonated fruit-flavored drinks and iced teas. But in a similar acquisition, 11 years before, he had outbid Pillsbury to buy Stokely-Van Camp, largely for its Gatorade, then a $90 million sports drink. Despite criticisms of that purchase, Gatorade went on to become a billion-dollar brand, and Smithburg was a hero. He was not to be a hero with Snapple.

THE COMPANY, QUAKER OATS

Quaker Oats had nearly $6.4 billion in fiscal 1995 sales, of which $1.7 billion was from foreign operations. Its brands were generally strong, in particular grocery products and beverage areas. In hot cereals, generations had used Quaker oatmeal, and it was still the No. 3 selling brand in the overall cereal category. Quaker's ready-to-eat cereals included Cap'n Crunch and Life brands. The firm was a leading competitor in the fast-growing rice cake and granola bar categories, and also in rice and pasta with its Rice-A-Roni, Pasta Roni, and Near East brands. Other products included Aunt Jemima frozen products, French toast, pancake mixes, and syrups; Celeste frozen pizza; as well as grits, tortilla flour, and corn meal.

With the purchase of Snapple, sales of its beverage operation would approach $2 billion or about one-third of total corporate sales. Gatorade alone accounted for $1.3 billion worldwide in fiscal 1995, and growth continued with sales in the United States increasing 7 percent over the previous year, while overseas the gain was a whopping 51 percent. In order to help pay for the Snapple acquisition, several mature but still moneymaking units were divested, including pet foods and chocolates.

THE SNAPPLE ACQUISITION

The brand, Snapple, had a modest beginning in 1972 in Brooklyn, N.Y., and its beverages were initially sold to health-food stores. As the healthy lifestyle became popu-

TABLE 15.1   **Snapple's Sales Growth, 1993–1996**

	1993	%	1994	%	1995	%	1996	%
			Sales (millions of dollars)					
1st quarter			$134		$112	–12%		
2nd quarter	$130		243	+87%	200	–18%	180	–10%
3rd quarter	203		191	–6%				–20%
4th quarter	118		105	–11%				

Source: 1995 Quaker Annual Report and various 1996 updates.

Note: While we do not have complete information for all the quarters, still the negative sales since the second quarter of 1994—before the Snapple acquisition—can be readily seen: Every quarter since then has seen losses from the same quarter the preceding year.

lar among certain segments of the general public, Snapple's sales for a time increased as much as 60 to 70 percent a year, especially in the Northeast and West Coast. In 1992, it was purchased for $27.9 million by Boston-based Thomas H. Lee Co., which took the now-trendy brand public and built it up to almost $700 million in sales.

Unlike Gatorade, however, Snapple faced formidable competitors, including Coke's Fruitopia and Pepsi's joint venture with Lipton, which used low prices to capture 31 percent of the iced-tea market. Snapple's growth rate had turned to declines by December 1994 when, in an outpouring of supreme confidence in his own judgment, Smithburg bought Snapple for $1.7 billion. Before long, many said he had paid about $1 billion too much. Table 15.1 shows the quarterly sales results of Snapple since June 1993 before the acquisition and after.

William Smithburg

At the time of the purchase, Smithburg was 56 years old but looked younger. He liked to wear suspenders stretched tightly over muscular shoulders that he had developed from years of tournament handball. He had been CEO at Quaker Oats since 1981 and had evolved from a flashy boy wonder to a seasoned executive. He was also a fitness buff, and perhaps this colored his zeal for products like Gatorade and Snapple.

His interest in fitness developed as a result of a childhood bout with polio. While he recovered with no permanent damage, the experience shaped his life: "As soon as I started to walk and run again, I said, 'I have to stay healthy,' and it just became part of my life."[1] In his long tenure as CEO, that passion shaped Quaker too. The company developed extensive fitness programs, including a heavily subsidized health club at headquarters. Quaker's product line also had increasingly emphasized low-fat foods compatible for the healthy lifestyle.

Indicative of Smithburg's personality, after graduating from DePaul University in 1960 with a BS in economics and marketing, he defied his father by quitting his first job only three days later. He decided to enroll in Northwestern's business school.

[1] Greg Burns, "Crunch Time At Quaker Oats," *Business Week*, September 23, 1996, p. 72.

With an MBA in hand he joined the Leo Burnett ad agency, and later, McCann Erickson. After five years of ad agency experience, he went to Quaker as brand manager for frozen waffles in 1966. There it took him ten years to become executive vice-president of U.S. grocery products, Quaker's biggest division. Five years later, in 1981, he became CEO and was named chairman two years after that.

The same year he became chairman, he acquired Stokely-Van Camp, overbidding Pillsbury's $62-per-share bid with a $77 offer, which carried a price tag of $238 million. His own investment banker considered this too steep, and critics in the business press abounded. But Smithburg had done his homework, and his intuition was prescient. He recognized the potential in Stokely's Gatorade, a sport drink meant to replenish lost salts and fluids of athletes. "I'd been drinking Gatorade myself, and I knew the product worked."[2] A $90 million brand in 1983, by 1996 this was a $1.3 billion-dollar brand and held 80 percent of the growing sport-drink market.

Somehow, Smithburg did not do his homework well with Snapple, despite its seeming similarity to Gatorade.

Rationale for the Snapple Purchase

Snapple was the largest acquisition in Quaker's history. The *Quaker Oats 1995 Annual Report* discussed the rationale for this purchase and the "growth opportunity it offers to shareholders";

> Snapple appeals to all ages with its incomparable flavor variety in premium iced teas and juice drinks. Current sales are concentrated in the Northeast and West Coast. So, the rest of the country presents fertile territory for developing the brand. Because of its excellent cold-channel distribution, the Snapple brand has taught us a great deal about reaching consumers outside our traditional grocery channels. We can apply this knowledge to Gatorade thirst quencher, thereby enhancing its availability as well.[3]

So Smithburg saw great opportunity to expand distribution of Snapple geographically from its present regional concentration. He thought it had wide appeal and that it could enhance sales of the already highly successful Gatorade.

Snapple beverages held good regional market positions in the premium ready-to-drink tea and single-serve juice drink categories. It was seemingly well positioned if consumer preferences continued to shift to all-natural beverages—and away from highly carbonated, artificially flavored, and chemically preserved soft drinks.

Apparently, not the least of the reasons for Smithburg's infatuation with Snapple was that it had a "sexy aura," even though problems were already emerging when he bought it. He liked to contrast it with Quaker's pet food: Pet food "was a dead, flat business with five or six big companies beating their brains out in it."[4] So it was not surprising that the pet food business, which had been acquired less than nine years before, was sold a few months after Snapple was acquired.

[2] Ibid., p. 74.
[3] *Quaker Oats 1995 Annual Report*, p. 6.
[4] Burns, p. 74.

Other speculations as to why Smithburg chased Snapple, besides misreading the growth potential, were that he wanted to make Quaker, which was a hotly rumored acquisition candidate, less vulnerable to a takeover. Some even speculated that Smithburg became bored with Quaker and sought the excitement of a splashy deal.[5]

PROBLEMS

One would think that Snapple's resemblance to Gatorade would bring instant compatibility and efficiencies in marketing the two brands. After all, with the proven success of Gatorade, Quaker had become the third-largest beverage company, after only Coca-Cola and Pepsi. And like Gatorade, Snapple was a flavored, noncarbonated drink. Surely this was a compatible marriage.

But this was not the case. Only after it bought Snapple did Quaker fully realize that Snapple's production and distribution systems were completely different from Gatorade's.

Quaker's production and distribution of Gatorade was state of the art. Its computers were closely integrated with those of its largest distributors and automatically kept these distributors well stocked, but not overstocked, with Gatorade.

The advertising of Gatorade was also markedly different. Several hundred million dollars a year was spent for Gatorade, with highly successful ads featuring Chicago Bulls star, Michael Jordan (Jordan was also a personal friend of Smithburg). Snapple's advertising, on the other hand, had run out of steam and was notably ineffective.

The production, distribution, and marketing efforts of Snapple at the time of the purchase were haphazard. Bottling was contracted to outsiders, and this resulted in expensive contracts for excess capacity when demand slowed. Snapple's 300 distributors delivered directly to stores; Gatorade's distributors delivered to warehouses. Quaker's efforts to consolidate the two distribution systems only created havoc. It tried to take the supermarket accounts away from Snapple distributors and give them to Gatorade, directing that the Snapple people concentrate on convenience stores and mom-and-pop retailers. Not surprising, Snapple distributors refused this downsizing of their operations. Eventually, Quaker backed down. But efforts at creating coordination and distribution efficiencies for 1995 were seriously delayed.

At the same time, Quaker failed to come up with a new business plan for Snapple in time for the peak 1995 season, which began in April. Tim Healy, president of a Snapple distributor in Chicago, noted: "There was no marketing plan, no initiatives, and no one to talk to (at Quaker)."[6]

The result was that 1995 sales of Snapple fell 9 percent, and there was a $100 million loss.

[5] Ibid.

[6] Scott McMurray, "Drumming Up New Business: Quaker Marches Double Time to Put Snap Back in its Snapple Drink Line," *U.S. News & World Report*, April 22, 1996, p. 59.

CORRECTIVE EFFORTS, 1996

As the dismal results of 1995 became widely publicized, Quaker faced the urgent need to vindicate the purchase of Snapple and somehow resurrect its failing fortunes. To aid the distributors, the company streamlined operations to reduce from two weeks to three days the time it took to get orders from bottlers to distributors. To do so, it coordinated its computers with the top 50 distributors, who represented 80 percent of Snapple's sales, so that it could replenish their inventory automatically, the way it was doing with Gatorade.

The company also introduced some packaging and product changes that it hoped would be more appealing to dealers and to customers. It brought out 32- and 64-ounce plastic bottles of Snapple for families, along with 12-packs and 4-packs in glass bottles. It reduced the number of flavors from 50 to 35 and made taste improvements in some of the retained flavors. At the same time seasonal products were introduced, such as cider tea for Halloween.

To develop distributor enthusiasm, a two-day meeting had been held in San Diego. Quaker brought in comedian Bill Cosby to entertain and Gen. Norman Schwarzkopf to motivate with a stirring speech on leadership. Then distributors were told that highly visible Snapple coolers would be placed in supermarkets, convenience stores, and schools—just like Coke and Pepsi.[7]

The weakness in the 1995 advertising also received, hopefully, corrective action. Quaker enlisted the creativity of Spike Lee, who had designed hyperkinetic TV commercials for Nike. While the campaign kept Snapple's "Made from the best stuff on earth," the new ads focused on Snapple's hope to become America's third choice in soft drinks, behind Coke and Pepsi, with such slogans as, "We want to be No. 3," and "Threedom = freedom." The goal of the advertising campaign, Smithburg explained, was to maintain Snapple's "funky" image while broadening its appeal beyond the East and West Coast markets.[8]

Still, sales languished. In late July, a huge nationwide sampling campaign was undertaken. In a $40 million effort, millions of bottles of the fruit-juice and ice-tea lines were given away during the height of the selling season, hopefully to spur consumer interest regardless of cost.

RESULTS OF 1996 EFFORTS

Unfortunately, the results of the summer giveaways were dismal. Instead of gaining market share during the important summer selling months, Snapple lost ground.

Snapple tea sales fell 14 percent, and juice sales fell 15 percent. This compared poorly with industry tea sales that also dropped but only 4 percent, and industry juice sales that fell 5 percent during a particularly cool summer in the Northeast.[9]

---

[7] Zina Moukheiber, "He Who Laughs Last," *Forbes,* January 1, 1996, p. 42.

[8] Ibid., p. 60.

[9] "Snapple Continues to Lose Market Share Despite Big Giveaway," *Wall Street Journal,* October 8, 1996, p. B9.

Relentless media scrutiny even found fault with the way in which Snapple was being given away. One critic observed the sampling at a New Jersey concert in which 16-ounce cans were handed out only 20 feet from the entrance in front of signs prohibiting food or drink beyond the gate. Most people barely had time to taste the drink before throwing it away. Furthermore, "for its brand undermining efforts, Quaker gets no consumer research either. Solution: In exchange for the self-serve sample, ask a few short ... questions."[10]

The reputation of Smithburg was being eroded, his early success with Gatorade not enough to weather much more adversity. Online, cyber critics assailed him. In conference calls with financial analysts, he was peppered with barbed questions about this $600 million beverage for which he paid $1.7 million. "Even my dad," Smithburg laughed, "He says, 'What are you doing with Snapple?'"[11]

Under pressure, Smithburg cast off president and chief operating officer, Philip Marineau, who he been grooming as heir apparent for many years. This departure was widely interpreted to be the result of Snapple's failure to justify its premium pricing, with Marineau the scapegoat. Nine months later, Donald Uzzi was replaced as president of Quaker's North America beverages unit. His successor was Michael Schott, former vice president of sales of Nantucket Nectars, a small, privately-held drink maker.

Some critics assumed that Smithburg's job was in jeopardy, that he could not escape personal blame for the acquisition snafu. Still, the past success of Smithburg with Gatorade continued to sustain him. The board of directors remained supportive, although they denied him any bonus for 1995. What made the continued loyalty of the board more uncertain was Quaker's stock price, which had fallen 10 percent since just before the acquisition, even as the Standard & Poor's 500-stock index had climbed to new highs.

If Snapple could not be revitalized, Smithburg had several options regarding it. All of these, of course, would be admissions of defeat and that a major mistake was made in acquiring Snapple. Any one of them might cost Smithburg his job.

One option would be to spin off the ailing Snapple to shareholders, perhaps under the wing of the booming Gatorade. Smithburg was no stranger to such maneuverings since he had divested retail, toy, and pet-food operations in his years as CEO. An outright sale could probably be made only at bargain-basement prices and would certainly underscore the billion-dollar mistake of Smithburg's purchase. A less extreme option would be to draw back from attempts to make Snapple a national brand and keep it as a regional brand in the Northeast and West Coast where it was well entrenched.

Perseverance

By early 1997, Smithburg still had not given up on Snapple. Quaker Oats announced it was pumping $15 million into a major 4-month sweepstakes promotion for Snapple's

---

[10] Gabe Lowry, "They Can't Even Give Snapple Away Right," *Brandweek*, September 30, 1996, p. 16.

[11] Burns, p. 71.

diet drinks, this to start right after the new year when consumers might be more concerned with undoing the excesses of the holiday season and when competitors would be less likely to advertise chilled drinks in cold weather. The theme was to be, "Escape with Taste," and among other winners would be 50 grand prize trips to the refurbished Doral Resort and Spa in Miami. If the campaign developed any momentum, it should carry over to a retooled image campaign planned immediately afterward in the spring.

This promotion was the first from new president Mike Schott, and it built on one product category that managed to grow 16 percent in convenience stores during the previous summer, even as core juices and teas slid drastically. The promotion plan was well received by distributors: "This one [promotion] is wonderfully thought out," one distributor said. "Diet drinks in the first quarter? It's a no-brainer."[12]

Since being named the brand's president late in the year, Schott had been visiting distributors to build up relations, offer greater support, and dispel rumors that Snapple was going to retrench to a regional brand. Still, Snapple's sales and profits showed no rebound.

On March 27, 1997, Smithburg finally threw in the towel; he sold the ailing Snapple to Nelson Peltz, chief executive of the smallish Triarc Cos., owner of RC Cola and Arby's restaurants. The price was shockingly low, only $300 million, or just over half of Snapple's $550 million in sales. This, for a brand Smithburg had paid $1.7 billion only three years before. The founder of Snapple, Leonard Marsh, who had previously sold his controlling interest, said that "they stole the company."[13]

Undoubtedly, Quaker was desperate to sell the money-draining Snapple, but at such a fire-sale price? As it turned out, the company had few options. Major suitors, such as PepsiCo, Coca-Cola, and Procter & Gamble, only wanted to consider a Snapple purchase along with Gatorade, Smithburg's crown jewel and most profitable brand.

On April 24, 1997, the *Wall Street Journal* reported that Quaker Oats had posted a $1.11 billion quarterly loss reflecting the final resolution of the Snapple affair, and that William Smithburg was stepping down. "Many investors have been asking for a long time why he hasn't stepped aside sooner," said one food-industry analyst.[14]

ANALYSIS

Beyond doubt, the price paid for Snapple was wildly extravagant. Demand was slumping, distribution inefficiencies had surfaced, and the advertising had run out of steam. We can understand Smithburg's reasoning, that he had bought Gatorade at a high price and turned it into a winner. Why shouldn't he do the same thing with Snapple? The price paid for Gatorade, $238 million for sales of $90 million at the time, was roughly comparable to the $1.7 billion for Snapple sales of almost $700 million.

---

[12] Gerry Khermouch, "Snapple Diet Line Gets $15 Mil Push," *Brandweek*, November 4, 1996, p. 1.

[13] I. Jeanne Dugan, "Will Triarc Make Snapple Crackle?" *Business Week*, April 28, 1997, p. 64.

[14] Michael J. McCarthy, "Quaker Oats Posts $1.11 Billion Quarterly Loss," *Wall Street Journal*, April 24, 1997, pp. A3, A12.

But we can surely fault Smithburg for not demanding that his subordinates analyze more thoroughly the compatibility of the two operations. There should have been no surprises after the sale that the distribution systems of Gatorade and Snapple were not compatible and maybe could not be made so. Furthermore, it seems only reasonable to expect for a purchase of this magnitude that adequate research and planning would also have been done concerning the promotional efforts of Snapple, whether they were adequate for the coming year or whether changes needed to be made, and if so, what changes. Should not stockholders expect that rather solid business plans would be in place before the acquisition was finalized by Quaker? Without such, the decision to let go of $1.7 billion seems rather like decision making by hunch and intuition. Perhaps it was.

The spinning of wheels in 1996, after the disastrous 1995, suggests that Smithburg had fallen prey to the decision-making error called *escalating commitment*. This is a resolve to increase efforts and resources to pursue a course of action that is *not* working, to be unable to "call it quits."[15]

See the following Information Box for advice by John Schermerhorn on not being trapped in an escalation commitment.

INFORMATION BOX

HOW TO AVOID THE ESCALATION TRAP

When should we call it quits, admit the mistake, and leave the scene as gracefully as possible, amid the cries of critics and the debris of sunk costs in a hopeless cause; and even embarrassment and shame and possible ouster by a board of directors tormented by irate investors? John Schermerhorn offers these guidelines to avoid staying in a lost cause too long:[16]

1. Set advance limits on your involvement in a particular course of action, and stick to it.
2. Make your own decisions; others may also be prone to escalation.
3. Carefully consider why you are considering continuing this course of action; unless there are sufficient reasons to continue, don't.
4. Consider the costs of continuing, and the savings in costs as a reason to discontinue.
5. Be on guard for escalation tendencies, especially where a big commitment has already been made.

Do you think Drucker's idea of an escalating commitment and Schermerhorn's suggestions for avoiding it have any downsides? In other words, when do you call it quits?

[16] John R. Schermerhorn, Jr., *Management, sixth edition*, New York: John Wiley, 1999, p. 67.

[15] Peter F. Drucker, "The Global Economy and the Nation-State," *Foreign Affairs,* vol. 76, September-October 1997, pp. 159–171.

You can imagine how the big commitment that had already been made for Snapple would have stimulated the escalating commitment to the fullest: "We have too much invested for this for fail."

If the product life cycle of Snapple had peaked before the Quaker purchase, this would account for the inability of Quaker management to reverse the downward trend of sales and profits. But such a possibility should surely have been considered before the acquisition decision. (See the following Information Box for a discussion of the product life cycle.)

One would think that the best minds in a major corporation, and any outside consultants used, should have been able to bring Snapple to more healthy national and

---

INFORMATION BOX

THE PRODUCT LIFE CYCLE

Just as people and animals do, products go through stages of growth and maturity—that is, life cycles. They are affected by different competitive conditions at each stage, ranging often from no competition in the early stages to intense competition later on. We can recognize four stages in a product's life cycle: introduction, growth, maturity, and decline.

Figure 15.1 depicts three different product life cycles. Number 1 is that of a standard item in which sales take some time to develop and then eventually begin a slow decline. Number 2 shows a life cycle for a product in which a modification of the product or else the uncovering of a new market rejuvenates the product so that it takes off on a new cycle of growth (the classic examples of this are Listerine, originally sold as a mild external antiseptic, and Arm & Hammer Baking Soda, which was repositioned as a deodorizer). Number 3 shows the life cycle for a fad item or one experiencing rapid technological change and intense competition. Notice its sharp rise in sales and the abrupt downturn.

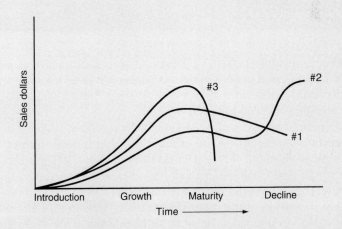

Figure 15.1. The Product Life Cycle

(continues)

THE PRODUCT LIFE CYCLE *(continued)*

Now, which life cycle most closely represented Snapple, at the time of the acquisition? Snapple was definitely on a downward trend, which began the summer before Quaker purchased it, and this downward trend continued and even accelerated through 1995 and 1996. (See Table 15.1.) Such suggests that Snapple had reached the maturity stage of its life cycle. As an admittedly trendy product, its curve in the worst scenario would resemble #3, the fad. An optimistic scenario would see a #2 curve, with strong efforts in 1997 bringing a rejuvenation. Perhaps the more likely life cycle is something akin to #1, with a slow downturn continuing for a lengthy period while aggressive efforts fail to stem the decline in an environment of more intense competition and less eager demand.

Do you agree with this prognosis? Why or why not?

international sales, or at least to a more profitable situation, even if the product life cycle had become less favorable. But in high-stake, near-crisis situations, prudent judgment may be abandoned as money is flung about in desperate efforts to turn things around. Often, such merely aggravates the situation, as was the case with the expensive and poorly planned $40 million sampling effort and the $15 million sweepstakes program.

Finally, it is worth emphasizing again that in the acquisition quest, extensive homework should be done. These are major, major decisions. Hundreds of millions of dollars, even billions, are at stake if an unwise acquisition has to be divested a few years later. In addition, there is the management time taken up with a poorly performing product line at the expense of other responsibilities.

UPDATE

Quaker's Gatorade remained a great strength of the company, having an estimated 78 percent of the sport-drink market. This made Quaker an attractive acquisition. In 2000, Coca-Cola expressed interest in buying Quaker but faced a sticker price of $16 billion that its board of directors, among them Warren Buffett, one of the country's most astute investors, decided to reject.

Just a few months later, PepsiCo bid $14.02 billion, which Quaker accepted. The deal was expected to close by the end of June 2001, but federal antitrust enforcers continued to raise objections. Federal Trade Commission (FTC) concern was that this merger would give Quaker's Gatorade brand even greater dominance once it became part of Pepsi's powerful distribution network. Coca-Cola's Powerade brand share was only 15 percent of the sport-drink market, while Pepsi's All-Sport, which the company agreed to sell, was a distant third. Opponents of the deal argued that it would enable Pepsi to gain too much clout with retailers, particularly convenience stores where Gatorade and other Pepsi products, such as Mountain Dew, were already strong. FTC approval was difficult to obtain, although the deal had already been approved by several foreign regulators, including the European Union's antitrust authority. Then on August 2, 2001, in a rare deadlocked 2-2 vote the FTC let PepsiCo proceed with the then $13.8 billion buyout of Quaker Oats Co.[17]

WHAT CAN BE LEARNED?

The Illusion of Compatibility

Bad acquisition decisions—in which the merger or acquisition turns out to be a mistake—often result from miscalculating the mutual compatibility of the two operations. Expectations are that consolidating various operations will result in significant cost savings. For example, instead of two headquarters' staffs, these can be reduced perhaps to a beefed-up single one. Sometimes even certain aspects of production can be combined allowing some facilities to be closed for greater cost efficiencies. Computer operations, sales forces, and distribution channels might be combined. But for these combinations and consolidations to be feasible, the two operations essentially should be compatible.

As we saw in the case, the distribution channels of Snapple and Gatorade were not compatible, and efforts to consolidate brought serious rancor by those who would be affected. Quaker had failed to do its homework and probe deeply enough to determine the real depth of compatibility, not merely assuming compatibility because of product similarities.

Certainly, we see many acquisitions and mergers of dissimilar operations: These are called *diversifications.* Some of these have little or no compatibility and may not provide significant opportunities for reducing costs. Instead, they may be made because of perceived growth opportunities, to lessen dependence on mature products, to smooth out seasonality, and so on. Unfortunately, many of these dissimilar diversifications prove to be disappointing and are candidates for divestiture some years later.

The Acquisition Contest

Once an acquisition candidate is identified, negotiations sometimes become akin to an athletic contest: Who will win? Not infrequently, several firms may be drawn to what they see as an attractive would-be acquisition, and a bidding war commences. Sometimes management of the takeover firm strongly resists. So, the whole situation evolves into a contest, almost a game. And aggressive executives get caught up in this game and sometimes overreach themselves in their struggle to win. No matter how attractive a takeover firm might be, if you pay way too much for it, this was a bad buy.

---

[17] *Source:* John R. Wilke and Betsy McKay, "PepsiCo Cites FTC For Further Delay of Quaker Deal," *Wall Street Journal,* June 11, 2001, p. B6; "FTC Allows PepsiCo to Buy Quaker Oats Despite Concerns," Associated Press as reported in *Cleveland Plain Dealer,* August 2, 2001, p. C5.

The Paradox of Perseverance—When Do We Give Up?

We admire people who persevere despite great odds: the student who continues with school even though family and work commitments may drag it out for ten years or more; the athlete who never gives up; the author who has a hundred rejection slips, but still keeps trying. So, how long should we persevere in what seems totally a losing cause? Isn't there such a thing as futility and unrealistic dreams, so that constructive efforts should be directed elsewhere? The enigma of futility has even been captured in classic literature with Don Quixote, the "Man from LaMancha," tilting his lance at windmills.

The line is blurred between perseverance and futile stubbornness, the escalating commitment of Peter Drucker. Circumstances vary too much for best decision certainty. Still, if a direct assault continues to fail, perhaps it is time to make an end run.

When Should a Weak Product Be Axed?

Weak products tend to take up too much management, sales force, and advertising attention, efforts that could better be spent making healthy products better and/or developing replacements. Publicity about such products may even cause customer misgivings and tarnish the company's image. This suggests that weak and/or unprofitable products or divisions ought to be gotten rid of, provided that the problems are enduring and not a temporary aberration.

Not all weak products should be pruned, however; rationale for keeping them may be strong. In particular, the weak products may be necessary to complete a line to benefit sales of other products. They may be desirable for customer goodwill. Some weak products may enhance the company's image or prestige. Although such weak products make no money in themselves, still their intrinsic value to the firm may be substantial. Other weak products may merely be unproven, too new in their product life cycle to have become profitable; in their growth and maturity stage they may contribute satisfactory profits. Finally, possibly a new business strategy will rejuvenate the weak product. That is the hope, and the proffered justification for keeping a weak product when its demise is overdue.

So, where did Snapple fit into this theoretical discussion? The only justification for procrastination would seem to be that business strategy alternatives to turn around the brand had not been exhausted. In the meantime, the image of Quaker Oats in the eyes of investors, and the reflection of this in stock prices, was being savaged.

Be Cautious with Possible Fad Product Life Cycles

With hindsight, we can classify Snapple's popularity as a short-term phenomenon. But it was heady and contagious while it lasted. Snapple transformed iced tea into a new-age product by avoiding the need for preservatives, adding fruit flavors, and introducing innovative wide-mouth, 16-ounce bottles. It also used Howard Stern, with his cult following, as its spokesperson.

The public offering of stock in 1993 was sensational. The original offering price was to be $14, but this was raised to $20; in the first day of trading the stock closed at $29. Two years later, Quaker paid $1.7 billion for a company whose founders paid just $500 to acquire the name. But the euphoric life cycle was turning down, and the cult following was distracted by imitators, such as Arizona Iced Tea, Mystic, and Nantucket Nectars, as well as Coke and Pepsi through alliances with Nestea and Lipton.

Perhaps what can be learned is that product life cycles are unpredictable—especially where they involve fad or cult followers who may be as fickle as the wind, and where imitation is easy. To bet one's firm on such an acquisition can be risky indeed. But in truth, Smithburg had faced a similar situation with Gatorade and won big. The moral: Decision making under uncertainty can be a crap shoot. But prudence suggests a more cautious approach.

CONSIDER

Can you think of any other learning insights?

QUESTIONS

1. Why do you think the great Snapple giveaway was ineffective?

2. Do you think Snapple could have been turned around? Why or why not?

3. Do you think the premium retail price for Snapple was a serious impediment? Why or why not?

4. "Pouring more money into a lost cause is downright stupid. Smithburg has got to go." Discuss.

5. "This isn't a case where a guy has gone from a genius to a dummy. Who's better at running the company?" Discuss this statement.

6. "What's all the fuss about? Snapple is going great on our college campus. It's a success, man." Do you agree? Why or why not?

7. Do you drink Snapple? If not, why not? Is so, how often—and how well do you like it?

HANDS-ON EXERCISES

Before

1. Be a Devil's Advocate. A major decision is at hand. You are a vice president of the beverage operation at Quaker. William Smithburg is proposing the acquisition of Snapple for some huge sum. Before this decision is made, you have been asked to array any contrary arguments to this expensive acquisition, in other words, to be a Devil's Advocate (one who takes a

contrary position for the sake of argument and clarification of opposing views). What concerns would you raise, and how would you defend them?

After

1. It is late 1996. You are the assistant to Michael Schott, who has just been named president of Snapple. He asks you to formulate a strategic plan for resurrecting Snapple for 1997. What do you propose? Be as specific as you can and be prepared to defend your recommendations.

2. Be a Devil's Advocate. The decision to sell Snapple for $300 million is on the table. What arguments would you array for *not* selling it at this low price? Be as persuasive as you can.

TEAM DEBATE EXERCISE

The acquisition of Snapple is accomplished. Now begins the assimilation. A major debate has ensured regarding whether Snapple should be consolidated with Gatorade, or whether it should remain an independent entity. Debate the two positions as persuasively as possible. Be sure and identify any assumptions made.

INVITATION TO RESEARCH

What is the situation with Snapple and with Smithburg today? Has Snapple prospered under its new ownership? Is Smithburg running any company? Is Gatorade still a formidable brand?

CHAPTER SIXTEEN

Newell Rubbermaid Destroys a Growth Mode

John McDonough, CEO of Newell, specialized in buying small marginal firms and improving their operations. In 10 years, he had bought 75 such firms and polished them by eliminating poorer products, employees, factories, and by stressing customer service. This format began to be called "Newellizing." It is hardly surprising that most of the acquisitions had strong brand names but mediocre customer service. Rubbermaid fit this mode, though it was by far the biggest acquisition and would nearly double Newell's sales.

Rubbermaid, manufacturer and marketer of high-volume, branded plastic and rubber consumer products and toys, had been a darling of investors and academicians alike. For ten years in a row, it placed in the *Fortune* survey of "America's Most Admired Corporations," and it was No. 1 in 1993 and 1994. It was ranked as the second most powerful brand in a Baylor University study of consumer goodwill and received the "Thomas Edison Award" for developing products to make people's lives better. Under CEO Stanley Gault, Rubbermaid's emphasis on innovation often resulted in a new product every day, thereby helping the stock routinely to return 25 percent annually.

Surprisingly, by the middle 1990s Rubbermaid began faltering, partly because of inability to meet the service demands of Wal-Mart, a major customer. Rubbermaid stock plummeted 40 percent from the 1992 high, leaving it ripe for a takeover. Newell Company acquired Rubbermaid on March 24, 1999, expecting to turn it around. But then Newell had to wonder.

THE ACQUISITION AND WOLFGANG SCHMITT

Former Rubbermaid CEO Wolfgang Schmitt felt a cloak of apprehension settling over him in May 1999. It was only 2 months after the merger with Newell had been completed, and things were not going as he expected.

Schmitt had become CEO a year after the legendary Stanley Gault retired in 1991. Gault had returned in 1980 to his hometown of Wooster, Ohio (Rubbermaid headquarters), after more than 31 years with the General Electric Company. During

Gault's tenure, Rubbermaid stock split four times to the delight of stockholders. It was a tough act to follow.

Schmitt often thought about this, but he was certainly a worthy successor to Gault. He had spent all his working life with Rubbermaid after graduating in 1966 from Otterbein College in Westerville, Ohio (about 60 miles from Wooster), with a degree in economics and business administration. A recruiter visiting the campus convinced him to join Rubbermaid, a rapidly growing company. He started as a management trainee and in 27 years worked his way up the corporate ranks to become chairman of the board and chief executive officer in 1993. He was proud of this accomplishment and thought his experience must be an inspiration to young people in the company: Any one of them could dream of becoming CEO, with hard work and loyalty. A significant highlight of his professional life came when he was invited back to Otterbein in November 1997 to inaugurate its Distinguished Executive Lecture Series.

During Schmitt's reign, Rubbermaid reached $2 billion in sales in 1994. When it celebrated its 75-year anniversary a year later, Schmitt set the company's sights on $4 billion in sales for the turn of the century. To do this, he knew it had to become a truly global company, and he instigated four foreign acquisitions that year.

He was an effective CEO; he knew he was. When the Newell Company, a slightly larger multinational firm, expressed an interest in merging, Schmitt thought he owed it to his stockholders, and to himself, to pursue this. After all, the two firms' houseware and hardware products and marketing efforts were compatible, and their combination would result in a $7-billion-a-year consumer products giant. Aiding Schmitt's decision to merge was a nice severance guarantee of $12 million after taxes in addition to his stock options. While Newell's CEO John McDonough would assume the CEO position of the merged corporation, Schmitt was to be a vice chairman and would work closely with McDonough to ensure the smooth merger and to help mold the new company.

Now, barely two months later, Schmitt had been shunted aside. He did not have an office at headquarters, his name was not listed on a new report of the seven highest-paid executives, and he was not even included in the list of directors reported to the Securities and Exchange Commission (SEC). He couldn't help feeling betrayed about no longer having a role in the operations of the company, after he had been so instrumental in bringing about the merger. At 55 years of age, he still had many productive years left. More than this, there was the principle of the thing: This was like a kick in the teeth.

But he was not alone. Three of Rubbermaid's five division presidents—the five divisions were Home Products, Little Tykes, Graco-Century, Curver, and Commercial Products—had already been replaced since the merger. Furthermore, in the Home Products division, only two of the top eight executives were still there.

NEWELL'S ASSESSMENT OF RUBBERMAID

If John McDonough of Newell was so unhappy with current Rubbermaid management and operations, why did he buy Rubbermaid in the first place—and for $6.3 billion dollars, more than two times current sales? At a shareholders' meeting a few months after the acquisition, McDonough tried to explain. He told them that Rubbermaid was a troubled company, but that once it's pulled into the revered operations of Newell, it can be great again.[1]

The shareholders were told that while jobs were being cut, the operations would be stronger in the long run. As a strength, McDonough noted that Rubbermaid commanded 94 percent brand loyalty and generated great customer traffic in stores. But Rubbermaid executives needed to slash unnecessary costs, introduce robotics, and reduce product variety. For example, was it necessary to have dozens of the same type of wastebasket?

Still, McDonough saw poor customer service as the biggest deficiency of Rubbermaid, the most unacceptable aspect of its operation, and the one that Newell could most easily correct. After all, Newell had achieved a 98.5 percent on-time delivery rate in dealings with Wal-Mart. He would see that Rubbermaid was brought up to this same performance standard.

Rubbermaid's Customer Service Problems

Perhaps a declining commitment to customer service dated back to the retirement of Gault, though Schmitt would likely dispute that. Customer service can erode without being obvious to top management. While some customers complain, many others simply switch their business to competitors. Still, Rubbermaid's lapses in customer service should have been obvious for years. After all, Wal-Mart was not tolerant with vendors not meeting its standards. When McDonough's people began digging deeper into Rubbermaid's operations, they found that the company wasn't even measuring customer service. This deficiency is almost the kiss of death when dealing with major retailers.

Up to the mid-1990s, about 15 percent of Rubbermaid's $2 billion-plus revenues came from Wal-Mart. Rubbermaid had had an impressive earnings growth of at least 15 percent a year to go along with 20 percent operating margins, much of this due to the generous space Wal-Mart gave its plastic and rubber products. This was to change abruptly.

In 1995, Wal-Mart refused to let Rubbermaid pass on much of its higher raw material costs and began taking shelf space away and giving it to smaller competitors who undersold Rubbermaid. This resulted in a major earnings drop (see Table 16.1) that forced Rubbermaid to shut nine facilities and cut 9 percent of its 14,000 employees. "When you hitch your wagon to a star, you are at the mercy of that star."[2]

Wal-Mart not only complained about poor deliveries but began taking more drastic action. Each day Wal-Mart gives suppliers such as Newell a two-hour time slot in which their trucks can deliver orders placed 24 hours before. Should the supplier miss the deadline, it pays Wal-Mart for every dollar of lost margin. Now such a fast replenishment of orders required that factories be tied in with Wal-Mart's computers. Rubbermaid began installing software to do this in 1996, and had spent $62 million by

---

[1] Teresa Dixon Murray, "Newell Details Its Plans for Rubbermaid," *Cleveland Plain Dealer*, May 27, 1999, p. C1.

[2] Matthew Schifrin, "The Big Squeeze," *Forbes*, March 11, 1996, p. 46.

TABLE 16.1   Rubbermaid Sales and Earnings, 1992–1997

	1992	1993	1994	1995	1996	1997
Sales (billions)	1.81	1.96	2.17	2.34	2.35	2.40
Net earnings (millions)	184	211	228	59	152	143
Earnings percentage of sales	10.2	20.0	18.9	4.9	14.2	13.8
Earnings per share	1.15	1.32	1.42	.38	1.01	.95

Source: Company reports

Commentary: This 6-year comparison of sales and the various profit indicators show rather starkly the decline in fortunes of Rubbermaid beginning in 1995. Sales remained practically static from 1995 on, although admittedly they were not growing very robustly in the 3 years before. The lack of growth occurred during a period of unprecedented economic prosperity.

The earnings comparisons show up worse. While acceptable earnings growth occurred up to 1995, they greatly worsened beginning in 1995. Not only were net earnings figures drastically reduced, but they showed little sign of recouping, even though there was some improvement from the bottom of 1995. Of course, net earnings as a percent of sales and per share also drastically declined from what they were in 1992–1994. Rubbermaid's major problems with Wal-Mart occurred in 1995.

1999, but still was often not even achieving 80 percent on-time delivery service. This was unacceptable to Wal-Mart, and returns and fines for poor service rose to 4.4 percent of sales in 1998.[3] Finally, Wal-Mart purged most of its stores of Rubbermaid's Little Tikes toy line, giving the space to a competitor, Fisher Price. See the Information Box for a discussion of the power of a giant retailer and the demands it can make.

Wal-Mart had such a high regard for the customer service of Newell that, upon hearing of the impending merger with Newell, again began carrying Little Tykes toys. McDonough vowed to get Rubbermaid's on-time delivery rate of 80 percent up to Newell's 98.5 percent, and he began ripping out Rubbermaid's computer system and writing off the entire $62 million. In addition, McDonough claimed to be able to squeeze $350 million of costs out of Rubbermaid, which would double its operating income.[4]

AFTER THE MERGER

Newell did not turn around and Newellize Rubbermaid quickly, and stockholders were shocked and disappointed. In a time of rising stock prices, Newell Rubbermaid's shares plunged 20 percent in one day in September 1999 as the now-giant consumer goods firm warned that third-quarter earnings would fall short of expectations. This was only the latest in a string of negatives, and Newell Rubbermaid's stock was to lose almost half of its value since the Rubbermaid acquisition in March. It blamed lower-than-expected sales of Rubbermaid's plastic containers and Little Tykes toys. Still, company officials maintained that "the integration process remains on plan."[5]

[3] Murray, p. C3.

[4] Michelle Conlin, "Newellizing Rubbermaid," *Forbes,* May 31, 1999, p. 118.

[5] James P. Miller, "Newell Rubbermaid Shares Fall 20% as an Earnings Short Fall Is Predicted," *Wall Street Journal,* September 7, 1999, p. A4.

INFORMATION BOX

THE DEMANDS OF A GIANT RETAILER

Giant retailers, especially the big discount houses, stand in a power position today relative to their vendors. Part of this power lies in their providing efficient access to the marketplace—imagine the problems of a large consumer goods manufacturer in trying to deal with thousands of small retailers rather than the few big firms that dominate their markets. These giant firms can account for 50 percent and more of many manufacturers' sales. However, if such a major customer is lost or not completely satisfied, a vendor's viability could be in jeopardy.

Retailers like Wal-Mart make full use of their power position. Take paying of invoices, for example. Many vendors give a 2 percent discount if bills are paid within ten days instead of thirty. Wal-Mart routinely pays its bills closer to thirty days and still takes the 2 percent discount. Wal-Mart has also led in "partnering" with its vendors. This "partnering" really means that vendors have to pick up more of the inventory management and merchandising costs associated with Wal-Mart stores, with most of these costs involved in providing fast replenishment so that the stores can maintain lean stocks without losing customer sales through stockouts.

So-called slotting fees are common in the supermarket industry, with manufacturers paying to get things on store shelves. It is estimated that some $9 billion annually changes hands in private, unwritten deals between grocery retailers and food and consumer goods manufacturers.[6]

The following is an example of a slotting fee stipulation of a supermarket chain:

Effective January 1, 1996

Our slotting fee is ... $2,500

An item authorized, will remain authorized for a minimum of six months, (as long as the basic cost does not go up substantially). Many times it is the "slotting fee" that determines whether we authorize an item or not.

With the coercive power of a big retailer, a vendor is practically forced to meet their demands no matter what the cost.

Do you think a big manufacturer, such as Coca-Cola, can be coerced by a big retailer? Why or why not? What might determine the extent of retailer coercion? Can a manufacturer coerce a retailer?

---

[6] John S. Long, "Specialty Items to Drive New Market," *Cleveland Plain Dealer*, October 6, 1999, p. F4.

A month later, coinciding with a Wal-Mart announcement that it was expanding vigorously in Europe, Newell Rubbermaid said it would focus on expanding overseas to serve domestic retailers who are moving abroad. The company had been getting a quarter of its sales outside the United States. "Our customers are going international," McDonough said. "We have the opportunity to follow them. It's a once-in-a-lifetime opportunity."[7]

The company also maintained that it had sharply reduced the number of late shipments of Rubbermaid products and expected to have 98 percent of orders shipped on time either in the present quarter or next.[8]

Was this a wise merger? Did Newell pay too much for a faltering Rubbermaid? It was hardly likely in the first year of a merger that management would admit to maybe making a mistake. But stockholders were betting with their money. Meantime, Wolfgang Schmitt pondered his exile and the erosion of value of his stock options.

DISAPPOINTMENT

John McDonough resigned as CEO in November 2000, after Newell Rubbermaid cut profit forecasts three times in the year after the Rubbermaid acquisition. Joseph Galli, a "master marketer," as *Forbes* proclaimed him, and the first outsider in the company's 99-year history, became the chief executive in January 2001.

Newell needed a rescuer. McDonough, whose forte was buying underperforming companies and Newellizing them, had met his match. This was the third year of flat or falling profits. For 2001, sales were off 2.4 percent and net income down 42 percent, with share prices reflecting this. The $6 billion purchase of Rubbermaid, its biggest deal, had brought Newell to its knees, and Rubbermaid remained the sickest division.

Joseph Galli

The 43-year-old Galli, in 19 years at Black & Decker, had built a reputation as a marketing wunderkind, a brand builder. He was running the company's crown jewel, the DeWalt brand, a high-margin line of power tools for skilled tradesmen and consumer do-it-yourselfers. Galli recruited teams of college graduates, dubbed "swarm teams," to be supermissionary salespeople hawking the DeWalt brand not only at store openings but at union halls and Nascar races as well. See the Information Box: Missionary Salespeople.

Galli brought amazing growth to DeWalt, pushing $60 million in sales in 1992 to more than $1 billion by 1999, in the process providing almost one quarter of the company's $4.6 billion sales. By age 38, Galli was the second-highest-paid executive at Black & Decker and in line for the top position except that the CEO was not ready to step down anytime soon.

Galli left to be president of Amazon.com, staying only a year, then became chief of VerticalNet for 167 days. Some were calling him a tumbleweed but conceded that if anybody could add sizzle to an unpretentious product line of such things as mop buckets, toilet brushes, and plastic containers, he might be the best.[9]

---

[7] "Newell Rubbermaid to Resume Acquisitions, Expand Overseas," *Cleveland Plain Dealer*, October 6, 1999, p. C2.

[8] Ibid.

[9] Bruce Upbin, "Rebirth of a Salesman," *Forbes*, October 1, 2001 pp. 95–104.

Galli spent his first three months at Newell Rubbermaid traveling the world and meeting every manager he could. His predecessor, John McDonough, was a diabetic whose leg was amputated in 1999 and who spent almost all his time at company head-quarters in Beloit, Wisconsin; in his first 6 months, Galli spent just 36 hours there.

Newell hadn't run a national ad campaign on television in three years. In 2000, the firm spent .7 percent on research and development. (Even conservative Colgate spent 2 percent on the innovation of adding a new color of dish detergent.) Sales of the Rubbermaid unit had declined every year since 1998 and were now at $1.8 bil-lion. No-name rivals were taking business away in major retailers such as Wal-Mart, Home Depot, Target, and Bed Bath & Beyond.

Galli tripled spending on new product development for Rubbermaid. He pro-moted the brand on prime-time TV for the first time in three years with a budget of $15 million, more than was spent in the previous ten years combined. He also bud-geted $40 million for swarm teams of well-paid college grads to push Newell Rubbermaid products at mass retailers, as they had done so successfully with power tools at Black & Decker.[10] Galli made his first acquisition in November 2002—buy-ing American Saw and Manufacturing Co., thus expanding into the hand-tool and power-tool market that he knew so well.[11] Could it be that Newell Rubbermaid was on the verge of a turnaround?

INFORMATION BOX

MISSIONARY SALESPEOPLE

Missionary or supporting salespeople do not normally try to secure orders. They are used by manufacturers to provide specialized services and create goodwill and more dealer push. They work with dealers, perhaps to develop point-of-service displays, train dealer salespeople to do a better job of selling the product, provide better communica-tion and rapport between distributor and manufacturer, and in general, aggressively pro-mote the brand. They are particularly important in selling to self-service outlets, such as supermarkets and discount stores, where with no retail clerks selling to customers, dis-plays, shelf space, and in-stock conditions have to be the selling tools.

The supermissionaries or swarm teams of Galli are small armies of energetic college recruits who also work NASCAR races, trade shows, new store openings, and the like. A typical supermissionary is given the use of a new Ford Explorer Sport Trac, a territory of 14 Wal-Marts, and a mission: Make sure Newell's pens, bowls, buckets, and blinds are neatly displayed, priced right, and piled high in prominent spots.[12]

Evaluate this statement: "Good customer service doesn't do you much good, but poor customer service can kill you."

---

[12] Upbin, p. 100.

---

[10] Ibid. p. 104.

[11] "Newell Rubbermaid To Buy American Saw in $450 Million Deal," *Wall Street Journal*, November 25, 2002, p. B6.

ANALYSIS

This case illustrates not only the risks of dealing with behemoth customers but also the rewards if you can satisfy their demands. After all, in better days Newell Rubbermaid prepared to follow Wal-Mart to Europe and be a prime supplier of its stores there. But a vendor has to have the commitment and ability to meet stringent requirements. If a 24-hour delivery cycle is demanded, the vendor must achieve this, regardless of costs. If selling prices are to be pared to the bone, efficiency must somehow be jacked up and production costs pruned, or else profitability may have to be sacrificed even to the point of extreme concern. Otherwise, the vendor can be replaced.

The alternative? To be content with far less revenues and a host of smaller accounts, or else to have such a brand name as to be partly insulated from price competition. Rubbermaid thought it had this, due to its public accolades of past years. Perhaps this contributed to its apathy regarding its delivery service. But Wal-Mart was hardly impressed with the superiority of this brand's products that cost more than alternative suppliers and could not be delivered on time.

But note that improving service and shortening replenishment time is not easily or cheaply done. Rubbermaid spent $62 million on computer technology to enable it to meet Wal-Mart's demands, but it was not enough. Better control of warehouse inventories and production schedules is essential. The vendor will need to carry more of the inventory burden traditionally assumed by the retailer and incur additional expenses and investment for more manpower and trucks and other equipment. Perhaps the most damning indictment of Rubbermaid's service deficiencies was how long these continued without being corrected. The problem initially surfaced in 1995, but by 1999 on-time deliveries had still not improved appreciably. What was Rubbermaid top management doing all this time? Wolfgang Schmitt can hardly escape the blame that in almost five years he had not corrected this serious problem with the most important customer.

The eagerness to merge that we saw in this case, by McDonough of Newell and Wolfgang Schmitt of Rubbermaid, may not always be in the best interests of shareholders, and certainly not of employees. Communities also suffer, as plants are closed and headquarters moved. It may even not be in the best interest of the executives involved, as Schmitt realized to his dismay—despite taking home a sizable severance package. But is this enough to make up for losing the power and prestige of a top management position, and all the perks that go with it? And what if the value of the stock in the severance package crashes as Schmitt found to his further dismay? And McDonough in his holdings?

In this era of merger mania, a more sober appraisal is needed by many firms. Not all mergers are in the best interests of both parties. Too many times a firm pays too much to acquire another firm, as we saw in the previous chapter where Quaker Oats bought Snapple for $1.7 billion and three years later got rid of it for $300 million. Frequently the glowing prospects of synergy do not work out. (See the following Information Box and a discussion of the allure and pitfalls of synergy in a merger.)

When an acquisition finally turns out to be unwise, especially where too much is paid for the acquired firm, the conclusion may be that someone fumbled the homework, that the research and investigation of the firm to be acquired was hasty, biased,

INFORMATION BOX

THE ALLURE OF SYNERGY IN A MERGER, AND THE PITFALLS

Synergy results from creating a whole that is greater than the sum of its parts that can accomplish more than the total of the individual contributions. In an acquisition, synergy occurs if the two or more firms, when combined, are more efficient, productive, and profitable than they were as separate operations before the merger. Sometimes this concept is referred to as $2 + 2 = 5$.

How can such synergy occur? If duplication of efforts can be eliminated, if operations can be streamlined, if economies of scale are possible, if specialization can be enhanced, if greater financial and managerial resources can be tapped—then a synergistic situation is likely to occur. Such an expanded operation should be a stronger force in the market than the individual single units that existed before.

The concept of synergism is the rationale for mergers and acquisitions. But sometimes combining causes the reverse: negative synergy, where the consequences are worse than the sum of individual efforts. If friction arises between the entities; if organizational missions are incompatible; if the new organizational climate creates fearful, resentful, and frustrated employees, then synergy is unlikely. And if greater managerial and financial resources are not realized—if indeed financial resources are depleted because of the interest overhead due to the acquisition—then synergy becomes negative. Furthermore, if because of sheer optimism or an uncontrolled acquisitive drive, more is paid for the acquisition than it is really worth, then a grand blunder has been made. Could that have been the case with the Rubbermaid acquisition?

Do you think a typical committee or group has more synergy than the same individuals working alone? Why or why not?

or downright incompetent. Admittedly, in some cases several suitors may be bidding for the same acquisition candidate, and this then becomes a contest: Who will make the winning bid? The only beneficiaries to such a situation—besides the consultants, lawyers, and investment bankers—are the shareholders of the firm to be acquired.

UPDATE

Early in 2003, Galli announced plans to move the headquarters of Newell Rubbermaid from the "cornfields surrounding the hometown of Freeport, Illinois" to Atlanta, "the city of the future," as Galli depicted it. He thought moving would be a signal that big changes were happening inside and out. He saw that the key to a new image was being in a city that symbolized change and innovation. It didn't hurt that Atlanta offered a sweet deal, potentially giving the company up to $25 million in breaks, as well as $1.3 million in cash for land and equipment purchases, as well as some tax relief.[13]

Galli's tenure since 2001 has not provided any breakthrough in sales, profits, and stock prices. The company had 2003 sales of about $7 billion, not much higher than the 2000 sales of $6.9 billion. For the first quarter of 2004, the net loss was $74.9 million on sales of $1.54 billion, and the share price was in the low $20s. Newell sold three subsidiaries in early 2004, part of its strategy to divest underperforming "non-strategic businesses." Now it was abandoning its growth-by-acquisition strategy "to reconfigure our portfolio, through divestitures and the exit of low-margin product lines," Galli announced.[14] Hardly a growth company anymore.

WHAT CAN BE LEARNED?

Customer Service Is Vital in Dealing with Big Customers

We saw in this case the consequences of not being able to meet the service demands of Wal-Mart. A vendor's very viability may depend on somehow gearing up to meet the service expectations. This should be a top priority if such a customer is not to be lost. Correcting the situation should be a matter of weeks or months, and not years.

The Well-Known Brand Name Does Not Always Compensate for Higher Prices or Poor Service When Dealing with Big Retailers

Generally, we think of a well-respected brand name as giving the vendor certain liberties, of insulating the vendor, at least somewhat, from vicious price competition and even excusing the vendor from some service standards such as prompt and dependable delivery. After all, a respected brand name gives an image of quality, which lesser brands do not have, as well as an assured body of loyal customers.

Well, Wal-Mart's dealings with Rubbermaid before the merger certainly disprove that notion.

How can this be? It still becomes a matter of power position. Not having Rubbermaid, or Little Tykes toys, was hardly damaging to Wal-Mart with its eager alternative suppliers. But the loss of Wal-Mart, even only the partial loss of being given less shelf space, was serious for Rubbermaid.

The Positive Aspects of Organizational Restructuring for Acquisitions Are Mixed

The idea of restructuring generally means downsizing. Some assets or corporate divisions may be sold off or eliminated, and the remaining organization thereby

---

[13] Peralte C. Paul and Patti Bond, "Out With the Old," Cox News, as reported in *Cleveland Plain Dealer*, March 8, 2003, pp. C1, C3.

[14] Marcia Pledger, "Newell Rubbermaid Continues Divesting," *Cleveland Plain Dealer*, May 9, 2004, p. G4.

streamlined. This usually means layoffs, plant closings, and headquarters relocations. In Rubbermaid's case, the small Ohio town of Wooster faced the loss of its headquarters and some 3,000 jobs. Of course, management's defense always is that while jobs are being cut, the operations will be stronger in the long run. Perhaps; but not always.

Where an organization has become fat and inefficient with layers of bureaucracy, some pruning of personnel and operations is necessary. But how much is too much, and how much is not enough? Certainly those personnel who are not willing to accept change may have to be let go. Weak persons and operations that show little probability of improvement need to be cut, just as the athlete who can't perform up to expectations can hardly be carried. Still, it is usually better to wait for sufficient information as to the "why" of poor performance before assigning blame for unsatisfactory operational results. (You may want to review Chapter 6 and the Scott Paper and Al Dunlap case for the worst scenario here.)

Periodic Housecleaning Produces Competitive Health

In order to minimize the buildup of deadwood, all aspects of an organization periodically ought to be objectively appraised. Weak products and operations should be pruned, unless solid justification exists for keeping them. Such justification might include good growth prospects or complementing other products and operations or even providing a desired customer service. In particular, staff and headquarters personnel and functions should be scrutinized, perhaps every five years, with the objective of weeding out the redundant and superfluous. Most important, these evaluations should be done objectively, with decisive actions taken where needed. While some layoffs may result, they might not be necessary if suitable transfers are possible.

Going back to Rubbermaid, the five-year-long tolerance of little improvement in customer service was inexcusable, and one would think that heads should roll (as undoubtedly some did and quickly when Newell took over).

Is There Life Without Wal-Mart for a Big Mass Market Consumer Goods Manufacturer?

Can such a large manufacturer be strong and profitable without selling to the giant retailers? Certainly other distribution channels are available in reaching consumers, such as smaller retailers, different types of retailers, wholesalers, and the Internet. For smaller manufacturers, some of these are viable alternatives to Wal-Mart, Target, Kmart, and the various large department store corporations.

Newell and Rubbermaid's products were diversified but still geared to rather pedestrian household and hardware consumer use, hardly the grist to create a fashion or fad demand. A limited distribution strategy, such as through boutiques, would hardly produce the sales volume needed. Only the mega-retailers could provide the mass distribution and sales volume needed. Of course, Wal-Mart was not the only large retailer, but it was the biggest. Kmart, Target, and the chain department stores were alternatives. But these tended to be just as demanding as Wal-

Mart. This suggests that somehow the demands of giant retailers had to be catered to, regardless of costs or inclinations for firms like Newell and Rubbermaid.

Missionary Salespeople Can Enhance Customer Service in Dealing with Large Retailers

Many vendors are realizing this today, and such sales-support staff are frequently used to provide the service, rapport, and feedback desirable in dealing with these most important clients. The vendor that provides the best such support may well win out over competitors. Furthermore, such missionaries may alert the vendor to emerging problems or competitive situations that need to be countered. Where they are swarm teams like Galli's, they can be a powerful tool in winning the battle for shelf space.

Once the Growth Mode Is Lost, It Is Difficult to Win Back

Newell and its albatross acquisition, Rubbermaid, certainly are examples of this. Both were high flying in the early 1990s, but even with Galli, a hot-shot marketer with his previous firm, he had not yet been able to turn around Newell Rubbermaid by 2005.

CONSIDER

Can you add any additional learning insights?

QUESTIONS

1. "Periodic evaluations of personnel and departments aimed at pruning 'deadwood' cause far too much harm to the organization. Such 'axing' evaluations should themselves be pruned." Argue this position as persuasively as you can.

2. Now gather your most persuasive arguments for such "axing" evaluations.

3. How do you account for Rubbermaid's inability to improve its delivery service to Wal-Mart? What factors do you see as contributing to this on-going deficiency?

4. Do you think Newell acted too hastily in discharging Schmitt and other top executives so soon after the merger? Why or why not?

5. Do you think Wal-Mart and the other large retailers are going too far in their demands on their suppliers? Where would you draw the line?

6. Stanley Gault's strategy of trying to introduce a new product every day was lauded as the mark of a successful firm permeated by innovative thinking. Do you agree with this?

7. Is it likely that a decades-old organization, such as Rubbermaid, would be bloated with excessive bureaucracy and overhead? Why or why not?

HANDS-ON EXERCISES

1. Be a Devil's Advocate (one who argues a contrary position). You have been asked by several concerned board members to argue against the avid "Newellizing" policy of John McDonough at the next board meeting. Marshal as many contrary or cautionary arguments as you can and present them as persuasively, yet as tactfully, as you can.

2. You are one of the three divisional presidents fired by McDonough in the first two months of the merger. Describe your feelings and your action plan at this point. (If you want to make some assumptions, state them specifically.)

3. You are a vice president of Rubbermaid, reporting to Wolfgang Schmitt in 1995. The first serious complaints have surfaced from Wal-Mart concerning unacceptable delivery problems. Schmitt has ordered you to look into the complaints and prepare a course of action. Be as specific as you can on how you would approach this and what recommendations you would make.

TEAM DEBATE EXERCISE

It is early 1998. The demands of Wal-Mart are intensifying, and Newell is making overtures to acquire Rubbermaid. Debate these two courses of action in this turn-about year for Rubbermaid: (1) We must gear up to meet Wal-Mart's demands, even though estimated costs of complying are $300 million dollars in a new computer network and other capital and operating costs versus (2) It is better to sacrifice the increasingly dictatorial Wal-Mart account and seek alternative distribution. (For this option you need to come up with some creative alternatives, and defend them.)

INVITATION TO RESEARCH

What is Wolfgang Schmitt doing after being ousted from an active role with Newell Rubbermaid? Have Newell Rubbermaid's fortunes improved yet under Galli's management, or has he been replaced? How about the stock price?

CHAPTER SEVENTEEN

Euro Disney: Bungling a Successful Format

With high expectations Euro Disney opened just outside Paris in April 1992. Success seemed ensured. After all, the Disneylands in Florida, California, and more recently, Japan, were all spectacular successes. But somehow all the rosy expectations became a delusion. The opening results cast even the future continuance of Euro Disney into doubt. How could what seemed so right be so wrong? What mistakes were made?

PRELUDE

Optimism

Perhaps a few early omens should have raised some cautions. Between 1987 and 1991, three $150 million amusement parks had opened in France with great fanfare. All had fallen flat, and by 1991, two were in bankruptcy. Now Walt Disney Company was finalizing its plans to open Europe's first Disneyland early in 1992. This would turn out to be a $4.4 billion enterprise sprawling over 5,000 acres 20 miles east of Paris. Initially, it would have six hotels and 5,200 rooms, more rooms than the entire city of Cannes, and lodging was expected to triple in a few years as Disney opened a second theme park to keep visitors at the resort longer.

Disney also expected to develop a growing office complex, this to be only slightly smaller than France's biggest, La Defense, in Paris. Plans also called for shopping malls, apartments, golf courses, and vacation homes. Euro Disney would tightly control all this ancillary development, designing and building nearly everything itself, and eventually selling off the commercial properties at a huge profit.

Disney executives had no qualms about the huge enterprise, which would cover an area one-fifth the size of Paris itself. They were more worried that the park might not be big enough to handle the crowds:

"My biggest fear is that we will be too successful."

"I don't think it can miss. They are masters of marketing. When the place opens, it will be perfect. And they know how to make people smile—even the French."[1]

Company executives initially predicted that 11 million Europeans would visit the extravaganza in the first year alone. After all, Europeans accounted for 2.7 million visits to the U.S. Disney parks and spent $1.6 billion on Disney merchandise. Surely, a park in closer proximity would draw many thousands more. As Disney executives thought more about it, the forecast of 11 million seemed most conservative. They reasoned that since Disney parks in the United States (population of 250 million) attract 41 million visitors a year, then if Euro Disney attracted visitors in the same proportion, attendance could reach 60 million with Western Europe's 370 million people. Table 17.1 shows the 1990 attendance at the two U. S. Disney parks and the newest Japanese Disneyland, as well as the attendance/population ratios.

Adding fuel to the optimism was the fact that Europeans typically have more vacation time than do U. S. workers. For example, 5-week vacations are commonplace for French and Germans, compared to two to three weeks for U.S. workers.

The failure of the three earlier French parks was seen as irrelevant. Robert Fitzpatrick, Euro Disney's chairman, stated, "We are spending 22 billion French francs before we open the door, while the other places spent 700 million. This means we can pay infinitely more attention to details—to costumes, hotels, shops, trash baskets—to create a fantastic place. There's just too great a response to Disney for us to fail."[2]

TABLE 17.1   Attendance and Attendance/Population Ratios of Disney Parks, 1990

	Visitors	Population	Ratio
	(millions)		
United States			
Disneyland (Southern California)	12.9	250	5.2%
Disney World/Epcot Center (Florida)	28.5	250	11.4%
Total United States	41.4	500	16.6%
Japan			
Tokyo Disneyland	16.0	124	13.5%
Euro Disney	?	310[a]	?

[a] Within a two-hour flight.

Source: Euro Disney, *Amusement Business Magazine.*

Commentary: Even if the attendance/population ratio for Euro Disney is only 10 percent, which is far below that of some other theme parks, still 31 million visitors could be expected. Euro Disney "conservatively" predicted 11 million the first year.

---

[1] Steven Greenhouse, "Playing Disney in the Parisian Fields," *New York Times*, February 17, 1991, Section 3, pp. 1, 6.
[2] Ibid. p. 6.

Nonetheless, a few scattered signs could be found that not everyone was happy with the coming of Disney. Leftist demonstrators at Euro Disney's stock offering greeted company executives with eggs, ketchup, and "Mickey Go Home" signs. Some French intellectuals decried the pollution of the country's cultural ambiance with the coming of Mickey Mouse and company: They called the park an American cultural abomination. The mainstream press also seemed contrary, describing every Disney setback "with glee." And French officials, in negotiating with Disney, sought less American and more European culture at France's Magic Kingdom. Still, such protests and bad press seemed contrived, unrepresentative, and certainly not predictive. Company officials dismissed the early criticism as "the ravings of an insignificant elite."[3]

The Location Decision

In the search for a site for Euro Disney, Disney executives examined 200 locations in Europe. The other finalist was Barcelona, Spain. Its major attraction was warmer weather. But its transportation system was not as good as around Paris, and it also lacked level tracts of land of sufficient size. The clincher for the decision for Paris was its more central location. Table 17.2 shows the number of people within two to six hours of the Paris site.

The beet fields of the Marne-la-Vallee area were the choice. Being near Paris seemed a major advantage, since Paris was Europe's biggest tourist draw. And France was eager to win the project to help lower its jobless rate and also to enhance its role as the center of tourist activity in Europe. The French government expected the project to create at least 30,000 jobs and to contribute $1 billion a year from foreign visitors.

To encourage the project, the French government allowed Disney to buy up huge tracts of land at 1971 prices. It provided $750 million in loans at below-market rates and also spent hundreds of millions of dollars on subway and other capital improvements for the park. For example, Paris's express subway was extended out to the park; a 35-minute ride from downtown cost about $2.50. A new railroad station

TABLE 17.2   Number of People Within 2–6 Hours of the Paris Site

Within a 2-hour drive	17 million people
Within a 4-hour drive	41 million people
Within a 6-hour drive	109 million people
Within a 2-hour flight	310 million people

Source: Euro Disney, *Amusement Business* magazine.

Commentary: The much more densely populated and geographically compact European continent makes access to Euro Disney much more convenient than it is in the United States.

[3] Peter Gumbel and Richard Turner, "Fans Like Euro Disney But Its Parent's Goofs Weigh the Park Down," *Wall Street Journal,* March 10, 1994, p. A12.

for the high-speed Train à Grande Vitesse was built only 150 yards from the entrance gate. This enabled visitors from Brussels to arrive in only 90 minutes. And when the English Channel tunnel opened in 1994, even London was only three hours and ten minutes away. Actually, Euro Disney was the second largest construction project in Europe, second only to construction of the English Channel tunnel.

Financing

Euro Disney cost $4.4 billion. Table 17.3 shows the sources of financing in percentages. The Disney Company had a 49 percent stake in the project, which was the most that the French government would allow. For this stake, it invested $160 million, while other investors contributed $1.2 billion in equity. The rest was financed by loans from the government, banks, and special partnerships formed to buy properties and lease them back.

The payoff for Disney began after the park opened. The company received 10 percent of Euro Disney's admission fees and 5 percent of the food and merchandise revenues. This was the same arrangement as Disney had with the Japanese park. But in the Tokyo Disneyland, the company took no ownership interest, opting instead only for the licensing fees and a percentage of the revenues. The reason for the conservative position with Tokyo Disneyland was that Disney money was heavily committed to building Epcot Center in Florida. Furthermore, Disney had some concerns about the Tokyo enterprise. This was the first non-American and cold-weather Disneyland. It seemed prudent to minimize the risks. But this turned out to be a significant blunder of conservatism, as Tokyo became a huge success, as the following Information Box on page 250 discusses in more detail.

Special Modifications

With the experiences of the previous theme parks, and particularly that of the first cold-weather park in Tokyo, Disney construction executives were able to bring state-of-the-art refinements to Euro Disney. Exacting demands were placed on French

TABLE 17.3   Sources of Initial Financing for Euro Disney (percent)

Total to Finance: $4.4 billion	100%
Shareholders equity, including $160 million from Walt Disney Co.	32
Loan from French government	22
Loan from group of 45 banks	21
Bank loans to Disney hotels	16
Real estate partnerships	9

Source: Euro Disney.

Commentary: The full flavor of the leverage is shown here, with equity comprising only 32% of the total expenditure.

INFORMATION BOX

THE TOKYO DISNEYLAND SUCCESS

Tokyo Disneyland opened in 1983 on 201 acres in the eastern suburb of Urazasu. It was arranged that an ownership group, Oriental Land, would build, own, and operate the theme park, with advice from Disney. The owners borrowed most of the $650 million needed to bring the project to fruition. Disney invested no money but received 10 percent of the revenues from admission and rides and 5 percent of sales of food, drink, and souvenirs.

While the start was slow, Japanese soon began flocking to the park in great numbers. By 1990, some 16 million a year passed through the turnstiles, about one-fourth more than visited Disneyland in California. In fiscal year 1990, revenues reached $988 million with profits of $150 million. Indicative of the Japanese preoccupation with things American, the park served almost no Japanese food, and the live entertainers were mostly American. Japanese management even apologized for the presence of a single Japanese restaurant inside the park: "A lot of elderly Japanese came here from outlying parts of Japan, and they were not very familiar with hot dogs and hamburgers."[4]

Disney executives were soon to realize the great mistake they made in not taking substantial ownership in Tokyo Disneyland. They did not want to make the same mistake with Euro Disney.

Would you expect the acceptance of the genuine American experience in Tokyo to be indicative of the reaction of the French and Europeans? Why or why not?

---

[4] James Sterngold, "Cinderella Hits Her Stride in Tokyo," *New York Times*, February 17, 1991, p. 6.

construction companies, and a higher level of performance and compliance resulted than many thought possible to achieve. The result was a major project on time, if not completely on budget. In contrast, the Channel tunnel was plagued by delays and severe cost overruns.

One of the things learned from the cold-weather project in Japan was that more needed to be done to protect visitors from such weather problems as wind, rain, and cold. Consequently, Euro Disney's ticket booths were protected from the elements, as were the lines waiting for attractions, and even the moving sidewalk from the 12,000-car parking area.

Certain French accents—and British, German, and Italian accents as well—were added to the American flavor. The park had two official languages, English and French, but multilingual guides were available for Dutch, Spanish, German, and Italian visitors. Discoveryland, based on the science fiction of France's Jules Verne, was a new attraction. A theater with a full 360-degree screen acquaints visitors with a sweep of European history. And, not the least modification for cultural diversity, Snow White spoke German, and the Belle Notte Pizzeria and Pasticceria were right next to Pinocchio.

Disney foresaw that it might encounter some cultural problems. This was one of the reasons for choosing Robert Fitzpatrick as Euro Disney's president. While American, he spoke French and had a French wife. However, he was not able to establish the rapport needed and was replaced in 1993 by a French native. Still, some of his admonitions that France should not be approached as if it were Florida fell on deaf ears.

RESULTS

As the April 1992 opening approached, the company launched a massive communications blitz aimed at publicizing the fact that the fabled Disney experience was now accessible to all Europeans. Some 2,500 people from various print and broadcast media were lavishly entertained while being introduced to the new facilities. Most media people were positively impressed with the inauguration and the enthusiastic spirit of the staffers. These public relations efforts, however, were criticized by some for being heavy-handed and for not providing access to Disney executives.

As 1992 wound down after the opening, it became clear that revenue projections were, unbelievably—not being met. But the opening turned out to be in the middle of a severe recession in Europe. European visitors, perhaps as a consequence, were far more frugal than their American counterparts. Many packed their own lunches and shunned the Disney hotels. For example, a visitor named Corine from southern France typified the "no spend" attitude of many: "It's a bottomless pit," she said as she, her husband, and their three children toured Euro Disney on a three-day visit. "Every time we turn around, one of the kids wants to buy something."[5] Perhaps investor expectations, despite the logic and rationale, were simply unrealistic.

Indeed, Disney had initially priced the park and hotels to meet revenue targets and assumed demand was there, at any price. Park admission was $42.25 for adults— higher than at the American parks. A room at the flagship Disneyland Hotel, at the park's entrance, cost about $340 a night, the equivalent of a top hotel in Paris. It was soon averaging only a 50 percent occupancy. Guests were not staying as long or spending as much on the fairly high-priced food and merchandise. We can label the initial pricing strategy at Euro Disney as *skimming pricing*. The Information Box on page 252 discusses skimming and its opposite, penetration pricing.

Disney executives soon realized they had made a major miscalculation. While visitors to Florida's Disney World often stayed more than four days, Euro Disney— with one theme park compared to Florida's three—was proving to be a two-day experience at best. Many visitors arrived early in the morning, rushed to the park, staying late at night, then checked out of the hotel the next morning before heading back to the park for one final exploration.

The problems of Euro Disney were not public acceptance (despite the earlier critics). Europeans loved the place. Since the opening, it attracted just under one million visitors a month, thus easily achieving the original projections. Such patronage

[5] Ailing Euro May Face Closure," *Cleveland Plain Dealer,* January 1, 1994, p. E1.

INFORMATION BOX

SKIMMING AND PENETRATION PRICING

A firm with a new product or service may be in a temporary monopolistic situation. If there is little or no present and potential competition, more discretion in pricing is possible. In such a situation (and, of course, Euro Disney was in this situation), one of two basic and opposite approaches may be taken in the pricing strategy: (1) skimming or (2) penetration.

Skimming is a relatively high-price strategy. It is the most tempting where the product or service is highly differentiated, since it yields high per-unit profits. It is compatible with a quality image. But it has limitations. It assumes a rather inelastic demand curve, in which sales will not be appreciably affected by price. And if the product or service is easily imitated (which was hardly the case with Euro Disney), then competitors are encouraged because of the high profit margins.

The penetration strategy of low prices assumes an elastic demand curve, with sales increasing substantially if prices can be lowered. It is compatible with economies of scale and discourages competitive entry. The classic example of penetration pricing was the Model T Ford. Henry Ford lowered his prices to make the car within the means of the general public, expanded production into the millions, and in so doing realized new horizons of economies of scale.

Euro Disney correctly saw itself in a monopoly position; it correctly judged that it had a relatively inelastic demand curve with customers flocking to the park regardless of rather high prices. What it did not reckon with was the shrewdness of European visitors: Because of the high prices, they shortened their stay, avoided the hotels, brought their own food and drink, and only sparingly bought the Disney merchandise.

What advantages would a lower price penetration strategy have offered Euro Disney? Do you see any drawbacks?

---

made it Europe's biggest paid tourist attraction. But large numbers of frugal patrons did not come close to enabling Disney to meet revenue and profit projections and cover a bloated overhead.

Other operational errors and miscalculations, most of these cultural, hurt the enterprise. A policy of serving no alcohol in the park caused consternation in a country where wine is customary for lunch and dinner. (This policy has since been reversed.) Disney thought Monday would be a light day and Friday a heavy one, and allocated staff accordingly, but the reverse was true. It found great peaks and valleys in attendance: The number of visitors per day in the high season could be ten times the number in slack times. The need to lay off employees during quiet periods came up against France's inflexible labor schedules.

One unpleasant surprise concerned breakfast. "We were told that Europeans don't take breakfast, so we downsized the restaurants," recalled one executive. "And guess what? Everybody showed up for breakfast. We were trying to serve 2,500 breakfasts at 350-seat restaurants. The lines were horrendous."[6]

Disney failed to anticipate another demand, this time from tour bus drivers. Restrooms were built for 50 drivers, but on peak days 2,000 drivers were seeking the facilities. "From impatient drivers to grumbling bankers, Disney stepped on toe after European toe."[7]

For the fiscal year ending September 30, 1993, the amusement park had lost $960 million in U.S. dollars, and the future of the park was in doubt. (As of December 31, 1993, the cumulative loss was 6.04 billion francs, or $1.03 billion.) Walt Disney made $175 million available to tide Euro Disney over until the next spring. Adding to the problems of the struggling park were heavy interest costs. As depicted in Table 17.3, against a total cost of $4.4 billion, only 32 percent of the project was financed by equity investment. Some $2.9 billion was borrowed primarily from 60 creditor banks, at interest rates running as high as 11 percent. Thus, the enterprise began heavily leveraged, and the hefty interest charges greatly increased the overhead to be covered from operations. Serious negotiations began with the banks to restructure and refinance.

ATTEMPTS TO RECOVER

The $960 million lost in the first fiscal year represented a shortfall of more than $2.5 million a day. The situation was not quite as dire as these statistics would seem to indicate. Actually, the park was generating an operating profit. But non-operating costs were bringing it deeply into the red.

Still, operations were far from satisfactory, although they were becoming better. It had taken 20 months to smooth out the wrinkles and adjust to the miscalculations about hotel demand and the willingness of Europeans to pay substantial prices for lodging, meals, and merchandise. Operational efficiencies were slowly improving.

By the beginning of 1994, Euro Disney had been made more affordable. Prices of some hotel rooms were cut—for example, at the low end, from $76 per night to $51. Expensive jewelry was replaced by $10 T-shirts and $5 crayon sets. Luxury sit-down restaurants were converted to self-service. Off-season admission prices were reduced from $38 to $30. And operating costs were reduced 7 percent by streamlining operations and eliminating over 900 jobs.

Efficiency and *economy* became the new watchwords. Merchandise in stores was pared from 30,000 items to 17,000, with more of the remaining goods being pure U.S. Disney products. (The company had thought that European tastes might prefer more subtle items than the garish Mickey and Minnie souvenirs, but this was found not so.) The number of different food items offered by park services was reduced more than 50 percent. New training programs were designed to remotivate the 9,000 full-time permanent employees, to make them more responsive to customers and

---

[6] Gumbel and Turner, p. A12.

[7] Ibid.

more flexible in their job assignments. Employees in contact with the public were given crash courses in German and Spanish.

Still, as we have seen, the problem had not been attendance, although the recession and the high prices had reduced it. Some 18 million people passed through the turnstiles in the first 20 months of operation. But they were not spending money as people did in the U. S. parks. Furthermore, Disney had alienated some European tour operators with its high prices, and it diligently sought to win them back.

Management had hoped to reduce the heavy interest overhead by selling the hotels to private investors. But the hotels only had an occupancy rate of 55 percent, making them unattractive to investors. While the recession was a factor in such low occupancy rates, most of the problem lay in the calculation of lodging demands. With the park just 35 minutes from the center of Paris, many visitors stayed in town. About the same time as the opening, the real estate market in France collapsed, making the hotels unsalable in the short term. This added to the overhead burden and confounded business plan forecasts.

While some analysts were relegating Euro Disney to the cemetery, few remembered that Orlando's Disney World showed early symptoms of being a disappointment. Costs were heavier than expected, and attendance was below expectations. But Orlando's Disney World turned out to be one of the most profitable resorts in North America.

PROGNOSIS

Euro Disney had many things going for it, despite the disastrous early results. In May 1994, a station on the high-speed rail running from southern to northern France opened within walking distance of Euro Disney. This should help fill many of the hotel rooms too ambitiously built. The summer of 1994, the 50th anniversary of the Normandy invasion, brought many people to France. Another favorable sign for Euro Disney was the English Channel tunnel's opening in 1994, which potentially could bring a flood of British tourists.

Furthermore, the recession in Europe was bound to end, and with it should come renewed interest in travel. As real estate prices become more favorable, hotels can be sold and real estate development around the park spurred.

Even as Disney Chairman Michael Eisner threatened to close the park unless lenders restructured the debt, Disney increased its French presence, opening a Disney store on the Champs Elysees. The likelihood of a Disney pullout seemed remote, despite the posturing of Eisner, since royalty fees could be a sizable source of revenues even if the park only breaks even after servicing its debt. With only a 3.5 percent increase in revenues in 1995 and a 5 percent increase in 1996, these could yield $46 million in royalties for the parent company. "You can't ask, 'What does Euro Disney mean in 1995?' You have to ask, 'What does it mean in 1998?'"[8]

---

[8] Lisa Gubernick, "Mickey N'est pas Fini," *Forbes*, February 14, 1994, p. 43.

ANALYSIS

Euro Disney, as we have seen, fell far short of expectations in the first 20 months of its operation, so much so that its continued existence was even questioned. What went wrong?

External Factors

A serious economic recession that affected all of Europe undoubtedly was a major impediment to meeting expectations. As noted before, it adversely affected attendance—although still not all that much—but drastically affected spending patterns with frugality being the order of the day for many visitors. The recession also affected real estate demand and prices, thus saddling Disney with hotels it had hoped to sell at profitable prices to eager investors, and thereby take the strain off its hefty interest payments.

The company assumed that European visitors would not be greatly different from those visitors, foreign and domestic, of U.S. Disney parks. Yet, at least in the first few years of operation, visitors were much more price conscious. This suggested that those within a two- to four-hour drive of Euro Disney were considerably different from the ones who traveled overseas, at least in spending ability and willingness.

Internal Factors

Despite the decades of experience with the U.S. Disney parks and the successful experience with the newer Japan park, Disney still made serious blunders in its operational planning, such as the demand for breakfasts, the insistence on wine at meals, the severe peaks and valleys in scheduling, and even such mundane things as sufficient restrooms for tour bus drivers. It had problems in motivating and training its French employees in efficiency and customer orientation. Did all these mistakes reflect an intractable French mind-set or a deficiency of Disney management? Perhaps both. But should not Disney management have researched all cultural differences more thoroughly? Further, the park needed major streamlining of inventories and operations after the opening. The mistakes suggested an arrogant mind-set by Disney management: "We were arrogant," concedes one executive. "It was like, 'We're building the Taj Mahal and people will come—on our terms.'"[9]

The miscalculations in hotel rooms and in pricing of many products, including food services, showed an insensitivity to the harsh economic conditions. But the greatest mistake was taking on too much debt for the park. The highly leveraged situation burdened Euro Disney with such hefty interest payments and overhead that the breakeven point was impossibly high and even threatened the viability of the enterprise. See the Information Box on page 256 for a discussion of the important inputs and implications affecting breakeven, and how these should play a role in strategic planning.

---

[9] Gumbel and Turner, p. A12

INFORMATION BOX

THE BREAKEVEN POINT

A breakeven analysis is a vital tool in making go/no go decisions about new ventures and alternative business strategies. This can be shown graphically as follows: Below the breakeven point, the venture suffers losses; above it, the venture becomes profitable.

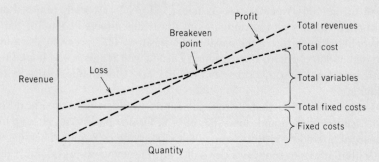

Let us make a hypothetical comparison of Euro Disney with its $1.6 billion in high interest loans (some of these as high as 11 percent) from the banks, and what the situation might be with more equity and less borrowed funds:

For this example, let us assume that other fixed costs are $240 million, that the average interest rate on the debt is 10 percent, and that average profit margin (contribution to overhead) from each visitor is $32. Now let us consider two scenarios: (a) the $1.6 billion of debt, and (b) only $0.5 billion of debt.

The number of visitors needed to breakeven are determined as follows:

$$\text{Breakeven} = \frac{\text{Total fixed costs}}{\text{Contribution to overhead}}$$

Scenario (a): Interest = 10% ($1,600,000,000) = $160,000,000
Fixed costs = Interest + $240,000,000
= 160,000,000 + 240,000,000
= $400,000,000

$$\text{Breakeven} = \frac{\$400,000,000}{\$32} = 12,500,000 \text{ visitors needed to breakeven}$$

Scenario (b) Interest = 10% (500,000,000) = $50,000,000
Fixed costs = 50,000,000 + 240,000,000
= $290,000,000

$$\text{Breakeven} = \frac{\$290,000,000}{\$32} = 9,062,500 \text{ visitors needed to breakeven}$$

Because Euro Disney expected 11 million visitors the first year, it obviously was not going to break even while servicing $1.6 billion in debt with $160 million in interest charges per year. The average visitor would have to be induced to spend more, thereby increasing the average profit or contribution to overhead.

In making go/no go decisions, many costs can be estimated quite closely. What cannot be determined as surely are the sales figures. Certain things can be done to affect the breakeven point. Obviously, it can be lowered if the overhead is reduced, as we saw in Scenario (b). Higher prices also result in a lower breakeven because of greater per-customer profits (but would probably affect total sales quite adversely). Promotion expenses can be either increased or decreased and affect the breakeven point; but they probably also have an impact on sales. Some costs of operation can be reduced, thus lowering the breakeven. But the hefty interest charges act as a lodestone over an enterprise, greatly increasing the overhead and requiring what may be an unattainable breakeven point.

Does a new venture have to break even or make a profit the first year to be worth going into? Why or why not?

Were such mistakes and miscalculations beyond what we would expect of reasonable executives? Probably not, with the probable exception of the crushing burden of debt. Any new venture is susceptible to surprises and the need to streamline and weed out its inefficiencies. While we would have expected such to have been done faster and more effectively from a well-tried Disney operation, European, and particularly French and Parisian consumers and employees showed different behavioral and attitudinal patterns than expected.

The worst sin that Disney management and investors could make would be to give up on Euro Disney and not to look ahead a few years. A hint of the future promise was Christmas week of 1993. Despite the first year's $920 million in red ink, some 35,000 packed the park most days. A week later on a cold January day, some of the rides still had 40-minute waits.

POSTSCRIPT

On March 15, 1994, an agreement was struck, aimed at making Euro Disney profitable by September 30, 1995. The European banks would fund another $500 million and make concessions such as forgiving 18 months interest and deferring all principal payments for three years. In return, Walt Disney Company agreed to spend about $750 million to bail out its Euro Disney affiliate. Thus, the debt would be halved, with interest payments greatly reduced. Disney also agreed to eliminate, for five years, the lucrative management fees and royalties it received on the sale of tickets and merchandise.

The problems of Euro Disney were still not resolved by mid-1994. The theme park and resort near Paris remained troubled. However, a new source for financing had emerged. A member of the Saudi Arabian royal family agreed to invest up to $500 million for a 24 percent stake in Euro Disney. Prince Alwaleed had shown considerable sophistication in investing in troubled enterprises in the past. Now his commitment to Euro Disney showed a belief in the ultimate success of the resort.

Finally, in the third quarter of 1995, Euro Disney posted its first profit, some $35 million for the period. This compared with a year earlier loss of $113 million. By now, Euro Disney was only 39 percent owned by Disney. It attributed the turnaround partly to a new marketing strategy in which prices were slashed at the gate and within the theme park in an effort to boost attendance and also to shed the nagging image of being overpriced. A further attraction was the new "Space Mountain" ride that mimicked a trip to the moon.

However, some analysts questioned the staying power of such a movement into the black. In particular, they saw most of the gain coming from financial restructuring in which the debt-ridden Euro Disney struck a deal with its creditors to temporarily suspend debt and royalty payments. A second theme park and further property development were seen as essential in the longer term, as the payments would eventually resume.

To the delight of the French government, plans were announced in 1999 to build a movie theme park, Disney Studios, next to the Magic Kingdom, to open in 2002. It was estimated that this expansion would attract an additional 4.2 million visitors annually, drawing people from farther afield in Europe. In 1998, Disneyland Paris had 12.5 million visitors, being France's No. 1 tourist attraction, beating out Notre Dame.

Also late in 1999, Disney and Hong Kong agreed to build a major Disney theme park there, with Disney investing $314 million for 43 percent ownership while Hong Kong contributed nearly $3 billion. Hong Kong's leaders expected the new park would generate 16,000 jobs when it opened in 2005, certainly a motivation for the unequal investment contribution.[10]

The Walt Disney Studios theme park opened in March 2002, as planned. It blended Disney entertainment with the history and culture of European film. Marketing efforts reflected a newfound cultural awareness, and efforts were focused largely on selling the new park through travel agents, whom Disney initially neglected in promoting Disneyland Paris. The timing could have been better, as theme parks were reeling from the recession and the threat of terrorist attacks. A second Disney part opened in Tokyo in 2001 and was a smash hit. But the new California Adventure park in Anaheim, Calif. had been a bust.[11]

By the end of 2004, Euro Disney was again facing record losses. Partly, this was because of the resumption of full royalty payments and management fees to Walt Disney Co. But deeper problems were besetting it. Attendance had remained flat at about 12.4 million. The new Disney Studios Park opened to expectations of 4 million visitors, but only 2.2 million came in 2004, and many complained that it did not have enough attractions. Three major new attractions are scheduled to open in 2006 to 2008, with two of these for the Studios Park. For the first three months of 2005, the

---

[10] "Hong Kong Betting $3 Billion on Success of New Disneyland," *Cleveland Plain Dealer,* November 3, 1999, p. C2; Charles Fleming, "Euro Disney to Build Movie Theme Park Outside Paris," *Wall Street Journal,* September 30, 1999, pp. A15, A21.

[11] Bruce Owwall, "Euro Disney CEO Named to Head Parks World-Wide," *Wall Street Journal,* September 30, 2002, p. B8; Paulo Prada and Bruce Orwall, "A Certain 'Je Ne Sais Quoi' at Disney's New Park," *Wall Street Journal,* March 12, 2002, pp. B1, B4.

popular Space Mountain was closed for upgrading. In this scenario, the company planned "regular admission-price increases." "The business model does not seem viable," observed one portfolio manager.[12]

UPDATE 2005

Something happened in January 2005. The French government realized that they really wanted Euro Disney to succeed. Despite the American bashing that came after President Bush's invasion of Iraq and President Jacques Chirac's calling the spread of American culture an "ecological disaster," another French preoccupation surfaced: the top priority of reducing France's high unemployment. Euro Disney's site was the biggest employer in the Paris region with 43,000 jobs, and it had created a booming urban sprawl on once-barren land.

Now Prime Minister Jean-Pierre Raffarin vowed not to let Euro Disney go bankrupt: "We are grateful to the American people and have lots of respect for their culture." A state-owned bank is contributing around $500 million in investments and loan concessions. The hope is that new and expensive attractions and a better economic climate will bring a turnaround. Still, if the Tower of Terror ride and other new attractions fail to attract millions of new visitors, Disney and the French government may have to pour more money into this venture that once seemed such a sure thing. Under consideration is to open Charles de Gaulle Airport to more low-cost Airlines to make Euro Disney a cheaper destination.[13]

Disney also has a lot at stake in the success of Euro Disney. Failure would hurt its global brand image as it prepares to expand into China and elsewhere in the Far East. Perhaps the lessons learned in Paris of trying to keep visitors longer while saving on fixed costs will transfer.

WHAT CAN BE LEARNED?

Beware the Arrogant Mind-Set, Especially When Dealing with New Situations and New Cultures

French sensitivities were offended by Disney corporate executives who often turned out to be brash, insensitive, and overbearing. A contentious attitude by Disney personnel alienated people and aggravated planning and operational difficulties. "The answer to doubts or suggestions invariably was: Do as we say, because we know best."[14]

[12] Jo Wrighton, "Euro Disney's Net Loss Balloons, Putting Financial Rescue at Risk," *Wall Street Journal,* November 10, 2004, p. B3.

[13] Jo Wrighton and Bruce Orwall, "Despite Losses and Bailouts, France Stays Devoted to Disney," *Wall Street Journal,* January 26, 2005, pp. A1, A6.

[14] Gumbel and Turner, p. A1.

Such a mind-set is a natural concomitant of success. It is said that success breeds arrogance, but this inclination must be fought against by those who would spurn the ideas and concerns of others. For a proud and touchy people, the French, this almost contemptuous attitude by the Americans fueled resentment and glee at Disney miscues. It did not foster cooperation, understanding, or the willingness to smooth the process. One might almost speculate that had not the potential economic benefits to France been so great, the Euro Disney project might never have been approved.

Great Success May Be Ephemeral

We often find that great successes are not lasting, that they have no staying power. Somehow the success pattern gets lost or forgotten or is not well rounded. Other times an operation grows beyond the capability of the originators. Hungry competitors are always in the wings, ready to take advantage of any lapse. As we saw with Euro Disney, having a closed mind to new ideas or needed revisions of an old success pattern—the arrogance of success—makes expansion into different environments more difficult and even risky.

While corporate Disney has continued to have good success with its other theme parks, competitors are moving in with their own theme parks in the United States and elsewhere. We may question whether this industry is approaching saturation, and we may wonder whether Disney has learned from its mistakes in Europe.

Highly Leveraged Situations Are Extremely Vulnerable

During most of the 1980s, many managers, including corporate raiders, pursued a strategy of debt financing in contrast to equity (stock ownership) financing. Funds for such borrowing were usually readily available, heavy debt had income tax advantages, and profits could be distributed among fewer shares so that return on equity was enhanced. During this time, a few voices decried the overleveraged situations of many companies. They predicted that when the eventual economic downturn came, such firms would find themselves unable to meet the heavy interest burden. Most lenders paid little heed to such lonesome voices and encouraged greater borrowing.

The widely publicized problems of some of the raiders in the late 1980s, such as Robert Campeau, who acquired major department store corporations, only to find himself overextended and lose everything, suddenly changed some expansionist lending sentiments. The hard reality dawned that these arrangements were often fragile indeed, especially when they rested on optimistic projections for asset sales, for revenues, and for cost savings to cover the interest payments. An economic slowdown hastened the demise of some of these ill-advised speculations.

Disney was guilty of the same speculative excesses with Euro Disney, relying far too much on borrowed funds, and assuming that assets, such as hotels, could be easily sold off at higher prices to other investors. As we saw in the breakeven box, hefty interest charges from such overleveraged conditions can jeopardize the viability of the enterprise if revenue and profit projections fail to meet the rosy expectations.

Be Judicious with the Skimming Price Strategy

Euro Disney faced the classical situation favorable for a skimming price strategy. It was in a monopoly position, with no equivalent competitors likely. It faced a somewhat inelastic demand curve, which indicated that people would come almost regardless of price. So why not price to maximize per-unit profits? Unfortunately for Disney, the wily Europeans circumvented the high prices by frugality. Of course, a severe recession exacerbated the situation.

The learning insight from this example is that a skimming price assumes that customers are willing and able to pay the higher prices and have no lower-priced competitive alternatives. It is a faulty strategy when many customers are unable, or else unwilling, to pay the high prices and can find a way to experience the product or service in a modest way.

CONSIDER

Can you think of other learning insights from this case?

QUESTIONS

1. How could the company have erred so badly in its estimates of spending patterns of European customers?

2. Could a better reading of the impact of cultural differences on revenues have been achieved?

3. What suggestions do you have for fostering a climate of sensitivity and goodwill in corporate dealings with the French?

4. How do you account for the great success of Tokyo Disneyland and the problems of Euro Disney? What are the key contributory differences?

5. Do you believe that Euro Disney might have done better if located elsewhere in Europe rather than just outside Paris? Why or why not?

6. "Mickey Mouse and the Disney park are an American cultural abomination." Evaluate this critical statement.

7. Consider how a strong marketing approach might be made to both European consumers and middlemen, such as travel agents, tour guides, even bus drivers.

8. Discuss the desirability of raising admission prices at the very time when attendance is static, profits are nonexistent, and new attractions are months and several years in the future.

ROLE PLAY

1. As the staff assistant to the president of Euro Disney, you already believe before the grand opening that the plans to use a skimming pricing strategy and to emphasize luxury hotel accommodations is ill advised. What argu-

ments would you marshal to try to persuade the company to offer lower prices and more moderate accommodations? Be as persuasive as you can.

2. It is six months after the opening. Revenues are not meeting target, and a number of problems have surfaced and are being worked on. The major problem remains, however, that the venture needs more visitors and/or higher expenditures per visitor. Develop a marketing strategy to improve the situation.

TEAM DEBATE EXERCISE

It is two years after the opening, and Euro Disney is a monumental mistake, profitwise. Two schools of thought are emerging for improving the situation. One is to pour more money into the project, build one or two more theme parks, and really make this another Disney World. The other camp believes more investment would be wasted at this time, that the need is to pare expenses to the bone and wait for an eventual upturn. Debate the two positions.

INVITATION TO RESEARCH

What is the situation with Euro Disney today? Are expansion plans going ahead? Have other theme parks been announced?

PART FIVE

NOTABLE MARKETING SUCCESSES

CHAPTER EIGHTEEN

Harley-Davidson—Creating An Enduring Mystique

This century-old firm has exhibited stark contrasts in its history. In its first 60 years it had destroyed all of its U. S. competitors and had a solid 70 percent of the motor-cycle market. Then in the early 1960s, its staid and unexciting market was shaken up, was rocked to its core, by the most unlikely invader. This intruder was a smallish Japanese firm that had risen out of the ashes of World War II and was now trying to encroach on U.S. territory.

Almost inconceivably, in just a few years Harley-Davidson's market share was to fall to 5 percent, and the total market was to expand many times over what it had been for decades. This foreign invader had furnished a textbook example of the awe-some effectiveness of carefully crafted marketing efforts. In the process, this con-frontation between Honda and Harley-Davidson was a harbinger of the Japanese invasion of the auto industry.

Eventually, by the late 1980s, Harley was to make a comeback. But only after more than two decades of travail and mediocrity. As it surged forward in the last of the old century, it had somehow built up a mystique, a cult following, for its big bikes. In January 7, 2002, *Forbes* declared Harley to be its "Company of the Year," a truly prestigious honor. But let us go back first to the dire days of the Japanese "invasion."

THE INVASION

Sales of motorcycles in the United States were around 50,000 per year during the 1950s, with Harley-Davidson, Britain's Norton and Triumph, and Germany's BMW accounting for most of the market. By the turn of the decade, Honda began to pen-etrate the U. S. market. In 1960, less than 400,000 motorcycles were registered in the United States. While this was an increase of almost 200,000 from the end of World War II 15 years before, it was far below the increase in other motor vehicles. But by 1964, only four years later, the number had risen to 960,000; two years later it was 1.4 million; and by 1971 it was almost 4 million.

In expanding the demand for motorcycles, Honda instituted a distinctly differ-ent strategy. The major elements of this strategy were lightweight cycles and an advertising approach directed toward a new customer. Few firms have ever experienced such a shattering of market share as did Harley-Davidson in the 1960s. (Although its market share declined drastically, its total sales remained nearly constant, indicating that it was getting none of the new customers for motorcycles.)

Reaction of Harley-Davidson to the Honda Threat

Faced with an invasion of its static U.S. market, how did Harley react to the intruder? They did not react! At least not until far too late. Harley Davidson considered themselves the leader in full-size motorcycles. While the company might shudder at the image tied in with their product's usage by the leather-jacket types, it took solace in the fact that almost every U.S. police department used its machines. Perhaps this is what led Harley to stand aside and complacently watch Honda make deep inroads into the American motorcycle market. The management saw no threat in Honda's thrust into the market with lightweight machines. The attitude was exemplified in this statement by William H. Davidson, the president of the company and son of the founder:

> Basically, we don't believe in the lightweight market. We believe that motorcycles are sport vehicles, not transportation vehicles. Even if a man says he bought a motorcycle for transportation, it's generally for leisure-time use. The lightweight motorcycle is only supplemental. Back around World War I, a number of companies came out with lightweight bikes. We came out with one ourselves. They never got anywhere. We've seen what happens to these small sizes.[1]

Eventually Harley recognized that the Honda phenomenon was not an aberration, and that there was a new factor in the market. The company attempted to fight back by offering an Italian-made lightweight in the mid-1960s. But it was far too late; Honda was firmly entrenched. The Italian bikes were regarded in the industry to be of lower quality than the Japanese. Honda and, toward the end of the 1960s other Japanese manufacturers, continued to dominate what had become a much larger market than ever dreamed.

AFTERMATH OF THE HONDA INVASION: 1965–1981

In 1965, Harley-Davidson made its first public stock offering. Soon after, it faced a struggle for control. The contest was primarily between Bangor Punta, an Asian company, and AMF, an American company with strong interests in recreational equipment including bowling. In a bidding war, Harley Davidson's stockholders chose AMF over Bangor Punta, even though the bid was $1 less than Bangor's $23 a share offer. Stockholders were leery of Bangor's reputation of taking over a company, squeezing it dry, and then scrapping it for the remaining assets. AMF's plans for expansion of Harley Davidson seemed more compatible.

[1] Tom Rowan, "Harley Sets New Drive to Boost Market Share," *Advertising Age,* January 29, 1973, pp. 34–35.

But the marriage was troubled: Harley-Davidson's old equipment was not capable of the expansion envisioned by AMF. At the very time that Japanese manufacturers—Honda and others—were flooding the market with high-quality motorcycles, Harley was falling down on quality. One company official noted that "quality was going down just as fast as production was going up."[2] Indicative of the depths of the problem at a demoralized Harley Davidson, quality-control inspections failed 50 to 60 percent of the motorcycles produced. This compared to 5 percent of Japanese motorcycles that failed their quality-control checks.

AMF put up with an average $4.8 million operating loss for eleven years. Finally, it called it quits and put the division up for sale in 1981. Vaughan Beals, vice president of motorcycle sales, still had faith in the company: He led a team that used $81.5 million in financing from Citicorp to complete a leveraged buyout. All ties with AMF were severed.

VAUGHAN BEALS

Beals was a middle-aged Ivy Leaguer, a far cry from what one might think of as being a heavy motorcycle aficianado. He had graduated from MIT's Aeronautical Engineering School and was considered a production specialist.[3] But he was far more than that. His was a true commitment to motorcycles, personally as well as professionally. Deeply concerned with AMF's declining attention to quality, he achieved the buyout from AMF.

The prognosis for the company was bleak. Its market share, which had dominated the industry before the Honda invasion, now was 3 percent. In 1983, Harley-Davidson would celebrate its 80th birthday; some doubted it would still be around by then. Tariff protection seemed Harley's only hope. And massive lobbying paid off. In 1983, Congress passed a huge tariff increase on Japanese motorcycles. Instead of a 4 percent tariff, now Japanese motorcycles would be subject to a 45 percent tariff for the coming five years.

The tariff gave the company new hope, and it slowly began to rebuild market share. Key to this was restoring confidence in the quality of its products. And Beals took a leading role in this. He drove Harley-Davidsons to rallies where he met Harley owners. There he learned of their concerns and their complaints, and he promised changes. At these rallies, a core of loyal Harley-Davidson users, called HOGs (for Harley Owners Group), were to be trailblazers for the successful growth and mystique to come.

Beals had company on his odyssey: Willie G. Davidson, grandson of the company's founder, and the vice president of design. Willie was an interesting contrast to the more urbane Beals. His was the image of a middle-age hippie. He wore a Viking helmet over his long, unkempt hair, while a straggly beard hid some of his wind-

---

[2] Peter C. Reid, *Well Made in America—Lessons from Harley-Davidson on Being the Best*, New York: McGraw-Hill, 1990, p. 10.

[3] Rod Willis, "Harley-Davidson Comes Roaring Back," *Management Review*, March 1986, pp. 20–27.

burned face. An aged leather jacket was compatible. Beals and Davidson fit in nicely at the HOG rallies.

THE STRUGGLE BACK

In December 1986, Harley-Davidson asked Congress to remove the tariff barriers, more than a year earlier than originally planned. The confidence of the company had been restored, and it believed it could now compete with the Japanese head to head.[4]

Production Improvements

Shortly after the buyout, Beals and other managers visited Japanese plants in Japan and Honda's assembly plant in Marysville, Ohio. They were impressed that they were being beaten not by "robotics, or culture, or morning calisthenics and company songs, [but by] professional managers who understood their business and paid attention to detail."[5] As a result, Japanese operating costs were as much as 30 percent lower than Harley's.

Beals and his managers tried to implement some of the Japanese management techniques. Each plant was divided into profit centers, with managers assigned total responsibility within their particular area. Just-in-time (JIT) inventory and a materials-as-needed (MAN) system sought to control and minimize all inventories both inside and outside the plants. Quality circles (QCs) were formed to increase employee involvement in quality goals and to improve communication between management and workers. See the Information Box on page 269 for further discussion of quality circles. Another new program called statistical operator control (SOC) gave employees the responsibility for checking the quality of their own work and making proper correcting adjustments. Efforts were made to improve labor relations by more sensitivity to employees and their problems as well as better employee assistance and benefits. Certain product improvements were also introduced, notably a new engine and mountings on rubber to reduce vibration. A well-accepted equipment innovation was to build stereo systems and intercoms into the motorcycle helmets.

The production changes between 1981 and 1988 resulted in:[6]

Inventory reduced by 67 percent

Productivity up by 50 percent

Scrap and rework down two-thirds

Defects per unit down 70 percent

In the 1970s, the joke among industry experts was, "If you're buying a Harley, you'd better buy two—one for spare parts."[7] Now this had obviously changed, but the change still had to be communicated to consumers, and believed.

[4] "Harley Back in High Gear," *Forbes,* April 20, 1987, p. 8.

[5] Dexter Hutchins, "Having a Hard Time with Just-in-Time," *Fortune,* June 19, 1986, p. 65.

[6] Hutchins, p. 66.

[7] Ibid.

INFORMATION BOX

QUALITY CIRCLES

Quality Circles were adopted by Japan in an effort to rid its industries of poor quality and junkiness after World War II. QCs are worker-management committees that meet usually weekly, to talk about production problems, plan ways to improve productivity and quality, and resolve job-related gripes on both sides.

At the height of their popularity they were described as "the single most significant reason for the truly outstanding quality of goods and services produced in Japan."[8] At one time, Mazda had 2,147 circles with more than 16,000 employees involved. They usually consisted of seven or eight volunteers who met on their own time to discuss and solve the issues they were concerned with. In addition to making major contributions to increased productivity and quality, QCs gave employees an opportunity to participate and gain a sense of accomplishment.[9]

The idea—like so many ideas adopted by the Japanese—did not originate with them: It came from two American personnel consultants. But the Japanese refined the idea and ran with it. In the 1980s, American industry, unable to match the quality of Japanese imports, saw QCs as the elixir in quality enhancement. Firms also found them a desirable way to promote teamwork, good feelings, and to avoid some of the adversarial relations stemming from collective bargaining and union grievances.

Despite the glowing endorsements for QCs, in the United States they were more a fad that quickly faded. Workers claimed they smacked of "tokenism" and were a facade and impractical, with no lasting benefits once the novelty had worn off. Others saw them as time wasted and, unlike Japan, few U.S. workers accepted the idea of participating in QCs on their own time.

How would you feel about devoting an hour or more to QC meetings every week or so, on your own time? If your answer is, "No Way," do you think this is a fair attitude on your part? Why or why not?

Invitation to Research: Can you find any U.S. firms that are still using quality circles?

---

[8] "A Partnership to Build the New Workplace," *Business Week,* June 30, 1980, p. 101.

[9] As described in a Mazda ad in *Forbes,* May 24, 1982, p. 5.

Marketing Moves

Despite its bad times and its poor quality, Harley had a cadre of loyal customers almost unparalleled. Company research maintained that 92 percent of its customers remained with Harley.[10] Despite such hard-core loyalists, the company had always had a serious public image problem. It was linked to an image of the pot-smoking, beer-drinking, woman-chasing, tattoo-covered, leather-clad biker: "When your company's logo is the number one requested in tattoo parlors, it's time to get

[10] Mark Marvel, "The Gentrified HOG," *Esquire,* July 1989, p. 25.

a licensing program that will return your reputation to the ranks of baseball, hot dogs, and apple pie."[11]

Part of Harley's problem had been with bootleggers ruining the name by placing it on unlicensed goods of poor quality. Now the company began to use warrants and federal marshalls to crack down on unauthorized uses of its logo at motorcycle conventions. And it began licensing its name and logo on a wide variety of products, from leather jackets to cologne to jewelry—even to pajamas, sheets, and towels. Suddenly retailers realized that these licensed goods were popular and were even being bought by a new customer segment, undreamed of until now: bankers, doctors, lawyers, and entertainers. This new breed of customers soon expanded their horizons to include the Harley-Davidson bikes themselves. They joined the HOGs, only now they became known as Rubbies—the rich urban bikers. And high prices for bikes did not bother them in the least.

Beals was quick to capitalize on this new market with an expanded product line with expensive heavyweights. In 1989, the largest motorcycle was introduced, the Fat Boy, with 80 cubic inches of V-twin engine and capable of a top speed of 150 mph. By 1991, Harley had 20 models, ranging in price from $4,500 to $15,000.

The Rubbies brought Harley back to a leading position in the industry by 1989, with almost 60 percent of the super heavyweight motorcycle market; by the first quarter of 1993, this had become 63 percent. See Figure 18.1. The importance of this customer to Harley could be seen in the demographic statistics supplied by the *Wall Street Journal* in 1990: "One in three of today's Harley-Davidson buyers are professionals or managers. About 60 percent have attended college, up from only 45 percent in 1984. Their median age is 35, and their median household income has risen sharply to $45,000 from $36,000 five years earlier."[12]

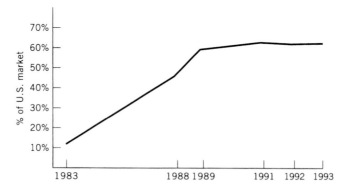

Figure 18.1 Harley-Davidson's Share of the U.S. Heavyweight Motorcycle Market, Selected Years, 1983–1993

Sources: Company annual reports; R. L. Polk & Company; Gary Slutsker, "Hog Wild," *Forbes,* May 24, 1993, pp. 45, 46.

[11] "Thunder Road," *Forbes,* July 18, 1983, p. 32.

[12] Robert L. Rose, "Vrooming Back," *Wall Street Journal,* August 31, 1990, p. 1.

In 1989, Beals stepped down as CEO, turning the company over to Richard Teerlink, who was chief operating officer of the Motorcycle Division. Beals, however, retained his position as chairman of the board. The legacy of Beals in the renaissance of Harley was particularly notable for his bringing it out of the internal production orientation that had long characterized the firm. See the following Information Box for a discussion of an internal versus an external (marketing) orientation.

INFORMATION BOX

INTERNAL VS. EXTERNAL (MARKETING) ORIENTATION

Managers sometimes focus primarily on internal factors, such as technology and cost cutting. They subsequently see the key to attracting customers being in improving production and distribution efficiency and lowering costs if possible. Henry Ford pioneered this philosophy in the early 1900s with his Model T. Harley stuck for decades with this orientation in the absence of competition. The internal orientation is most appropriate in three situations (with the third often being a dubious risk):

1. When demand for a product exceeds supply, such as in new technologies and in developing countries.
2. When the product cost is high and the market can be expanded only if costs can be brought down.
3. Where there is a present lack of significant competition, and no competitive threat is expected either because of severe entry requirements in the industry or because the market is limited.

Obviously, Harley-Davidson in the 1960s had made a major miscalculation with the third situation, assuming that the motorcycle market would be forever limited.

An external, or marketing, orientation recognizes the fallacy of the assumption that products will forever sell themselves "if we maintain our production and technological superiority." Looking outside the firm to the market environment results in giving major priority to determining customers' needs and wants, assessing how these may be changing as evidenced by shifts in buying patterns, and adapting products and services accordingly. The external focus also permits more responsiveness to other external forces, such as major competitive thrusts, changing laws and regulations, economic conditions, and the like. With such an external orientation, attention will more likely be directed to locating new opportunities brought about by changing conditions, rather than focusing on internal production and technology. Such an orientation is more geared to meeting and even anticipating change.

Do all firms need a marketing orientation? Can you think of any that probably do not and will not?

SUCCESS

By 1993, Harley-Davidson had a new problem, one born of success. Now it could not even come close to meeting demand. Customers faced empty showrooms, except perhaps for rusty trade-ins or antiques. Waiting time for a new bike could be six months or longer, unless the customer was willing to pay a 10 percent or higher premium to some gray marketer advertising in biker magazines.

Some of the 600 independent U.S. dealers worried that these empty showrooms and long waiting lists would induce their customers to turn to foreign imports, much as they had several decades before. But other dealers recognized that somehow Beals and company had engendered a brand loyalty unique in this industry, and perhaps in all industries. Assuaging the lack of big bike business, dealers were finding other sources of revenues. Harley's branded line of merchandise, available only at Harley dealers and promoted through glossy catalogs, had really taken off. Harley black leather jackets were bought eagerly at $500; fringed leather bras went for $65; even shot glasses brought $12—all it seemed to take was the Harley name and logo. So substantial was this ancillary business, that in 1992 non-cycle business generated $155.7 million in sales, up from $130.3 million in 1991.

Production

In one sense, Harley's production situation was enviable—it had far more demand than production capability. More than this, it had such a loyal body of customers that delays in product gratification were not likely to turn many away to competitors. The problem, of course, was that full potential was not being realized.

Richard Teerlink, the successor to Beals, expressed the corporate philosophy to expanding quantity to meet the demand: "Quantity isn't the issue, quality is the issue. We learned in the early 1980s, you do not solve problems by throwing money at them."[13]

The company increased output slowly. In early 1992, it was making 280 bikes a day; by 1993, this had risen to 345 a day. With increased capital spending, goals were to produce 420 bikes a day, but not until 1996.

Export Potential

Some contrary concerns with the conservative expansion plans of Teerlink surfaced regarding international operations. The European export market beckoned. Harleys had become very popular in Europe. But the company had promised its domestic dealers that exports would not go beyond 30 percent of total production, until the North American market was fully satisfied. Suddenly, the European big-bike market grew by an astounding 33 percent between 1990 and 1992. Yet because of its production constraints, Harley could only maintain a 9 to 10 percent share of this market. In other words, it was giving away business to foreign competitors.

---

[13] Gary Slutsker, "Hog Wild," *Forbes,* May 24, 1993, p. 46.

To enhance its presence in Europe, Harley opened a branch office of its HOG club in Frankfurt, Germany, for its European fans.

Specifics of the Resurgence of Harley-Davidson

Table 18.1 shows the trend in revenues and net income of Harley from 1982 through 1994. The growth in sales and profits did not go unnoticed by the investment community. In 1990, Harley-Davidson stock sold for $7; in January of 1993, it hit $39. Its market share of heavyweight motorcycles (751 cubic centimeters displacement and larger) had soared from 12.5 percent in 1983 to 63 percent by 1993. Let the Japanese have the lightweight bike market! Harley would dominate the heavyweights.

Harley acquired Holiday Rambler in 1986. As a wholly owned subsidiary, this manufacturer of recreational and commercial vehicles was judged by Harley management to be compatible with the existing motorcycle business as well as moderating some of the seasonality of the motorcycle business. The diversification proved rather mediocre. In 1992, it accounted for 26 percent of total corporate sales, but only 2 percent of profits.[14]

Big motorcycles, made in America by the only U.S. manufacturer, continued to be the rage. Harley's 90th anniversary was celebrated in Milwaukee on June 12,

TABLE 18.1   Harley-Davidson's Growth in Revenue and Income (millions of $), 1983–1994

Year	Revenue	Net Income
1982	$ 210	def. $25.1
1983	254	1.0
1984	294	2.9
1985	287	2.6
1986	295	4.3
1987	685	17.7
1988	757	27.2
1989	791	32.6
1990	865	38.3
1991	940	37.0
1992	1,100	54.0
1993	1,210	68.0
1994	1,537	83.0

Source: Company annual reports.

Commentary: The steady climb in sales and profits, except for a pause in 1985, is noteworthy. The total gain in revenues over these years was 631.9%, while income rose more than eightyfold since 1983.

---

[14] Company annual reports.

1993. As many as 100,000 people, including 18,000 HOGS, were there to celebrate. Hotel rooms were sold out for a 60-mile radius. Harley Davidson was up and doing real well.

More Recent Developments

The 1990s continued to be kind to Harley. Demand grew with the mystique as strong as ever. The company significantly increased its motorcycle production capacity with a new engine plant in Milwaukee completed in 1997 and a new assembly plant in Kansas City in 1998. It expected that demand in the United States would still exceed the supply of Harley bikes.

The following numbers show how motorcycle shipments (domestic and export) increased from 1993 to 1997 (in thousands of units):

	U.S.	Exports
1997	96.2	36.1
1993	57.2	24.5

Despite continuous increases in production, U.S. consumers still had to wait to purchase a new Harley Davidson bike, but the wait only added to the mystique.

The following shows the growth in revenues and income from 1993 to 1997:

	Revenues ($M)	Net Income ($M)
1997	1,763	174.0
1993	1,217	18.4

As an indication of the popularity of the Harley Davidson logo, Wolverine World Wide, original maker of Hush Puppies but now the largest manufacturer of footwear in the United States, entered into a licensing agreement with Harley to use its "sexy" name for a line of boots and fashion shoes to come out in late 1998.[15]

In its January 7, 2002 issue, *Forbes* declared Harley to be its "Company of the Year," a truly prestigious honor. In supporting its decision, Forbes noted that:

> In a disastrous year for hundreds of companies, Harley's estimated 2001 sales grew 15 percent to $3.3 billion and earnings grew 26 percent to $435 million. Its shares were up 40 percent in 2001, while the S&P stock averages dropped 15 percent. Since Harley went public in 1986, its shares have risen an incredible 15,000 percent. Since 1986, GE, generally considered the paragon of American business, had risen only 1,050 percent.

Jeffrey Bleustein, a 26-year company veteran and the current Harley CEO, was diversifying into small, cheaper bikes to attract younger riders, as well as women, who

---

[15] Carleen Hawn, "What's in a Name? Whatever You Make It," *Forbes*, July 27, 1998, p. 88.

had shunned the big lumbering machines and who represented only 9 percent of Harley riders. The cult image was stronger than ever. Half of the company's 8,000 employees rode Harleys, and many of them appeared at rallies around the country for pleasure and to promote the company. In 2002, there were 640,000 owners, the parts-and-accessories catalog numbered 720 pages, and the Harley-Davidson name was on everything from blue jeans to pickup trucks. Harley celebrated its 100th birthday in 2002, and some 250,000 riders were at the rally in Milwaukee.[16]

ANALYSIS

One of Vaughan Beals's first moves after the 1981 leveraged buyout was to improve production efficiency and quality control. This became the foundation for the strategic regeneration moves to come. In this quest, he borrowed heavily from the Japanese, in particular in cultivating employee involvement.

The cultivation of a new customer segment for the big bikes had to be a major factor in the company's resurgence. To some, discovering that more affluent consumers embraced the big, flashy Harley motorcycles was a surprise of no small moment. After all, how could you have two more incompatible groups than the stereotyped black-jacketed cyclists and the Rubbies? Perhaps part of the change was due to high-profile people such as Beals and some of his executives frequently participating at motorcycle rallies and charity rides. Technological and comfort improvements in motorcycles and their equipment added to the new attractiveness. Dealers were also coaxed to make their stores more inviting.

Along with this, expanding the product mix not only made such Harley-branded merchandise a windfall for company and dealers alike but also piqued the interest of upscale customers in motorcycles themselves. The company was commendably aggressive in running with the growing popularity of the ancillary merchandise and making this well over a $100 million revenue booster.

Some questions remained. How durable was this popularity, both of the big bikes and the complementary merchandise, with this affluent customer segment? Would it prove to be only a passing fad? If so, then Harley needed to seek diversifications as quickly as possible, even though the Holiday Rambler Corporation had brought no notable success by 1992. Diversifications often bring disappointed earnings compared with a firm's core business.

Another question concerned Harley's slowness in expanding production capability. Faced with a burgeoning demand, was it better to go slowly, to be carefully protective of quality, and to refrain from heavy debt commitments? This had been Harley's most recent strategy, but it raised the risk of permitting competitors to gain market share in the United States and especially in Europe. The following Issue Box discusses aggressive versus conservative planning.

---

[16] Jonathan Fahey, "Love Into Money," *Forbes*, January 7, 2002, pp. 60–65.

ISSUE BOX

SHOULD WE BE AGGRESSIVE OR CONSERVATIVE IN OUR PLANNING?

The sales forecast—the estimate of sales for the periods ahead—serves a crucial role because it is the starting point for all detailed planning and budgeting. A volatile situation presents some high-risk alternatives: Should we be optimistic or conservative?

On one hand, with conservative planning in a growing market, a firm risks underestimating demand and being unable to expand its resources sufficiently to handle the potential. It may lack the manufacturing capability and sales staff to handle growth potential, and it may have to abdicate a good share of the growing business to competitors who are willing and able to expand their capability to meet the demands of the market.

On the other hand, a firm facing burgeoning demand should consider whether the growth is likely to be a short-term fad or a more permanent situation. A firm can easily become overextended in the buoyancy of booming business, only to see the collapse of such business jeopardizing its viability.

Harley's conservative decision was undoubtedly influenced by concerns about expanding beyond the limits of good quality control. The decision was probably also influenced by management's belief that Harley-Davidson had a loyal body of customers who would not switch despite the wait.

Do you think Harley-Davidson made the right decision to expand conservatively? Why or why not? Defend your position.

WHAT CAN BE LEARNED?

A Firm Can Come Back from Adversity

The resurrection of Harley Davidson almost from the point of extinction proves that adversity can be overcome. It need not be fatal or forever. This should be encouraging to all firms facing difficulties, and to their investors. Harley, however, is noteworthy in the time it took to turnaround: more than several decades before a Vaughan Beals came on the scene as change maker.

What does a turnaround require? Above all, it takes a leader who has the vision and confidence that things can be changed for the better. The change may not necessitate anything particularly innovative. It may involve only a rededication to basics, such as better quality control or an improved commitment to customer service brought about by a new positive attitude of employees. But such a return to basics requires that a demoralized or apathetic organization be rejuvenated and remotivated. This calls for leadership of a high order. If the core business has still been maintained, it at least provides a base to work from.

Preserve the Core Business At All Costs

Every viable firm has a basic core or distinctive position—sometimes called an *ecological niche*—in its business environment. This unique position may be due to its particular location, or to a certain product. It may come from somewhat different operating methods or from the customers served. Here, a firm is better than its competitors. This strong point is the basic core of a company's survival. Though it may diversify and expand far beyond this area, the firm should not abandon its main bastion of strength.

Harley almost did this. Its core—and indeed, only—business was its heavyweight bikes sold to a limited and loyal, though not at the time particularly savory, customer segment. Harley almost lost this core business by abandoning reasonable quality control to the point that its motorcycles became the butt of jokes. To his credit, upon assuming leadership Beals acted quickly to correct the production and employee motivation problems. By preserving the core, Beals could pursue other avenues of expansion.

The Power of a Mystique

We first discussed this in Chapter 12 in describing how Gateway Computer hoped to gain devoted followers as it thought Apple had. But it is worth repeating here, even though few products are able to gain a mystique or cult following. Coors beer did for a few years in the 1960s and early 1970s, when it became the brew of celebrities and the emblem of the purity and freshness of the West. In the cigarette industry, Marlboro rose to become the top seller from a somewhat similar advertising and image thrust: the Marlboro man. The Ford Mustang had a mystique at one time. Somehow the big bikes of Harley-Davidson developed a more enduring mystique as they appealed to two disparate customer segments: the HOGS and the Rubbies. Different they might be, but both were loyal to their Harleys. The mystique led to "logo magic": Simply put the Harley-Davidson name and logo on all kinds of merchandise and watch the sales take off.

How does a firm develop (or acquire) a mystique? There is no simple answer, no guarantee. Certainly a product has to be unique, but though most firms strive for this differentiation, few achieve a mystique. Image-building advertising, focusing on the target buyer, may help. Perhaps even better is image-building advertising that highlights the people customers might wish to emulate. But what about the black-leather-jacketed, perhaps bearded, cyclist?

Perhaps in the final analysis, acquiring a mystique is more accidental and fortuitous than something that can be deliberately orchestrated. Two lessons, however, can be learned about mystiques: First, they do not last forever. Second, firms should run with them as long as possible and try to expand the reach of the name or logo to other goods, even unrelated ones, through licensing.

CONSIDER

What additional learning insights can you see coming from this Harley Davidson resurgence?

QUESTIONS

1. Do you think Beals' rejuvenation strategy for Harley-Davidson was the best policy? Discuss and evaluate other strategies that he might have pursued.

2. How durable do you think the Rubbies' infatuation with the heavyweight Harleys will be? What leads you to this conclusion?

3. A Harley-Davidson stockholder criticizes present management: "It is a mistake of the greatest magnitude that we abdicate a decent share of the European motorcycle market to foreign competitors, simply because we do not gear up our production to meet the demand." Discuss.

4. Given the resurgence of Harley-Davidson in the 1990s, would you invest money now in the company? Discuss, considering as many factors bearing on this decision as you can.

5. "Harley-Davidson's resurgence is only the purest luck. Who could have predicted, or influenced, the new popularity of big bikes with the affluent?" Discuss.

6. "The tariff increase on Japanese motorcycles in 1983 gave Harley-Davidson badly needed breathing room. In the final analysis, politics is more important than management in competing with foreign firms." What are your thoughts?

HANDS-ON EXERCISES

1. Be a Devil's Advocate (one who opposes a position to establish its merits and validity). Your mutual fund has a major investment in Harley-Davidson, and you are concerned with Vaughn Beals's presence at motorcycle rallies, hobnobbing with black-jacketed motorcycle gangs. He maintains this is the way to cultivate a loyal core of customers. Argue against Beals's practices.

2. As a vice president at Harley-Davidson in the 1990s, you believe the recovery efforts should have gone well beyond the heavyweight bikes into lightweights. What arguments would you present for this change in strategy, and what specific recommendations would you make for such a new course of action? What contrary arguments would you expect? How would you counter them?

3. As a staff assistant to Vaughan Beals when he first took over, you have been charged to design a strategy to bring a mystique to the Harley-Davidson name. How would you propose to do this? Be as specific as you can, and defend your reasoning.

TEAM DEBATE EXERCISE

A major schism has developed in the executive ranks of Harley-Davidson. Many executives believe a monumental mistake is being made not to gear up production to meet the burgeoning worldwide demand for Harleys. Others see the present go-slow approach to increasing production as more prudent. Persuasively support your position and attack the other side.

INVITATION TO RESEARCH

What is the situation with Harley-Davidson today? Has the cult following remained as strong as ever? How are the new lightweight bikes faring? Are many women being attracted to Harleys? Have any new competitors emerged?

CHAPTER NINETEEN

Vanguard—Success in Taking the Road Less Traveled

Vanguard Group has become the largest mutual fund family in the world, besting Fidelity Investments. While Fidelity had been increasing its fund assets about 20 percent a year, Vanguard was growing at 33 percent. Fidelity advertised heavily, while Vanguard did practically no advertising, spending a bare $8 million for a few ads to get people to ask for prospectuses. The Kaufmann Fund, 100th Vanguard's size, spent that much for advertising, and General Mills spent twice as much just to introduce a new cereal, Sunrise.[1]

What is Vanguard's secret? How wise is it with such a consumer product to spurn advertising? The answer lies in the vision and steadfastness of John C. Bogle, the founder and now retired chairman.

JOHN BOGLE AND THE CREATION OF VANGUARD

In 1950, as a junior at Princeton, Bogle was groping for a topic for his senior thesis. He wanted a topic that no one had written about in any serious academic paper. In December 1949, he read an article in *Fortune* on mutual funds. At that time, all mutual funds were sold with sales commissions often 8 percent of the amount invested, and this was taken off the top as a front-end load. (This meant that if you invested $1,000, only $920 would be earning you money. Today, we find no funds with a front-end load more than 6.5 percent, so there has been some improvement.) In addition, these funds had high yearly overheads or expense ratios. As Bogle thought about this, he wondered why funds couldn't be bought without salespeople or brokers and their steep commissions, and if growth could not be maximized by keeping overhead down.

Right after graduation he joined a tiny mutual fund, Wellington Management Company and moved up rapidly. In 1965, at age 35, he became the chief executive. Unwisely, he decided to merge with another firm, but the new partners turned out to

---

[1] Thomas Easton, "The Gospel According to Vanguard," *Forbes*, February 8, 1999, p. 115.

be active managers (buying and selling with a vengeance), generating high overhead costs. The relationship was incompatible with Bogle's beliefs, and in 1974 he was fired as chief executive.

He decided to go his own way and change the "very structure under which mutual funds operated" into a fund distribution company mutually owned by shareholders. The idea came from his Princeton thesis and included such heresies as "reduction of sales loads and management fees" and "giving investors a fair shake" as the rock on which the new enterprise would be built. He chose the name "Vanguard" for his new company, after the great victory of Lord Nelson over Napoleon's fleet with his flagship, *HMS Vanguard.* Bogle launched the Vanguard Group of Investment Companies on September 26, 1974, and he hoped "that just as Nelson's fleet had come to dominate the seas during the Napoleonic wars, our new flagship would come to dominate the mutual fund sea."[2]

But success was long in coming. Bogle brought out the first index fund the next year, a fund based on the Standard & Poor's 500 Stock Price Index, and named it Vanguard 500 Index Fund. It was designed to mirror the market averages and thus required minimal management decisions and costs. It flopped initially. Analysts publicly derided the idea, arguing that astute management could beat the averages every time, though they ignored the costs of high-priced money managers and frequent trading.

At the millennium 25 years later, this Vanguard flagship fund that tracks the 500 stocks on the Standard & Poor's Index had more than $75 billion in assets and had beat 86 percent of all actively managed stock funds in 1998, and an even higher percentage over the past decade. By early 2000, it overtook Fidelity's famed Magellan Fund as the largest mutual fund of all. The relative growth between Magellan and Vanguard's 500 Index is shown in Table 19.1.

The Vanguard family of funds had become the world's largest no-load mutual fund group, with 12 million shareholders and $442 billion in assets as of the beginning of 1999. Fidelity, partly load and partly no-load, had nearly $700 billion, but the gap was closing fast.

TABLE 19.1   Relative Growth Comparisons of the Two Largest Mutual Funds

	Assets (millions $)		5-Year Gain
	6/30/94	6/30/99	(percentage)
Fidelity Magellan	$33,179	$97,594	194.2%
Vanguard 500 Index	8,443	92,644	997.3

Source: Company reports.

Commentary: Especially notable is the tremendous growth of Vanguard's 500 Index Fund in the last five years, growing from $8 billion in assets to over $92 billion.

[2] John C. Bogle, *Common Sense on Mutual Funds,* (New York: John Wiley, 1999), pp. 402–403.

Bogle, the Messiah

A feature article in *Forbes'* February 8, 1999 issue had this headline:

> The Gospel According to Vanguard
>
> How do you account for the explosive success of that strange business called Vanguard? Maybe it isn't really a business at all. It's a religion.[3]

Bogle's religion was low-cost investing and service to customers. He believed in funds being bought and not sold, thus no loads or commissions to salespeople or brokers. Customers had to seek out and deal directly with Vanguard. The engine was frugality with the investor-owner's best interests paramount. This was not advertised, not pasted on billboards, but the gospel was preached in thousands of letters to shareholders, editors, Securities & Exchange Commission members, and congressmen. Bogle made many speeches, comments to the news media, appearances on such TV channels as CNBC, and wrote two best-selling books. With his gaunt face and raspy voice, he became the zealot for low-cost investing and the major critic of money managers who trade frenetically, in the process running up costs and tax burdens for their investors. As the legions of loyal and enthusiastic clients grew, word-of-mouth from past experiences, and favorable mentions in business and consumer periodicals such as *Forbes, Wall Street Journal, Money,* and numerous daily newspapers, as well as TV stations, brought a groundswell of new and repeat business to Vanguard.

Bogle turned 70 in May 1999 and was forced to retire from Vanguard's board. The new chairman, John J. Brennan, 44, seemed imbued with the Bogle philosophy and vision. He said, "We're a small company, and we haven't begun to explore our opportunities, yet." He noted that there's Europe and Asia, to say nothing of the trillions of dollars held in non-Vanguard funds. "It's humbling."[4]

GREAT APPEAL OF VANGUARD

Performance

Each year *Forbes* presents "Mutual Funds Ratings" and "Best Buys." The Ratings lists the hundreds of mutual funds that are open end, that is, can be bought and sold at current net asset prices.[5] The Best Buys are those select few that *Forbes* analysts judged to "invest wisely, spend frugally, and you get what you pay for," and that perform best in shareholder returns over up and down markets. Vanguard equity and bond funds dominate *Forbes'* Best Buys:

---

[3] Easton, p. 115.

[4] Easton, p. 117.

[5] Footnote: A far smaller number of mutuals are closed-end funds that have a fixed number of shares and are traded like stocks. These generally have higher annual expenses yet sell at a discount from net asset value. We will disregard these in this case.

Of 43 U.S. equity funds listed in the various categories, 12 are Vanguard funds. Of 70 bond funds, 27 are Vanguard.[6]

Forbes explains that "the preponderance of Vanguard funds in our Best Buy Tables is a testament to the firm's cost controls ... Higher expenses, for most other fund families, are like lead weights. Why carry them?"[7] Table 19.2 shows representative examples of the substantially lower expenses of Vanguard funds relative to others on the Best Buy list.[8]

TABLE 19.2   Comparative Expense Ratios of Representative Mutual Funds

	Annual Expenses per $100
Balanced Equity Funds:	
Vanguard Wellington Fund	0.31
Columbia Balanced Fund	0.67
Janus Balanced Fund	0.93
Ranier Balanced Portfolio	1.19
Index Equity Funds:	
Vanguard 500 Index	.18
T. Rowe Price Equity Index 500	.40
Dreyfus S&P 500 Index	.50
Gateway Fund	1.02
Municipal Long-Term Bonds:	
Vanguard High Yield Tax Exempt	.20
Dreyfus Basic Muni Bond	.45
Strong High Yield Muni Bond	.66
High-Yield Corporate Bonds:	
Vanguard High Yield Corp.	.29
Fidelity High Income	.75
Value Line Aggressive Income	.81
Ivesco High Yield	.86

Source: Company records as reported in *Forbes Mutual Fund Guide,* August 23, 1999.

Commentary: The great cost advantage of Vanguard shows up very strikingly here. It is not a slightly lower expense ratio, but one that is usually three or four times lower than similar funds. Take, for example, the category of Index Equity Funds, where the goal is to simply track the Index averages, which suggests passive management rather than free-wheeling buying and selling. Yet, Vanguard's costs are far below the other funds; in one case, the Gateway fund is five times higher.

[6] *Forbes,* August 23, 1999, pp. 128, 136–7.

[7] Ibid, p. 136.

[8] Ibid., pp. 128, 137.

Looking at total averages, the typical mutual fund has an expense ratio of 1.24 percent of assets annually. The ratio for Vanguard's 101 funds is .28 percent, almost a full percentage point lower.[9]

How does Vanguard achieve such a low expense ratio? We noted before the reluctance to advertise at all; nor does it have any mass sales force. Its commitment has been to pare costs to the absolute minimum. But there have been other economies.

Fidelity and Charles Schwab have opened numerous walk-in sales outposts. Certainly these bring more sales exposure to prospective customers. But are such sales promotion efforts worth the cost? Vanguard decided not. It had one sales outpost in Philadelphia, but closed it to save money.

Vanguard discouraged day traders and other market timers from in-and-out trading of its funds. It even prohibited telephone switching on the Vanguard 500 Index; redemption orders had to come by mail. Why such market timing discouragement? Frequent redemptions run up transaction costs, and a flurry of sell orders might impose trading costs that would have to be borne by other shareholders as some holdings might have to be sold.

Not the least of the economies is what Bogle calls passive investing, tracking the market rather than trying to actively manage the funds by trying to beat the market. The funds with the highest expense ratios are hedge funds and these usually are the most active traders, with heavy buying and selling. Yet they seldom beat the market but squander a lot of money in the effort and burden shareholders with sizable capital gains taxes because of the flurry of transactions. Still, the common notion prevails that more is better, that the more expensive car or service must be better than its less expensive alternative. See the Information Box on page 285 for another discussion of the price-quality perception.

Another factor also contributes to the great cost advantage of Vanguard. It is a mutual firm, organized as a nonprofit owned by its customers. Almost all other financial institutions, except TIAA-CREF (and we will discuss this shortly), have stock ownership with its heavy allegiance to profit maximization.

Customer Service

Many firms espouse a commitment to customer service. It is the popular thing to do, rather like motherhood, apple pie, and the flag. Unfortunately, pious platitudes do not always match reality. Vanguard's commitment to service seems to be more tangible.

Service to customers is often composed of the simple things, such as just answering the phone promptly and courteously, or responding to mail quickly and completely, or giving complete and unbiased information. Vanguard's 2,000 phone representatives are ready to answer the phone by the fourth ring. During a market panic or on April 15 when the tax deadline stimulates many inquiries, CEO John Brennan brings a brigade of executives with him to help man the phones. Vanguard works to make its monthly statements to investors as complete and easy-to-understand as possible, and it leads the industry in this.

---

[9] Easton, p. 116.

INFORMATION BOX

THE PRICE-QUALITY PERCEPTION—REVISITED

We had a similar box in Chapter 11 on Perrier and will have again in Chapter 22. But the topic is worth further discussion. In the Perrier case, we considered whether high-priced bottled water was that much better than regular tap water or lower-priced bottled water and concluded that it usually was not. The same thing applies to perfume, to beer and liquor, and to many other consumer products. "You get what you pay for," is a common perception, and its corollary is that you judge quality by price: The higher the price, the higher the quality. But this notion leads many consumers to be taken advantage of, and for top-of-the-line brands and products to command a higher profit margin than lower-priced alternatives. Admittedly, sometimes we are led to the more expensive brand or item for the prestige factor.

When it comes to money management, by no means do high fees mean better quality; the reverse is usually true. And prestige should hardly be a factor since we are not inclined to show off our investments like we might a new car. Does a high-overhead index fund deliver better performance than a cheap one, than Vanguard? Not at all. And hedge funds as we noted before seldom even beat the averages despite running up some of the highest expenses in the mutual fund industry. Looking at Table 19.2, which shows typical expense ratios of Vanguard and its competitors, are the other funds doing a better job than Vanguard with their expenses three to five times higher? No, because their high expense ratios take away from any performance advantage, even if frequent trading resulted in somewhat better gains, and that seldom is achieved.

If Vanguard advertised its great expense advantage aggressively to really get the word out, do you think it would win many more customers? Why or why not?

The philosophy of a customer-service commitment was espoused by Bogle. "Our primary goal: to serve, to the best of our ability, the human beings who are our clients. To serve them with candor, with integrity, and with fair dealing. To be the stewards of the assets they have entrusted to us. To treat them as we would like the stewards of our own assets to treat us."

Bogle described a talk he gave to Harvard Business School in December 1997 on how "our focus on human beings had enabled Vanguard to become what at Harvard is called a 'service breakthrough company.' I challenged the students to find the term *human beings* in any book they had read on corporate strategy. As far as I know, none could meet the challenge. But 'human beingness' has been one of the keys to our development."[10]

Not the least of the consumer, best interests has been a commitment to holding down taxable transactions for shareholders. Vanguard has led the industry with tax-

[10] Bogle, pp. 423,424.

managed funds aimed at minimizing the capital gains that confront most mutual fund investors to their dismay at the end of the year.

COMPETITION

Why is Vanguard's low-expense approach not matched by competitors? All the other fund giants that sell primarily to the general public are for-profit companies. Are they willing to sacrifice profits to win back Vanguard converts? Hardly likely. Are they willing to reduce their hefty marketing and advertising expenditures? Again, hardly likely. Why? Because advertising, not word-of-mouth, is vital to their visibility and to seeking out customers.

TIAA-CREF

One potential competitor looms, another low-cost fund contender. TIAA-CREF, which manages retirement money for teachers and researchers, in 1997 launched six no-load mutual funds that are now open to all investors. The funds' annual expenses range from 0.29 percent to 0.49 percent, comparable with Vanguard's. A significant potential attraction over Vanguard is that each fund's investment minimum is just $250, compared with Vanguard's usual minimum of $3,000. As of late August 1999, the combined assets of the six TIAA-CREF funds was $1.5 billion, far less of course, than the near $500 billion of Vanguard.

TIAA-CREF is also run solely for the benefit of its shareholders, being another mutual, with the long-term aim of providing fund-management services at cost. Still, there is some doubt that expense ratios can be kept low, should the new funds fail to attract enough investors.

Is this a gnat against the giant Vanguard? Perhaps; however, the low investment requirement of only $250 should certainly attract cost-conscious investors who cannot come up with the $3,000 that Vanguard requires on most of its funds. Still, six fund choices versus the more than 100 of Vanguard is not very attractive yet. Efforts to be as tax efficient as Vanguard are also unknown.

ANALYSIS

The success of Vanguard with its disavowal of most traditional business strategies flies in the face of all that we have come to believe. It suggests that heavy advertising expenditures may at least be questioned as not always desirable—and what a heresy this is. It suggests that relying on word-of-mouth and whatever free publicity can be garnered may sometimes be preferable to advertising. All you need is a superior product or service. It supports the statement that textbooks like to shoot down: "If you build a better mousetrap, people will come." Conventional wisdom maintains that without advertising to get the message out, this better mousetrap will fade away from lack of buyer knowledge and interest. But the planning of Bogle and Vanguard to tread a different path and not be dissuaded, despite the critics, illustrates a remarkable and enduring commitment first formulated almost three decades ago.

How do we reconcile Vanguard with the commonly accepted notion that communication is essential to get products and services to customers (except perhaps when selling solely to the government or to a single customer)?

Maybe we should not try to fit Vanguard into such traditional beliefs. Maybe it is the exception, the anomaly, in its seeming repudiation of them. Still, let us not be too hasty in this judgment.

I do not believe that Vanguard contradicts traditional principles of marketing and business strategy. Rather, it has revealed another approach to the communication component: the effective use of word-of-mouth publicity. If we have a distinctive product that can be tangibly demonstrated as superior in relative cost advantages to competitors, then demand may be stimulated without mass advertising. Word-of-mouth, enhanced or developed through formal publicity—from media, public appearances, and publications—can replace massive advertising expenditures of competitors. But is there a downside to all this? Let us examine the role of word-of-mouth in more detail in the following Information Box.

INFORMATION BOX

THE POTENTIAL OF WORD-OF-MOUTH AND UNPAID PUBLICITY

Word-of-mouth advertising, by itself, is almost always frowned on by the experts. It is the sign of the marginal firm, one without sufficient resources, so they say, to do what is needed to get established. Such a firm is bound to succumb to competitors who are better managed and better resourced. The best they can say for word-of-mouth advertising is that if the firm can survive for an unknown number of years, and if it really, really has a superior product or service, then it might finally attain some modest success.

Compared to spending for advertising, word-of-mouth takes far longer to have any impact, and firms seldom have the staying power to wait years, so the belief holds. The best strategy would be to have both, with healthy doses of advertising to jumpstart the enterprise and let favorable word-of-mouth reinforce the advertising.

As we have seen, Bogle and his Vanguard repudiated the accepted strategy, yet became highly successful. Still, it took time, even decades. If you look at Table 19.1, in 1994 after 16 years, the flagship Index 500 fund had reached $8 billion in assets; not bad, but far below the heavily advertised Magellan fund of Fidelity. The growth of the Index 500 fund has accelerated only in recent years. Would more advertising have shortened the period?

Bogle would maintain that such advertising would have destroyed the uniqueness of Vanguard by making its expenses like other funds. He would also likely contend that the favorable publicity enhanced the word-of-mouth influence of satisfied shareholders, and thus there was no need for expensive advertising. But in the early years of Vanguard, it did not have much favorable publicity. On the contrary, it took experts a long time to admit that a low-expense fund with passive management could do as well or better than aggressively managed funds with a lot of buying and selling and big trading and marketing expenses.

So the success of Vanguard without much formal advertising attests to the success of word-of-mouth heavily seasoned by favorable free publicity. But was it too conservative, especially in the early years?

Do you think Vanguard should have advertised more, especially in its early days? Why or why not? If yes, how much more do you think it should have spent?

Vanguard illustrates a commendable application of one important marketing principle: the desirability of uniqueness or product differentiation. It differentiated itself from competitors in two respects: (1) its resolve and ability to bring out a low-priced product and at the same time one of good quality and (2) its achievement of good customer service despite the low price.

Even today, after several decades of competitors seeing this highly effective strategy, Vanguard still is virtually unmatched in its uniqueness, except for one newcomer that is hardly a contender but could be a factor should Vanguard let down its guard and be tempted to seek more profits.

Prognosis—Can Vanguard Continue As Is?

Is it likely Vanguard can continue its success pattern without increasing advertising and other costs and becoming more like its competitors? Why should it change? It has become a giant with its low-cost strategy. The last decade saw a growing momentum created by favorable word-of-mouth and publicity that made the need for heavy advertising and selling efforts far less than in the early years. It took bravery, or audacity, in those early years not to succumb to the Lorelei beguilement that advertising and commission selling was the only viable strategy. Something would be lost if Vanguard changes its strategy and uniqueness and becomes a higher-cost imitation of its competitors.

If Vanguard is so good, why are so many investors still doing business with the higher-cost competitors? We can identify four groups of consumers who are noncustomers of Vanguard:

1. Those who have not studied the statistics and editorials of publications like *Forbes* and *Wall Street Journal,* and are not aware of the Vanguard advantage.

2. Those who are naive in investing and content to let someone else—brokers or bankers—advise them and reap the commissions.

3. Those who are swayed by the massive advertisements of firms like Fidelity, Dreyfus, Rowe Price, and others.

4. Those who put their faith in the price-quality perception: the higher the price the higher the quality, with quality guaranteeing higher investor returns.

In addition to continued investments of its ardent customers, Vanguard should find potential in the gradual eroding of the commitment of these four consumer groups. Of course, the overseas markets also offer a huge and virtually untapped potential for Vanguard.

WHAT CAN BE LEARNED?

Marketing Can Be Overdone

The success of Vanguard shows that marketing can be overdone. Too much can be spent for advertising, without realizing congruent benefits. Sales expenses and branch office overhead may get out of line. Yet few firms think they dare reduce such costs lest they be competitively disadvantaged. For example, it is the brave executive who reduces advertising in the face of increases by competitors, though the results of the advertising may be impossible to measure with any accuracy. Still, despite the success of Vanguard in downplaying advertising, one has to wonder how much faster the growth might have been by budgeting more dollars for selling, at least in the early years.

Can Word-of-Mouth Do the Job of Advertising by Itself?

In Vanguard's case, word-of-mouth combined with favorable unpaid publicity from the media brought it to the largest mutual fund family in the industry. However, the time it took for word-of-mouth, even eventually with good publicity, to build demand has to be a negative. Without such favorable publicity, it would have taken far longer.

The Benefits of Frugality

There is far too much waste in most institutions, business and nonbusiness. Some waste comes from undercontrolled costs and such extravagances as lavish expense accounts, entertainment, and expenditures that do little to benefit the bottom line. Other factors may be a top-heavy bureaucratic organization saddled with layers of staff personnel, and/or too many debt payments due to heavy investments in plant and equipment or mergers. Heavy use of advertising may not always pay off enough to justify the expenditures, as we saw in Chapter 3 when Coca Cola was outspending Pepsi by $100 million but was still losing market share. In money management, trading costs may get far out of line.

Vanguard shows the benefit of austerity in greatly reduced expense ratios for its funds compared to competitors. At last, more and more astute investors are recognizing this unique cost advantage that not only gives a better return on their investment dollars but some of the best customer service in the industry.

The Power of Differentiation

Firms seek to differentiate themselves, to come up with products or ways of doing business that are unique in some respect from competitors. This is a paramount quest of business strategy and accounts for the massive expenditures for advertising. Too often, such attempts to find uniqueness are fragile, not very substantial, and easily lost or countered by competitors. Sometimes, though, they can be rather enduring, as for example the quality-image perception perpetrated by advertisements featuring the lonely Maytag repairman, as described in Chapter 13. If a firm can effectively differentiate itself from competitors, it gains a powerful advantage and may even be able to charge premium prices.

While Vanguard seemingly disregarded marketing, John Bogle found a powerful and enduring way to differentiate through low-cost quality products and superb customer service. For decades no competitor has been able to match this attractive uniqueness.

Beware Placing Too Much Faith in the Price-Quality Relationship

We are drawn to judge quality by a product's price relative to other choices. Often this is justified, although the better quality may not always match the higher price. In other words, the luxury item may not be worth the much higher price, except for the significant psychological value that some people see in the prestige of a fine brand name. Unfortunately, there are some products and services where the higher price does not really reflect higher quality, better workmanship, better service, and the like. Then we are taken advantage of with this price-quality perception. Beware of always judging quality by price.

CONSIDER

Can you think of additional learning insights?

QUESTIONS

1. "The success of Vanguard is due to media exploitation of what would otherwise be a very ordinary firm." Discuss.

2. Why do you think people continue to buy front-end load mutual funds with 5 to 6 percent commission fees when there are numerous no-load funds to be had?

3. Do you think Bogle's shunning advertising was really a success or was it a mistake?

4. Was Vanguard's failure to open walk-in sales outposts a mistake and an example of misplaced frugality? Why or why not?

5. What are the differences in passive and active fund management? How significant are these?

6. "Vanguard seems too good. There must be a downside." Discuss.

7. What is a service breakthrough company?

8. Can publicity ever take the place of massive advertising expenditures?

HANDS-ON EXERCISES

1. You are an executive assistant to John Brennan, the new CEO of Vanguard now that Bogle has retired. Brennan is thinking of judiciously adding some marketing and advertising expenditures to the paucity that Bogle had insisted on. He has directed you to draw up a position paper on the merits of adding some advertising and even some walk-in sales outposts such as other big competitors have already done.

2. You are John Brennan, CEO. It is 2006, and TIAA-CREF is turning out to be a formidable competitor and is gaining fast on your first-place position in the industry. What actions would you take and why? Discuss all ramifications of these actions that you can think of.

TEAM DEBATE EXERCISES

1. You are a member of the board of directors of Vanguard. John Bogle is approaching the retirement age as set forth in the company policies. However, he wants to continue as chairman of the board, even though he is willing to let Brennan assume active management. Debate the issue of whether to force Bogle to step down or bow to his wishes.

2. Debate the no-advertising policy of Bogle.

INVITATION TO RESEARCH

Is Vanguard still No. 1 in the mutual fund industry? Has it increased its advertising expenditures? Has Brennan made any substantial changes?

CHAPTER TWENTY

Southwest Airlines—
"Try to Match Our Prices"

In 1992, the airlines lost a combined $2 billion, matching a dismal 1991, and bringing their three-year red ink total to a disastrous $8 billion. Three carriers—TWA, Continental, and America West—were operating under Chapter 11 bankruptcy, and others were lining up to join them. But one airline, Southwest, was profitable as well as rapidly growing—with a 25 percent sales increase in 1992 alone. Interestingly enough, this was a low-price, bare bones operation, run by a flamboyant CEO, Herb Kelleher. He had found a niche, a strategic window of opportunity and, oh, how he milked it! See the Information Box on page 293 for further discussion of a strategic window of opportunity and its desirable accompaniment, a SWOT analysis.

HERBERT D. KELLEHER

Herb Kelleher impresses one as an eccentric. He likes to tell stories, often with himself as the butt of the story, and many involve practical jokes. He admits he sometimes is a little scatterbrained. In his cluttered office, he displays a dozen ceramic wild turkeys as a testimonial to his favorite brand of whiskey. He smokes five packs of cigarettes a day. As an example of his zaniness, he painted one of his 737s to look like a killer whale in celebration of the opening of Sea World in San Antonio. Another time, during a flight he had flight attendants dress up as reindeer and elves, while the pilot sang Christmas carols over the loudspeaker as he gently rocked the plane. Kelleher is a "real maniac," said Thomas J. Volz, vice-president of marketing at Braniff Airlines. "But who can argue with his success?"[1]

Kelleher grew up in Haddon Heights, N.J., the son of a Campbell Soup Company executive. He graduated from Wesleyan University and New York University law school, then moved to San Antonio in 1961, where his father-in-law helped him set up a law firm. In 1968, he and a group of investors put up $560,000 to found Southwest; of this amount, Kelleher contributed $20,000.

---

[1] Kevin Kelly, "Southwest Airlines: "Flying High with 'Uncle Herb'," *Business Week,* July 3, 1989, p. 53.

INFORMATION BOX

STRATEGIC WINDOW OF OPPORTUNITY AND SWOT ANALYSIS

A strategic window is an opportunity in the marketplace, not presently well served by competitors, that fits well with the firm's competencies. Strategic windows often last for only a short time (although Southwest's strategic window has been much more durable), before they are filled by alert competitors.

Strategic windows are usually found by systematically analyzing the environment, examining the threats and opportunities it holds. The competencies of the firm, its physical, financial, and people resources—management and employees and their strengths and weaknesses—should also be assessed. The objective is to determine what actions might or might not be appropriate for that particular enterprise and its orientation. This is commonly known as a SWOT analysis: analyzing the strengths and weaknesses of the firm and assessing the opportunities and threats in the environment.

This analysis may be a formal part of the planning process, or it may also be informal and even intuitive. We can suspect that Herb Kelleher instinctively sensed a strategic window in short hauls and lowest prices. Although he must have recognized the danger that his bigger competitors would try to match his prices, he believed that with his simplicity of operation he would be able to make a profit while bigger airlines were racking up losses.

Why do you think the major airlines so badly overlooked the possibilities in short hauls at low prices?

In the early years, he was the general counsel and a director of the fledgling enterprise. But in 1978, he was named chairman, despite his having no managerial experience, and in 1981 he became CEO. His flamboyance soon made him the most visible aspect of the airline. He starred in most of its TV commercials. A rival airline, America West, charged in ads that Southwest passengers should be embarrassed to fly such a no-frills airline, whereupon Kelleher appeared in a TV spot with a bag over his head. He offered the bag to anyone ashamed to fly Southwest, suggesting it could be used to hold "all the money you'll save flying us."[2]

He knew many of his employees by name, and they called him "Uncle Herb" or "Herbie." He held weekly parties for employees at corporate headquarters. And he encouraged such antics by his flight attendants as organizing trivia contests, delivering instructions in rap, and awarding prizes for the passengers with the largest holes in their socks. But such wackiness had a shrewd purpose: to generate a gung-ho spirit to boost productivity. "Herb's fun is infectious," said Kay Wallace, president of the

[2] Kelly, p. 53.

Flight Attendants Union Local 556. "Everyone enjoys what they're doing and realizes they've got to make an extra effort."[3]

THE BEGINNINGS

Southwest was conceived in 1967, folklore tells us, on a napkin. Rollin King, a client of Kelleher, then a lawyer, had an idea for a low-fare, no-frills airline to fly between major Texas cities. He doodled a triangle on the napkin, labeling the points Dallas, Houston, and San Antonio.

The two tried to go ahead with their plans but were stymied for more than three years by litigation, battling Braniff, Texas International, and Continental over the right to fly. In 1971, Southwest won, and it went public in 1975. At that time, it had four planes flying between the three cities. Lamar Muse was president and CEO from 1971 until he was fired by Southwest's board in 1978. Then the board of directors tapped Kelleher.

At first, Southwest was in the throes of life-and-death low-fare skirmishes with its giant competitors. Kelleher liked to recount how he came home one day "beat, tired, and worn out. So I'm just kind of sagging around the house when my youngest daughter comes up and asks what's wrong. I tell her, 'Well, Ruthie, it's these damned fare wars.' And she cuts me right off and says, 'Oh, Daddy, stop complaining. After all, you started 'em.'"[4]

For most small firms, competing on a price basis with much larger, well endowed competitors is tantamount to disaster. The small firm simply cannot match the resources and staying power of such competitors. Yet Southwest somehow survived. Not only did it initiate the cut-throat price competition, but it achieved cost savings in its operation that the larger airlines could not. The question then became: How long would the big carriers be content to maintain their money-losing operations and match the low prices of Southwest? And the big airlines eventually blinked.

In its early years, Southwest faced other legal battles. Take Dallas and Love Field. The original airport, Love Field, is close to downtown Dallas, but it could not geographically expand at the very time when air traffic was increasing mightily. So, a major new facility, Dallas/Fort Worth International airport, superseded it in 1974. This boasted state-of-the-art facilities and enough room for foreseeable demand, but it had one major drawback: it was 30 minutes farther from downtown Dallas. Southwest was able to avoid a forced move to the new airport and to continue at Love. But in 1978, competitors pressured Congress to bar flights from Love Field to anywhere outside Texas. Southwest was able to negotiate a compromise, now known as the Wright Amendment, that allowed flights from Love Field to the four states contiguous to Texas. In retrospect, the Wright Amendment forced onto Southwest a key ingredient of its later success: the strategy of short flights.[5]

---

[3] Richard Woodbury, "Prince of Midair," *Time*, January 25, 1993, p. 55.

[4] Charles A. Jaffe, "Moving Fast by Standing Still," *Nation's Business*, October 1991, p. 58.

[5] Bridget O'Brian, "Southwest Airlines Is a Rare Air Carrier: It Still Makes Money," *Wall Street Journal*, October 28, 1992, p. A7.

GROWTH

Southwest grew steadily, but not spectacularly, through the 1970s. It dominated the Texas market by appealing to passengers who valued price and frequent departures. Its one-way fare, for example, between Dallas and Houston was $59 in 1987 versus $79 for unrestricted coach flights on other airlines.

In the 1980s, Southwest's annual passenger traffic count tripled. At the end of 1989, its operating costs per revenue mile—the industry's standard measure of cost-effectiveness—was just under 10 cents, which was about 5 cents per mile below the industry average.[6] Although revenues and profits were rising steadily, especially compared with the other airlines, Kelleher took a conservative approach to expansion, financing it mostly from internal funds rather than taking on debt.

Perhaps the caution stemmed from an ill-fated acquisition in 1986. Kelleher bought a failing long-haul carrier, Muse Air Corp. for $68 million and renamed it TransStar. (This carrier had been founded by Lamar Muse after he left Southwest.) But by 1987, TransStar was losing $2 million a month, and Kelleher shut down the operation.

By 1993, Southwest had spread to 34 cities in 15 states. It had 141 planes and these each made 11 trips a day. It used only fuel-thrifty 737s and still concentrated on flying large numbers of passengers on high-frequency, one-hour hops at bargain fares (average $58). Southwest shunned the hub-and-spoke systems of its larger rivals and took its passengers directly from city to city, often to smaller satellite airfields, rather than congested major metropolitan fields. With rock-bottom prices, and no amenities, it quickly dominated most new markets it entered.

As an example of Southwest's impact on a new market, it came to Cleveland, Ohio, in February 1992, and by the end of the year was offering 11 daily flights. In 1992, Cleveland Hopkins Airport posted record passenger levels, up 9.74 percent from 1991. "A lot of the gain was traffic that Southwest Airlines generated," noted John Osmond, air trade development manager.[7]

In some markets, Southwest found itself growing much faster than projected, as competitors either folded or else abandoned directly competing routes. For example, in Phoenix, America West Airlines cut back service in order to conserve cash after a Chapter 11 bankruptcy filing. Of course, Southwest picked up the slack, as it did in Chicago when Midway Airlines folded in November 1992. And in California, Southwest's arrival led to several large competitors abandoning the Los Angeles-San Francisco route, unable to meet Southwest's $59 one-way fare. Before Southwest, fares had been as high as $186 one way.[8]

Now cities that Southwest did not serve were petitioning for service. For example, Sacramento, California, sent two county commissioners, the president of the chamber of commerce and the airport director, to Dallas to petition for service.

---

[6] Jaffe, p. 58.

[7] "Passenger Flights Set Hopkins Record," *Cleveland Plain Dealer,* January 30, 1993, p. D3.

[8] O'Brian, p. A7.

Kelleher consented a few months later. In 1991, the airline received 51 similar requests.[9]

A unique situation was developing. On many routes, Southwest's fares were so low they competed with buses, and even with private cars. By 1991, Kelleher did not even see other airlines as his principal competitors: "We're competing with the automobile, not the airlines. We're pricing ourselves against Ford, Chrysler, GM, Toyota, and Nissan. The traffic is already there, but it's on the ground. We take it off the highway and put it on the airplane."[10]

Following are several tables and graphs that depict various aspects of Southwest's growth and increasingly favorable competitive position. See Tables 20.1, 20.2, and 20.3, and Figure 20.1. While total revenues of Southwest were still less than the major airlines in the industry, its growth pattern indicated a major presence, and its profitability was second to none.

Tapping California

The formidable competitive power of Southwest was perhaps never better epitomized than in its 1990 invasion of populous California. By 1992, it had become the

TABLE 20.1 Growth of Southwest Airlines: Various Operating Statistics, 1982–1991

Year	Operating Revenues ($ millions)	Net Income ($ millions)	Passengers Carried (thousands)	Passenger Load Factor
1991	$1,314	$26.9	22,670	61.1%
1990	1,187	47.1	19,831	60.7
1989	1,015	71.6	17,958	62.7
1988	880	58.0	14,877	57.7
1987	778	20.2	13,503	58.4
1986	769	50.0	13,638	58.8
1985	680	47.3	12,651	60.4
1984	535	49.7	10,698	58.5
1983	448	40.9	9,511	61.6
1982	331	34.0	7,966	61.6

Source: Company annual reports.

Commentary: Note the steady increase in revenues and in numbers of passengers carried. Although the net income and load factor statistics show no appreciable improvement, these statistics are still in the vanguard of an industry that has suffered badly in recent years. See Table 20.2 for a comparison of revenues and income with the major airlines.

[9] Ibid.

[10] Subrata N. Chakravarty, "Hit 'Em Hardest with the Mostest," *Forbes,* September 16, 1991, p. 49.

TABLE 20.2   Comparison of Southwest's Growth in Revenues and Net Income with Major Competitors, 1987–1991

	1991	1990	1989	1988	1987	% 5-Year Gain
Operating Revenue Comparisons ($ millions)						
American	$9,309	$9,203	$8,670	$7,548	$6,369	46.0
Delta	8,268	7,697	7,780	6,684	5,638	46.6
United	7,850	7,946	7,463	7,006	6,500	20.8
Northwest	4,330	4,298	3,944	3,395	3,328	30.1
Southwest	1,314	1,187	1,015	860	778	68.9
Net Income Comparisons (millions)						
American	(253)	(40)	412	450	225	
Delta	(216)	(119)	467	286	201	
United	(175)	73	246	426	22	
Northwest	10	(27)	116	49	64	
Southwest	27	47	72	58	20	

Source: Company annual reports.

Commentary: Southwest's revenue gains over these 5-years outstripped those of its largest competitors. While the percentage gains in profitability are hardly useful because of the erratic nature of airline profits during these years, Southwest stands out starkly as the only airline to be profitable each year.

second largest player, after United, with 23 percent of intrastate traffic. This was achieved by pushing down fares as much as 60 percent on some routes. The big carriers, which had tended to surrender the short-haul niche to Southwest in other markets, suddenly faced a real quandary in competing in this "Golden State." Now Southwest was being described as a "500 pound cockroach, too big to stamp out."[11]

TABLE 20.3   Market Share Comparison of Southwest and Its Four Major Competitors, 1987–1991

	1991	1990	1989	1988	1987
Total Revenues:					
American, Delta, United, Northwest	$29,757	$29,144	$27,857	$24,633	$21,835
Southwest Revenues	$1,314	$1,187	$1,015	$860	$778
Percentage of big four	4.4	4.1	3.6	3.5	3.6

Increase in Southwest's market share, 1987–1991: 22%

Source: Company annual reports.

[11] Wendy Zellner, "Striking Gold in the California Skies," *Business Week*, March 30, 1992, p. 48.

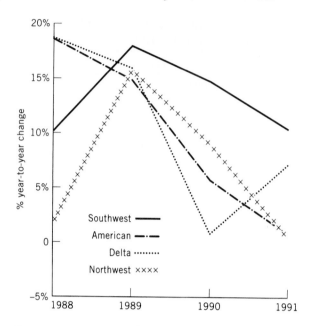

Figure 20.1. Year-to-year percentage changes in revenues, Southwest and its three major competitors, 1988–1991.

The California market was indeed enticing. Some eight million passengers each year flew between the five airports in metropolitan Los Angeles and three in the San Francisco Bay area, this being the busiest corridor in the United States. It was also one of the pricier routes as the low fares of AirCal and Pacific Southwest Airlines had been eliminated when these two airlines were acquired by American and US Air.

Into this situation Southwest charged, with low fares and frequent flights. While airfares dropped, total air traffic soared 123 percent in the quarter Southwest entered the market. Competitors suffered, as American lost nearly $80 million at its San Jose hub, while US Air still lost money even though it cut service drastically. United, the market leader, quit flying the San Diego-Sacramento and Ontario-Oakland routes where Southwest had rapidly built up service. The quandary of the major airlines was all the greater since this critical market fed traffic into the rest of their systems, especially the lucrative transcontinental and trans-Pacific routes. They could hardly abdicate California to Southwest. American, for one, considered creating its own no-frills shuttle for certain routes. But the question remained: could anyone stop Southwest, with its formula of lowest prices, lowest costs, and frequent schedules? And, oh yes, good service and fun.

INGREDIENTS OF SUCCESS

Although Southwest's operation under Kelleher had a number of rather distinctive characteristics contributing to its success pattern and its seizing of a strategic window of opportunity, the key factors appear to be cost containment, employee commitment, and conservative growth.

Cost Containment

Southwest has been the lowest-cost carrier in its markets. While its larger competitors might try to match its cut-rate prices, they could not do so without incurring sizable losses. Nor did they seem able to trim their costs to match Southwest. For example, in the first quarter of 1991, Southwest's operating costs per available seat mile (i.e., the number of seats multiplied by the distance flown) were 15 percent lower than America West, 29 percent lower than Delta, 32 percent lower than United, and 39 percent lower than US Air.[12]

Many aspects of the operation contributed to these lower costs. With all its planes being a single aircraft type, Boeing 737, costs of training, maintenance, and inventory could be reduced. And since a plane earns revenues only when flying, Southwest was able to achieve a faster turnaround time on the ground than any other airline. Although competitors take upwards of an hour to load and unload passengers, then clean and service the planes, some 70 percent of Southwest's flights have a turnaround time of 15 minutes, while 10 percent have even pared the turnaround time to 10 minutes.

In areas of customer service, Southwest curbed costs as well. It offered peanuts and drinks but no meals. Boarding passes were reusable plastic cards. Boarding time was minimal because there were no assigned seats. Southwest subscribed to no centralized reservation service. It did not even transfer baggage to other carriers; that was the passengers' responsibility. Admittedly, such customer service frugalities would be less acceptable on longer flights—and this helped to account for the difficulty competing airlines had in cutting their costs to match Southwest's. Still, if the price is right, many passengers might also opt for no frills on longer flights.

Employee Commitment

Kelleher was able to achieve an esprit de corps unmatched by other airlines despite the fact that Southwest employees were unionized. But there was no adversarial relationship with unions, so that Southwest was able to negotiate flexible work rules, with flight attendants and even pilots helping with plane cleanup. Employee productivity continued to be very high, permitting the airline to be leanly staffed. Kelleher resisted the inclination to hire extravagantly when times were good, necessitating layoffs during leaner times. This contributed to employee feelings of security and loyalty. The low-key attitude and sense of fun that Kelleher engendered helped, perhaps more than anyone could have foreseen. Kelleher declared, "Fun is a stimulant to people. They enjoy their work more and work more productively."[13]

---

[12] Chakravarty, p. 50.
[13] Ibid.

Conservative Growth Efforts

Not the least of the ingredients of success was Kelleher's conservative approach to growth. He resisted the temptation to expand vigorously—for example, to seek to fly to Europe or get into head-to-head competition with larger airlines with long-distance routes. Even in its geographical expansion, conservatism prevailed. The philosophy of expansion was only to do so when enough resources could be committed to go into a city with ten to twelve flights a day, rather than just 1 or 2. Kelleher called this "guerrilla warfare," with efforts concentrated against stronger opponents in only a few areas, rather than dissipating strength by trying to compete everywhere.

Even with a conservative approach to expansion, the company showed vigorous but controlled growth. Its debt, at 49 percent of equity, was the lowest among U.S. carriers. Southwest also had the airline industry's highest Standard & Poor's credit rating, A minus.

GALLOPING TOWARD THE NEW MILLENNIUM

In its May 2, 1994, edition, prestigious *Fortune* magazine devoted its cover story to Herb Kelleher and Southwest Airlines. It raised an intriguing question: "Is Herb Kelleher America's Best CEO?" It called him a "people-wise manager who wins where others can't."[14] The operational effectiveness of Southwest continued to surpass all rivals, for example, in such productivity ratios as cost per available seat mile, passengers per employee, and employees per aircraft. Only Southwest remained consistently profitable among the big airlines, by the end of 1998 having been profitable for 26 consecutive years. Operating revenue had grown to $4.2 billion (it was $1.3 billion in 1991—see Table 20.2), and net income was $433 million, up from $27 million in 1991.

In 1999, Herb Kelleher was named CEO of the Year by *Chief Executive* magazine.

Geographical Expansion

Late in October 1996, Southwest launched a carefully planned battle for East Coast passengers that would drive down air fares and pressure competitors to back away from some lucrative markets. It chose Providence, Rhode Island, just 60 miles from Boston's Logan Airport, thus tapping the Boston-Washington corridor. The Providence airport escaped the congested New York and Boston air-traffic-control areas, and from the Boston suburbs was hardly a longer trip than that to Logan Airport. Experience had shown that air travelers would drive considerable distance to fly with Southwest's cheaper fares.

As Southwest entered new markets, most competitors refused any longer to try to compete pricewise—they simply could not cut costs enough to compete. Their alternative then was either to pull out of these short-haul markets, or be content to

---

[14] Kenneth Labich, "Is Herb Kelleher America's Best CEO," *Fortune*, May 2, 1994, pp. 45–52.

let Southwest have its market share while they tried to hold on to other customers by stressing first-class seating, frequent-flyer programs, and other in-flight amenities.

In April 1997, Southwest quietly entered the transcontinental market. From its major connecting point of Nashville, Tennessee, it began nonstops both to Oakland, California, and to Los Angeles. With Nashville's direct connections with Chicago, Detroit, Cleveland, Providence, and Baltimore-Washington, as well as points south, this afforded, *one-stop,* coast-to-coast service, with fares about half as much as the other major airlines.

Two other significant moves were announced in late 1998. One was an experiment. On Thanksgiving Day, a Southwest 737-700 flew *nonstop* from Oakland, California, to the Baltimore-Washington Airport, and back again. It provided its customary no-frills service, but a $99 one-way fare, the lowest in the business. The test was designed to see how pilots, flight attendants, and passengers would feel about spending five hours in a 737, with only peanuts and drinks served in flight. The older 737s lacked the fuel capacity to fly coast-to-coast nonstop, but with Boeing's new 737-700 series, this was no problem. The Thanksgiving Day test was a precursor of more nonstop flights, as Southwest had firm orders for 129 of the new planes to be delivered over the next seven years. This would enable it to compete with the major carriers on their moneymaking transcontinental flights.

In November 1998, plans were also announced for starting service to MacArthur Airport at Islip, Long Island, which would enable Southwest to tap into the New York City market. By late 1999, it was flying to 54 cities in 29 states. Table 20.4 list these cities.

TABLE 20.4 Cities Served by Southwest October 1999

Albuquerque	Ft. Lauderdale	Midland/Odessa	Rio Grande Valley (South Padre Island/Harlingen)
Amarillo	Hartford, CT[a]	Nashville	
Austin	Houston (Hobby & Bush Intercontinental)	New Orleans	Sacramento
Baltimore-Washington		Oakland	St. Louis
Birmingham	Indianapolis	Oklahoma City	Salt Lake City
Boise	Islip (Long Island)	Omaha	San Antonio
Burbank	Jackson, MS	Ontario, CA	San Diego
Chicago (Midway)	Jacksonville	Orange County	San Francisco
Cleveland	Kansas City	Orlando	San Jose
Columbus	Little Rock	Phoenix	Seattle
Corpus Christi	Los Angeles (LAX)	Portland	Spokane
Dallas (Love Field)	Louisville	Providence, RI	Tampa
Detroit (Metro)	Lubbock	Raleigh–Durham	Tucson
El Paso	Manchester, NH	Reno/Tahoe	Tulsa

[a] Service to Hartford, Connecticut, began October 31, 1999.

UPDATE TO 2005

By mid-2002, with the 9/11 disaster still affecting airline travel, Southwest was the only major carrier that had been operating profitably in the 18 months since. U. S. airlines were posting losses of as much as $8 billion in 2002—eclipsing the record in 2001 of $7.7 billion, with the loss in the more profitable business travel being particularly acute. The high-cost airlines faced enormous pressure from low-fare carriers, most notably Southwest, but also from Internet sites that allowed bargain hunting. Southwest was now the nation's sixth largest airline, and it had been profitable for 29 consecutive years.

In June 2001, just months before the September 11 attacks, Herb Kelleher retired. He was replaced by James Parker, who had joined Southwest in 1986, and Parker readily admitted he was no Herb Kelleher. His immediate challenge was to contain operating costs of soaring liability insurance and unionized workers agitation for raises to match rich contracts negotiated at other airlines before September 11. However, the bankruptcies of United Airlines and US Airways in late 2002 highlighted the need for airlines to slash billions in operating costs, notably through labor givebacks of extravagant union contracts, and this helped subdue new labor demands.[15]

In the increasingly brutal airline market, even Southwest was getting squeezed. It still remained profitable and its seat capacity for the first half of 2004 was up 29 percent from four years earlier, but because of mounting price competition, revenue had risen only 18 percent during this time. It still remained profitable while the world-wide airline industry had incurred losses of about $30 billion since 2001. But Southwest now faced price competition from a new breed of low-price competitors, such as JetBlue Airways, which also offered such amenities as inflight TV. The bigger airlines also were posing greater competition as they had substantially lowered their costs and their ticket prices. Some pilots on major airlines, with their compensation givebacks, were even making less than Southwest pilots. In this environment, CEO James Parker abruptly retired after only three years on the job. He was replaced in July 2004 by Gary Kelly, former chief financial officer of Southwest.

In early 2005, Southwest announced its invasion of the Pittsburgh market, taking advantage of US Airways' major service cuts there. This was the latest move in Southwest's continuing buildup in the East. It had entered the Philadelphia market in May 2004, where traffic rose more than 51 percent and average fares fell more than 37 percent with its arrival. Pittsburgh now had six low-cost carriers and the dominant hub position of US Airways has eroded.[16]

---

[15] Daniel Fisher, "Is There Such a Thing as Nonstop Growth? *Forbes,* July 8, 2002, pp. 82, 84.

[16] Melanie Trottman, "At Southwest, New CEO Sits in a Hot Seat," *Wall Street Journal,* July 19, 2004, pp. B1, B3; Melanie Trottman, "Southwest Feels Squeeze," *Wall Street Journal,* August 23, 2004, p. B3; Melanie Trottman, "Southwest Will Fill US Airways' Pittsburgh Gap," *Wall Street Journal,* January 6, 2005, p. D9.

WHAT CAN BE LEARNED?

The Power of Low Prices, and Simplicity of Operation

If a firm can maintain prices below its competitors, and do so profitably and without sacrificing quality of service, then it has a powerful advantage. We noted in the previous chapter, the great advantage Vanguard had with its lowest expense ratio in the mutual fund industry. Here, Southwest also achieved this with its simplicity of operation and no-frills, but dependable service. Competition on the basis of price is seldom used in most mature industries (although the airline industry has been an exception), primarily because competitors can quickly match prices with no lasting advantage to anyone. As profits are destroyed, only customers benefit, and then only in the short run before the industry realizes the futility of price competition. (With new and rapidly changing industries, price competition is effective as productivity and technology improve and marginal competitors are driven from the market.)

The effectiveness of the cost controls of Southwest, however, shows the true competitive importance of low prices. Customers love the lowest-price producer, *if* the provider does not sacrifice too much quality, comfort, and service. While there was some sacrifice of service and amenities with Southwest, most customers found this acceptable because of the short-haul situation; and dependable and reasonable service was still maintained.

An intriguing factor regarding the relationship of customer satisfaction and price is explored in the Information Box: The Key to Customer Satisfaction: Meeting Customer Expectations on page 304.

The Power of a Niche Strategy

Directing marketing efforts toward a particular customer segment or niche can provide a powerful competitive advantage. This is especially true if no competitor is directly catering to this niche or is likely to do so with a concerted effort. Such an untapped niche then becomes a strategic window of opportunity.

Kelleher revealed the niche strategy of Southwest: While other airlines set up hub-and-spoke systems in which passengers are shunted to a few major hubs from which they are transferred to other planes going to their destination, "We wound up with a unique market niche: we are the world's only short-haul, high-frequency, low-fare, point-to-point carrier … We wound up with a market segment that is peculiarly ours, and everything about the airline has been adapted to serving that market segment in the most efficient and economical way possible.[17] See the Information Box on page 305 for a discussion of the criteria needed for a successful niche or segmentation strategy.

Southwest has been undeviating in its pursuit of its niche. For years, while others tried to copy, none were able to fully duplicate it. For years, Southwest was the nation's only high-frequency, short-distance, low-fare airline. As an example of

[17] Jaffe, p. 58.

INFORMATION BOX

THE KEY TO CUSTOMER SATISFACTION: MEETING CUSTOMER EXPECTATIONS

Southwest consistently earns high ratings for its customer satisfaction, higher than those of its giant competitors. Yet these major airlines all offered more food service than Southwest's peanuts and drinks. They also provided such additional amenities as advance seat assignments, in-flight entertainment on longer flights, the opportunity to upgrade, and a comprehensive frequent-flyer program. Yet Southwest gets the highest points for customer satisfaction.

Could something else be involved here?

Let's call this *expectations*. If a customer has high expectations, perhaps because of a high price and/or the advertising promising high-quality, luxury accommodations, dependable service, or whatever, then if product or service does not live up to these expectations, customer satisfaction dives. Turning to the airlines, customers are not disappointed in the service of Southwest because they don't expect luxury; Southwest does not advertise this. They expect no frills, but pleasant and courteous treatment by employees, dependable and safe flights, and the low prices. On the other hand, expectations are higher for the bigger carriers with their higher prices. This is well and good for the first- or business-class service. But for the many who fly coach?

Do you think there is a point where a low-price/no frills strategy would be detrimental to customer satisfaction? What might it depend on?

Source: This idea of expectations affecting customer satisfaction was suggested by Ed Perkins for Tribune Media Services and reported in "Hotels Must Live Up to Promises," *Cleveland Plain Dealer,* November 1, 1998, p. K11.

its virtually unassailable position, Southwest accounted for more than two-thirds of the passengers flying within Texas, and Texas is the second largest market outside the West Coast. When Southwest invaded California, some San Jose residents drove an hour north to board Southwest's Oakland flights, skipping the local airport where American had a hub. And in Georgia, so many people were bypassing Delta's huge hub in Atlanta and driving 150 miles to Birmingham, Alabama, to fly Southwest that an entrepreneur started a van service between the two airports.[18]

Unlike many firms, Southwest did not permit success to dilute its niche strategy. It has not attempted to fly to Europe or South America or match the big carriers in offering amenities in coast-to-coast flights. In curbing such temptations, it has not sacrificed growth potential. It still has many U.S. cities to embrace. Despite its price advantage now being countered by low-price competitors and

[18] O'Brian, A7.

INFORMATION BOX

CRITERIA FOR SELECTING NICHES OR SEGMENTS

In deciding what specific niches to seek, these criteria should be considered:

1. *Identifiability.* Is the particular niche identifiable so that those persons who constitute it can be isolated and recognized? It was not difficult to identify the short-route travelers, and while their numbers may not have been readily estimated, this was soon to change as demand burgeoned for Southwest's short-haul services.

2. *Size.* The segment must be of sufficient size to be worth the efforts to tap. And again, the size factor proved to be significant: Southwest soon offered 83 flights daily between Dallas and Houston.

3. *Accessibility.* For a niche strategy to be practical, promotional media must be able to reach the segments without much wasted coverage. Southwest had little difficulty in reaching its target market through billboards, newspapers, etc.

4. *Growth potential.* A niche is more attractive if it shows some growth characteristics. The growth potential of short-haul flyers proved to be considerably greater than for airline customers in general. Partly the growth reflected customers won from other higher-cost and less-convenient airlines. And some of the emerging growth reflected customers' willingness to give up their cars to take a flight that was almost as economical and certainly more comfortable.

5. *Absence of vulnerability to competition.* Competition, present and potential, must certainly be considered in making specific niche decisions. By quickly becoming the low-cost operator in its early routes, and gradually expanding without diluting its cost advantage, Southwest became virtually unassailable in its niche. The bigger airlines with their greater overhead and less flexible operations could not match Southwest prices without going deeply into the red. And the more Southwest became entrenched in its markets, the more difficult it was to pry it loose. But nothing remains forever. Today Southwest's position is less unassailable.

Assume you are to give a lecture to your class on the desirability of a niche strategy, and you cite Southwest as a classic example. But suppose a classmate asks: "If a niche strategy is so great, why didn't the other airlines practice it?" How will you respond?

even some major airlines desperately trying to reduce their overheads to better compete with discount carriers on certain routes, Southwest was still the market leader in its niche.

Seek Dedicated Employees

Stimulating employees to move beyond their individual concerns to a higher level of performance, a truly team approach, was by no means the least of Kelleher's accomplishments. Such an esprit de corps enabled planes to be turned around in fifteen minutes instead of the hour or more of competitors; it brought a dedication to serving customers far beyond what could ever be expected of a bare-bones, cut-price operation; it brought a contagious excitement to the job obvious to customers and employees alike.

Kelleher's extroverted, zany, and down-home personality certainly helped in cultivating such dedicated employees. So did his legendary ability to remember employee names, his sincere interest in the employees, as well as company parties. Flying in the face of conventional wisdom, which says an adversarial relationship between management and labor is inevitable with the presence of a union, Southwest achieved its great teamwork while being 90 percent unionized. It helped, though, that Kelleher started the first profit-sharing plan in the U.S. airline industry in 1974, with employees eventually owning 13 percent of the company stock.

Whether such a worker dedication can pass the test of time, and the test of increasing size, is uncertain. Kelleher retired, and his two successors have different personalities. Yet here is a model for an organization growing to large size and still maintaining employee commitment. In the next case, we will examine the leadership style of Sam Walton and the growth of Wal-Mart to become the largest retailer.

The attainment of dedicated employees is partly a product of the firm itself, and how it is growing. A rapidly growing firm—especially when such growth starts from humble beginnings, with the firm as an underdog—promotes a contagious excitement. Opportunities and advancements depend on growth. And where employees can acquire stock in the company and see their shares rising, potential financial rewards seem almost infinite. Success tends to create a momentum that generates continued success.

CONSIDER

Can you identify additional learning insights that could be applicable to other firms in other situations?

QUESTIONS

1. In what ways might airline customers be segmented? Which segments or niches would you consider Southwest's prime targets? Which segments probably would not be?

2. Discuss the pros and cons for expansion of Southwest beyond short hauls. Which arguments do you see as most compelling?

3. Evaluate the effectiveness of Southwest's unions.

4. On August 18, 1993, a fare war erupted. To initiate its new service between Cleveland and Baltimore, Southwest announced a $49 fare (a sizable reduction from the then-standard rate of $300). Its rivals, Continental and

US Air, retaliated. Before long, the price was $19, not much more than the tank of gas it would take to drive between the two cities—and the airlines also supplied a free soft drink. Evaluate the implications of such a price war for the three airlines.

5. A price cut is the most easily matched marketing strategy and usually provides no lasting advantage to any competitor. Identify the circumstances when you see it desirable to initiate a price cut and potential price war.

6. Do you think it is likely that Southwest will remain dominant in its niche despite the array of discount carriers? Why or why not?

7. What is your forecast for the competitive environment of the airline industry ten years from now?

ROLE PLAY

1. Herb Kelleher has just retired, and you are his successor. Unfortunately, your personality is far different from his: you are an introvert and far from flamboyant, and your memory for names is not good. What would be your course of action to try to preserve the great employee dedication of the Kelleher era? How successful do you think you will be? Did the board make a mistake in hiring you?

2. Herb Kelleher has not retired. He is going to continue until 70, or later. Somehow, his appetite for growth has increased as he has grown older. He has charged you with developing plans for expanding into longer hauls, and maybe to South and Central America, and even to Europe. Be as specific as you can in developing such expansion plans.

   Kelleher has also asked for your evaluation of these plans. Be as persuasive as you can in presenting this evaluation.

3. How would you feel personally about a five-hour transcontinental flight with only a few peanuts, and no other food or movies? Would you be willing to pay quite a bit more to have more amenities?

TEAM DEBATE EXERCISE

The Thanksgiving Day nonstop transcontinental experiment went fairly well, although customers and even flight attendants expressed some concern about the long, five-hour flight with no food and no entertainment. No one complained about the price.

Debate the two alternatives of going ahead slowly with the transcontinental plan with no frills, or adding a few amenities, such as some food, reading material, or whatever else might make the flight less tedious. You might even want to debate the third alternative of dropping this idea entirely at this time.

INVITATION TO RESEARCH

What is Southwest's current situation? What is its market share in the airline industry? Is it still maintaining a high growth rate? Has the decision been made to expand the nonstop transcontinental service, and have any changes been made in the no-frills service for this? How about international flights? Have other discount carriers, such as JetBlue, made any sizable inroads in Southwest's niche?

CHAPTER TWENTY-ONE

Wal-Mart: The Unstoppable

*I*n March 1992, Sam Walton passed away after a two-year battle with bone cancer. Perhaps the most admired businessman of his era, he had founded Wal-Mart Stores with the concept of discount stores in small towns and had brought it to the lofty stature of the biggest retailer in the United States, and then the world—ahead of the decades-long leaders, Sears and JCPenney—and in 1990, pushed ahead of an earlier great discount-store success, Kmart.

Walton's successors continued his legacy well. By the end of fiscal 1998, Wal-Mart's sales of $137.6 billion made it one of the largest corporations in the world; by 2002 sales were $217.8 billion, and it had knocked ExxonMobil out of first place.

Yet a growing number of people were questioning how Wal-Mart was using its gargantuan power, some seeing it becoming the antithesis of fair competition through questionable practices toward suppliers, competitors, employees, and communities themselves. Was Wal-Mart becoming too big? Would its growth rate ever slow?

THE EARLY YEARS OF SAM WALTON

Samuel Moore Walton was born in Kingfisher, Oklahoma, on March 29, 1917. He and his brother, James, born three years later, were reared in a family that valued hard work and thrift. They grew up in Missouri in the depths of the Great Depression.

By the time Walton entered eighth grade in Shebina, Oklahoma, he was already exhibiting the character traits that would dominate his future life: quiet and soft spoken, but a natural leader who became class president and captain of the football team. He even became the first Eagle Scout in Shebina's history.

At the University of Missouri, Walton excelled in academics and athletics. He worked his way through college by delivering newspapers, working in a five-and-dime store, lifeguarding, and waiting tables at the university.

After his graduation in 1940, Walton joined the JCPenney Company and became a management trainee at the Des Moines, Iowa, store. There he applied his work ethic, competed to become Penney's most promising new man and became imbued with the Penney philosophy of catering to smaller towns and having "associates" instead of employees or clerks. He also met J. C. Penney himself and was intrigued with his habit of strolling around stores and personally meeting and observing customers and salespeople. After 18 months, Walton left Penney's for the U.S. Army, but what he had learned in the Penney store in Des Moines was to shape his future ideas.

WAL-MART'S GROWTH TO THE BIGGEST RETAILER

Sam Walton was discharged from the Army in August 1945. By chance, he stumbled on an opportunity to buy the franchise of a Ben Franklin variety store in Newport, Arkansas, and he opened it a month later. The lease arrangement with the building's owner did not work out, so he eventually relocated in Bentonville, Arkansas, in 1950. During the 1950s and early 1960s, Walton increased his number of Ben Franklin franchises to fifteen. In the winter of 1962, he proposed at a Ben Franklin board meeting that the company should aggressively turn its efforts to discounting, citing the great potential of this emerging retail phenomenon. The company refused to consider such an innovative idea, so Walton and his brother went ahead anyway. They opened a Discount City in Rogers, Arkansas, in 1962; and then a second store in Harrison, Arkansas, in 1964. They incorporated the business as Wal-Mart Stores on October 3l, 1969, and it became a publicly held company a year later. In 1970, Walton also opened his first distribution center and general office: a 72,000 square-foot complex in Bentonville, Arkansas. In 1972, Wal-Mart became listed on the New York Stock Exchange.

In 1976, Walton severed ties with Ben Franklin in order to concentrate on expanding Wal-Mart. His operations now extended to small towns in Arkansas, Missouri, Kansas, and Oklahoma. The essence of Walton's management philosophy during these building years was that of an old-fashioned entrepreneur; Walton personally roamed through his own stores, as well as those of competitors, always looking for new ideas in mass merchandising to maximize sales at attractive prices.

Rather than confronting the major retailers—department stores, chains such as Penney's and Sears, and the strong discounters such as Kmart—Walton confined his efforts to the smaller cities, ones major retailers shunned as having insufficient market potential. But he saw these small markets as a strategic window of opportunity, untapped by any aggressive firms.

Growth accelerated. By the end of 1975, Walton had 104 stores with nearly 6,000 employees and annual sales of $236 million, which generated $6 million net profit. The next year, the number of stores increased to 125, employees to 7,500, and sales to $340 million, with $11.5 million in profit.

Table 21.1 compares the growth of sales and number of stores of Wal-Mart with Kmart, its major competitor, from 1980 to 1990, the decade that ended with Wal-Mart forging ahead to become the biggest retailer. By the end of 1990, Wal-Mart had 1,573 stores located in 35 states.

Some of these new stores were Wal-Mart SuperCenters, considerably larger than regular Wal-Marts, having a warehouse-style food outlet under the same roof as the discount store. While such food stores carried items comparable to products in a regular urban supermarket, the assortment and service were superior to most direct competitors in the smaller cities. The key advantage of adding food to general-mer-

TABLE 21.1   Comparison of Growth in Sales and Number of Stores, Wal-Mart and Kmart, 1980–1990

	Kmart		*Wal-Mart*	
	Sales (millions)	Number of Stores	Sales (millions)	Number of Stores
1980	$14,204	1,772	$1,643	330
1981	16,527	2,055	2,445	491
1982	16,772	2,117	3,376	551
1983	18,597	2,160	4,667	642
1984	20,762	2,173	6,401	745
1985	22,035	2,332	8,451	859
1986	23,035	2,342	11,909	980
1987	25,627	2,273	15,959	1,114
1988	27,301	2,307	20,649	1,259
1989	29,533	2,361	25,810	1,402
1990	32,070	2,350	32,602	1,573

Source: Company annual reports.

Commentary: Several of these statistics are of particular interest. First, the comparison of the sales from 1980 to 1990, slightly more than one decade, of Wal-Mart and Kmart, show the tremendous growth rate of Wal-Mart, starting at little more than 10 percent of Kmart sales figures to forge ahead by 1990. And Kmart was no slouch during this period.

   Second, Wal-Mart achieved its leadership in total sales with almost 800 fewer stores than Kmart had. This means that Wal-Mart's stores were achieving much higher sales volume than Kmart's, a fact that is further borne out by the statistics in Table 21.3.

chandise discount stores was greater traffic: Because customers shop weekly for groceries, they are exposed to other merchandise in the stores far more than would otherwise be the case.

   Wal-Mart by now was also opening another category of stores: Sam's Wholesale, also known as Sam's Clubs. First introduced in 1984, by 1991 there were 148. This wholesale club concept came about as regular discount stores seemed to be reaching saturation in some locations. The wholesale warehouse went a step further in discounting.

   Sam's Clubs were large, ranging up to 135,000 square feet. Each store was a membership-only operation, and qualified members included businesses and members of certain groups, such as government employees and credit union members. Although the stores were huge, they carried less than 5 percent of the total variety of items carried by regular discount stores. Assortments were limited to fast-moving home goods and apparel, generally name brands, with prices 8 to 10 percent over cost, well under those of discount stores and department and specialty stores. Sam's Clubs were the initial entry for Wal-Mart into the big metropolitan markets it had avoided in its early years.

TABLE 21.2 10-Year Comparison of Gross Revenues, Percentage of Operating Margin, and Return on Equity for Wal-Mart and Its Competitors[a]

| | Wal-Mart | | | Kmart | | | Sears | | | JCPenney | | |
| | % Operating | | | % Operating | | | % Operating | | | % Operating | | |
Year	Gross Revenue	Profit Margin	Equity Return %	Gross Revenue	Profit Margin	Equity Return %	Gross Revenue	Profit Margin	Equity Return %	Gross Revenue	Profit Margin	Equity Return %
1981	$2,445.0	5.6	25.6	$16,527.0	2.2	9.0	$27,357	7.2	8.2	$11,860	7.5	13.2
1982	3,376.3	7.8	25.4	17,040.0	4.3	10.1	30,020	8.8	10.1	11,414	8.3	13.3
1983	4,666.9	8.3	26.6	18,878.9	6.0	16.7	35,883	9.7	14.4	12,078	8.7	13.1
1984	6,400.9	8.5	27.5	21,095.9	6.7	15.4	38,828	10.5	14.1	13,451	7.8	11.4
1985	8,451.5	7.2	25.6	22,420.0	6.2	14.4	40,715	9.5	11.5	13,747	7.7	9.8
1986	11,909.1	7.1	26.6	23,812.1	5.7	14.5	44,282	9.1	10.4	15,151	8.6	11.0
1987	15,959.3	6.8	27.8	25,626.6	5.8	15.7	48,439	8.5	12.1	15,747	9.1	14.6
1988	20,649.0	6.4	27.8	27,301.4	6.5	16.0	50,251	9.2	3.0	15,296	8.3	20.4
1989	25,810.7	6.5	27.1	29,532.7	5.8	6.5	53,794	9.2	10.6	16,405	9.2	18.4
1990	32,601.6	6.0	24.1	32,070.0	5.4	14.0	55,971	7.4	7.0	16,365	2.4	15.6

[a] Gross revenue is in $ billions.

Source: Company annual reports.

Commentary: The comparison with major competitors shows Wal-Mart far exceeding its rivals in revenue growth. The operating profit percentage exceeds Kmart's for most years, but Sears and Penney look better here. However, the true measure of profitability is return on equity, and here Wal-Mart shines: It indeed is a very profitable operation, while offering consumers attractive prices.

TABLE 21.3 Average Sales per Store,
Wal-Mart and Kmart, 1980–1990

	Kmart	Wal-Mart
1980	$8,015,801	$4,978,788
1981	8,042,338	4,979,633
1982	7,922,532	6,127,042
1983	8,609,722	7,269,470
1984	9,554,533	8,591,946
1985	9,448,970	9,838,184
1986	9,835,611	12,152,040
1987	11,274,527	14,325,852
1988	11,833,983	16,401,111
1989	12,508,682	18,409,415
1990	13,646,808	20,726,001

Source: Computed from Table 21.1

Commentary: The great increase in sales per store for Wal-Mart is particularly noteworthy. In 1980, Wal-Mart's average store's sales was hardly one-half that of an average Kmart. By 1990 the average Wal-Mart store was generating more than 50% more sales than an average Kmart.

In December 1987, Wal-Mart opened its newest merchandising concept, Hypermart USA, in Garland, Texas, a suburb of Dallas. The hypermart offered a combination of groceries and general merchandise in over 200,000 square feet of selling space. The stores also included a variety of fast-food and service shops, such as beauty shops, shoe repair, and dry cleaners. Thus, an atmosphere was created of one-stop shopping. But in spite of optimistic beginnings, the hypermarket idea proved unsuccessful, and it was replaced with the scaled-down version, the SuperCenter.

For a comparison of sales and profitability of Wal-Mart with Kmart, Sears, and Penney's from 1980 to 1990, see Table 21.2. Note that profitability comparisons include operating profit as a percentage of sales, and the more valid measure of profitability, the return on equity, that is, the return on the money invested in the enterprise. From this table, we see the awesome growth of Wal-Mart in sales and profitability compared with its nearest competitors. Table 21.3 shows another operational comparison, this time the average sales per store for Wal-Mart and Kmart. And again, the comparison shows the great growth performance of Wal-Mart.

THE FUTURE WITHOUT SAM WALTON

On March 17, 1992, President Bush awarded Sam Walton the Medal of Freedom, this a capstone among his other honors, which included Man of the Year, Horatio Alger Award in 1984, and "Retailer of the Decade" in 1989. Unfortunately, Walton did not live long to enjoy this high honor; he died of cancer nine days later, on March 26, 1992, just four days short of his 75th birthday.

David Glass, 53 years old, assumed the role of president and chief executive officer. Glass was known for his hard-driving managerial style. He had gained his retail experience at a small supermarket chain in Springfield, Missouri, and joined Wal-Mart as executive vice president for finance in 1976. He was named president and chief operating officer in 1984, while Sam Walton kept the position of chief executive officer. About the transition, Glass said:

> There's no transition to make, because the principles and basic values he (Walton) used in founding this company were so sound and so universally accepted … We'll be fine as long as we never lose our responsiveness to the customer.[1]

A new generation now was entrusted to continue the successful growth as Wal-Mart entered tougher competitive environments of U.S. metropolitan areas, and then the world. By 1995, sales were $82 billion, and only three *Fortune* 500 companies had higher sales: General Motors, Ford, and Exxon.

INTO THE NEW MILLENNIUM

In 2001, Wal-Mart knocked off ExxonMobil to become the world's biggest firm in revenues, with sales of $217.8 billion to ExxonMobil's $187.5 billion. General Motors' sales were $177.3 billion and Ford in 4th place had sales of $162.4 billion.[2]

Table 21.4 shows selected statistics of operating performance at the beginning and end of the decade 1992-2002. Wal-Mart's former closest retail rivals had been left in the dust by 2002, as can be starkly seen below:

	Revenues (billions)	% Change Since 2001
Sears	$41.1	0.3
Target	39.9	8.1
Kmart	36.9	1.1
Penney	32.0	0.5
Wal-Mart	217.8	13.8

Its nearest rival up to 1990, the one that dominated the retail environment in the early days of Wal-Mart, was Kmart. But Kmart slid into Chapter 11 bankruptcy and only recently emerged from bankruptcy and merged with Sears. See Chapter 9 for some of the ramifications of that merger.

As it approached the millennium, and was only a short step away from becoming the world's largest firm, Wal-Mart turned to other growth opportunities. It bought Asda Group PLC, a large British supermarket chain, thereby expanding its interna-

[1] Susan Caminiti, "What Ails Retailing," *Fortune,* January 30, 1989, p. 61.
[2] "Sales Super 500," *Forbes*, April 15, 2002, p. 168.

TABLE 21.4   Wal-Mart Selected Growth Statistics
from 1993 to 2002

	2002	1993
Net sales (millions)	$217,799	$55,484
Net income (millions)	6,671	1,995
Number of associates	1,383,000	434,000
Number of U.S. Wal-Mart stores	1,647	1,848
Number of U.S. Supercenters	1,066	34
Number of U.S. Sam's Clubs	500	256
International units	1,170	10

Source: Wal-Mart annual reports.

Commentary: Here we see a four-fold increase in sales in these 10 years. Income had only a little more than a three-fold increase, but this was still impressive. Of particular interest is the decrease in number of U.S. Wal-Mart stores in producing these increases, but the big growth was in Supercenters and Sam's Clubs, and the biggest of all was in international units, but then Wal-Mart had barely entered the international arena in 1993.

tional presence. In the United States, it not only accelerated building discount-grocery SuperCenters but also expanded its smallish, (40,000 square foot) Neighborhood Markets designed to fill the gaps between convenience stores and Wal-Mart's big SuperCenters. Wal-Mart also bought a small savings bank in Oklahoma that could pave the way for bringing to banking its low prices for such services as check cashing, credit cards, and loans.

Overseas expansion created the most waves. European merchants and labor unions ran scared, but consumers stood to benefit enormously: "Its low-pricing policies and customer-friendly attitude is likely to change the face of British retailing and its reputation for high prices and surly service," one scribe wrote.[3]

Threat of Wal-Mart led two rival French retailers to merge in a $16-billion-dollar deal, though the combined company would still be far smaller than Wal-Mart. The battle was perhaps fiercest in Germany, where Wal-Mart had 95 stores. Competitors began staying open longer and improving customer courtesy. However, regulators in Germany closely monitored whether prices were too low, while powerful trade unions worried that price wars would result in store closures and job losses.

To reduce costs, Wal-Mart began buying globally, negotiating one price for stores worldwide. In so doing, it changed the organization to combine some domestic and international operations including buying, new store planning and marketing.[4]

[3] Ernest Beck, "The Wal-Mart Is Coming! And Shopping for the British May Never Be the Same," *Wall Street Journal,* June 16, 1999, p. A23.

[4] Emily Nelson, "Wal-Mart Revamps International Unit to Decrease Costs," *Wall Street Journal,* August 10, 1999, p. A6; David Woodruff and John Carreyrou, "French Retailers Create New Wal-Mart Rival," *Wall Street Journal,* August 31, 1999, p. A14.

Invasion of Foreign Markets

With few prime sites in the United States remaining untapped for stores, Wal-Mart aggressively sought to expand worldwide, but these efforts were not very successful. For example, in Germany Wal-Mart still had losses five years after buying two local chains to gain entry into this market. German consumers were very price sensitive, and Wal-Mart failed to beat competitors who quickly undercut Wal-Mart and beefed up their private-label goods. Even Wal-Mart's use of greeters was met with disdain by German shoppers. These experiences cast doubt on the Wal-Mart model in all international markets.

More than 80 percent of Wal-Mart's international revenue came from Canada, Mexico, and the U.K. In China, it struggled with a primitive supply chain. In Japan, it faced a powerful but backward retail ecosystem. While Wal-Mart has done well in Mexico, it faced stronger competitors in the huge markets of Brazil and Argentina. It made some mistakes along the way. It entered Hong Kong in 1994 and left two years later after bad decisions on merchandise selection and location. It entered Indonesia in 1996 but fled after a Jakarta store was looted and torched in the 1997-98 riots. In South Korea, its SuperCenters misread local tastes and locations were too far outside city centers.

Wal-Mart's impact on the world went beyond its store openings overseas. It imported many goods from low-wage countries such as China, thereby eliminating manufacturing jobs and depressing wage growth in the United States. But by selling goods for less, Wal-Mart raised living standards and created 800,000 jobs worldwide, in addition to the labor needed for construction and distribution in these countries.[5]

INGREDIENTS OF SUCCESS

Management Style and Employee Orientation

Sam Walton cultivated a management style that emphasized individual initiative and autonomy over close supervision. He constantly reminded employees that they were vital to the success of the company, that they were essentially "running their own business," that they were "associates" or "partners" in the business, rather than simply employees.

In his employee relations philosophy, Walton borrowed from James Cash Penney, founder of the JCPenney Company, and his formulation of the "Penney idea" in 1913. This Penney idea also stressed the desirability of constantly improving the human factor, of rewarding associates through participation in what the business produces, and of appraising every policy and action as to whether it squares with what is right and just.

Walton emphasized bottoms-up communication, thereby providing a free flow of ideas throughout the company. For example, the "people greeter" concept (described in the Information Box: Greeters) was implemented in 1983 as a result of a suggestion

---

[5] Bruce Upbin, "Wall-to-Wall Wal-Mart," *Forbes,* April 12, 2004, pp. 76–85.

INFORMATION BOX

GREETERS

All customers entering Wal-Mart stores encounter a store employee assigned to welcome them, give advice on where to find things, and help with exchanges or refunds. These "greeters" thank people exiting the store, while unobtrusively observing any indications of shoplifting.

Many retailers staff exits and entrances; what makes Wal-Mart's greeters unique is their friendliness and patience. Wal-Mart has found that retirees supplementing pensions usually make the best greeters and are most appreciated by customers. As noted before, this idea was suggested by an employee (associate); Sam Walton liked the idea, and it became a company-wide practice.

Do you personally like the idea of a store employee greeting you as you enter and leave an establishment? On balance, do you think the greeter idea is a plus or a minus? Explain.

received from an employee in a store in Louisiana. This idea proved so successful that it has been adopted by Kmart, some department stores, and even shopping malls.

Another example of listening to employees' ideas came when an assistant manager in an Alabama store ordered too many marshmallow sandwiches, or Moon Pies. The store manager told him to use his imagination to sell the excess, so John Love came up with an idea to create the first World Championship Moon Pie Eating Contest. It was held in the store's parking lot and became so successful that it became a yearly event, drawing spectators not only from the community but from all over Alabama as well as surrounding states.[6]

In 1972, Wal-Mart instituted a profit-sharing plan with associates sharing in the company's yearly profits. As one celebrated example of the benefits of such profit sharing, Shirley Cox had worked as an office cashier earning $7.10 an hour. When she retired after 24 years, her profit sharing amounted to $220,127.[7] In addition, associates may participate in a payroll stock purchase plan with Wal-Mart contributing part of the cost.

The Sam Walton philosophy was to create a friendly, "down-home," family atmosphere in his stores. He described it as a "whistle while you work philosophy," one that stressed the importance of having fun while working because you can work better if you enjoy yourself. He was concerned about losing this atmosphere: "The bigger Wal-Mart gets, the more essential it is that we think small. Because that's exactly how we have become a huge corporation—by not acting like one."[8]

---

[6] Don Longo, "Associate Involvement Spurs Gains," *Discount Store News*, December 18, 1989, p. 83.

[7] Example cited in Vance H. Trimble, *Sam Walton: The Inside Story of America's Richest Man*, New York: Dutton, 1990, p. 233.

[8] Ibid, pp. 104, 105.

Another incentive spurred employees to reduce shrinkage (i.e., the loss of merchandise due to shoplifting, carelessness, and employee theft). Employees were given $200 each a year if shrinkage limits were met, and they became detectives watching shoppers and each other. In 1989, Wal-Mart's shrinkage rate was 1 percent of sales, well below the industry average.[9]

A rather simple way to make employees feel part of the operation was regular sharing of statistics about the store's performance, including profits, purchases, sales, and markdowns. Many employees thought of Wal-Mart as their own company.

Not the least of the open and people-oriented management practices was what Walton called MBWA, Management by Walking Around. Managers, from store level to headquarters, walked around the stores to stay familiar with what was going on, to talk to the associates, and to encourage associates to share their ideas and concerns. Such interactions brought a personal touch usually lacking in large firms.

Not surprisingly, unions have not fared well at Wal-Mart. Walton argued that in his "family environment," associates had better wages, benefits, and bonuses than any union could get for them. In addition, the bonuses and profit sharing were inducements far better than those a union could negotiate.

State of the Art Technology

The decentralized management style led to a team approach to decision making. A huge telecommunications system permitted headquarters to easily communicate with stores. In addition, home-office management teams, using company airplanes, visited stores to assess their operations and any problems and to coordinate needed merchandise transfers among stores. A master computer tracked the company's complex distribution system.

Small Town Invasion Strategy

Adopting a strategy similar to that of the JCPenney Company over half a century before, Wal-Mart for many years shunned big cities and kept to smaller towns where competition consisted only of local merchants and small outlets of a few chains, such as Woolworth, Gamble, and Penney.

These merchants typically offered only limited assortments of merchandise, had no Sunday or evening hours, and charged substantially higher prices than would be found in the more competitive environments of bigger cities. Larger retailers, especially discount stores, had shunned such small towns as not affording enough potential to support the sales volume needed for the low-price strategy. But Wal-Mart found abundant potential with customers flocking from surrounding towns and rural areas for its variety of goods and prices. (In the process of captivating these consumers, Wal-Mart wrecked havoc on the existing small-town merchants. See the Issue Box: Impact of Wal-Mart on Small Towns for a discussion of the sociological impact of Wal-Mart on small towns.) The company honed its skills in such markets isolated from aggressive competitors, and then flexed its muscles and moved confi-

[9] Charles Berstein, "How to Win Employee and Customer Friends," *Nation's Restaurant News,* January 30, 1989, p. F3.

ISSUE BOX

IMPACT OF WAL-MART ON SMALL TOWNS

During most of its growth years, Wal-Mart pursued a policy of opening stores on the outskirts of small rural towns, usually with populations between 25,000 and 50,000. Attractive in prices and assortment of goods, a Wal-Mart store drew customers from miles around and was often the biggest employer in the town, giving jobs to 200 to 300 locals.

But the dominating presence of Wal-Mart was a mixed blessing for many communities. Small-town merchants were devastated and unable to compete. Downtowns became decaying vestiges of what perhaps a few months previously had been prosperous centers. But consumers benefited.

Wal-Mart brought trade-offs and controversy: Was rural America better or worse off with the arrival of Wal-Mart? While most experts saw the economic development brought on by Wal-Mart as more than offsetting the business destruction it caused, few could dispute the sociological trauma.

What is your assessment of the desirability of Wal-Mart coming into a rural small town? How might your assessment differ depending on your particular position or status in that community?

dently into the big cities, whose retailers were as fearful of Wal-Mart as the thousands of small-town merchants had been.

Controlling Costs

Sam Walton was a stickler for holding down costs in order to offer customers the lowest prices. Cost control started with vendors, and Wal-Mart gained a reputation of being hard to please, of constantly pressuring suppliers to give additional price breaks and advertising, and to provide prompt deliveries. (In Chapter 16, Newell Rubbermaid, we saw the difficulty vendors faced in trying to meet Wal-Mart's demands.) In further efforts to buy goods at the lowest possible prices, Wal-Mart attempted to bypass middlemen and sales reps and buy all goods direct from manufacturers. In so doing, a factory presumably would save money on sales commissions of 2 to 6 percent and was expected to pass this savings on to Wal-Mart. Understandably, this aroused a heated controversy from groups representing sales reps.

Wal-Mart achieved great savings with its sophisticated distribution centers and its own fleet of trucks that enabled it to buy in bulk directly from suppliers. Most goods were processed through one of the company's distribution centers. For example, take the distribution center in Cullman, Alabama, situated on 28 acres with 1.2 million square feet. Some 1,042 employees loaded 150 outbound Wal-Mart trailers a day and unloaded 180. On a heavy day, laser scanners routed 190,000 cases of goods on an 11-mile-long conveyor.[10]

[10] John Huey, "America's Most Successful Merchant," *Fortune,* September 23, 1991, p. 54.

Each warehouse used the latest in optical scanning devices, automated materials-handling equipment, bar coding, and computerized inventory. With a satellite network, messages could be quickly flashed between stores, distribution centers, and corporate headquarters in Bentonville, Arkansas. Hand-held computers assisted store employees in ordering merchandise. These advanced technologies cut distribution expenses to half those of most chains.

Wal-Mart had previously been able to achieve great savings in advertising costs, compared to major competitors. While discount chains typically spent 2 to 3 percent of sales for advertising, Wal-Mart held it to less than 1 percent of sales. Some of this difference reflected low media rates in its small-town markets. But advertising costs were also kept low in larger markets by using very little local advertising, relying instead on national TV institutional commercials showing prices being slashed and Wal-Mart as a good and caring firm. See the Issue Box: Institutional Advertising? for a discussion.

ISSUE BOX

SHOULD WE USE INSTITUTIONAL ADVERTISING?

Institutional advertising is nonproduct advertising designed to create goodwill for the firm rather than immediate and specific product sales. While the intent is laudable, the payoff is murky since it is difficult to measure good will and its effect on sales. With specific product advertising, of course, a retailer can determine the effectiveness of an ad by the specific sales it produces compared to previous periods when the product was not advertised. We suggest that most institutional advertising is based on faith—faith that enough people will see the ad or commercial and gain a favorable attitude toward the company, the assumption being that a favorable attitude translates into more sales.

Wal-Mart's heavy use of institutional commercials on TV originally was two pronged: (1) showing its employees as friendly and helpful people, not only to customers but to the community at large and (2) showing prices enthusiastically being slashed. As Wal-Mart confronted more and more negative publicity, it increased its institutional advertising as never before, trying to reinforce the image of Wal-Mart as a good citizen. In January 2005, CEO Lee Scott authorized full-page ads in more than 100 newspapers around the nation to highlight the message that Wal-Mart provides great opportunity for employee advancement with stores providing mainly full-time jobs that come with a broad benefits package.[11]

Despite the greater use of institutional advertising, the criticisms just would not go away, as we will discuss in the next section.

Be a Devil's Advocate (One who argues a contrary position for the sake of testing a decision). Argue as persuasively as you can that, while Wal-Mart's institutional advertising may have improved the image, this did not conclusively translate into additional sales.

[11] Chuck Bartels, Associated Press, as reported in "Wal-Mart Hits Critics with Media Blitz," *Cleveland Plain Dealer,* January 14, 2005, pp. C1, C5.

Wal-Mart's operating and administrative costs reflected a rigidly enforced, spartan operation. A lean headquarters organization and a minimum of staff assistants compared with most other retailers completed the cost-control philosophy and reflected the frugal thinking of Sam Walton that dated back to his early days.

A DARKER SIDE

Despite the good-citizen image that Walton sought to cultivate, Wal-Mart has provoked controversy almost from its beginnings. As it honed its skills and resources, and moved into more and more small towns, its impact on these local communities was profound. As we have discussed in a previous Box, many downtowns were devastated as local merchants could not compete with this giant newcomer opening on the outskirts of town. Still, most people thought Wal-Mart brought more good than bad to their community—although some communities voted to keep Wal-Mart out.

Today, Wal-Mart is the most powerful firm in the world with its size and buying clout, and this invites allegations that it may be crossing the line of unfair competition. Suppliers have felt the power of Wal-Mart and the price and service demands that it imposed on those wishing to do business with it. For many of these suppliers, losing Wal-Mart's business was life threatening; they had to meet its dictates, or else.

Wal-Mart led the retail industry in "partnering" with its vendors. If this were truly a two-way relationship it would be of mutual benefit and would be an example of a symbiotic relationship in which both parties gain from the success of each other. However, Wal-Mart's "partnering" more often meant that vendors had to assume most of the inventory management and merchandising costs associated with their products in Wal-Mart stores; it also compelled them to guarantee fast replenishment, often saddling them with huge costs, so that the stores could maintain lean stocks. The power position of Wal-Mart made some of these demands on vendors a do-it-or-else situation: "If you can't do it, we'll find another vendor."

In 1988, Wal-Mart entered grocery retailing, and in only four years, by 2002, became the nation's largest grocer with over $53 billion in grocery sales. Its nonunionized workforce and legendary efficiency enabled it to drive prices down in all markets it entered—good for customers, but deadly for rivals. In the decade of the 1990s, 29 grocery chains sought bankruptcy-court protection, with Wal-Mart the catalyst in 25 of these cases.[12]

In recent years, Wal-Mart found toys to be a big traffic generator, especially at the important Christmas season and expanded its emphasis on toys until it bested Toys "R" Us to become the biggest toy retailer.

During Christmas 2003, Wal-Mart moved to increase its market share even more. It drastically reduced prices on many of the hottest toys in late September, long before the peak selling season. This essentially denied its smaller competitors a profitable Christmas season as they were forced to match these low prices or lose most of

[12] Patricia Callahan and Ann Zimmerman, "Price War in Aisle 3," *Wall Street Journal*, May 27, 2003, pp. B1, B16.

their customers. As a result, two major toy chains, famed FAO Schwarz, along with its Zany Brainy and Right Start stores, and KB Toys filed for bankruptcy protection, unable to profitably match Wal-Mart's prices. Wal-Mart could afford to sell these popular toys at a loss to generate traffic for its other merchandise. But its smaller competitors could not. Toys "R" Us, the nation's second-largest toy chain behind Wal-Mart, also suffered.[13]

Despite Wal-Mart's profit sharing and bonuses, scattered allegations surfaced about dictatorial employee relations and refusal to pay earned overtime. Wal-Mart led in pruning employee health benefits by requiring a six-months wait for hourly workers to be eligible for benefits, while deductibles ranged up to $1,000, triple the norm. It refused to pay for flu shots, eye exams, child vaccinations, and numerous other treatments normally covered by other employers, nor would it usually pay for treatment of pre-existing conditions in the first year of coverage. As a result, Wal-Mart spent 40 percent less per employee for health care than the national average. To Wal-Mart's credit, some saw its approach to health care as a positive influence at a time when health care costs were soaring.[14]

Wal-Mart has also been the target of lawsuits accusing it of bias toward women and not paying employees for all the hours they worked. The company vigorously fought such court actions, and as we saw in the Box on institutional advertising, had in early 2005 begun a massive media blitz to defend itself. Joseph Sellers, an attorney in a gender-discrimination suit, observed, "It is hard to reconcile Wal-Mart's claim that it is serving everybody when it systematically underpaid and under-promoted its 1.6 million women employees for over a decade."[15]

In late 2003, Wal-Mart faced serious allegations of subcontracting its daily cleaning chores, in many stores, to firms that employed illegal immigrants, at low wages, with no overtime or benefits, and without collecting payroll taxes. These illegalities purportedly saved the company millions. If company executives knew of such practices, they could be indicted. In a company so tightly controlled, some wondered if company executives could have been oblivious.[16]

Going into 2004, Wal-Mart faced increasing criticisms and lawsuits. These had been granted class-action status in Massachusetts, California, Indiana, and Minnesota, and 35 similar lawsuits were pending. Allegations were that Wal-Mart understaffed its stores, banned overtime, and consequently required workers to continue to work after their shifts, as well as during rest and meal breaks, without compensation. Wal-Mart denied that it required workers to work without pay.

The Los Angeles City Council was trying to prevent Wal-Mart from opening its SuperCenters in the city. Similar bans on these giant stores had been approved in the San Francisco Bay area, as well as communities from Atlanta to Albuquerque. City leaders feared that such stores would drive down local wages as rival businesses strug-

---

[13] Lisa Bannon, "An Icon's Last Christmas?" *Wall Street Journal*, December 12, 2003, pp. B1, B2.

[14] Bernard Wysocki, Jr. and Ann Zimmerman, "Wal-Mart Cost-Cutting Finds a Big Target in Health Benefits," *Wall Street Journal*, September 30, 2003, pp. A1, A16.

[15] Bartels, p. C5.

[16] Dan K. Thomasson, "Underpriced and Overgrown," *Cleveland Plain Dealer*, November 15, 2003, p. B7.

gled to survive, wipe out more jobs than they created, and leave more people without health insurance, thereby putting additional burden on overtaxed public hospitals and clinics.

Wal-Mart fought back aggressively by taking the battle to the ballot box. A spokesman declared, "The reality is that this is not some huge grass-roots uprising. Most communities in the state do not believe the government should be restricting the shopping choices of their residents."[17]

COMMENTARY

Wal-Mart is a success story of no small moment. It has certainly been good for consumers and for the country and is a symbol of one-man's vision. Yet we may raise the question: In its quest for providing customers with lowest prices, has it become guilty of predatory practices, of crossing the line in coercing suppliers, and using its size to deliberately drive out less efficient competitors? Have its executives been guilty of going too far in hard-nosed cost cutting? Has it practiced gender discrimination? Is it polluting the environment with abandoned old box stores?

Of late, more questions are being raised as to how much Wal-Mart can continue to grow. It already has almost $300 billion in sales. The following Issue Box discusses Wal-Mart's growth prospects and their impact.

ISSUE BOX

IS THERE A LIMIT TO WAL-MART'S GROWTH?

Geoffrey Colvin, senior editor of *Fortune,* has postulated what would be the operational statistics if Wal-Mart were to grow at the same rate in the next 15 years as it has in the last 15 years, and the results are mind boggling. Its revenues would be $3.2 trillion, the size of Japan's total economic output, or the size of France's and Britain's economies combined. If its workforce would grow for the next 15 years at the same rate it has in the past 15, Wal-Mart would employ 8.2 million people: This would be equivalent to all the working population of Los Angeles, San Francisco, and six other large American cities being employed by Wal-Mart. Looking at such figures, can anyone doubt that Wal-Mart's growth rate will decelerate? Colvin sees three forces "that look almost certain to do the job:"

Societal Resistance

Wal-Mart is already feeling the heat emanating from its size. Its unprecedented PR campaign of full-page ads in 100 newspapers suggests that. Critical media attention has

(continues)

[17] "Wal-Mart Suit Gets Class-Action Status in Massachusetts," *Wall Street Journal,* January 19, 2004, p. A2; and Rene Sanches, "L.A. Isn't Buying Wal-Mart's Sales Job," *Washington Post,* reported in *Cleveland Plain Dealer,* February 4, 2004, p. C2.

IS THERE A LIMIT TO WAL-MART'S GROWTH? *(continued)*

exploded in recent years, neighborhoods and towns are agitating against allowing another Wal-Mart in their communities, over 5,000 lawsuits are pending against it, and at least one crusader (or agitator, depending on your point of view), Albert Norman, is making a good living rousing merchants, townspeople, unions, and environmental groups to rise up against new additional Wal-Marts. He also decries Wal-Mart's "boneyard," 371 empty hulks of former Wal-Mart stores.[18]

It is not improbable that labor unions and small businesses will persuade Congress to enact some kind of small-business protection. Colvin also raises an interesting speculation: "As Wal-Mart expands into ever more lines of business, maybe consumers will limit the dollars they're willing to hand to one company."

Competition

While most businesses quail when confronted with a new Wal-Mart in their vicinity, there is enough anecdotal evidence that some can prosper in the shadow of Wal-Mart. Particularly in overseas markets, Wal-Mart is often finding a very difficult time of it. Competition may rise up to delimit the growth rate of Wal-Mart in the future.

Cultural Exhaustion

We have had massive firms in earlier decades—such as Sears, General Motors, IBM, AT&T, U.S.Steel, Standard Oil—and their dominance is no more. A few have been broken up by antitrust efforts. But most have seen a withering of their driving spirit, their eagerness to innovate, their flexibility—they have rather become encumbered with bureaucracy, enamored with process rather than execution. A 3Cs mind-set of vulnerability—complacency, conservatism, and conceit—have overtaken great firms in the past. While Wal-Mart still seems to be resisting this, it may be vulnerable in the not-distant future.

Do you agree Colvin's speculations? Why or why not?

Take a Devil's Advocate position against Albert Norman. Present as many arguments against his criticisms of Wal-Mart as you can—in other words, defend Wal-Mart.

Source: Geoffrey Colvin, "Wal-Mart's Growth Will Slow Down—Eventually," *Fortune,* February 7, 2005, p. 48.

[18] "Giant Slayer," *Forbes,* September 6, 2004, pp. 73–76.

WHAT CAN BE LEARNED

Take Good Care of People

Sam Walton was concerned with two groups of people: his employees and his customers. By motivating and even inspiring his employees, he found that customers also were well served. Somehow in the exigencies of business, especially big business, this emphasis on people tends to be pushed aside. Walton made caring for people common practice.

By listening to his employees, by involving them, by exhorting them, and by giving them a real share of the business—all the while stressing friendliness and concern for customers—Walton fostered a business climate almost unique in any large organization. In addition to providing customers with the friendliest of employees, his stores also offered honest values and great assortments and catered to the concerns of many middle-income Americans for the environment and American jobs.

But is Walton's philosophy eroding?

Go for the Strategic Window of Opportunity

Strategic windows of opportunity sometimes come in strange guises. They represent areas of overlooked or untapped potential business by existing firms. But in the formative and early growth years of Wal-Mart, no window could ever have seemed less promising than the one Walton milked to perfection and to great growth. Small towns and cities in many parts of rural America were losing population and economic strength, partly because of the decline in family farms and the accompanying infrastructure of small businesses. It was hardly surprising that the major discount chains focused their growth efforts on large metropolitan areas. Although many small towns had Penney's and Sears outlets as well as Woolworth, Gamble, and Coast to Coast stores, these were often old and marginal stores in the backstream of corporate consciousness. This retail environment was one of small stores with limited assortments of merchandise and relatively high prices.

Here Walton saw something no other merchants had: that the limited total market potential meant a dearth of competition. He also saw the potential being far greater than the population of the small town and its immediate surroundings. Indeed, a Wal-Mart store in a rather isolated rural community could draw customers from many miles away.

Do such windows of opportunity still exist today? You bet they do for the entrepreneur with vision, an ability to look beyond the customary, and the courage to follow up on his or her vision.

Consider the Marriage of Old-Fashioned Ideas and Modern Technology

Walton embraced this strategy and made it work throughout his organization, even as it grew to large size. In the forefront of retailers, in the use of communication technology and computerized distribution, he still was able to motivate his employees to offer friendly and helpful customer services to a degree that few large retailers have consistently achieved.

Other firms can benefit from the example of Wal-Mart in cultivating homespun friendliness with awesome technology, and competitors are trying to emulate. The particular difficulty that many are finding, however, is in achieving consistency.

Beware the Arrogance of Power

Wal-Mart is no longer a humble company. Maybe it hasn't been since the days of Sam Walton. (Other firms fall into the same mind-set: for example, Euro Disney in Chapter 17, Coca-Cola in Chapter 3, and Boeing in Chapter 4 before AirBus tamed it.) It is difficult not to succumb to this arrogant attitude—which can permeate an entire organization—to the detriment of relations with employees, customers, suppliers, the communities with which it does business, and eventually even the government (despite heavy lobbying and political pandering). Such arrogance must be combated, must not be permitted to become obvious, for it makes for huge public relations problems and negative press relations.

How is arrogance to be combated? It starts at the top, and only then can percolate down through the rest of the organization until it reaches those persons who have contact with customers and the various other publics with which the firm deals. Any large firm is highly visible and actions that might be overlooked for smaller firms can sometimes mushroom to serious proportions. When a firm is the biggest in the world, and knows it, and uses its power to drive hard bargains and coerce dissenters—such as vocal opponents of a proposed new store in their community—then it sets itself up for a public relations situation that even if it wins, denigrates its public image.

For the large and powerful firm, its public image should be of major importance. Many decisions should be made with the probable impact on public image in mind.

Buy American and Environmental Programs Help the Public Image

As foreign manufacturers increasingly took market share away from American producers—in the process destroying some American jobs—public sentiment mounted for import restrictions to save jobs. In March 1985, Walton became concerned about what seemed to him a national problem. He ordered his buyers to find products that American manufacturers had stopped producing because they couldn't compete with foreign imports. Thus began Walton's Buy American program, which became a cooperative effort between retailers and domestic manufacturers to reestablish the competitive position of American-made goods in price and quality. At the time, Magic Chef, 3M, Farris Fashions, and many other manufacturers joined Walton's crusade, as Wal-Mart pledged to support domestic production for items ranging from film to microwave ovens to flannel shirts and other apparel. Regardless of the great controversy over the desirability of free trade, many middle-class Americans applauded the leadership of Wal-Mart in this widely publicized "Buy American" policy. Now the policy has quietly slipped away, and cheaper imports are the rule.

Wal-Mart also became a leader in challenging manufacturers to improve their products and packaging in order to protect the environment. As a result, manufacturers made great improvements in eliminating excessive packaging, converting to recyclable materials, and getting rid of toxic inks and dyes. Has this policy been abandoned?

Other environmental activities at the time included participation in Earth Day events, with tree plantings, information booths, and videos to show customers how to improve their environment. Wal-Mart had also been active in fund-raising for local environmental and charitable groups, and in adopt-a-highway programs, in which store personnel volunteered at least one day a month to collect trash and clean up local highways and beaches.

The firm that acts for environmental protection stands to benefit in customer relations and, not the least, from positive media attention. Firms catering to the general public—as Wal-Mart certainly is—should be alert to their increasing concerns and where possible take on a leadership role.

Can a Firm Become Too Big?

We cannot answer this. But we can warn of the dangers of bigness as far as the public interest and trusting relationships are concerned. The phrase, "arrogance of power," describes the temptation of bigness. Some would even see this as a natural evolution of size. Years ago, such major firms as U.S. Steel and Standard Oil were broken up because enough people believed they had become too big; General Motors for years also feared this, until foreign competition destroyed its dominance. Could Wal-Mart be approaching this as it increasingly dominates certain sectors of the retail scene? When it can tyrannize its suppliers, drive competitors in the food and toy industries into bankruptcy, bring fear to others as it searches for new areas to assert its power—may it be in danger of losing its humanity?

CONSIDER

Can you identify additional learning insights that could be applicable to firms in other situations?

QUESTIONS

1. How might you attempt to compete with Wal-Mart if you were:
    (a) a small hardware merchant?
    (b) a small men's clothing store?
    (c) a supermarket?
    (d) a toy store?
2. Do you think Wal-Mart is vulnerable today to governmental intervention, and if so, in what way? If you do not think it is vulnerable, do you see any limits to its growth?
3. When you shop at Wal-Mart, do you usually find the employees far superior in friendliness and knowledge to those of other retailers? If not, what are your conclusions regarding Wal-Mart's employee relations programs?
4. What weaknesses do you see Wal-Mart as having either now or potentially? How can the company overcome them?

5. Can discounting go on forever? What are the limits to growth by price competition?

6. Discuss Wal-Mart's business practices (especially in regard to unions, invading small towns, and supplier relations) in terms of their ethical ramifications for the industry and for society. Should students be encouraged to emulate these practices?

7. Do you think Wal-Mart today is a benevolent and humane firm? Why or why not? Is it completely ethical?

8. Do you think Wal-Mart's Buy American program should be reestablished? Why or why not?

INVITATION TO ROLE PLAY

1. Be a Devil's Advocate (one who argues a contrary position). The decision is being made to phase out the hypermarts. Argue as persuasively as you can that Wal-Mart is being too hasty and that the hypermart concept should be continued, if necessary with some changes.

2. You are an ambitious Wal-Mart store manager. Describe how you might design your career path to achieve a high executive position. Be as creative as you can.

3. You are the principal adviser to David Glass, who replaced Sam Walton as chief executive. Even though Wal-Mart has expanded aggressively overseas in recent years, he still thinks the greatest potential lies in foreign markets. He has charged you to develop a strategy to make greater inroads. What do you advise, and why? (Hint: you may need to do some research as to Wal-Mart's overseas presence at this time, and what specific problems it seems to be encountering in some countries.)

TEAM DEBATE EXERCISES

1. Debate the notion of Wal-Mart aggressively seeking to enter small communities, such as in rural New England, where many people oppose this. Should Wal-Mart bow to the public pressure (which the company deems to be from a small minority of vehement agitators), or should it carry on with "right on its side."

2. Can the great growth of Wal-Mart continue indefinitely? Debate the pros and cons of this.

3. Is Wal-Mart today in danger of losing its humanity?

INVITATION TO RESEARCH

Has Wal-Mart faltered since 2005? Are there any ominous signs on the horizon? Has the management style and employee relations changed since that described in the case? Are any stores unionized? Is the Buy American program still in effect? What has been the resolution of the subcontracting daily cleaning chores?

ENTREPRENEURIAL
ADVENTURES

CHAPTER TWENTY-TWO

Boston Beer—Is Greater Growth Possible?

Jim Koch was obsessed with becoming an entrepreneur. He wasn't quite sure where he should do his entrepreneuring. Maybe the brewing industry? Years before, his great-great-grandfather, Louis Koch, had concocted a recipe at his St. Louis brewery that was heavier, more full-bodied than such beers as Budweiser or Miller. However, it was much more expensive to produce than mass-market beers. It involved a lengthy brewing and fermentation process and such premium ingredients as Bavarian hops that cost many times more than those regularly used by other brewers.

Jim had a well-paying job with the prestigious Boston Consulting Group. He had been with them for six-and-a-half years already, but still he was haunted by that dream of becoming his own man. Of late, the thought pursued him that maybe the brewing industry might be ripe for a new type of product and a new approach, a good-tasting brew something like his ancestor's. He wondered if he might have a strategic window of opportunity in a particular consumer segment: men in their mid-twenties and older who were beer aficionados and would be willing to pay a premium for a good-tasting beer. What he couldn't be certain of was how large this segment was, and he knew from his consulting experience that too small a segment doomed a strategy. So, were there enough such sophisticated drinkers to support the new company that he envisioned?

In 1984, he thought he detected a clue that this might indeed be the case: Sales were surging for import beers such as Heineken and Beck's with their different tastes. Didn't this portend that enough Americans would be willing to pay substantially more for a full-bodied flavor?

As he studied this more, he also came to believe that these imports were very vulnerable to well-made domestic brews. They faced a major problem in maintaining freshness with a product that goes sour rather quickly. He knew that the foreign brewers, in trying to minimize the destructive influence of the time lag between production and consumption, were adding preservatives and even using cheaper ingredients for the American market.

Some small local brewers offered stronger tastes. But they were having great difficulty producing a lager with consistent quality. And he sensed they were squandering their opportunity. Although they could produce small batches of well-crafted beer, albeit of erratic quality, what they mainly lacked was ability and resources to aggressively market their products.

He thought now that he had indeed found the right niche, a strategic window of opportunity, for becoming an entrepreneurial success. See the following Information Box for further discussion of a strategic window of opportunity and its desirable accompaniment, a SWOT Analysis.

He decided to take the plunge and gave up his job

INFORMATION BOX

STRATEGIC WINDOW OF OPPORTUNITY AND SWOT ANALYSIS—REVISITED AGAIN

(We also discussed this in Chapter 20, the Southwest Airline case, but it is worth reviewing again.) A strategic window is an opportunity in the marketplace, an opportunity that no competitor has yet recognized, and one that fits well with the firm's competencies. Strategic windows often last for only a short time before they are filled by alert competitors, but sometimes they may be more lasting if competitors deem it difficult to enter the particular niche. Potential competitors may pass because of price or image advantages they see the first firm as having, or perhaps because they judge—correctly or incorrectly—that the niche does not have sufficient potential.

SWOT Analysis

Strategic windows may be found by systematically analyzing the environment, examining the opportunities and threats it poses. The firm's competencies, its strengths and weaknesses, should be assessed. These competencies would include its physical and financial resources and, not the least, its people resources—management and employees. The objective is to determine whether the competencies of the firm might be appropriate for a particular course of action.

This then is the SWOT analysis:

Analyzing: Strengths and
        Weaknesses of the firm, and
        Opportunities and
        Threats in the environment

Although SWOT analysis may be a formal part of the planning, it may also be informal and even intuitive. We suspect that Jim Koch, having worked six-and-a-half years with a prestigious consulting firm would have formalized this analysis. In the next case, OfficeMax, Michael Feuer may have been more informal and intuitive in his assessment of entrepreneurial opportunity.

Why do you think all the big brewers overlooked the possibilities of the highest-priced end of the market?

Amassing sufficient capital to start a new venture is the common problem with almost all entrepreneurs, and so it was with Koch. Still, he was better off than most. He had saved $100,000 from his years with Boston Consulting, and he persuaded family and friends to chip in another $140,000. But while this might be enough to start a new retail or service venture, it was far less than the estimated $10 million or more needed to build a state-of-the-art brewery.

Koch got around this major obstacle. Instead of building or buying he contracted an existing firm, Pittsburgh Brewing Company, to brew his beer. It had good facilities, but more than this, its people had the brewing skills coming from more than 20 years of operation. He would call his new beer Samuel Adams, after a Revolutionary War patriot who was also a brewer.

PROBLEMS

A mighty problem still existed, and the success of the venture hinged on this. Koch would have to sell his great-tasting beer at $20 a case to break even and make a reasonable profit. But this was 15 percent more than even the premium imports like Heineken. Would anyone buy such an expensive beer, and one that didn't even have the cachet of an import? See the Information Box: Competing on Price, Revisited.

INFORMATION BOX

COMPETING ON PRICE, REVISITED: THE PRICE/QUALITY PERCEPTION

In the Vanguard and Southwest Airlines cases, we examined the potent strategy of offering the lowest prices in their industries—if this could be done profitably due to a lower expense and overhead structure than competitors.

Here, Boston Beer was attempting to compete while having some of the highest prices in the industry. Was this the height of foolishness? Why would anyone pay prices higher even than the expensive imported beers, just for a different taste?

The highest price can convey an image of the very highest quality. We as consumers have long been conditioned to think this. With cars, we may not be able to afford this highest quality, such as an Infiniti, Lexus, or Mercedes convertible. But with beer, almost anyone can afford to buy the highest-price brew sometimes, maybe to influence guests or to simply enjoy a different taste that we are led to think is better.

Sometimes such a price/quality perception sets us up. It might be valid, or might not be. This is especially true where quality is difficult to ascertain, such as with beer and liquor, with bottled water, with perfume, as well as other products with hidden ingredients and complex characteristics.

Have you have ever fallen victim to the price/quality misperception? How does one determine quality for an alcoholic beverage such as vodka, gin, and scotch, as well as beer? By the taste? The advertising claims? Anything else?

It fell to Koch as the fledgling firm's only salesperson to try to acquaint retailers and consumers with his new beer, this unknown brand with the very high price. "I went from bar to bar," he said. "Sometimes I had to call 15 times before someone would agree to carry it."[1]

He somehow conjured up enough funds for a $100,000 ad campaign in the local market. Shunning the advertising theme of the big brewers that, almost without exception, stressed the sociability of the people drinking their brand, Koch's ads attacked the imports: "Declare your independence from foreign beer," he urged. And the name Samuel Adams was compatible with this cry for independence. Foreign brews were singled out as not having the premium ingredients and quality brewing of Samuel Adams. Koch appeared on most of his commercials, saying such things as: "Hi, I'm Jim Koch ... It takes me all year to brew what the largest import makes in just three hours because I take the time to brew Samuel Adams right. I use my great-great-grandfather's century-old recipe, all malt brewing and rare hops that cost ten times what they use in the mass-produced imports."[2]

Gradually, his persistence in calling on retailers and his anti-import ads, some of which garnered national attention in such periodicals as *Newsweek* and *USA Today*, induced more and more bartenders and beer drinkers to at least try Samuel Adams. Many liked it, despite the high price. (Or, perhaps, because of it?)

Now his problem became finding distributors, and this proved particularly daunting for a new firm in this industry where major brands often had a lock on existing wholesalers. The situation was so bad in Boston—no wholesaler would carry Samuel Adams, even though it was a local brand—that Boston Beer bought a truck and delivered the cases itself.

Koch slowly expanded his distribution one geographical area at a time, from Boston into Washington, D.C., then to New York, Chicago, and California, taking care that production could match the steady expansion without sacrificing quality. He brought in his secretary at Boston Consulting, Rhonda Kaliman, to assist him in building a sales organization. This grew from less than a dozen sales reps in 1989 to 70 nationwide by 1994, more than any other microbrewer and about the same number as Anheuser-Busch, the giant of the industry. Now, Samuel Adams salespeople could give more personalized and expert attention to customers than competitors whose sales reps often sold many beverage lines.

Sales soared 63 percent in 1992 when the company went national and achieved distribution in bars and restaurants in 48 states. In a continual search for new beer ideas, Boston Beer added a stout, a wheat beer, and even a cranberry lambic, a type of beer flavored with fruit. Adding to the growing popularity were numerous industry awards and citations Samuel Adams had received since 1984. It was not only voted the Best Beer in America four times at the annual Great American Beer Festival but also received six gold medals in blind tastings.

In April 1994, Jim Koch and two of his brewmasters were testing their entry into the Great American Beer Festival—"Triple Bock." They had not yet tried to market

---

[1] Jenny McCune, "Brewing Up Profits," *Management Review,* April 1994, p. 18.
[2] Ibid., p. 19.

this creation, although their expectations were high. But this was so different. It boasted a 17 percent alcoholic content with no carbonation, and they planned to package it in a cobalt bottle with a cork. It was meant to be sipped as a fine brandy. "It's a taste that nobody has ever put into a beer," Koch said.[3] Too innovative? Jim and his colleagues pondered this as they sipped on this beautiful spring day.

THE BREWING INDUSTRY IN THE 1990S

In 10 years, Boston Beer had forged ahead to become a major contender in its industry and the largest U. S. specialty brewer. But a significant change in consumer preferences was confronting the industry in the 1990s. The big brands that had been so dominant, to the extent that smaller brewers could not compete against their production efficiencies, now were seeing their market shares decline. The brand images they had spent millions trying to establish were in trouble. Many were cutting prices in desperate attempts to keep and lure consumers. For example, special price promotions in some markets were offering 12-packs of Budweiser, Coors, and Miller for just $1.99.

The shifting consumer preferences, and the severe price competition with their regular brands, were compelling the big brewers to seek the types of beers that would command higher prices. Imports were still strengthening, growing at an 11 percent rate between 1993 and 1994. But microbrews seemed the wave of the future, with prices and profit margins that were mouthwatering to the big barons of the industry.

Consequently, the major breweries came up with their own craft brands. For example, Icehouse, a name that conveys a fake microbrewery image to a beer was actually produced in megabreweries by Miller Brewing. So too, the pseudo-import Killian's Irish Red was made by Coors in Golden, Colorado. Killian's, stocked in retailer's import cases and commanding a high price, muscled its way abreast of Samuel Adams as the largest specialty beer in the United States.

The brewing industry was desperately trying to innovate. But no one saw anything revolutionary on the horizon, not like the 1970s, when light beer made a significant breakthrough in the staid industry. Now, "ice" beers became the gimmick. First developed in Canada, these are beers produced at temperatures a little colder than ordinary beer. This gives them a slightly higher alcohol content. Whether because of this, or the magic of the name "ice," these products captured almost 6 percent of total industry sales in 1994, more than all the imports combined. But, still, the potential was limited.

Anheuser-Busch, with a still dominant 44 percent of U.S. beer sales despite its 9 percent sales volume slide in the early 1990s, asserted its reluctance to change: "The breweries that we have are designed to produce big brands. Our competition can't compete with big brands. That's why they've had to introduce lots of little brands."[4]

---

[3] Ibid, p. 20.
[4] Patricia Sellers, "A Whole New Ballgame in Beer," *Fortune*, September 19, 1994, p. 86.

But even Anheuser, despite its words, was sneaking into microbrewing by buying into Redhook Ale Brewery, a Seattle microbrewery that sold 76,000 barrels of beer in 1993, versus Anheuser's 90 million. Anheuser's distributors applauded this move as a badly needed step in giving them higher-profit, prestige brands. When Anheuser tip-toed into this market, other giants began to look for microbreweries to invest in.

This troubled Jim Koch: "I'm afraid of the big guys. They have the power to dominate any segment they want." Then he expressed his faith and confidence: "Still, my faith is that better beer will win out."[5]

THE CONTINUING SAGA OF BOSTON BEER

In August 1995, Boston Beer announced an initial public stock offering (IPO) of 5.3 million shares, of which 990,000 shares would be made available directly to the public through a coupon offer. This selling of shares to the general public was unlike any other IPO and, as such, caught the fancy of the national press.

The company put clip-and-mail coupons on Samuel Adams 6-packs and other beer packages. These offered customers a chance to buy 33 shares of stock at a maximum price of $15, or $495 total. Only one subscription was allowed per customer, and these were honored on a first-come, first-served basis. The success was overwhelming. First distributed in October, by the first of November the offering was oversubscribed. The company expected that the total funds generated from the IPO would be $75 million.[6] But when the new stock offering finally came out on November 20, 1995, heavy demand led to it being priced at $20 a share. Two days later it was selling on the New York Stock Exchange for $30. Interestingly, its stock symbol is SAM.

Boston Beer was riding a high. It reported an impressive 50 percent growth in 1994 over 1993, brewing 700,000 barrels and becoming the largest microbrewery in the country. The entire microbrewing industry was producing more than double the volume in 1990. By now Boston Beer had 12 different beers including six seasonals and was distributing in all 50 states through 300 wholesalers. Its newest beer, the 17-percent alcohol content Triple Bock, had been introduced to the market.[7]

Most of Boston Beer's production continued to be contract brewed. In early 1995, it did encounter difficulties with Pittsburgh Brewing, the first of the three contract breweries it was now using. Because of an alleged overdraft of $31 million by its owner, Michael Carlow, who was accused of fraud, the brewery was to be auctioned off. Jim Koch stoutly professed having no interest in buying the brewery and that any problems of Pittsburgh Brewery would have no affect on Boston Beer.[8]

See the following Information Box for a discussion of contracting out rather than building production facilities.

---

[5] Ibid.

[6] "Boston Beer's Plan for Offering Stock," *New York Times*—National Edition, August 26, 1995, p. 20.

[7] "Little Giants," *Beverage-World*, December 1994, p. 26.

[8] "Sam Adams Brewer May Be On Block," *Boston-Business-Journal*, February 24, 1995, p. 3.

INFORMATION BOX

THE MERITS OF EXPANDING SLOWLY AND KEEPING FIXED COSTS TO A MINIMUM

There is much to be said for any enterprise, new or old, to keep its fixed overhead to a minimum. If it can escape having to commit large sums to physical plant and production facilities, its breakeven point is far less, which means that fewer sales are needed to cover expenses and interest payments, leaving more to go into profits. In the event of adversity, such a firm can retrench much more nimbly than if burdened with heavy overhead. In every such decision of renting or buying, the economics of the particular situation need to be carefully analyzed.

Arguments against such contracting out usually maintain that efficiency will be sacrificed since direct control is lacking. So, this argument would maintain that Pittsburgh Brewing could not do as good a job as Boston Beer could have done itself. Yet the empirical evidence is that Boston's contract brewers were giving it the high standards it wanted. It set the standards and insisted on them being met, or it would find another contract brewery.

Still, the "edifice complex" tantalizes many top executives, as well as hospital and school administrators, who see the stone and mortar of their buildings and factories as conveying tangible evidence of their own importance and accomplishments. They will claim that such is important to the public image of their organization.

Given the approximately $100 million that Boston Beer received from its IPO, would you predict some of this would go for "stones and mortar?"

TOWARD THE MILLENNIUM

By 1998, Samuel Adams had become the seventh-largest brewer overall and was the largest independent craft brewer, in the sector that had grown 39 percent in a five-year period, while U.S. beer total shipments remained virtually flat. Samuel Adams Boston Lager, the company's flagship product, grew faster than the overall craft beer sector and accounted for the majority of Boston Beer's sales in 1997.

For 1997, revenues were $184 million, down 3.8 percent from the year before, but a major increase from the $77 million in 1994, the year before Boston went public. Net income at $7.6 million was a decline of 9.9 percent from the year before, but this compared with $5.3 million in 1994.

Boston Beer produced more than two dozen styles of beer and was selling in all 50 states and several foreign countries. Its sales force was still the largest of any craft brewer, and one of the largest in the domestic beer industry.

The acute disappointment had to be the stock market valuation of its shares. An exuberant public reaction to the initial stock offering had bid the price up to $30 a share. Almost immediately, the share price began a slow decline. By late 1998, shares were trading around $8.

The situation had not improved significantly by the millennium. Indeed, the growth that had so bedazzled Koch and early investors seemed only an illusion. Samuel Adams had been the forefather of microbrews, but this specialty market had now spawned 3,000 microbrews, all competing within the $3 billion beer market—a market that represented just 3 percent of the U.S. beer market—with a mind-boggling array of ciders, ales, stouts, and so-called better beers. "After people got inundated with so many choices ... they kind of stepped back," said one industry analyst.[9]

Koch drastically cut back his assortment of different brews, concentrating only on best sellers: the flagship lager and four seasonal brews. He went through four advertising agencies in six years trying to find the right pitch, but without much success. Experts were wondering if Koch would eventually sell out to a big brewer such as Miller. By mid-2001, the stock price ranged from $8 to $10 a share, still a disaster for its IPO investors.

UPDATE

Table 22.1 shows the trend in revenues and net income for 1998 through 2002. Sales and profits show little growth trend during this five-year period. The stock price has ranged between $10 and $18 a share for 2003.

In August—National Beer Month—of 2002, Koch led a ten-city "Liquid Lunch" taste-test tour, pitting three Samuel Adams beers and local craft beers from each of the cities against leading international brews, such as Heineken, Corona, and Guinness. The beers were scored according to appearance, aroma, flavor, mouthfeel, and overall impression. The taste testers included beer enthusiasts, consumers, journalists, and winners from local radio station promotions.

TABLE 22.1   Boston Beer Revenue and Net Income, 1998–2002 (millions)

	1998	1999	2000	2001	2002
Revenue	$183.5	176.8	190.6	186.8	215.4
Net Income	7.9	11.1	11.2	7.8	8.6

Source: Company annual reports

Commentary: Here we see a company with practically no growth, even though revenue for 2002 was the highest ever. But it was not accompanied by the highest net income; that was back in 1999 and 2000. But these statistics do show a stable company, one comfortably established in its own niche. Unfortunately, this is little consolation for those investors who bought at the initial public stock offering (IPO) at $20 a share, or bought a few days later at $30 a share, expecting big growth.

[9] Hillary Chura, "Boston Beer Crafts Strategy: Slumping Brewer Abandons Some of Its Specialty Beers," *Advertising Age,* November 8, 1999, p. 20.

In one-on-one taste tests, Samuel Adams was preferred over the imports in all thirty blind taste-offs. Many of the local brews also bested their foreign competition. Koch's crusade against imports received a good promotional push. He declared: "These imports have been considered the world standards ... But I believe when you take away the fancy bottles and marketing mystique of imported beer, you discover that Samuel Adams and other American brewers simply make better tasting beers."[10]

In January 2005, Jim Koch announced that he would spend nearly $7 million modernizing an old brewery in Cincinnati to restore roots deep in Ohio's German heritage. Koch's father had once apprenticed in the brewery, and now the expansion would mean that nearly two-thirds of Samuel Adams beer would be produced and bottled in Ohio by the end of 2005. The mayor and other city officials downed bottles of beer with Koch to toast the economic coup of gaining 100 new jobs. Boston Beer's annual sales remained at about $208 million a year. "Anheuser spills more in a day than we make in a year," Koch quipped.[11]

ANALYSIS

Entrepreneurial Character

Although many entrepreneurial opportunities come in the retail and service industries, mostly because these typically require less start-up investment, Jim Koch saw the possibility in beer, even without a huge wallet. He started with $100,000 of his own money and $140,000 from friends and relatives. He had the beer recipe and determination. By contracting out the production to an existing brewery with unused production capacity, the bulk of the start-up money could be spent on nonproduction concerns, such as advertising.

His determination to gain acceptance of his beer, despite its high price and lack of foreign cachet, is characteristic of most successful entrepreneurs. They press on, despite obstacles in gaining acceptance. They have confidence that their product or concept is viable. They are not easily discouraged.

At the same time, Koch believed he had something unique, a flavor and quality that neither domestic nor imported brews could deliver. He had the audacity to further make his product unique by charging even higher prices than the imports, thus conveying an image of highest quality.

His search for uniqueness did not end with the product. He developed an advertising theme far different from that of other beers by stressing quality and aggressively attacking the imports: "Declare your independence from foreign beer." And he was the spokesman on TV and radio commercials, giving a personal and charismatic touch.

[10] Boston Beer Company News, August 25, 2000, www.samadams.com.
[11] Bill Sloat, "Samuel Adams Brewer Expanding in Cincinnati," *Cleveland Plain Dealer,* January 7, 2005, pp. C1, C3.

As Boston Beer moved out of regional into national distribution, Koch developed a sales force as large as Anheuser-Busch, the giant of the industry. His grasping of uniqueness even went to Boston Beer's initial public stock offering, in which customers were invited to buy into the company through coupons on 6-packs. And it was oversubscribed in only a few weeks.

Controlled Growth (Aggressive Moderation)

The temptation for any firm, but especially for newer, smaller firms, when demand seems to be growing insatiably is to expand aggressively: "We must not miss this opportunity." Such optimism can sow the seeds of disaster, when demand suddenly lessens because of a saturated market and/or new competition. And our firm is left with too much plant and other fixed assets, and a burdensome overhead.

Controlled growth—we might also call this "aggressive moderation"—is usually far better. Now a firm is not shunning growth, even vigorous growth, but is controlling it within its present resources, not overextending itself. Boston Beer showed this restraint by expanding within its production capability, adding several more contract brewers as needed. It expanded market by market at the beginning, only moving to a new geographical area when it could supply it. First was Boston, then Washington D.C., then New York, Chicago, California, and finally all 50 states.

Besides husbanding resources, material and personnel, aggressive moderation is compatible with the tightness of controls needed to ensure high-quality product and service standards. Even more than this, moderation allows a firm to build the accounting and financial standards and controls needed to prevent the dangerous buildup of inventories and expenses.

Limits on Potential

It is difficult to perceive, in the heady days of growth for a new firm, that the growth potential is sorely limited without drastic and risky changes. Limits on potential usually are due to two factors:

1. Ease of entry into the industry, which encourages a host of competitors. This turned out to be especially true with the influx of microbrewers, to 3,000 in just a few years.

2. Finite potential in demand. (This also affected the high tech industry and the collapse of the NASDAQ at the turn of the millennium.) Demand for specialty beer, while at first robust and rising, was certainly not going to take over the mainstream beer market.

Given the rush to microbreweries in an environment of limited demand, the aspirations of Jim Koch to be a dominant force in the brewing industry had to be curbed. He could still be a profitable firm and do well in his niche, but he would never be a challenge beyond that. Perhaps that is enough for most entrepreneurs. They can hardly expect to grasp the golden ring of complete market dominance.

WHAT CAN BE LEARNED?

The Price-Quality Perception, Again

We have a curious phenomenon today regarding price. More consumers than ever are shopping at discount stores because they supposedly offer better prices than other retailers. Airlines competing with lowest prices, such as Southwest and JetBlue, are clobbering higher-cost carriers. As is Dell with PCs. Yet for many products, especially those that are complex and have hidden ingredients, a higher price than competitors is the major indicator of higher quality. Boston Beer certainly confirms that higher price can successfully differentiate a firm. Especially if the taste is robustly different, and if the theme of highest quality is constantly stressed in advertising.

Perhaps the moral is that both low prices and high prices can be successful. A strategy of lowest prices, however, tends to be more vulnerable since competitors can so easily and quickly match these low prices (not always profitably, of course), while a high-price strategy stressing quality tends to attract less competitors. But it will also attract less customers, as with higher priced goods such as office furniture. The high-price strategy should generally be more successful with products that are relatively inexpensive to begin with, such as beer, and ones where the image of prestige and good taste is attractive.

The Challenge of the Right Approach to Growth

In the analysis section, we discussed the desirability of *controlled growth or aggressive moderation* and noted that Boston Beer practiced this well. There are some who would challenge such a slowness in grabbing opportunities. Exuberant expansion instead is advocated, when and if the golden opportunity is presented (some would call this "running with the ball"). Operations should be expanded as fast as possible in such a situation, some would say. But there are times when caution is advised.

Risks lie on all sides as we reach for these opportunities. When a market begins to boom and a firm is unable to keep up with demand without greatly increasing capacity and resources, it faces a dilemma: Stay conservative in the expectation that the burgeoning potential will be short lived, and thereby abdicate some of the growing market to competitors, or expand vigorously and take full advantage of the opportunity. If the euphoria is short lived, and demand slows drastically, the firm is then left with expanded capacity, more resource commitment than needed, high interest and carrying costs, and perhaps even jeopardized viability because of overextension. Above all, however, a firm should not expand beyond its ability to maintain organizational and accounting control over the operation. To do so is tantamount to letting a sailing ship brave the uncertainties of a storm under full canvas.

Keep the Breakeven Point as Low as Possible, Especially for New Ventures

Fixed investments in plant and equipment raise the breakeven point of sales needed to cover overhead costs and make a profit. (For a review of breakeven, see the Breakeven Box in Chapter 17 Euro Disney.) Boston Beer kept its breakeven point low by using contract breweries. Now this would have been a mistake if the quality of production at these breweries was erratic or not up to Boston Beer expectations. Excellent and dependable quality were indeed vital requirements if it were to succeed in selling its high-priced beer. But by working closely with experienced brewers, quality control apparently was no problem.

Certainly the lower breakeven point makes for less risk. And the future is always uncertain, despite research and careful planning. Mistakes will be made. The environment is constantly changing as to customer attitudes and preferences, and particularly in actions of competitors.

When a decision involves high stakes and an uncertain future—which translates into high risks—is it not wiser to approach the venture somewhat conservatively, not spurning the opportunity, but also not committing major resources and efforts until success appears more certain?

The Importance of Maintaining Quality

For a high-priced product, a brief letdown in quality control can be disastrous to the image. The story is told of Jim Koch ordering a draft of his own Samuel Adams at a restaurant across from Lincoln Center in New York City. He was horrified at the taste. He called the manager and they went to the basement and looked at the keg. "It was two-and-a-half months past its pull date." The manager quickly changed the past-its-prime keg, which the distributor, intentionally or not, had sold the restaurant.[12] Sometimes a lapse in quality is not the fault of the manufacturer, but of a distributor or dealer. Whoever is at fault, the brand image is tarnished. And it is difficult to resurrect a reputation of poor or uncertain quality.

For Investors, Consider the Risk of Initial Public Offerings (IPOs)

IPOs are often bid up to unreasonable prices in public enthusiasm with new offerings. While Boston Beer did well as a niche brewer, and dominated its niche, it has to be a major disappointment to its investors who bought in at the beginning. Perhaps the better investor strategy is to wait for public enthusiasm to calm down before taking a stake in a new enterprise.

CONSIDER

Can you think of other learning insights?

---

[12] Example related in McCune, p. 16.

QUESTIONS

1. Have you ever tried one of the Boston Beer brews? If so, how did you like the taste? Did you think it was worth the higher price?

2. The investment community evidently thought Boston Beer had great growth probabilities to have bid up the initial price so quickly. Why do you suppose so many fell into this trap? Or was Jim Koch a poor executive in not bringing Boston Beer up to their expectations?

3. "The myriad specialty beers are but a fad. People will quickly tire of an expensive, strong-flavored beer. Much of it is just a gimmick." Discuss.

4. What problems do you see retailers facing with the burgeoning number of different beers today? What might be the implications of this?

5. Playing the Devil's Advocate (one who takes an opposing view for the sake of argument and deeper analysis), critique the strategy of charging some of the highest prices in the world for your beer.

6. We saw the detection of a problem with the freshness of a beer at a restaurant by Jim Koch himself. How can Boston Beer prevent such incidents from happening again? Can such distributor negligence or shortsighted actions be totally prevented by Boston Beer?

7. Do you think Boston Beer can continue to compete effectively against the giant brewers who are now moving with their infinitely greater resources into the specialty beer market with their own microbrews? Why or why not?

8. In 1998, Boston Beer produced more than two dozen styles of beer. Now it is down to just a few. Do you see any problems with this?

HANDS-ON EXERCISES

1. You are Jim Koch. You have just learned that Michael Feuer, founder of OfficeMax, described in Chapter 23, has grown his entrepreneurial endeavor to a $1.8 billion enterprise in just seven years. It has taken you ten years to grow Boston Beer to a $50 million firm. You are depressed at this but determined to greatly increase your company's growth. How would you go about setting Boston Beer on this great growth path? Be as specific as you can. What dangers do you see ahead?

2. It is 1986 and Boston Beer is beginning its growth after hiring Pittsburgh Brewery to produce its beer. Jim Koch has charged you with coordinating the efforts at Pittsburgh Brewery, paying particular attention to assuring that your quality standards are rigidly maintained. How would you go about doing this?

TEAM DEBATE EXERCISE

Debate how Boston Beer should commit the $100 million it received in late 1995 from the public stock offering. In particular, debate whether the bulk of the proceeds should go to building its own state-of-the-art brewery, or something else.

INVITATION TO RESEARCH

How is Boston Beer faring today? Has its expansion accelerated or stalled? Is it facing any particular problems? Has the stock price risen to the $30 initial issuance price? Are any merger rumors circulating?

CHAPTER TWENTY-THREE

OfficeMax—To the End

*M*ichael Feuer had a passion to be an entrepreneur. He realized this passion was rather late in coming, but by age 42 he was bored with the corporate life. Still, perhaps it had been there all along, this passion.

He had started with Fabri-Centers of America, a 600-store chain, 17 years before, and had quickly rose through the ranks. He liked to describe himself in those days as suffering from the Frank Sinatra syndrome—"I wanted to do it my way." And he got tired of what he called CYB, "covering your backside," which he saw most executives spending too much of their time trying to do, at the expense of total effectiveness. If he only had his own business he could escape these drains on career satisfaction and constraints on his potential. However, he couldn't accept the common notion of the true entrepreneur as one who has enormous self-confidence, enough to give up the security of the paycheck and go off on his or her own. "I'm not a true entrepreneur because I suffer acutely from what I call 'F of F,' the fear of failure."[1]

In his pursuit of entrepreneurship, Feuer turned down a number of big-money corporate jobs and the perks that go with them. Increasingly he felt an overwhelming urge to be his own man, to succeed or fail on his own terms. He soon realized, however, the reality of starting a small business from scratch and the contrast with what might have been if he had chosen the corporate option.

THE START

OfficeMax officially began on April Fools Day, April 1, 1988. The most precious asset at the time was a blank sheet of paper. But the concept, laid out that day on paper, was simple: create an exciting office products superstore that featured breadth and depth of merchandise, present it in a contemporary manner with professional, friendly service, and then offer prices 30 to 70 percent less than those at more traditional office supply retailers.

---

[1] Until late 1993, little had been written about the success of OfficeMax. Much of the early material and quotes have come from speeches that Feuer made to various business and graduate business school classes.

Michael Feuer and his partner had recognized a flaw—another of those strategic windows of opportunity (see Chapters 20 and 22)—in the existing system for marketing office products and they resolved to exploit it, if they could convince enough investors to give them the resources needed. The traditional channel of distribution for this merchandise was from manufacturers to wholesalers or distributors, and finally to stationers, who were usually small retailers. This rather lengthy channel imposed markups at each stage of the distribution and resulted in relatively higher prices for the end user. Feuer saw this as archaic, akin to the "old-time mom-and-pop groceries on every corner," which were eventually replaced by more efficient and much lower-priced supermarkets. These for the most part bypassed wholesalers and distributors and went directly to manufacturers. While Feuer was not unique in recognizing office products' flawed method of distribution, he was in the forefront.

Feuer and his partner Robert Hurwitz (who became no longer active in the firm on a full-time basis) were able to mass $3 million from 50 investors, some friends, family members, and a number of doctors and lawyers. The two partners did not use any debt financing, nor did they seek venture capitalists. They shunned these most common sources of capital for new firms, not wanting to give up some control of their enterprise; neither did they want to answer to skeptics and defend every major decision. However, for many promising small businesses, venture capital can provide needed startup funds difficult to obtain otherwise. See the Information Box on page 347 for more discussion of venture capitalists and their role in fostering small enterprises.

While Feuer and Hurwitz recognized what seemed an attractive market opportunity, they were not the only ones to do so. In May 1988, an industry trade paper listed all the embryonic firms in the emerging office products superstore industry. OfficeMax rated No. 14 on a list of 15. "We would have been dead last, but another company had started a week later than we did, although neither one of us had any stores."[2]

Feuer and Hurwitz established headquarters offices in a tiny 500-square-foot brick warehouse. It had little heat or air conditioning. The company owned only a few pieces of office furniture, a coffee-maker, and a copy machine, but no fax. The restroom had to be unisex since there was only space for one toilet. They had recruited seven people who were only half-jokingly told that they needed to have small appetites because there was little money to pay them. But Feuer promised that they would share in the financial success of the company, and for these seven their faith and hope for the future was enough. Feuer liked to tell the story of how he reinterviewed a candidate for a vice-president's position who had turned him down in 1988. Had he accepted the job, then he would have been a multi-millionaire by 1993.

THE FIRST YEAR

Even with $3 million of seed money from the 50 investors, OfficeMax had limited resources for what it proposed to do. A major problem now was to convince manufacturers to do business with this upstart of a firm in Cleveland. Most manufacturers

---

[2] John R. Brandt, "Taking It to the Max," *Corporate Cleveland*, September 1988, p. 17.

INFORMATION BOX

VENTURE CAPITALISTS: AID TO ENTREPRENEURS

The biggest roadblock to self-employment is financing. Banks tend to be unreceptive to funding unproven new ventures, especially for someone without a track record. Given that most would-be entrepreneurs have limited resources from which to draw, where are they to get the financing needed?

Feuer and Hurwitz bypassed conventional sources of financing by finding 50 willing investors. For many other would-be entrepreneurs venture capitalists may be the answer.

Venture capitalists are wealthy individuals (or firms) looking for extraordinary returns for their investments. At the same time, they are willing to accept substantial risks. Backing nascent entrepreneurs in speculative undertakings can be the route to a far greater return on investment than possible otherwise—provided that the venture capitalist chooses wisely who to stake. This decision is much easier after a fledgling enterprise has a promising start. Then venture capitalists may stand in line for a piece of the action. But until then, the entrepreneur may struggle to get seed money.

How do these sources of funding choose among the many business ideas brought to them? "They look at the people, not the ideas," says Arthur Rock, one of the foremost venture capitalists. "Nearly every mistake I've made has been because I picked the wrong people, not the wrong idea."[3]

For a would-be entrepreneur seeking venture capital, then, the most important step may be in selling yourself, in addition to your idea. Intellectual honesty is sometimes mentioned by venture capitalists as a necessary ingredient. This may be defined as a willingness to face facts rigorously and not be deluded by rosy dreams and unrealistic expectations.

Those who win the early support of venture capitalists will likely have to give away a good piece of the action. Should the enterprise prove successful, the venture capitalist will expect to share in the success. Indeed, the funds provided by a venture capitalist may be crucial to even starting, or they may mean the difference in being adequately funded or so poorly funded that failure is almost inevitable.

Selling a definitive business plan to a prospective venture capitalist is usually a requirement for such financing. In the process, of course, you are selling yourself. You may want to do this exercise: choose a new business idea, develop an initial business plan, and attempt to persuasively present it to a would-be investor.

---

[3] John Merwin, "Have You Got What It Takes?" *Forbes*, August 3, 1981, p. 61.

---

were satisfied with the existing distribution channels and were reluctant to grant credit to a revolutionary newcomer with hardly a store to its name.

The key to winning the support of these manufacturers lay in convincing them that OfficeMax had such a promising future that it could offer them far more business potential than they would ever have with their present distributors—that

OfficeMax would soon be a 30-, 50-, even 300-store chain in a few years. "We explained to them that it was in *their* best interest to help us today—to guarantee a place with us tomorrow."

To make its message credible, OfficeMax needed to create an image of stability and of a firm poised to jump. To help convey this image, Feuer convinced a major Cleveland bank to grant the company an unsecured line of credit. There was only one condition: OfficeMax had to promise that it would never use it. But this impressive-looking line of credit, bespeaking the faith that a major bank seemingly had in the embryonic firm, brought respect from manufacturers. Then OfficeMax even went so far as to ask them for unheard-of terms of sale—such as 60, 90, even 120 days with a discount.

Xerox was somehow persuaded to grant a year's payment delay for purchases. Many other manufacturers also accepted the outlandish requests. The bold promise of growth was realized, as many manufacturers, five years later, found OfficeMax to be their best customer. OfficeMax became so important at Xerox that the account became handled by a divisional president and chief financial officer.

The first store was opened July 5, 1988, three months after the enterprise itself was started. This was an amazingly short time to fine-tune the concept, find a site, remodel as needed, and merchandise and staff the store. Feuer explained that the firm urgently needed some cash to survive, hence the desperate efforts to bring the first unit on line. In addition to providing needed cash flow, they needed the first store to confirm the viability and promise of the superstore concept to investors and suppliers alike.

This the first store quickly did. Customers eagerly embraced the great variety yet lowest prices of the superstore, more commonly known today as a category killer store, for office products. The only publicity had been a newspaper story two days before. Yet, the store racked up $6,400 in sales that first day.

In the next 90 days, stores two and three were opened, also in metropolitan Cleveland. The fourth store was opened in Detroit, not far from the executive offices of Kmart, destined a few years later to become a majority shareholder. Within six months, the company was breaking even before corporate expenses.

As Feuer described his work schedule in those early days, he typically was in the corporate office from 7:00 a.m. to 7:00 p.m., stopping at his home just long enough to change into nondescript clothing before going to the first store, where he could inconspicuously observe the shopping activity there and talk to customers, asking them what they liked and didn't like about the store. He liked to recount how he would even follow customers who left without buying anything out to the parking lot to ask them why OfficeMax did not meet their needs.

Following the example of Feuer, from its inception the company has had a strong commitment to its customers. For example, OfficeMax accepted collect calls from customers. Any complaints had to be resolved in less than 24 hours, complete with an apology from OfficeMax. The company's objective was to build loyalty. "We're not embarrassed to say that we were wrong—and the customer was right."

As the company began making a small profit, Feuer's worst nightmare was that the accounting had been "screwed up," and that OfficeMax was on the verge of bankruptcy without realizing it. With this tormenting thought, he went back to the existing shareholders after six months to raise additional capital. The early success of the enterprise enabled them to raise the per-share price 75 percent over the original placement.

By the end of the first full year, OfficeMax had six stores operational in Ohio and Michigan, with total sales of $13 million. The stores were profitable due to an undeviating cost-consciousness.

GROWTH CONTINUES

By early 1990, 2 years into the operation, OfficeMax had 17 stores in operation. Unexpectedly, Montgomery Ward proposed a merger between OfficeMax and Office World, a similar operation that Ward had funded along with a number of venture capitalists. Office World had been started with what seemed to OfficeMax executives as almost a king's ransom. But it proceeded to lose $10 million in a very short time. In the negotiations, OfficeMax was in the power position, and it acquired Office World and its seven Chicago locations on rather attractive terms: Its major concession was to relinquish two of its ten board seats to Montgomery Ward and the venture capitalists, but it acquired along with the stores several million dollars in badly needed cash.

By the summer of 1990, OfficeMax had about $25 million in cash, with 30 stores in operation. It raised another $8 million in a third private placement, at a share price 600 percent higher than the original investors had paid just two years before. Corporate offices were now moved into a building with space for men's and women's restrooms.

Feuer began an aggressive new expansion program, calling for opening 20 additional stores. Competition was heating up in this new superstore industry, and several competitors had gone public to raise funds for more rapid expansion. Several others had gone bankrupt.

The Kmart Connection

The biggest threat facing OfficeMax now came from news that Kmart was poised to roll out its new Office Square superstore chain, which would be a direct threat to OfficeMax. With all the resources of Kmart—financial, managerial, and real estate expertise and influence—Feuer and company saw themselves being crushed and driven into Lake Erie. Feuer consoled himself that being left penniless would at least be character building.

Mostly as a defensive strategy, Feuer sought to open talks with Kmart. Kmart top executives proved to be receptive, and in November 1990 an agreement was negotiated in which Kmart made an investment of about $40 million in return for a 22 percent equity stake in OfficeMax. As part of the agreement, the feared Office Square became a possession of OfficeMax, and Kmart received one seat of the board of OfficeMax.

Now the expansion program could begin accelerating, with Kmart's full cooperation and support. So good was the rapport that within ten months of the initial transaction, discussions were started concerning a broader business relationship with Kmart.

As the original goals of the business were being realized, it was perhaps time to cash in some of the chips, so Michael Feuer thought. Two options seemed appropriate for the original investors: (1) go public or (2) structure a new deal with Kmart. The company decided to go with Kmart. Kmart agreed to buy out all of the shareholders, with the exception of 50 percent of the shares of Feuer and partner Hurwitz, for a total market capitalization of about $215 million. This was up from zero just 42 months earlier. What made the deal particularly attractive was the fact that while 92 percent of OfficeMax was sold to a well-heeled parent, it could still retain total autonomy.

Onward and Upward, Without Kmart

By the end of July 1995, OfficeMax had 405 superstores in more than 150 markets in 41 states and Puerto Rico. The typical store was 23,500 square feet and had 6,000 items. Faster growth had been achieved through two major acquisitions: the 46-store Office Warehouse chain and the 105-store BizMart chain.

Sales were primarily to small and medium-sized businesses employing under a hundred employees, home office customers, and individual consumers. But institutions such as school boards and universities were also targets, and the low prices of OfficeMax were powerful inducements. A new program was established for next-day delivery of office supplies, based on calls to telephone centers with toll-free lines.

The company was planning to open up to 20 new FurnitureMax stores, which were to be 8,000 to 10,000 square feet additions to existing OfficeMax stores devoted to office furniture. It was also testing five to ten new CopyMax stores. Along with a multimedia advertising strategy, the company now had a 220-page merchandise catalog featuring about 5,000 items with toll-free telephone ordering.

Meanwhile, Kmart was seeking additional money to provide badly needed facelifts for its stores in a desperate attempt to hold off the mighty Wal-Mart. This led Kmart to sell its share of OfficeMax, as well as some of its other subsidiaries, in order to raise a needed $3 billion in cash. This was finalized in July 1995. OfficeMax netted $110 million to be used to fund its store expansion. Its future as a public company rather than a subsidiary of Kmart now presented a heady dream to Feuer and his investors. The Information Box on page 351 discusses the prescription for great wealth in going public.

In fiscal 1995 (year ending January 31) revenues were over $1.8 billion. Net income was $30.4 million, up 181 percent from the year before. Figures 23.1 and 23.2 show the growth in sales and in number of stores.

STORM CLOUDS

In 1996, OfficeMax became only the fourth company up to that time to exceed $3 billion in revenues in less than nine years. As of September 1998, it had 769 stores in 48 states and Puerto Rico. Through joint ventures, it also had nine stores in Mexico and a first store in Japan. In addition, there were 129 CopyMax outlets targeting the esti-

INFORMATION BOX

THE PRESCRIPTION FOR GREAT WEALTH FOR ENTREPRENEURS

An entrepreneur often has much to gain by going public with an enterprise after a few years if it shows early success and a promising future. The entrepreneur keeps a portion of the stock and offers the rest to the public. With an attractive new venture, the offering price may be high enough to make the entrepreneur an instant multi-millionaire.

Take Office Depot, for example. This was the largest office supply superstore chain in North America, although not that much bigger than OfficeMax. It was listed on the New York Stock Exchange, with its 94,143,455 shares of common stock sold for about $39 a share, giving a total market value of about $3.7 billion. If OfficeMax went public and had a similar relative market value, and if Feuer and Hurwitz held 8 percent of the total capitalization, they would be worth about $296 million, or almost $150 million apiece.

What rationale do you see for Feuer's decision to structure a new deal with Kmart rather than go public? Do you agree with his rationale?

mated $9 billion print-for-pay industry, as well as 129 FurnitureMax stores tapping the estimated $12 billion office furniture industry.[4]

In 1999, it planned to open 120 new superstores in the United States on top of the 150 opened in 1998. Revenues had steadily climbed to $3.765 billion in 1997,

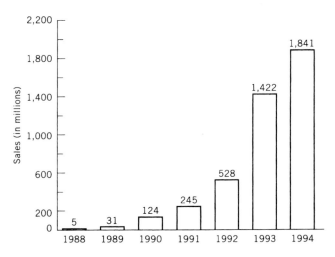

Figure 23.1 Sales growth (fiscal years ending Jan. 31 of the next year). In 1988, OfficeMax projected 1993 sales of less than $100 million; actual 1993 sales were 14 times larger.

[4] *1998 OfficeMax Annual Report.*

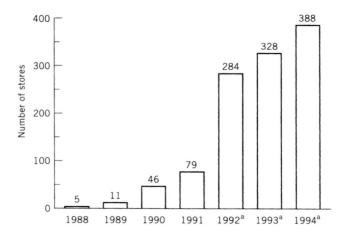

Figure 23.2   Growth in number of stores (fiscal years ending Jan. 31 of the next year). OfficeMax's 1988 business plan called for fifty stores by 1993; the company ended the year with nearly seven times that number.

ᵃ Includes BizMart stores.

while net income had grown to $89.6 million, an increase of 30 percent from 1996.[5] Over the three-year period from January 31, 1994 to January 31, 1997, OfficeMax's market share compared to its largest competitor, Office Depot, rose from 30.1 percent to 35.9 percent, as shown below:

	Fiscal 1997	Fiscal 1994
Office Depot revenues	$6.716 billion	$4.266 billion
OfficeMax revenues	3.765	1.841
Market share of OfficeMax relative to Office Depot	35.9%	30.1%

Yet OfficeMax's stock price had fallen precipitously to under $10 a share by September 1998. By late 1998, analysts began attacking OfficeMax as it was showing up more poorly than competitors Office Depot and Staples. In particular, sales were lagging at its older stores, and OfficeMax warned that third- and fourth-quarter earnings would not hit expectations, mostly because of heavy price cutting on computers. Critics were quick to point out that Office Depot and Staples were not so adversely affected.[6]

The situation worsened as businesses began cutting back in a slowing economy in 2000, and the office-supply industry faced a saturated market—too many stores from years of vigorous expansion in the 1990s.

[5] Ibid.

[6] For example, "OfficeMax Opens New Stores While Sales Lag at Old Ones," *Cleveland Plain Dealer*, October 29, 1998, p. C2.

The fourth quarter of 2000, which should have been the strongest quarter of the year, was particularly nasty. OfficeMax posted an $85 million loss, while Office Depot and Staples posted $168 million and $112 million losses respectively. All announced sharp cuts in expansion and closings of underperforming stores. OfficeMax, now grown to 995 stores, planned 50 store closings. Company stock was trading around $2 a share.

THE END

On July 14, 2003, OfficeMax announced that it had agreed to be acquired by Boise Cascade Corp., a big lumber and paper company. In a $1.15 billion buyout, OfficeMax shareholders would get $9 a share, about a 25 percent premium over the current share price. Feuer himself would stand to make $22.3 million from the shares he held, in addition to at least five years of his $983,000 salary for having a consulting role in the new operation.

Feuer had actively sought a buyer since Fall 2002, having concluded that he had taken the company about as far as he could with his resources, and with being the smallest firm in office-products retailing. In spite of all his efforts, OfficeMax had had eight losing quarters before regaining profitability in late 2002. He felt worst about those investors who had enthusiastically joined him when he took his enterprise public in 1994. Their faith in him was largely unrewarded, and many of these investors were his friends, and they had paid $19 a share then. In the bad days of 2000 and 2001, their shares had sunk 92 percent to $1.56 at the lowest point. Perhaps he had been too ambitious, had opened too many stores more than OfficeMax was able to assimilate. These brought a hefty debt load that became an unhealthy burden. Now, he had finally turned the company to profitability, but the stock price remained only a fraction of what it had been a few years earlier and was well below the $19 a share many of these people paid.

Feuer reflected on the drawbacks of being a distant third in a strongly competitive industry. He had never been able to gain a foothold with the large customers his rivals had. No, his main customer base was consumers and small businesses; the profitable volume was just not there.

Boise had been endeavoring to move away from the severe price competition of being a commodity supplier to distributors and get into the more profitable business of selling paper products to end users. It had already made more than 40 acquisitions in recent years to expand its office products business, and this offered the potential of tapping into the larger customer base.

Would this turn out to be one of the few mergers "made in heaven" or another of the ill-fated ones? At least Feuer came out of his 15 years of entrepreneurship a very wealthy man.[7]

---

[7] Jim Carlton, "Boise Cascade Expects OfficeMax to Shore Up Profit," *Wall Street Journal*, July 15, 2003, p. B5; Teresa Dixon Murray and Janet H. Cho, "Michael Feuer Drove OfficeMax and Himself," *Cleveland Plain Dealer*, July 20, 2003, pp. A1, A10.

LATE-BREAKING NEWS

Boise had to be disappointed in its acquisition of OfficeMax and its total commitment to a retail operation and abandonment of its lumber and paper manufacturing. February 14, 2005, the company announced the resignation of CEO Christopher Milliken, on the job for less than four months. He was the third senior executive to leave OfficeMax this year, amid a growing accounting scandal. Investigation had uncovered improper billings, errors in rebates and other payments from vendors in 2004, that necessitated restating operating income for three quarters. The scandal came to light after the firm had posted disappointing Christmas season results and lowered its profit forecast.

ANALYSIS

Here we see what initially was an outstanding entrepreneurial success. The growth rate in only a few years rivaled the best at that time. In the same year that OfficeMax was started, 685,095 other new businesses were also formed in the United States, but more than half of these eventually failed. Of the survivors, only a small percentage would ever achieve a net worth over $50 million. Only a handful would ever reach $200 million. What made OfficeMax so uniquely successful?

It was not that it had identified a great idea and nurtured it exclusively. While OfficeMax launched on to a business opportunity arising from the archaic distribution structure of the office-supplies industry, it was far from unique in this identification. Indeed, the concept of category-killer stores was in the ascendancy for all kinds of retail goods.[8] The competition could become intense when category killer stores competed with each other. Eventually, only three chains of superstores remained in the office-products industry, and OfficeMax was one of these, although the smallest. Why did OfficeMax succeed so well, while most of its competitors failed or were acquired?

Much of the success was due to the efforts of the principal founder, Michael Feuer. His vision was to retain control of the nascent enterprise by shunning venture capitalists and debt financing. While the money initially raised, $3 million, would seem adequate for most ventures, for a category killer chain it was barely sufficient. But severe austerity combined with the promise of great future rewards motivated employees and suppliers. This required optimism and an enthusiastic selling job by Feuer. And it also required a trusting relationship with investors, employees, and suppliers.

Great attention to customer service, to cost containment to the point of austerity, to the myriad details needed for opening stores with adequate employees and merchandise in severe deadline situations—all these were part of the success package. Building on the growth without losing sight of the austerity heritage was perhaps even more important as the enterprise grew from a few stores to 20, 50, and more.

---

[8] A category killer store gets its name from the strategy of carrying such a huge assortment of merchandise at good prices in a particular category of goods that they practically destroy traditional merchants of such goods.

Of particular interest for any growing enterprise is the opportunity to make attractive acquisitions of former competitors who have fallen into desperate straits. The successful firm is in a position to quickly build on the bones of former competitors who could not make it.

Alas, some of the early virtues of austerity and moderate borrowing (and consequent modest interest expenses) were disregarded in the heady rush to expansion in the late 1990s. A saturated market and an economic slowdown forced retrenchment, not only for OfficeMax but for its bigger competitors as well.

WHAT CAN BE LEARNED?

Successful Entrepreneurship Is Not Easy

Not many who opt to go into business for themselves expect this to be an easy road, a comfortable and lazy lifestyle. Yet the work ethic of successful entrepreneurs can be awesome, even for those prepared for long hours and worries in the night. Michael Feuer customarily put in 12- to 18-hour days between corporate headquarters and keeping in close touch with stores, customers, and suppliers. He would wake up at 3 a.m. to stare at the ceiling while wondering if he made the right decision. He felt a responsibility to his employees, even after they had grown from the seven original ones whose jobs depended on his decisions. By the end of 1993, he had more than 19,000 reasons to worry in the night.

Would he have been less successful with a more moderate work ethic? Maybe. But the personal stake in a growing business drives many entrepreneurs to become workaholics even to the point of sacrificing other aspects of their lives, including family.

There Is Power in a Growth Image, Even If It Is Only an Illusion

In perhaps one of the most crucial moves taken in the early and most vulnerable months of the embryonic enterprise, Feuer and his people were able to sell bankers and manufacturers on the great growth prospects for the company, that "we would rapidly become a 20-,50-, or even 300-store chain. We explained that it was in their best interest to help us today—to guarantee a place with us tomorrow."

What makes a strong growth company so attractive to investors, creditors, suppliers, and employees? Part of the attractiveness certainly is that everyone likes to be associated with a winner. The greatest appeal of growth companies is their economic promise. This embraces investors, of course, because their investment grows with the business. Creditors and suppliers see more and more business coming their way as the company grows ever larger. And employees see great career opportunities continually opening up in a rapidly growing organization.

Perhaps in creating the image of OfficeMax as a company on the threshhold of great growth, Feuer was simply very persuasive. But perhaps many of the people he talked with were so eager to be convinced and to be offered the opportunity to get in on the ground floor of what might be the stuff of dreams that they would accept even grandiose conjecture.

Go the Extra Miles in Customer Relations

It is easy for an organization to proclaim its dedication to customer service and good customer relations. Too often, however, such is only lip service, pious pronouncements without real substance. OfficeMax went far beyond lip service. Feuer and his executives, at least in the early years, sought close contact with customers in stores, even to the point of following them to the parking lot to see what might have been lacking in the merchandise or service that discouraged a purchase. The company accepted collect calls from customers, who might have problems or complaints or special needs. A promise of satisfaction of all complaints within 24 hours, the guiding "How can we make you happy?" question in all customer dealings, and readiness to apologize, attest to a customer commitment beyond the ordinary. With few exceptions, all businesses depend on customer loyalty and repeat business for their success. Perhaps in office products, where many customers are businesses, customer loyalty is all the more important. But it is easy to delude yourself and an organization that the loss of any single customer is not all that important, and that the firm must guard against being taken advantage of by unreasonable customers. Where should a firm, particularly a retailer, draw the line? Can any retailer be too liberal in the handling of customer complaints?

Again, the Power of "Lean and Mean"

In several earlier cases, we noted problems of bloated bureaucracies and/or uncontrolled spending, and the dire effect on profitability. We examined several highly successful firms, notably Southwest Airlines and Vanguard, that followed a policy of continued frugality despite increasing size. The temptation with great growth is to let down the barriers and open the spending spigots. OfficeMax resisted this urge in the early years but then got caught up in the frenzy of opening stores as fast as it could.

Again, Dedicated Employees Can Give a Powerful Advantage

As with Southwest Airlines, OfficeMax, in its early years, was able to stimulate employees to move beyond individual concerns to a higher level of performance, a true team approach. This dedication, and the vague promise of future great expectations, brought employees to OfficeMax for very low wages, some turning down much higher paying jobs for the dream that might or might not come to pass. The dedication of these employees made it possible to open the first store from scatch barely three months after the company was founded, with other stores quickly following.

   The hope for great growth, a trusted leader, and an organization geared to a team effort seem to be most compatible in producing dedicated employees. One suspects there is also a close relationship in lean and mean organizations, where a limited bureaucracy and management levels bring ease of communication. Unfortunately, for a maturing OfficeMax, such motivational factors began to wan. The hope for great growth had to be more soberly appraised in a competitive environment where OfficeMax was No. 3 behind two other aggressive competitors and a rapidly-becoming saturated market.

Beware Market Saturation

How many office supply superstores can one metro area handle and still enable all outlets to prosper? Especially when there is little to choose from among the major competitors? OfficeMax, Staples, and Office Depot all have large box stores, widest possible assortment of goods, reasonably low prices, and all push employees to be friendly, knowledgeable, and to provide the best possible service. In such an environment with little distinctiveness possible, market saturation or overstoring becomes a real problem. It hurts profitability, until weaker competitors leave the market, and certainly curbs the growth potential.

CONSIDER

Can you identify other learning insights coming from this case?

QUESTIONS

1. In the hiring process, how would you identify candidates who are most likely to become dedicated employees?

2. Can a firm be too liberal in handling customer complaints?

3. "OfficeMax is No. 3 in its industry. This is a severe disadvantage, as it can never match the resources of its two larger competitors." Evaluate this assertion.

4. Do you think Feuer was being entirely ethical when he sold manufacturers on the desirability of doing business with OfficeMax in the very early days of the company? Why or why not?

5. Do you see any limitations to the future of category killer stores?

6. Can you think of some types of merchandise where category killer stores are unlikely to be successful?

7. Feuer put in 12-to 18-hour days regularly in the early years. Do you think he would have been as successful with less of a work ethic? Why or why not?

8. Be a Devil's Advocate. Argue against Feuer's plans to sell out to Boise.

9. Would you personally have been willing to work for OfficeMax in the early days, with very low pay, primitive accommodations, long hours—but maybe for a dream?

ROLE PLAY

1. You own a small office supply store. Business has been steady and sufficient for a good living for you and your family up to now. Now an OfficeMax has opened less than a mile away. Discuss how you possibly can compete against such a superstore when you cannot come close to matching their variety of goods or their prices.

2. You are the assistant to Feuer. He wants you to draw up plans for targeting large institutions and businesses. Be as specific as you can, making assumptions where needed, and persuasively support your recommendations.

TEAM DEBATE EXERCISE

On October 25, 1995, the largest office-products retailer, Office Depot, announced it was planning to open a dozen stores on OfficeMax's home turf, metropolitan Cleveland where OfficeMax has its headquarters and 17 stores. "When we enter a major market, our usual policy is to go in rather quickly and saturate the market with six to a dozen to twenty stores within the first couple of years," Office Depot said. Michael Feuer was unfazed. "We think the advantage we have is such a fierce sense and focus of local pride. I don't think there will be much of a test," he said. Debate the challenge OfficeMax now faces: it should be worried, because the market already is close to saturation; it should not be worried since the market potential is still increasing and it can outcompete Office Depot.[9]

INVITATION TO RESEARCH

What is the situation with OfficeMax and its acquisition by Boise? From what you can ascertain, has it been a fairly successful merger? What is Feuer doing?

---

[9] Bill Lubinger, "Office Depot Is Taking on Office Max," *Cleveland Plain Dealer*, October 25, 1995, p. C1.

CHAPTER TWENTY-FOUR

Conclusions:
What Can Be Learned?

*I*n considering mistakes, three things are worth noting: (1) Even the most successful organizations make mistakes but survive as long as they maintain a good "batting average" of satisfactory decisions; (2) Mistakes should be effective teaching tools for avoiding similar errors in the future; and (3) Firms can bounce back from adversity, and turnaround.

We can make a number of generalizations from these mistakes and successes. Of course, we recognize that marketing is a discipline that does not lend itself to laws or axioms. Examples of exceptions to every principle or generalization can be found. However, the decision maker does well to heed the following insights. For the most part, they are based on specific corporate and entrepreneurial experiences and should be transferable to other situations and other times.

INSIGHTS REGARDING OVERALL ENTERPRISE PERSPECTIVES

Importance of Public Image

The impact, for good or bad, of an organization's public image was a common thread through a number of cases—for example, Nike, Southwest Airlines, Vanguard, Disney, Maytag, Perrier, and Harley-Davidson.

Nike shows the power of an image that was compatible with the product and attractive to the target market. The carefully nurtured association with some of the most esteemed male and female athletes in the world—many of whom its customers were eager to emulate—if only in their dreams—propelled Nike and its swoosh logo to dominance in the athletic apparel industry. Still, we saw a positive image become tarnished for Nike.

Southwest's image of friendliness, great efficiency, and unbeatable prices propelled it to an unassailable position among short-haul airlines. Now it seeks to expand its image to longer hauls. Vanguard has also used its image of frugality and great customer service in the mutual fund industry to propel it to the top with relatively little advertising. Harley-Davidson was able to develop its image one step further—to a mystique with a devoted cult following. Gateway Computer tried to upgrade its Holstein cow image to a mystique, but without success.

Some images were less favorable. Disney found its image did not travel well to Paris, nor did Maytag's quality image to the United Kingdom. Perrier responded aggressively to a contamination problem by making a major product recall but lost its image of quality.

The importance of a firm's public image should be undeniable. Yet some continue to disregard their image and either act in ways detrimental or else ignore the constraints and opportunities that a reputation affords.

Power of the Media

We have seen or suspected the power of the media in a number of cases. Coca-Cola, Firestone and Ford, and Vanguard are obvious examples. This power is often used critically—to hurt a firm's public image. The media can fan a problem or exacerbate an embarrassing or imprudent action. In particular, this media focus can trigger the herd instinct, in which increasing numbers of people join in protests and public criticism. And the media, in its zeal, can sometimes cross the line, as in singling out Nike for all the employment abuses in Third World countries. But in Vanguard's case, positive media attention minimized the need for much advertising.

We can make these five generalizations regarding image and its relationship with the media:

1. It is desirable to maintain a stable, clear-cut image and undeviating objectives.
2. It is difficult and time-consuming to upgrade an image.
3. An episode of poor quality can leave a lasting stigma.
4. A good image can be quickly lost if a firm relaxes in an environment of aggressive competition.
5. Well-known firms are especially vulnerable to critical public scrutiny and must use great care in safeguarding their reputations.

Need for Growth Orientation—But Not Reckless Growth

The opposite of a growth commitment is a status quo mind-set, uninterested in expansion and the problems and work involved. Harley-Davidson's downfall in the 1950s was its contentment with the status quo; Sunbeam's lack of growth led to the ill-fated choice of "Chainsaw Al" Dunlap to get things moving again.

In general, how tenable is a low-growth or no-growth philosophy? Although at first glance it seems workable, it usually sows the seeds of its own destruction. Almost four decades ago the following caution was made:

> Vitality is required even for survival; but vitality is difficult to maintain without growth, at least in the American business climate. The vitality of a firm depends on the vigor and

ambition of its members. The prospect of growth is one of the principal means by which a firm can attract able and vigorous recruits.[1]

Consequently, if a firm is perceived as not growth minded, its ability to attract able people diminishes. Customers see a growing firm as reliable, eager to please, and constantly improving. Suppliers and creditors tend to give preferential treatment to a growing firm because they hope to retain it as a customer when it reaches large size.

In other cases, firms had strong growth commitments, but somehow their growth in bureaucratic overhead let competitiveness slip and they fell back, sometimes after decades of market dominance. Boeing comes to mind here, as does Newell Rubbermaid, reaping the consequences of reckless growth and unwise diversifications. Then we have the bungled growth efforts of Maytag's Hoover Division in the United Kingdom. Good financial judgment must not be sacrificed to the siren call of growth.

Therefore, an emphasis on growth can be carried too far. Somehow the growth must be kept within the abilities of the firm to handle it. OfficeMax's eagerness to open many more stores contributed to its downfall. Even McDonald's found that less emphasis on increasing the number of outlets brought more pleased shareholders and franchisees. Several examples, such as Vanguard, Southwest Airlines, and Wal-Mart showed how firms could grow rapidly without losing control.

We can make several generalizations about the most desirable growth perspectives:

1. Growth targets should not exceed the abilities and resources of the organization. Growth at any cost—especially at the expense of profits and financial stability—must be shunned. In particular, tight controls over inventories and expenses should be established, and performance monitored closely.

2. The most prudent approach to growth is to keep the organization and operation as simple and uniform as possible, to be flexible should sales not meet expectations, and to keep the breakeven point as low as possible, especially for new and untried ventures. Vanguard, Southwest Airlines, and Wal-Mart's great competitive advantages lie in their much lower overhead than anyone else in their industries. Boston Beer is another example of giving priority to a low breakeven point.

3. Concentrating maximum efforts on the expansion opportunity is like an army exploiting a breakthrough. The concentration strategy—such as that of Southwest Airlines and McDonald's until recently—usually wins out over more timid competitors who diffuse efforts and resources. But such concentration is more risky than spreading efforts.

4. Rapidly expanding markets pose dangers from too conservative and overly optimistic sales forecasts. The latter may overextend resources and jeopardize viability should demand contract; the former opens the door to more aggressive competitors. There is no right answer to this dilemma, but management should be aware of the risks and the rewards of both extremes.

[1] Wroe Alderson, *Marketing Behavior and Executive Action*, Homewood, IL: Irwin, 1957, p. 59.

5. A strategy emphasizing rapid growth should not neglect other aspects of the operation. For example, older stores should not be ignored in the quest to open new ones.

6. Decentralized management is more compatible with rapid growth than centralized, because it puts less strain on home-office executives. However, delegation must have well-defined standards and controls as well as competent subordinates. Otherwise, the Maytag Hoover fiasco may be repeated.

7. The safety and integrity of the product and firm's reputation must not be sacrificed in pursuit of growth and profits. This is especially important when customers' health and safety may be jeopardized, such as Ford and Firestone encountered with the Ford Explorer.

Beware the Rush to Merge

Some have called this rush to merge *merger mania.* Mergers and acquisitions often work out badly for employees, communities, even stockholders. Only the top executives, lawyers, bankers, and consultants usually come out ahead. As we go to print, a huge merger of Procter & Gamble and Gillette was announced. The payday of this merger for James Kilts, CEO of Gillette, received wide attention from the media as well as government officials. It was reported to be at least $185 million.[2]

We have seen three cases where acquisitions turned out horrendous: Newell Rubbermaid, Snapple, and Maytag. The unfulfilled promise from the Hewlett-Packard merger with Compaq, led to Carly Fiorina's firing in February 2005. The success of the Kmart/Sears merger remains questionable, with the final verdict years away. *Forbes* magazine reported on some recent large mergers that were losers:

- Daimler-Benz buys Chrysler, May 1998, for $46 billion.

  "A perfect fit," said Juergen Schrempp, CEO of Daimler

  Outcome: Combined market value down 50 percent.

- AT&T buys Tele-Communications, June 1998, for $48 billion.

  "Undisputed leader in ... the fastest-growing segments of the communications services industry."

  Outcome: Cable businesses sold for half original price.

- America Online buys Time Warner, January 2000, for $173 billion.

  "We did wrestle a little bit with valuations ... but most of the time was spent on social issues."

  Outcome: Times Warner stock off from $73 to $18.

  ("Seemed Like a Good Idea at the Time," *Forbes,* February 28, 2005, p.38.)

---

[2] Charles Forelle and Mark Maremont, "Gillette CEO Payday May Be Richer," *Wall Street Journal,* February 3, 2005, p. B2.

Some cautions: Don't rush into the merger or acquisition.

Beware of optimistic projections for mergers.

Assumptions should be defended in merger decisions.

Really examine compatibility of the two firms.

Beware overpaying for an acquisition.

Strategic Windows of Opportunity

Several of the great successes we examined resulted from exploiting strategic windows of opportunity. Southwest found its opportunity by being so cost-effective that it could offer cut-rate fares and highly dependable short-haul service that no other airline could match. Similarly, Vanguard found its strategic niche with the lowest expense ratios and overhead in the mutual fund industry. Sam Walton certainly found a strategic window in the small towns of rural America in the early decades of Wal-Mart.

We make these generalizations regarding opportunities and strategic windows:

1. Opportunities often exist when a traditional way of doing business has prevailed in the industry for a long time—maybe the climate is ripe for a change.

2. Opportunities often are present when existing firms are not entirely satisfying customers' needs.

3. Innovations are not limited to products but can involve customer services as well as such things as methods of distribution.

4. For industries with rapidly changing technologies—usually new industries—heavy research and development expenditures are usually required if a firm is to avoid falling behind its competitors. But heavy R&D does not guarantee being in the forefront, as shown by Hewlett-Packard and the competitors of Dell Computer.

Power of Judicious Imitation

Some firms are reluctant to copy successful practices of their competitors; they want to be leaders, not followers. But successful practices or innovations may need to be copied if a firm is not to be left behind. Sometimes the imitator outdoes the innovator. Success can lie in doing the ordinary better than competitors.

Nike achieved its initial success by imitating many of the successful practices of the entrenched German competitor, Adidas. Somehow the competitors of McDonald's for decades were unable to imitate its undeviating insistence on rigorous standards and controls over all aspects of the operation.

For 50 years, Boeing was the innovator in the commercial-jet industry, sometimes taking big risks to do so. It biggest risk was in the 1960s when it almost bankrupted itself to build the 747 that was twice the size of any other plane in commercial use. Now Airbus is the innovator with its huge plane, the 600-seat and more A-360. Boeing decided not to follow Airbus's lead.

We can make this generalization: It makes sense for a company to identify the characteristics of successful competitors (and even similar but noncompeting firms) that contributed to their success, and then adopt these characteristics if they are compatible with the imitator's resources. Let someone else do the experimenting and risk taking. The imitator faces some risk in waiting too long, but this usually is far less than the risk of being an innovator.

Managing Change and Crises

Crises are unexpected happenings that pose threats, moderate to catastrophic, to the organization's well-being. We described three crisis cases in Part II: Firestone/Ford, Perrier, and Scott Paper/Sunbeam. Other cases as well also involved crises: Boeing, Merck, Euro Disney, Coca-Cola, Maytag, and Rubbermaid Newell. Some firms—such as Coca-Cola, Merck, and Euro Disney—handled their crisis reasonable well, although we can question how such crises were allowed to happen in the first place. However, Firestone/Ford, Maytag, and Perrier either overreacted or underreacted and failed badly in salvaging the situation. And Al Dunlap's savaging of Sunbeam and Scott Paper can be condemned.

Most crises can be prevented if a company takes precautions. This suggests being alert to changing conditions, having contingency plans, and practicing risk avoidance. For example, it is prudent to not have key executives traveling on the same air flight to insure key executives so that their incapacity will not endanger the organization, and to set up contingency plans for a strike, an equipment failure or plant shutdown, the loss of a major distributor, unexpected economic conditions, or a serious lawsuit. Some risks, of course, can be covered by insurance, but others probably not. The mettle of any organization may be severely tested by an unexpected crisis. This is especially true after 9/11: In an age of terrorism, virtually anything is possible.

Crises and significant environmental changes—such as Merck faced with the damning disclosures about Vioxx—may necessitate some shifts in the organization and the way of doing business. Firms should avoid making hasty or disruptive moves or, at the other extreme, responding too late and too grudgingly. The middle ground is usually best. Advanced planning can help a company minimize trauma and enact effective solutions. This advanced planning should include worst-scenario situations.

Vulnerability to Competition and the Three C's

Competitive advantage can be short lived, success does not guarantee continued success, and innovators as well as long-dominant firms can be overtaken and surpassed. With Harley-Davidson, Boeing, and Disney we saw the three C's syndrome of complacency, conservatism, and conceit that often characterizes the mind-set of leading organizations in their industries. We suggest that a constructive attitude of never underestimating competitors be fostered by:

- Bringing fresh blood into the organization for new ideas and different perspectives.
- Establishing a strong commitment for customer service and satisfaction with periodic feedback.

- Periodically making a corporate self-analysis designed to detect weaknesses as well as opportunities in their early stages.
- Continually monitoring the environment and being alert to any changes.

The environment is dynamic, often with subtle and hardly recognizable changes. Still, these changes may eventually have profound effects on ways of doing business, and a firm should be alert in order to protect its position as well as seize opportunities.

Environmental Monitoring

The dynamic business environment may involve changes in customer preferences and needs, in competition, and in the economy. It may involve changes even in international events—such as nationalism in Canada, NAFTA, OPEC machinations, Middle East continuing problems, changes in Eastern Europe and South Africa, advances in Pacific Rim countries in productivity and quality control and, of course, the new threat of terrorism. Pepsi, in South America, failed to realize the intricacies of penetrating and protecting its several markets there. Toys "R" Us failed to anticipate how quickly the big box discounters could invade its industry. Even McDonald's did not recognize that the fast-food industry was at long last becoming saturated, and the growth it had known for half a century was a thing of the past.

How can a firm stay alert to subtle and insidious or more obvious changes? It needs *sensors* to constantly monitor the environment. A marketing or economic research department may provide such sensors, but in many instances a formal organizational entity is not really necessary to provide primary monitoring. *Executive alertness* is essential. Most changes do not occur suddenly and without warning. Information can come from feedback by customers, sales representatives, and suppliers; news of relevant changes and projections in business journals; and even simple observations of what is happening in stores, advertising, prices, and new technologies. Unfortunately, in the urgency of dealing with day-to-day operating problems, executives can overlook or disregard changing environmental factors that may affect present and future business.

Consider the following generalizations regarding vulnerability to competition:

1. Initial market advantage tends to be rather quickly countered by competitors.
2. Countering by competitors is more likely to occur when an innovation is involved than when the advantage comes from more commonplace effective management and marketing techniques, such as superb customer service.
3. An easy-entry industry is particularly vulnerable to new and aggressive competition, especially if the market is expanding. In new industries, severe price competition usually weeds out marginal firms.
4. Long-dominant firms become vulnerable to upstart competitors because of their complacency, conservatism, and even conceit. They frequently are resistant to change and myopic about the environment.

5. Careful monitoring of performance trends of similar operating units at *strategic control points* can detect weakening positions before situations become serious. (This point is discussed further in the next section.)

6. In expanding markets, increases in sales may hide a deteriorating competitive situation. Market share data is more important.

7. A no-growth policy, or a temporary absence from the marketplace, even if fully justified by extraordinary circumstances, invites competitive inroads. Example: Perrier.

Effective Organization

We can identify several organizational attributes that can help or hinder effectiveness.

Management by Exception

With diverse and far-flung operations, it becomes difficult to closely supervise all aspects. Successful managers therefore focus their attention on performances that deviate significantly from the expected norms at *strategic control points*. Such points should include market share, profitability measures, turnover ratios, various expense ratios, and the like, broken down by individual operational units. Trend information is important: is performance getting better or worse? Subordinates can be left to handle ordinary operations and less significant deviations, so that the manager is not overburdened with details.

Management by exception failed, however, with Maytag and its overseas Hoover division. Seemingly, no budget restraints and approvals were needed for expenditures over a certain amount. The lack of such approval requirements can be directly blamed for the reprehensible promotional plans. By the time results came in, it was too late.

The Deadly Parallel

As an enterprise becomes larger, a particularly effective organizational structure is to have operating units of comparable characteristics. Sales, expenses, and profits can then be more readily compared, enabling strong and weak performances to be identified so that appropriate action can be taken. Besides providing control and performance evaluation, this *deadly parallel* structure fosters intra-firm competition that can stimulate best efforts. For the deadly parallel to be used effectively, operating units must be fairly equalized, perhaps by size or through quotas or similar categories of sales potential. This is not difficult to achieve with retail units, since departments and stores can be divided into sales volume categories—often designated as A, B, and C units—and operating results compared within the category. The deadly parallel can also be used with sales territories and certain other operating units for which sales and applicable expenses and ratios can be directly measured and compared with similar units.

Lean and Mean

A new climate is sweeping our country's major corporations. In one sense it is good: It enhances their competitiveness. But it can be destructive. Vanguard, Southwest

Airlines, Wal-Mart, Boston Beer, and OfficeMax (in its formative years) are examples of the lean-and-mean movement. Lean-and-mean firms develop flat organizations with few management layers, thus keeping overhead low, improving communication, involving employees in greater self-management, and fostering an innovative mind-set.

In contrast, we saw the organizational bloat of Boeing, with its many management levels, entrenched bureaucracies, and massive overhead. A virtual cause-and-effect relationship exists between the proportion of total overhead committed to administration/staff and the ability to cope with change and innovate. It is like trying to maneuver a huge ship: Bureaucratic weight slows the response time.

The problem with the lemming-like pursuit of the lean-and-mean structure is knowing how far to downsize without cutting into bone and muscle. As thousands of managers and staff specialists can attest, productivity gains have not always been worth the loss of jobs, the destruction of career paths, and the possible sacrifice of long-term potential. The extreme example of this was Dunlap's decimating of Scott Paper and Sunbeam.

Resistance to Change

People, as well as organizations, do not embrace change well. Change is disruptive; it destroys accepted ways of doing things and muddles familiar authority and responsibility patterns. Previously important positions may be downgraded or even eliminated, and people who view themselves as highly competent in a particular job may be forced to assume unfamiliar duties amid the fear that they cannot master the new assignments. When the change involves wholesale terminations in a major downsizing, as with Euro Disney, Scott/Sunbeam, and Boeing in its down cycles, the resistance and fear of change can become so great that efficiency is seriously jeopardized.

Normal resistance to change can be eased by good communication with participants about forthcoming changes, thus dampening rumors and fears. Acceptance of change is helped if employees are involved as fully as possible in planning the changes, if their participation is solicited and welcomed, and if assurances can be given that positions will not be impaired, only changed. Gradual rather than abrupt changes also make a transition smoother.

In the final analysis, however, making needed changes and embracing new opportunities should not be delayed or canceled because of possible negative repercussions on the organization. If change is desirable, as it often is with long-established bureaucratic organizations, then it should be done without delay. Individuals and organizations can adapt to change—it just takes some time.

SPECIFIC MARKETING STRATEGY INSIGHTS

Strengths and Limitations of Advertising

The cases provide several insights regarding the effectiveness of advertising, but they also present unanswered questions and contradictions. At the time of Coca-Cola's blunder with its New Coke, it was spending $100 million more for advertising than Pepsi and all the while losing market share. Vanguard became the star of the mutual fund industry with virtually no advertising, unlike its competitors, relying instead on word-of-mouth and free publicity. Such outcomes raise doubts about the power of advertising.

However, the right theme can bring success as shown by Nike's great success with celebrity endorsements in creating an image irresistible to many of its customers. Merck and its competitors in the drug industry aroused great demand with their massive advertising expenditures. Then we have a case where promotional efforts were too effective: Maytag Hoover's promotional campaign created more customer demand than it could possibly handle.

Thus the great challenge of advertising. We never know for sure how much should be spent to reach planned objectives, perhaps of increasing sales by a certain percentage or gaining market share. But, despite the inability to measure directly the effectiveness of advertising, only the brave—or foolhardy—executive stands pat in the face of increased promotional efforts by competitors.

We draw these conclusions: There is no ensured correlation between expenditures for advertising and sales success. But the right theme or message can be powerful. In most cases, advertising can generate initial trial. But if the other elements of the marketing strategy are relatively unattractive, customers will not be won or retained.

Limitations of Marketing Research

Marketing research is touted as the key to better decision making, the mark of sophisticated professional management. The popular belief is that the more money spent for marketing research, the less chance for a bad decision. But there is no guarantee of that, as we saw with Coca-Cola.

At best, marketing research increases the batting average of good decisions—maybe only by a little, sometimes by quite a bit. To be effective, research must be current and unbiased. Customer attitudes can change significantly if months elapse between the research and the product introduction. The several million dollars spent in taste-test research for Coca-Cola hardly reassures us about the validity of even current marketing research. Admittedly, results of taste tests are difficult to rely on, simply due to the subjective nature of taste preferences. Still, the Coca-Cola research did not even uncover the latent and powerful loyalty toward tradition and gave a false "go" signal for the new flavor.

We do not imply that marketing research has little value. Most flawed studies would have been worthwhile with better design and planning. Marketing research should have enabled Disney to better structure its pricing and other strategies to unique conditions facing its Euro Disney project.

Surprisingly, many successful new ventures initially used little formal research. Vanguard, Southwest Airlines, Wal-Mart—even McDonald's and Nike in their early days, apparently relied on entrepreneurial hunch rather than sophisticated research. Why have we not seen more extensive use of marketing research for new ventures? Consider the following major reasons:

- Most of the founding entrepreneurs did not have marketing backgrounds and, therefore, were not familiar and confident with such research.

- Available tools and techniques are not always appropriate to handle some problems and opportunities. There may be too many variables to ascertain their full impact, and some of these variables will be intangible and impossible to measure precisely. Much research consists of collecting past and present data that, although helpful in predicting a stable future, are little help in charting revolutionary new ventures. If risks are higher without marketing research for new ventures, these may be offset by the potential for great rewards.

The Importance of Price as an Offensive Weapon

Price promotions are the most aggressive marketing strategy and the one most desirable from the customer's viewpoint. We saw three notable marketing successes that geared their major strategy on lower prices than competitors: Vanguard, Southwest Airlines, and Wal-Mart. In another case, Euro Disney, high prices were detrimental in meeting performance goals. Low-price competition—price wars—were cutting into the profits of McDonald's and its competitors. Still, with Perrier a high-price strategy was key to its marketing success before the crisis, as consumers perceived the high price as indicative of high quality. The high-price strategy—higher even than most imports—was also a positive differentiation for Boston Beer.

The major disadvantage of price competition is that other firms are almost forced to meet the price cutter's prices—in other words, such a strategy is easy to match. Consequently, when prices fall for an entire industry, no firm has any particular advantage and all suffer diminished profits. Thus, price cutting gave no competitive advantage, so the thinking went. But we saw three major successes with price competition, but these came from greater operating efficiencies and lower overhead costs that still permitted good profits, while most competitors could not meet their prices without losing money.

In general, other marketing strategies are better for most firms—strategies such as better quality, better product and brand image, better service, and improved warranties—all these aspects of nonprice rather than price competition.

At the same time, we have to recognize that in new industries, ones characterized by rapid technological change and production efficiencies, severe price competition is the norm, and it weeds out marginal operations. Even a substantial position in such an industry may not insulate a firm from price competition that can jeopardize its viability.

Analytical Tools for Marketing

We identified several of the most useful analytical tools for marketing decision making. In Disney, we discussed *breakeven analysis*, a highly useful tool for making go/no-go decisions about new ventures and alternative business strategies. In Maytag, the *cost-benefit analysis* might have prevented the bungled promotion in England.

The Southwest case introduced us to the SWOT (strengths, weaknesses, opportunities, threats) analysis. While these analyses do not guarantee the best decisions, they do bring order and systematic thinking into the art of marketing decision-making.

Franchising

Franchising provides the vehicle for great growth in number of stores and other outlets. The growth comes from the lower investment needed for expansion by having independent franchisees put up much of the capital for new outlets. However, franchisee relations can present problems, as McDonald's recently found. In particular, its efforts to hold the line on prices and menus, and meeting desired standards for service and cleanliness, were difficult to achieve.

A Kinder, Gentler Stance?

In several cases, we could identify an arrogant mind-set as leading to difficulties. The French did not appreciate the arrogance of Disney, and the Euro Disney project was almost a disaster. Arrogance may have played a role in the Firestone/Ford Explorer disaster, and also in Merck's reluctance to accept early research warnings about Vioxx. The size of Wal-Mart has sometimes led to arrogance in its dealings with others.

At the other extreme, is there room in today's competitive environment for a kinder, gentler stance by a business firm? While a firm normally comes into contact with numerous parties, let us consider this question with regard to suppliers and distributors, customers, and employees.

Relations with Suppliers and Distributors

With the movement toward just-in-time deliveries in the search for more efficiency and cost containment, manufacturers and retailers are placing greater demands on suppliers. Those who cannot meet these demands will usually lose out to competitors able to do so. The big manufacturer or retailer can demand ever more from smaller suppliers, since it is in the power position and the loss of its business could be overwhelming. We saw the problems of Rubbermaid in being unable to meet the service demands of Wal-Mart. At the least, the big customer deserves priority attention since its business is so important to any supplier. Reebok's callousness in disregarding the new product concerns of Foot Locker led to its being supplanted by a hard-charging Nike in the sneaker wars of the early 1990s.

Some of the big retailers today, such as Wal-Mart, Home Depot, and supermarket chains, impose "slotting fees." A slotting fee essentially is a toll charged by the retailer for the use of its space; suppliers pay this up-front if they wish to be represented in the retailer's stores. Other demands include driving cost prices down to rock bottom, even if this destroys the supplier's profits, and insisting that the supplier take responsibility for inventory control, even stocking shelves, as well as providing special promotional support. It is common for big customers to make suppliers wait longer to be paid while the cash discount for prompt payment is routinely taken.

While organizations such as Wal-Mart argue that the use of clout leads to greater marketing efficiencies and lower consumer prices, it can be carried too far. The term *symbiotic relationship* describes the relationship between the various channel-of-distribution members: All benefit from the success of the product, and it should be to their mutual advantage to work together. The manufacturer and the dealers and distributors thus should represent a valued partnership. They are on the same side; they are not in competition with one another.

Yet we have seen in several instances that a manufacturer created sour distributor-dealer relations. Pepsi was not closely attuned to the concerns of its longtime Venezuela bottler and lost distribution in that entire country. And McDonald's callously disregarded concerns of its domestic franchisees in its eager quest to open more and more outlets. Would a kinder, gentler approach to the other members of the channel-of-distribution team have prevented or resolved these problems?

Relations with Customers

Most firms pay lip service to customer satisfaction, but some go much further in this regard than others. The participation of Harley-Davidson at rallies and other events helped develop a cult following. While not exactly gaining a cult following, Vanguard has created a loyal and enthusiastic body of customers. A symbiotic relationship can also be seen as applying to manufacturer-customer relations: They both stand to win from highly satisfied customers. And again, isn't a kinder, gentler relationship a positive?

Giving Employees a Sense of Pride and a Caring Management

Kelleher of Southwest Airlines certainly developed this esprit de corps, and this helped account for Southwest's great cost advantage. Ray Kroc of McDonald's fostered harmonious franchisee relations as McDonald's began its great growth, although such relations dimmed in recent years.

On the other hand, Boeing's problems with its peaks and valleys of layoffs and hiring destroyed any hope of widespread pride and esprit de corps among its employees, except perhaps for a nucleus. A sense of pride was certainly latent for a firm with such a national symbol, but management did not cultivate it in present-day Boeing.

ETHICAL CONSIDERATIONS

A firm tempted to walk the low road in search of greater short-run profits may eventually find that the risks far outweigh the rewards. Even more risky is not to admit mistakes and product safety risks, as was the reluctance of Ford and Firestone to admit and accept blame for product safety deficiencies that cost hundreds of lives. Merck may have been close to the edge of unethical behavior in its refusal to consider early research reports and concerns of physicians about the safety of Vioxx, even though it prided itself on its high ethical principles.

While we cannot delve very deeply into social and ethical issues[3] these insights are worth noting:

---

[3] For more depth of coverage, see R. F. Hartley, *Business Ethics, Mistakes and Successes,* (New York: John Wiley) 2005.

- A firm can no longer disavow itself from the possibility of critical ethical scrutiny. Activist groups often publicize alleged misdeeds long before governmental regulators will.

- Trial lawyers are quick to pounce on anything that might bring big payoffs from deep-pocketed defendants.

- The media will help fan public scrutiny and criticism of alleged misdeeds.

Should a firm attempt to resist and defend itself? The overwhelming evidence is to the contrary. The bad press, the continued adversarial relations, and the effect on public image are hardly worth such a confrontation. The better course of action may be to back down as quietly as possible, repugnant though that may be to a management convinced of the reasonableness of its position. Better rapport with the media may be gained by corporate openness and cooperation, with company top executives readily available to the press.

GENERAL INSIGHTS

Impact of One Person

In many of the cases one person had a powerful impact on the organization. Sam Walton of Wal-Mart is perhaps the most outstanding example, but we also have Ray Kroc of McDonald's, who converted a small hamburger stand into the world's largest restaurant operation. Other examples are Herb Kelleher of Southwest Airlines, tormentor of the mighty airlines, and Phil Knight of Nike, who could never break the four-minute mile in college but went on to bring Nike world leadership in running and other athletic gear. Let us not forget John Bogle, the founder and crusader of the Vanguard Fund Family, and his gospel of frugality. For turnaround accomplishments, virtually and undeservingly unknown is Leonard Hadly, who quietly turned around Maytag after the disaster with its United Kingdom subsidiary.

One person can also have a negative impact on an organization. How can we forget "Chainsaw Al" Dunlap. The impact of one person, for good or ill, is one of the recurring marvels of history, whether business history or world history.

Prevalence of Opportunities for Entrepreneurship Today

Despite the maturing of our economy and the growing size and power of many firms in many industries, opportunities for entrepreneurship are more abundant than ever. Opportunities exist not only for the change-maker or innovator, but also for the person who only seeks to do things a little better than existing, and complacent, competition.

Most entrepreneurial successes are unheralded, although dozens have been widely publicized, such as Bill Gates of Microsoft, and Michael Dell and Ted Waitt, founders of their computer firms. Wal-Mart and Southwest Airlines, and even McDonald's and Vanguard, are not so many years away from their beginnings. Opportunities are there for the dedicated with venture capital to support promising new businesses helping many fledgling enterprises. As a new business shows early promise, initial public offerings (IPOs) (i.e., new stock issues) become important sources of capital, and great wealth for the entrepreneurs.

But entrepreneurship is not for everyone. The great venture capitalists look at the person, not the idea. Typically they distribute their seed money to resourceful people who are courageous enough to give up security for the unknown consequences of their embryonic ventures, who have great self confidence, and who demonstrate a tremendous will to win. Our two entrepreneurs in the Boston Beer and OfficeMax cases exemplify this (although Michael Feuer claimed he never had any self confidence—"he always had an acute fear of failing.")

Conclusion

We learn from mistakes and from successes, although every marketing problem and opportunity seems cast in a unique setting. One author has likened marketing strategy to military strategy:

> Strategies which are flexible rather than static embrace optimum use and offer the greatest number of alternative objectives. A good commander knows that he cannot control his environment to suit a prescribed strategy. Natural phenomena pose their own restraints to strategic planning, whether physical, geographic, regional, or psychological and sociological.[4]

He later adds:

> Planning leadership recognizes the unpleasant fact that, despite every effort, the war may be lost. Therefore, the aim is to retain the maximum number of facilities and the basic organization. Indicators of a deteriorating and unsalvageable total situation are, therefore, mandatory ... No possible combination of strategies and tactics, no mobilization of resources ... can supply a magic formula which guarantees victory; it is possible only to increase the probability of victory.

Thus, we can pull two concepts from military strategy to help guide marketing strategy: the desirability of flexibility in an unknown or changing environment and the idea that a basic core should be maintained during crises. The first suggests that the firm should be prepared for adjustments in strategy as conditions warrant. The second suggests that there is a basic core of a firm's business that should be the final bastion to fall back on for regrouping if necessary. Harley-Davidson certainly had such a core as it saw its market share fall from 70 percent to 5 percent: its heavy machines. Gateway also moved back to its basic PC core, shedding its retail stores and other electronics; whether this basic core will keep Gateway viable remains to be seen.

---

[4] Myron S. Heidingsfield, *Changing Patterns in Marketing*, Boston: Allyn & Bacon, 1968, p. 11.
[5] Ibid.

Regarding the basic core of a firm, every viable firm has some distinctive function or "ecological niche" in the business environment:

> Every business firm occupies a position which is in some respects unique. Its location, the product it sells, its operating methods, or the customers it serves tend to set it off in some degree from every other firm. Each firm competes by making the most of its individuality and its special character.[6]

Woe to the firm that loses its ecological niche.

QUESTIONS

1. Design a program aimed at mistake avoidance. Be as specific, as creative, and as complete as possible.
2. Would you advise a firm to be an imitator or an innovator? Why?
3. "There is no such thing as a sustainable competitive advantage." Discuss.
4. How would you build controls into an organization to ensure that similar mistakes do not happen in the future?
5. Array as many pros and cons of entrepreneurship as you can. Which do you see as most compelling?
6. Do you agree with the thought expressed in this chapter that a firm confronted with strong criticism should abandon the product or the way of doing business? Why or why not?
7. We have suggested that the learning insights discussed in this chapter and elsewhere in the book are transferable to other firms and other times. Do you completely agree with this? Why or why not?
8. Do you agree or disagree with the author's contention that a kinder, gentler stance toward channel members would be desirable and profitable? Why or why not?

HANDS-ON EXERCISE

Your firm has had a history of reacting rather than anticipating changes in the industry. As the staff assistant to the CEO, you have been assigned the responsibility of developing adequate sensors of the marketplace. How will you go about developing such sensors?

TEAM DEBATE EXERCISE

Debate the extremes of forecasting for an innovative new product: conservative versus aggressive.

---

[6] Alderson, p. 101.